The LICENSABLE BEAR™

Big Book

of

Officially Licensed

Fun!

ABOUT COMICS   **Thousand Oaks, California**

The Licensable Bear™*Big Book of Officially Licensed Fun!*
Copyright 2008 About Comics
All writing copyright 2004-2008 Nat Gertler
Art for all stories copyright their respective artists
Mister U.S. is copyright by and a trademark of Nat Gertler and Mark Lewis
Liberty Girl™ is copyright Heroic Publishing, Inc. Used with permission.
Licensable Bear™ and his likeness are trademarks of About Comics.

For all rights inquiries, please contact: RIGHTS@ABOUTCOMICS.COM

Contains material originally publishing in *Licensable Bear*™ issues 1-4, *Wild About Comics* 1, *Many Happy Returns*
1, and *Liberty Comics* issue 2 (digital edition).

ISBN: 0-9790750-6-8
ISBN-13: 978-0-9790750-6-3

Published by About Comics, Thousand Oaks, CA. WWW.ABOUTCOMICS.COM

First printing: September, 2008

1 2 3 4 5 6 7 8 9   17 16 15 14 13 12 11 10 09 08

Printed in Canada

Table of
Licensable Bear™-Approved
Contents

all stories written by Nat Gertler

FROM *LICENSABLE BEAR*™ ISSUE 4

FROM *MANY HAPPY RETURNS* ISSUE 2008

FROM *WILD ABOUT COMICS* ISSUE 1

FROM ABOUT COMICS' 2005 HOLIDAY CARD

BITS AND ALSO PIECES

Tones on "Licensable Bear™ Goes on a Bus" and "Licensable Bear™ Rests" by Mark Lewis. Tones on "Licensable Bear™, Finder of Lost Consumers" and "Licensable Bear™ Perpetuates Freedom" by Eric Erbes. Tones on "Licensable Bear™ Learns the Truth," "Licensable Bear™ Checks the Goods," and "Licensable Bear™ Defends Himself" by Ryan Estrada. Tones on "Licensable Bear™ Recommends Another" by Nimrod Reshef. Tones on "Licensable Bear™ Gets a Return Visit" by Jim MacQuarrie. All other toning by Nat Gertler.

Lettering on "Licensable Bear™ Goes on a Bus" by Mark Lewis. Lettering on "Licensable Bear™ Cuts a Ribbon" by Bradley Walton. Lettering on "Licensable Bear™ Goes to Japan" by Rusty Haller. Lettering on "Licensable Bear™'s Nightmare" by Alexander Grecian. All other lettering by Nat Gertler.

LICENSABLE BEAR™ GOES ON A BUS

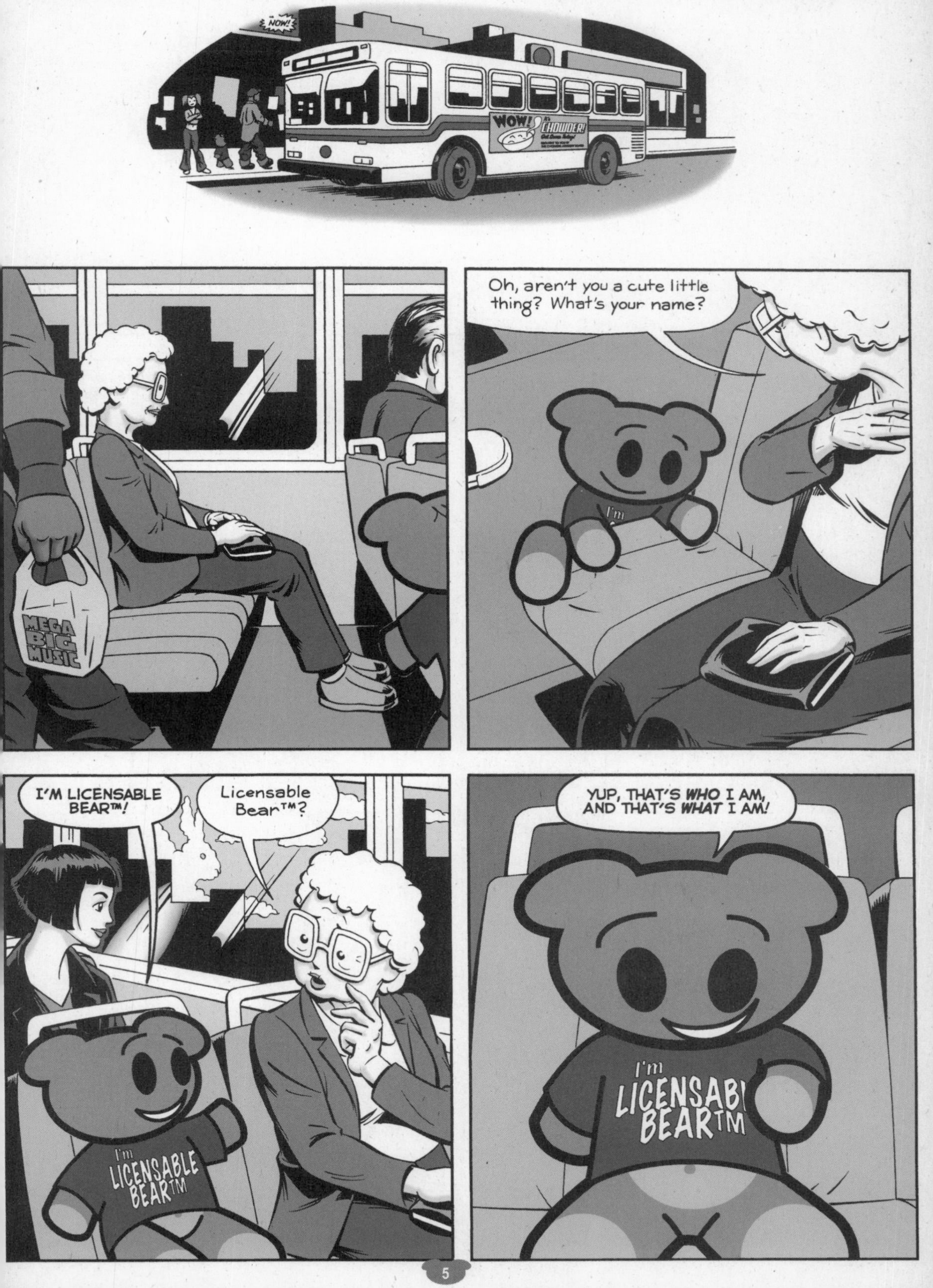

NOW!
WOW! It's CHOWDER!
MEGA BIG MUSIC
Oh, aren't you a cute little thing? What's your name?
I'M LICENSABLE BEAR™!
Licensable Bear™?
I'm LICENSABLE BEAR™
YUP, THAT'S *WHO* I AM, AND THAT'S *WHAT* I AM!
I'm LICENSABL BEAR™

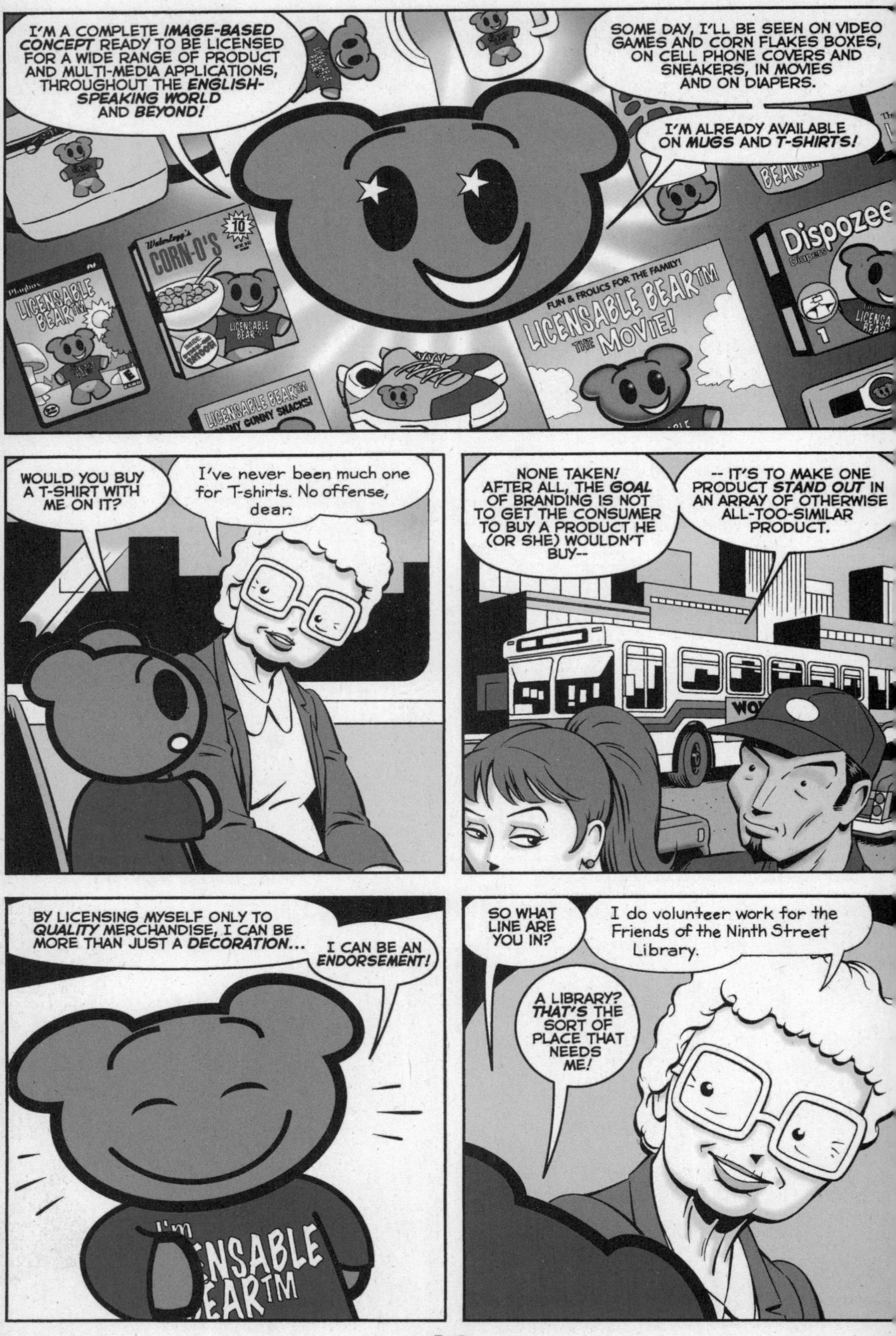
I'M A COMPLETE IMAGE-BASED CONCEPT READY TO BE LICENSED FOR A WIDE RANGE OF PRODUCT AND MULTI-MEDIA APPLICATIONS, THROUGHOUT THE ENGLISH-SPEAKING WORLD AND BEYOND!
SOME DAY, I'LL BE SEEN ON VIDEO GAMES AND CORN FLAKES BOXES, ON CELL PHONE COVERS AND SNEAKERS, IN MOVIES AND ON DIAPERS.
I'M ALREADY AVAILABLE ON MUGS AND T-SHIRTS!
CORN-O'S
LICENSABLE BEAR™
FUN & FROLICS FOR THE FAMILY!
LICENSABLE BEAR™ THE MOVIE!
Dispozee
WOULD YOU BUY A T-SHIRT WITH ME ON IT?
I've never been much one for T-shirts. No offense, dear.
NONE TAKEN! AFTER ALL, THE GOAL OF BRANDING IS NOT TO GET THE CONSUMER TO BUY A PRODUCT HE (OR SHE) WOULDN'T BUY--
-- IT'S TO MAKE ONE PRODUCT STAND OUT IN AN ARRAY OF OTHERWISE ALL-TOO-SIMILAR PRODUCT.
BY LICENSING MYSELF ONLY TO QUALITY MERCHANDISE, I CAN BE MORE THAN JUST A DECORATION...
I CAN BE AN ENDORSEMENT!
SO WHAT LINE ARE YOU IN?
I do volunteer work for the Friends of the Ninth Street Library.
A LIBRARY? THAT'S THE SORT OF PLACE THAT NEEDS ME!

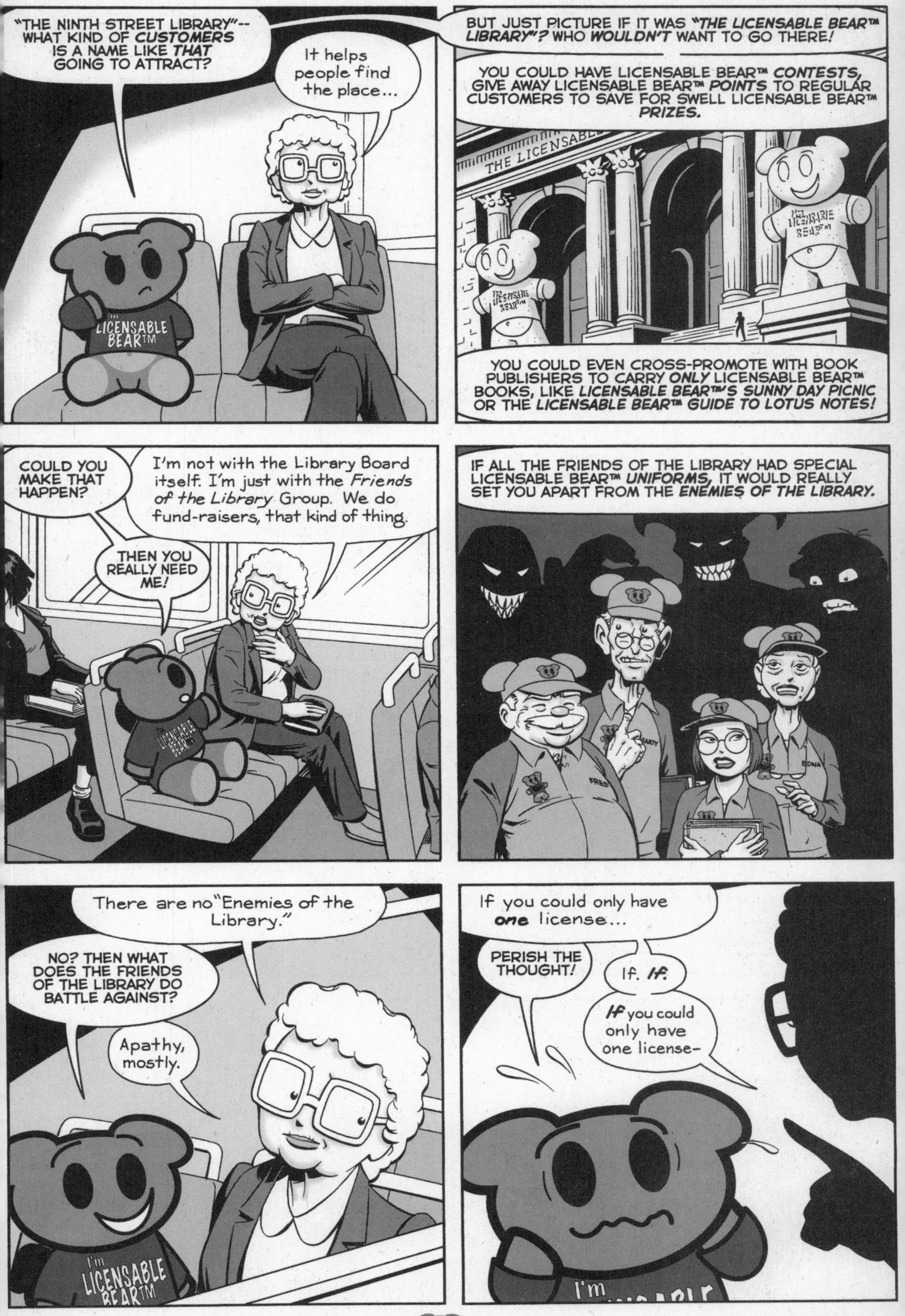

"THE NINTH STREET LIBRARY"-- WHAT KIND OF *CUSTOMERS* IS A NAME LIKE *THAT* GOING TO ATTRACT?
It helps people find the place...
I'M LICENSABLE BEAR™
BUT JUST PICTURE IF IT WAS *"THE LICENSABLE BEAR™ LIBRARY"?* WHO *WOULDN'T* WANT TO GO THERE!
YOU COULD HAVE LICENSABLE BEAR™ *CONTESTS,* GIVE AWAY LICENSABLE BEAR™ *POINTS* TO REGULAR CUSTOMERS TO SAVE FOR SWELL LICENSABLE BEAR™ *PRIZES.*
THE LICENSABLE
YOU COULD EVEN CROSS-PROMOTE WITH BOOK PUBLISHERS TO CARRY *ONLY* LICENSABLE BEAR™ BOOKS, LIKE *LICENSABLE BEAR™'S SUNNY DAY PICNIC* OR THE *LICENSABLE BEAR™ GUIDE TO LOTUS NOTES!*
COULD YOU MAKE THAT HAPPEN?
I'm not with the Library Board itself. I'm just with the *Friends of the Library* Group. We do fund-raisers, that kind of thing.
THEN YOU REALLY NEED *ME!*
IF ALL THE FRIENDS OF THE LIBRARY HAD SPECIAL LICENSABLE BEAR™ *UNIFORMS,* IT WOULD REALLY SET YOU APART FROM THE *ENEMIES OF THE LIBRARY.*
FRED
EDNA
There are no "Enemies of the Library."
NO? THEN WHAT DOES THE FRIENDS OF THE LIBRARY DO BATTLE AGAINST?
Apathy, mostly.
I'm LICENSABLE BEAR™
If you could only have **one** license...
PERISH THE THOUGHT!
If. ***If.***
If you could only have one license-
I'm

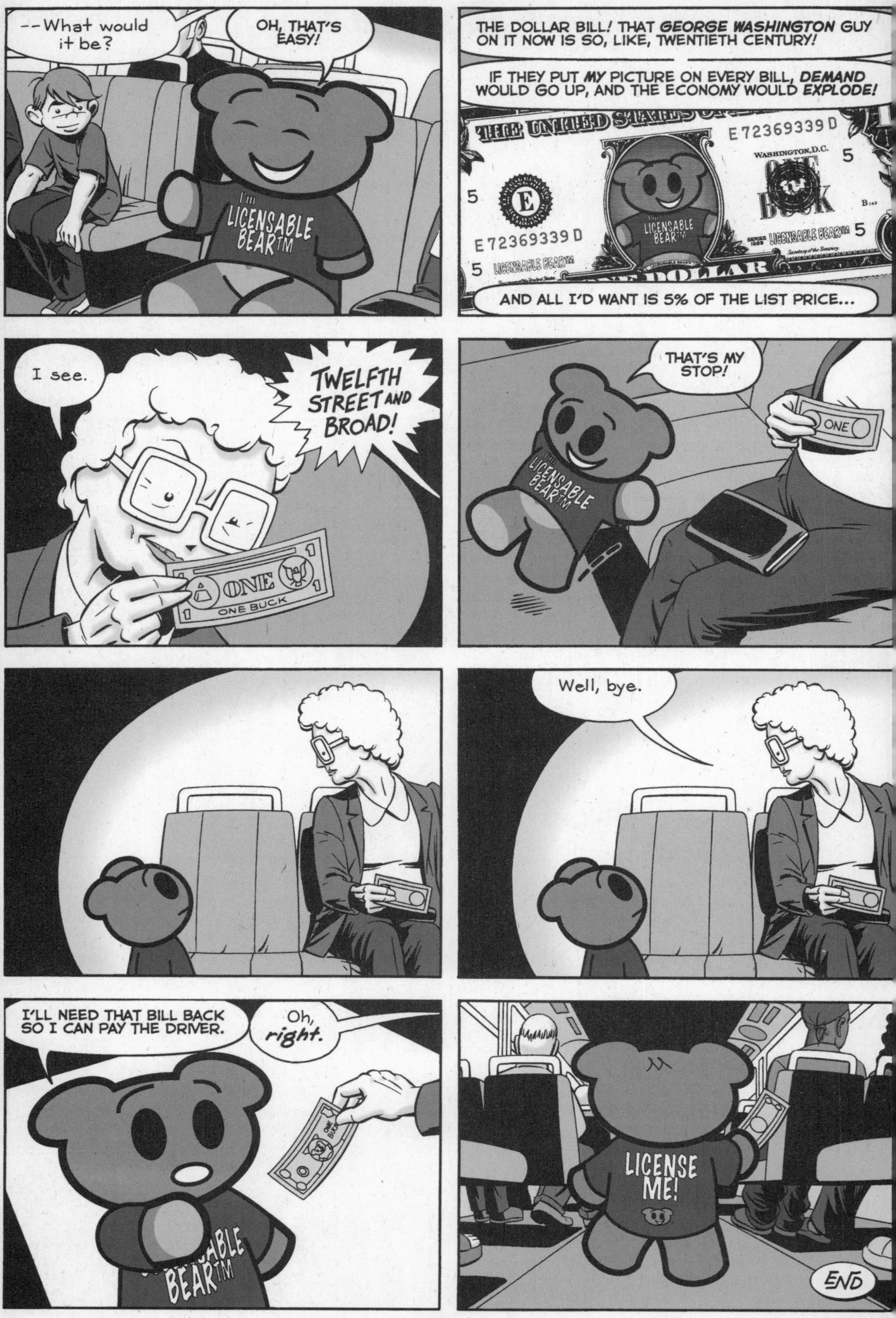
--What would it be?
OH, THAT'S EASY!
I'm LICENSABLE BEAR™
THE DOLLAR BILL! THAT GEORGE WASHINGTON GUY ON IT NOW IS SO, LIKE, TWENTIETH CENTURY!
IF THEY PUT MY PICTURE ON EVERY BILL, DEMAND WOULD GO UP, AND THE ECONOMY WOULD EXPLODE!
THE UNITED STATES
E72369339D
WASHINGTON, D.C.
ONE BUCK
LICENSABLE BEAR™
AND ALL I'D WANT IS 5% OF THE LIST PRICE...
I see.
TWELFTH STREET AND BROAD!
ONE
ONE BUCK
THAT'S MY STOP!
ONE
I'm LICENSABLE BEAR™
Well, bye.
I'LL NEED THAT BILL BACK SO I CAN PAY THE DRIVER.
Oh, right.
BEAR™
LICENSE ME!
END

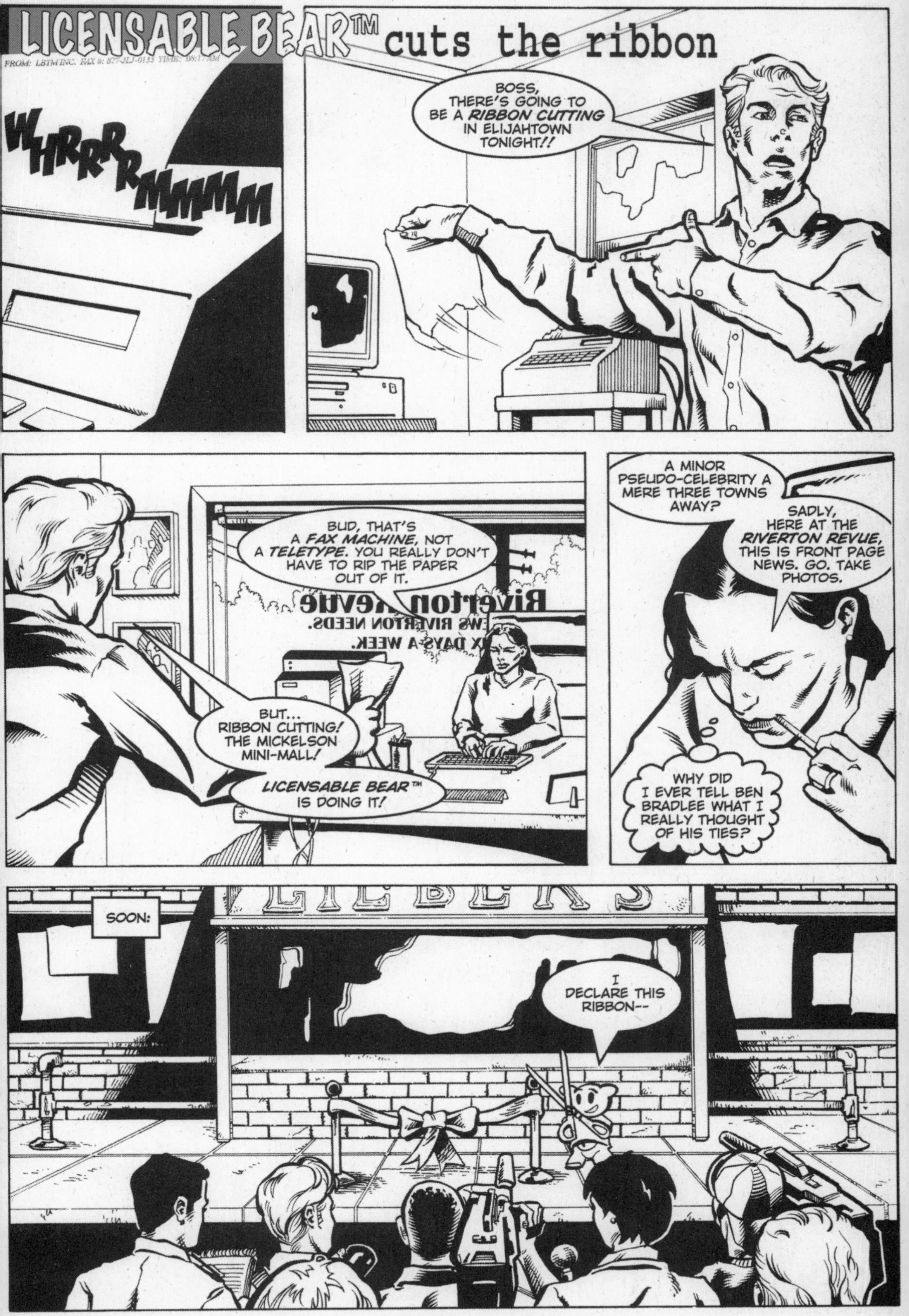
LICENSABLE BEAR™ cuts the ribbon
FROM: LBTM INC. FAX #: 877-JLJ-0133 TIME: 08:17AM
WHRRRRMMMMM
BOSS, THERE'S GOING TO BE A *RIBBON CUTTING* IN ELIJAHTOWN TONIGHT!!
BUD, THAT'S A *FAX MACHINE,* NOT A *TELETYPE.* YOU REALLY DON'T HAVE TO RIP THE PAPER OUT OF IT.
BUT... RIBBON CUTTING! THE MICKELSON MINI-MALL!
LICENSABLE BEAR™ IS DOING IT!
A MINOR PSEUDO-CELEBRITY A MERE THREE TOWNS AWAY?
SADLY, HERE AT THE *RIVERTON REVUE,* THIS IS FRONT PAGE NEWS. GO. TAKE PHOTOS.
WHY DID I EVER TELL BEN BRADLEE WHAT I REALLY THOUGHT OF HIS TIES?
SOON:
I DECLARE THIS RIBBON--

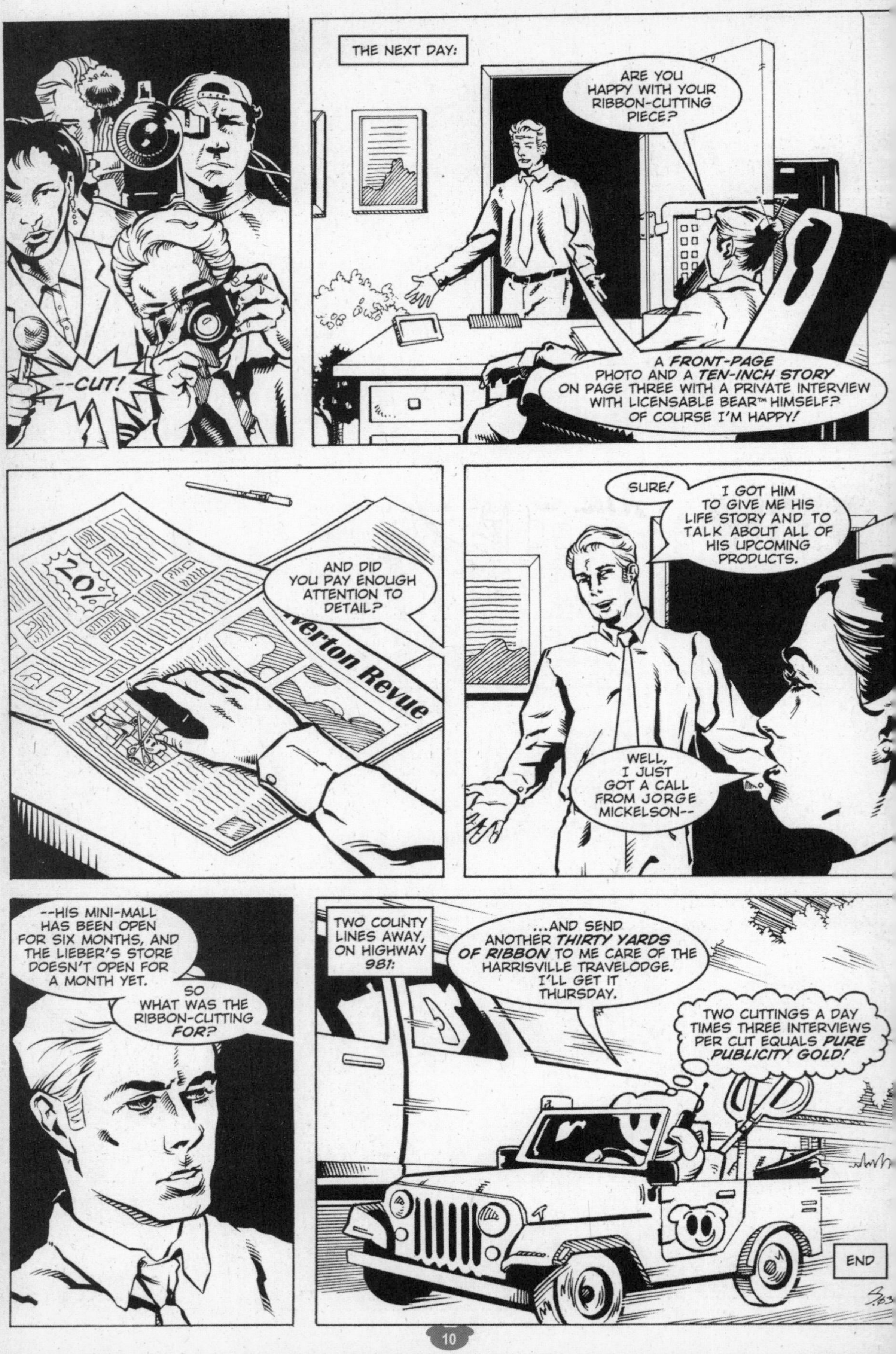
--CUT!
THE NEXT DAY:
ARE YOU HAPPY WITH YOUR RIBBON-CUTTING PIECE?
A FRONT-PAGE PHOTO AND A TEN-INCH STORY ON PAGE THREE WITH A PRIVATE INTERVIEW WITH LICENSABLE BEAR™ HIMSELF? OF COURSE I'M HAPPY!
20%
Averton Revue
AND DID YOU PAY ENOUGH ATTENTION TO DETAIL?
SURE!
I GOT HIM TO GIVE ME HIS LIFE STORY AND TO TALK ABOUT ALL OF HIS UPCOMING PRODUCTS.
WELL, I JUST GOT A CALL FROM JORGE MICKELSON--
--HIS MINI-MALL HAS BEEN OPEN FOR SIX MONTHS, AND THE LIEBER'S STORE DOESN'T OPEN FOR A MONTH YET.
SO WHAT WAS THE RIBBON-CUTTING FOR?
TWO COUNTY LINES AWAY, ON HIGHWAY 981:
...AND SEND ANOTHER THIRTY YARDS OF RIBBON TO ME CARE OF THE HARRISVILLE TRAVELODGE. I'LL GET IT THURSDAY.
TWO CUTTINGS A DAY TIMES THREE INTERVIEWS PER CUT EQUALS PURE PUBLICITY GOLD!
END

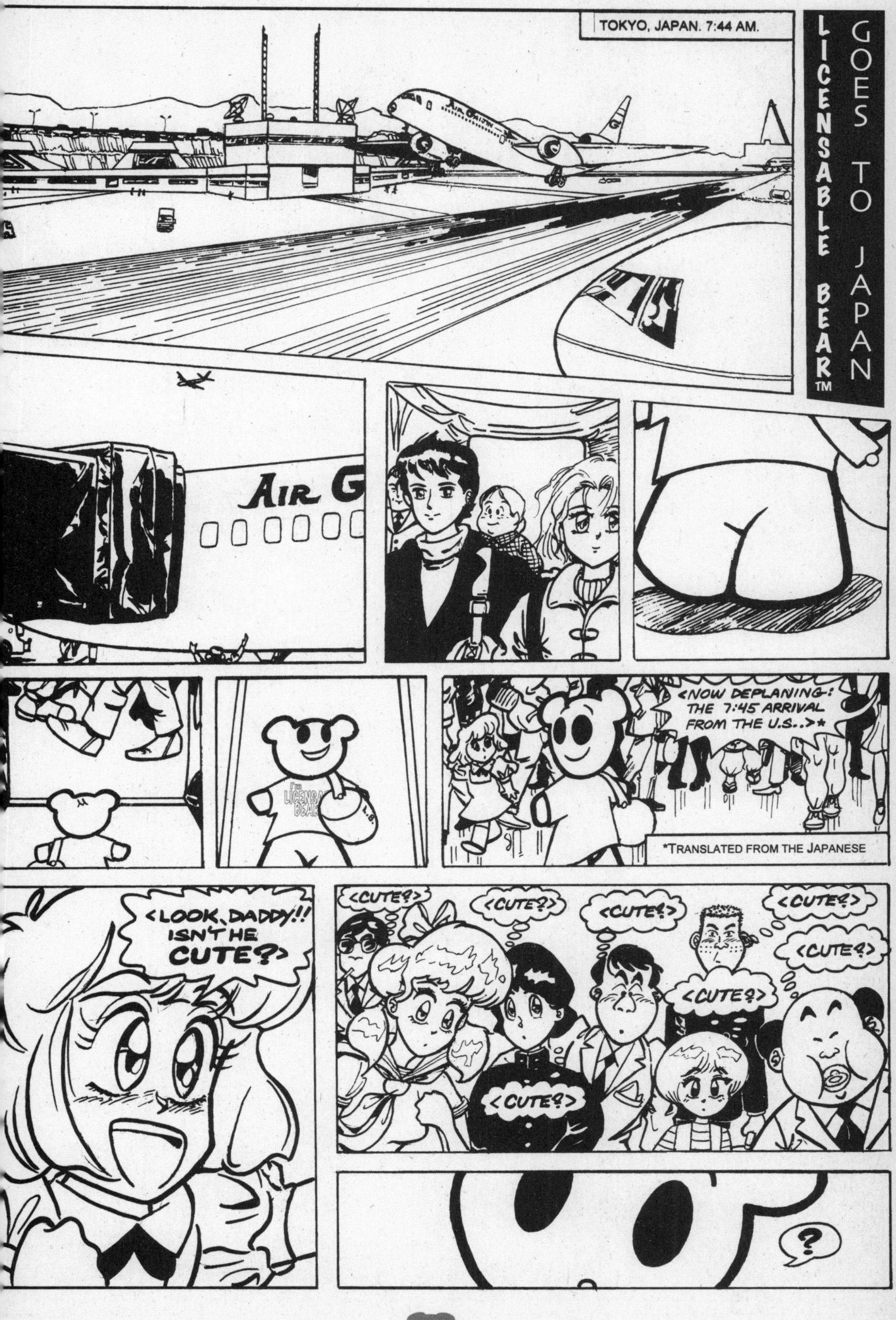
LICENSABLE BEAR™ GOES TO JAPAN
TOKYO, JAPAN. 7:44 AM.
AIR G
I'm LICENSABLE BEAR
L.B.
<NOW DEPLANING: THE 7:45 ARRIVAL FROM THE U.S..>*
*TRANSLATED FROM THE JAPANESE
<LOOK, DADDY!! ISN'T HE CUTE?>
<CUTE?>
<CUTE?>
<CUTE?>
<CUTE?>
<CUTE?>
<CUTE?>
<CUTE?>
?

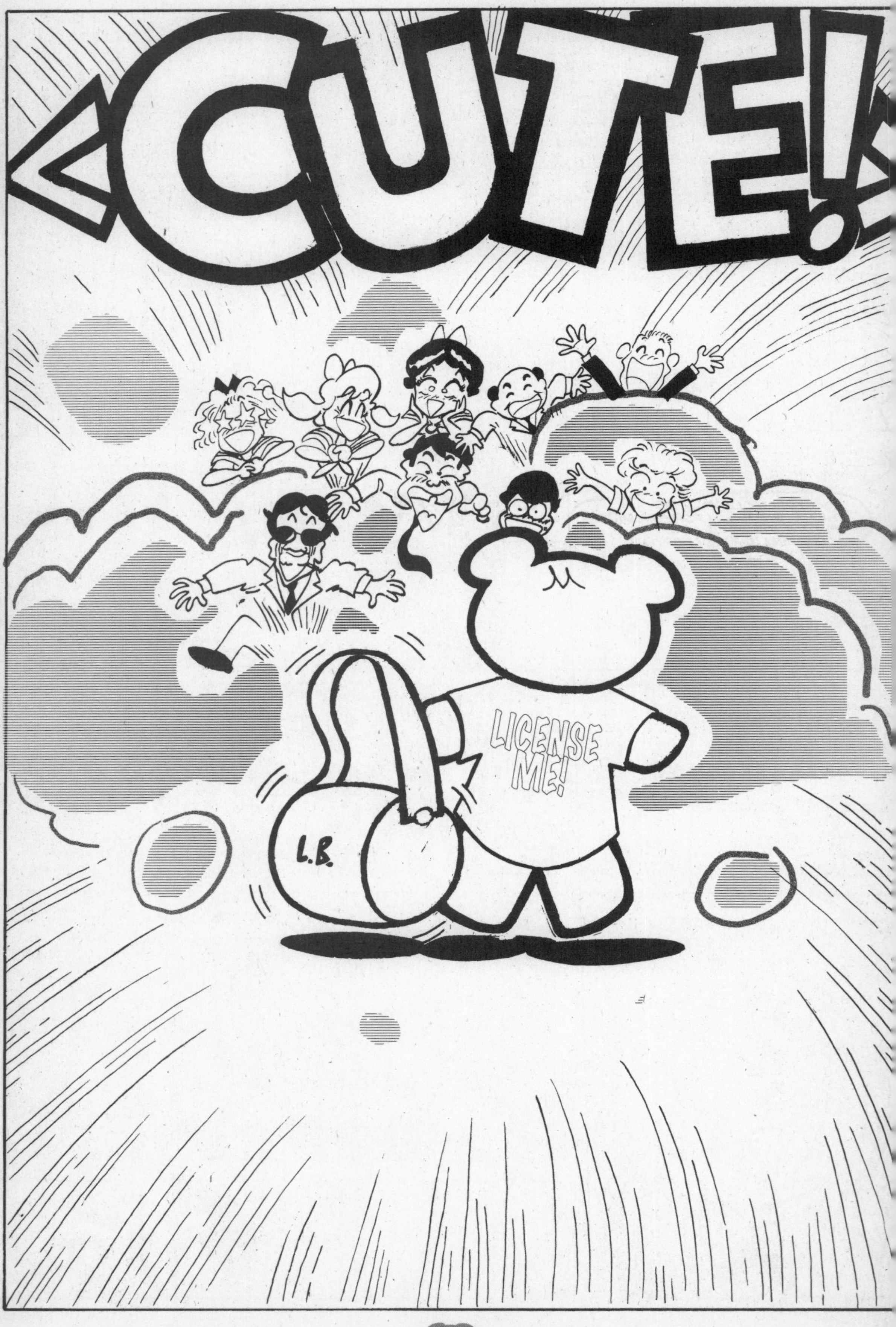
CUTE!
LICENSE ME!
L.B.

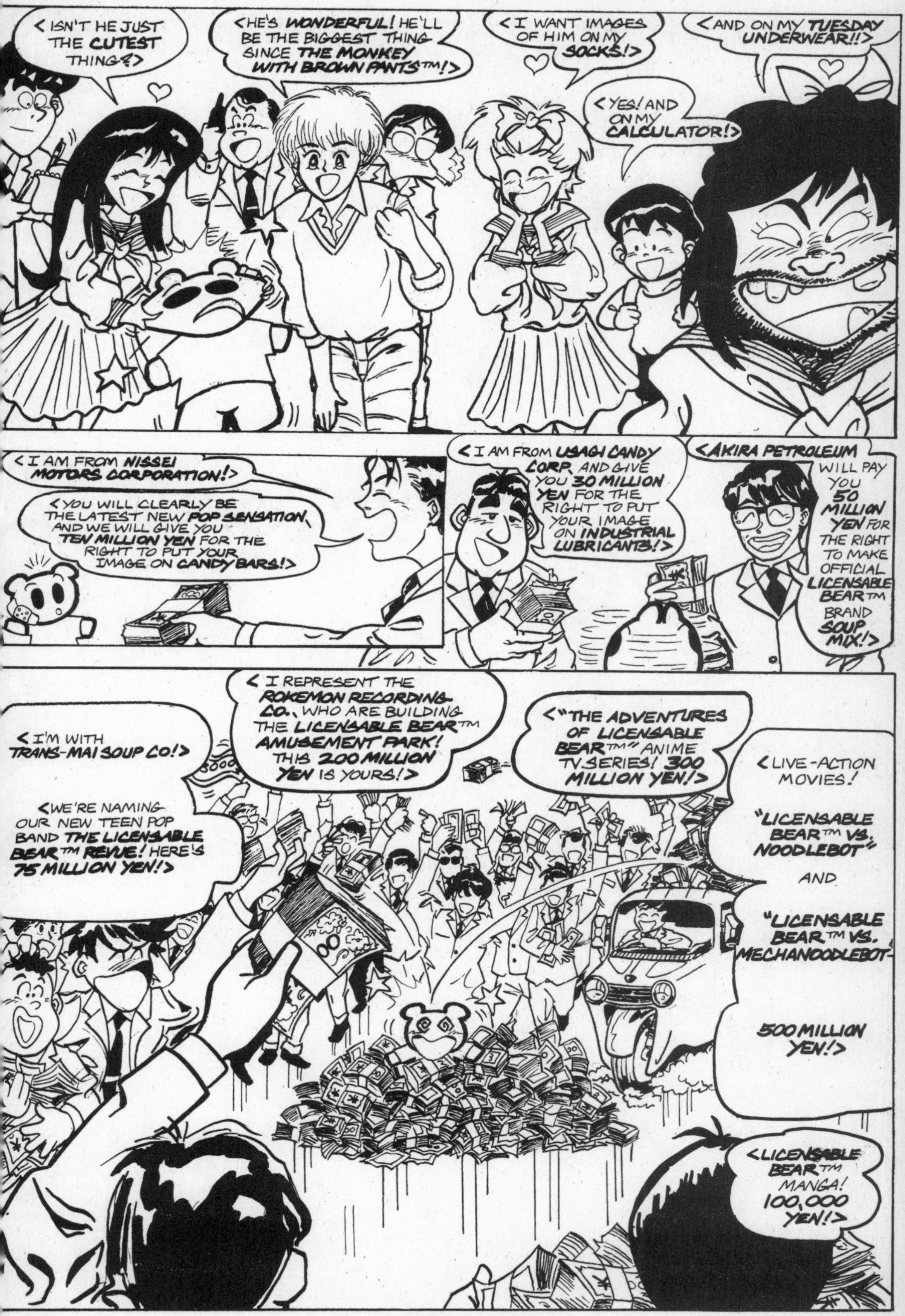

<ISN'T HE JUST THE CUTEST THING?!>
<HE'S WONDERFUL! HE'LL BE THE BIGGEST THING SINCE THE MONKEY WITH BROWN PANTS™!>
<I WANT IMAGES OF HIM ON MY SOCKS!>
<AND ON MY TUESDAY UNDERWEAR!!>
<YES! AND ON MY CALCULATOR!>
<I AM FROM NISSEI MOTORS CORPORATION!>
<YOU WILL CLEARLY BE THE LATEST NEW POP SENSATION, AND WE WILL GIVE YOU TEN MILLION YEN FOR THE RIGHT TO PUT YOUR IMAGE ON CANDY BARS!>
<I AM FROM USAGI CANDY CORP. AND GIVE YOU 30 MILLION YEN FOR THE RIGHT TO PUT YOUR IMAGE ON INDUSTRIAL LUBRICANTS!>
<AKIRA PETROLEUM WILL PAY YOU 50 MILLION YEN FOR THE RIGHT TO MAKE OFFICIAL LICENSABLE BEAR™ BRAND SOUP MIX!>
<I'M WITH TRANS-MAI SOUP CO!>
<I REPRESENT THE ROKEMON RECORDING CO., WHO ARE BUILDING THE LICENSABLE BEAR™ AMUSEMENT PARK! THIS 200 MILLION YEN IS YOURS!>
<"THE ADVENTURES OF LICENSABLE BEAR™" ANIME TV SERIES! 300 MILLION YEN!>
<WE'RE NAMING OUR NEW TEEN POP BAND THE LICENSABLE BEAR™ REVUE! HERE'S 75 MILLION YEN!>
<LIVE-ACTION MOVIES! "LICENSABLE BEAR™ VS. NOODLEBOT" AND "LICENSABLE BEAR™ VS. MECHANOODLEBOT" 500 MILLION YEN!>
<LICENSABLE BEAR™ MANGA! 100,000 YEN!>

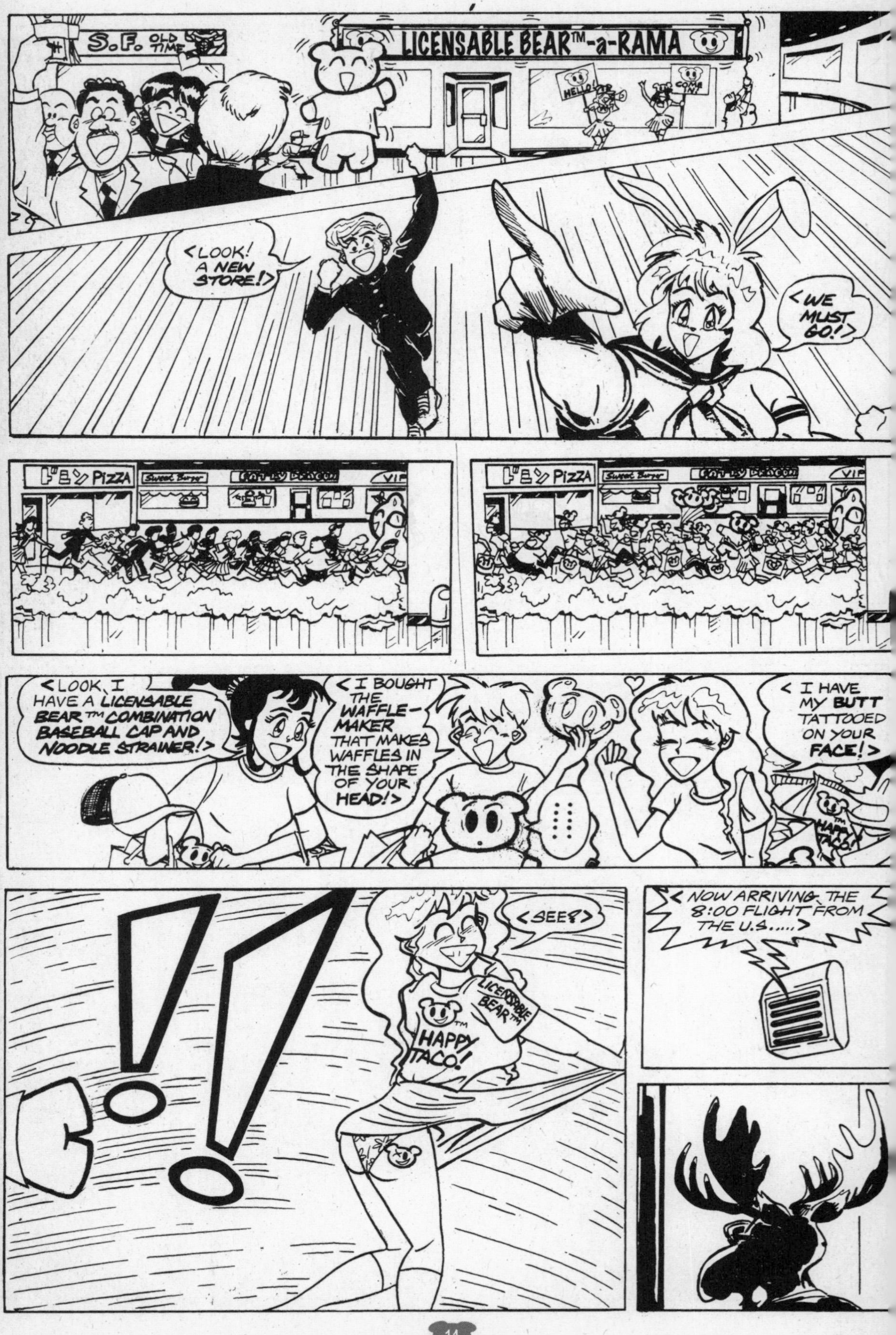
S.F. OLD TIME
LICENSABLE BEAR™-a-RAMA
HELLO!
COME IN!
<LOOK! A NEW STORE!>
<WE MUST GO!>
PIZZA
Sweet Burger
PIZZA
Sweet Burger
<LOOK, I HAVE A LICENSABLE BEAR™ COMBINATION BASEBALL CAP AND NOODLE STRAINER!>
<I BOUGHT THE WAFFLE-MAKER THAT MAKES WAFFLES IN THE SHAPE OF YOUR HEAD!>
<I HAVE MY BUTT TATTOOED ON YOUR FACE!>
HAPPY TACO!
<SEE?>
LICENSABLE BEAR™
HAPPY TACO!
<NOW ARRIVING THE 8:00 FLIGHT FROM THE U.S.....>

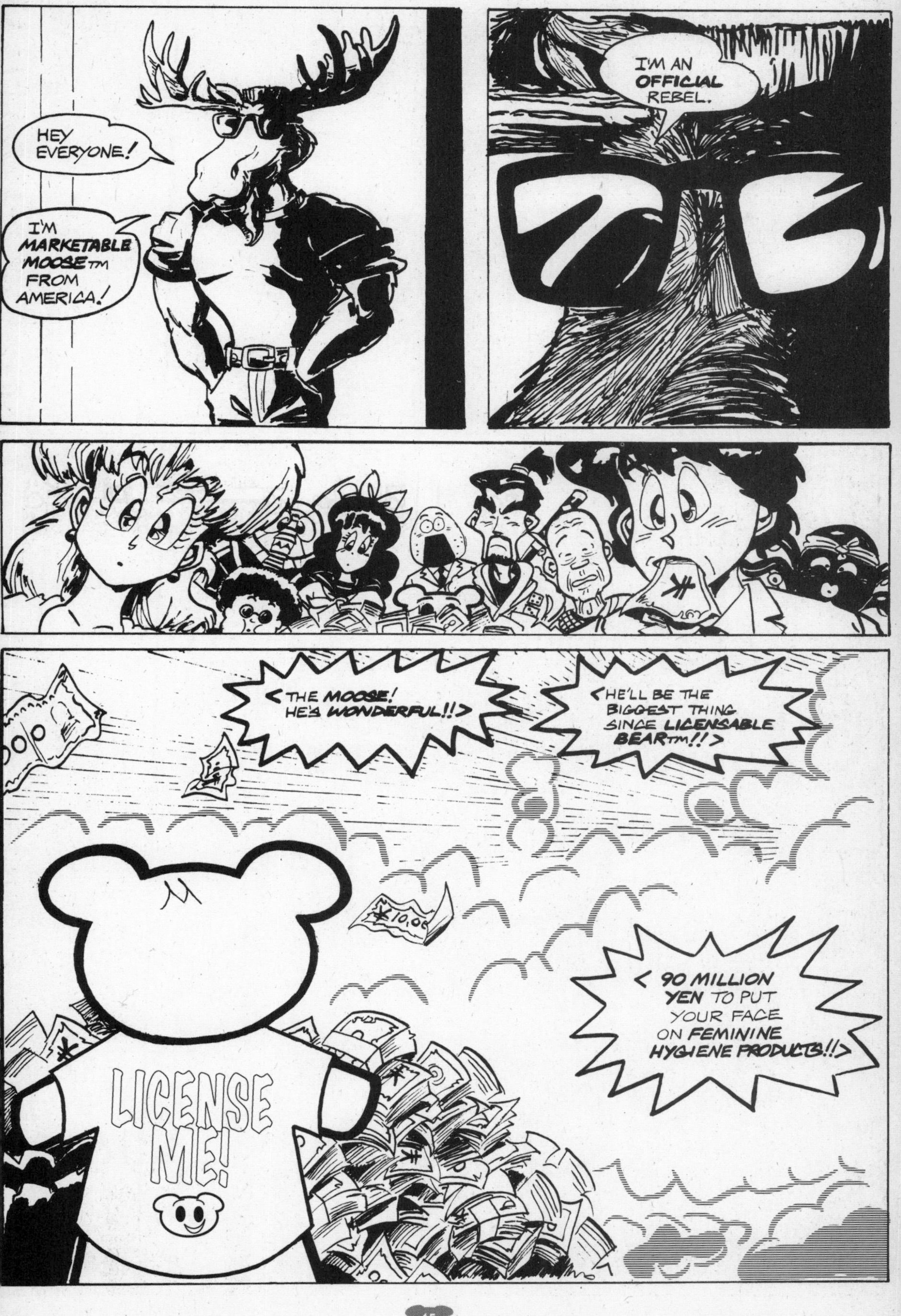
HEY EVERYONE!
I'M MARKETABLE MOOSE™ FROM AMERICA!
I'M AN OFFICIAL REBEL.
<THE MOOSE! HE'S WONDERFUL!!>
<HE'LL BE THE BIGGEST THING SINCE LICENSABLE BEAR™!!>
< 90 MILLION YEN TO PUT YOUR FACE ON FEMININE HYGIENE PRODUCTS!!>
LICENSE ME!

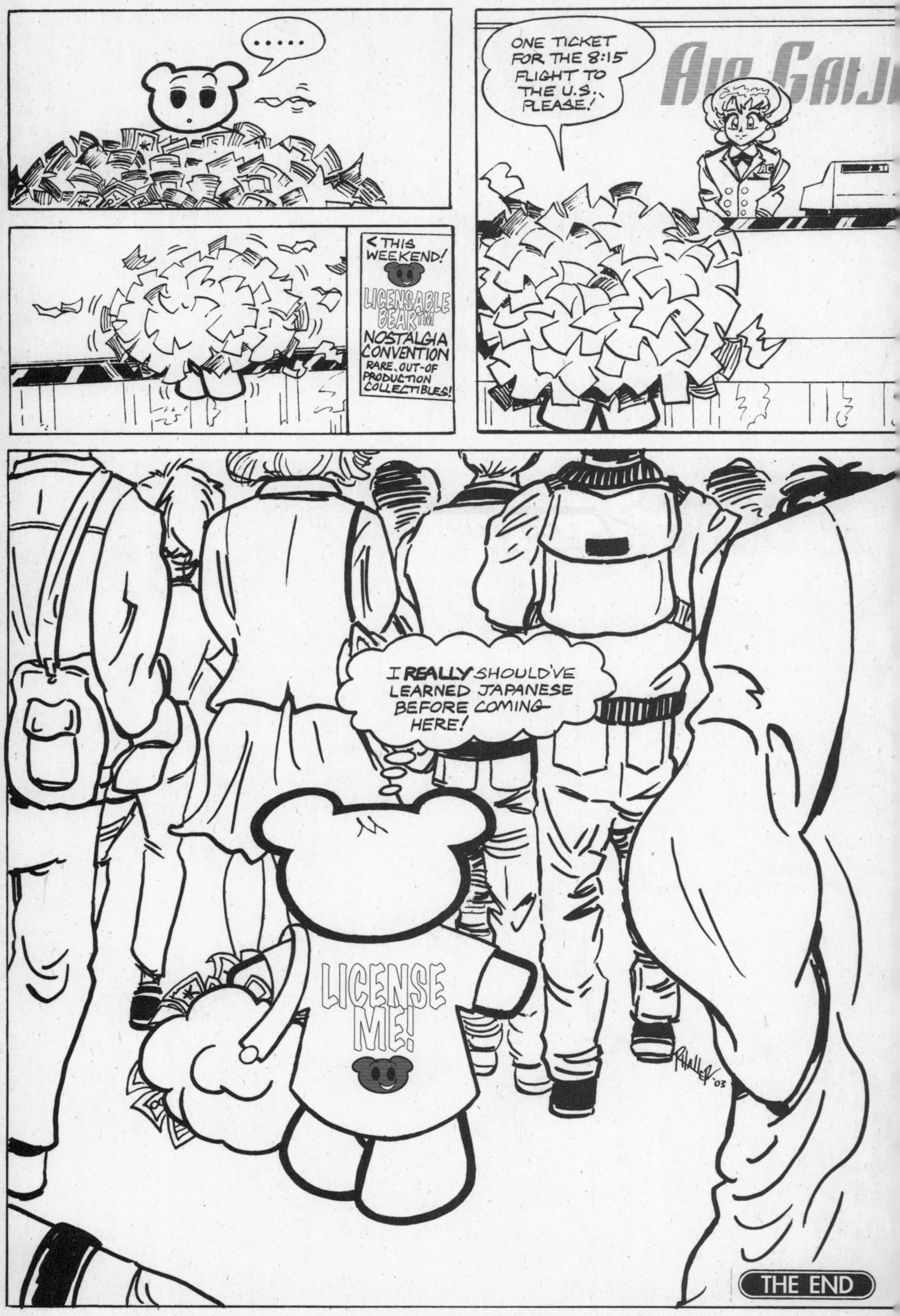
. . . . . .
ONE TICKET FOR THE 8:15 FLIGHT TO THE U.S., PLEASE!
AIR GAIJI
< THIS WEEKEND!
LICENSABLE BEAR TM
NOSTALGIA CONVENTION
RARE, OUT-OF PRODUCTION COLLECTIBLES!
I **REALLY** SHOULD'VE LEARNED JAPANESE BEFORE COMING HERE!
LICENSE ME!
THE END

LICENSABLE BEAR™ tries Video Dating

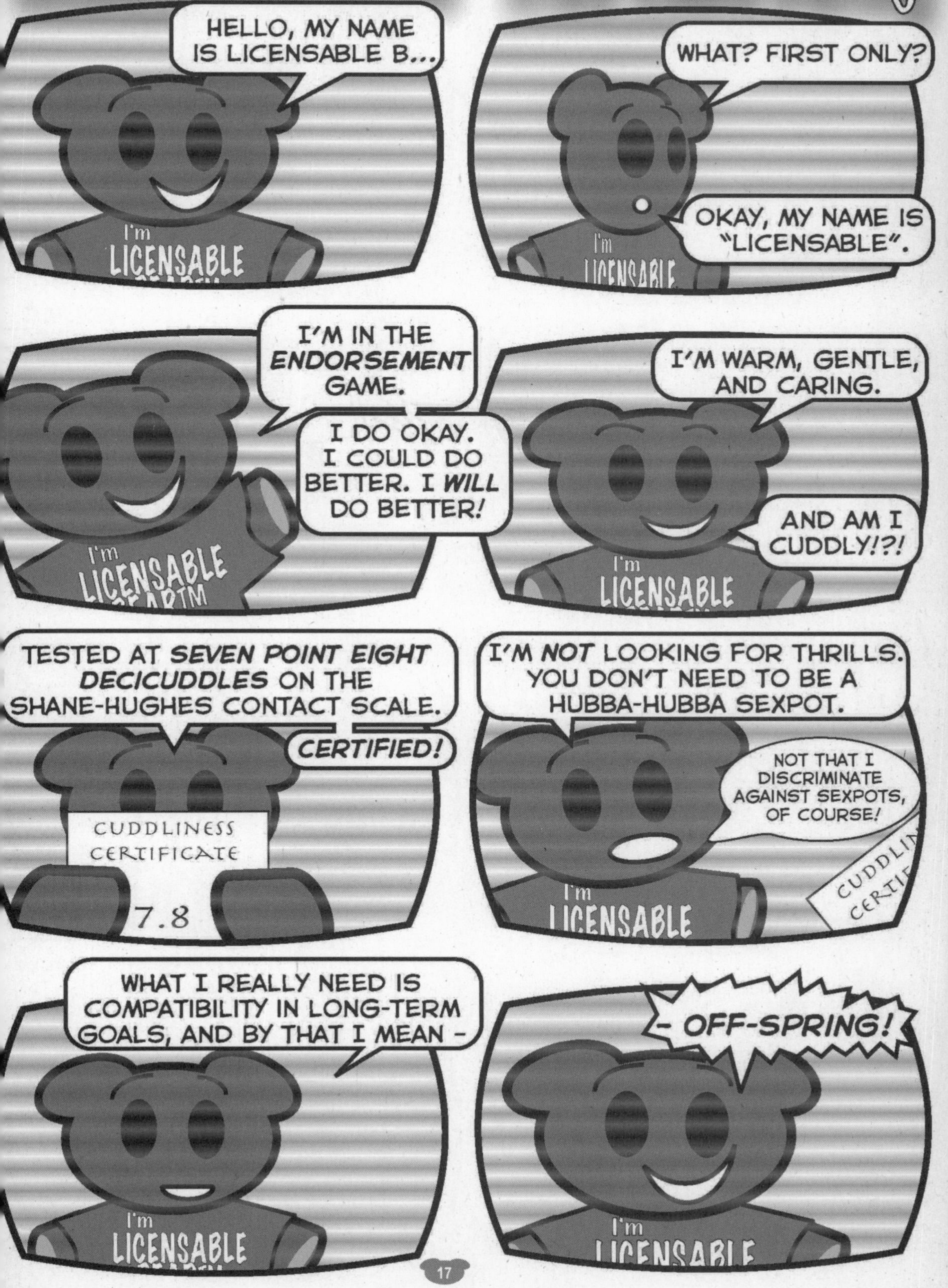
HELLO, MY NAME IS LICENSABLE B...
WHAT? FIRST ONLY?
OKAY, MY NAME IS "LICENSABLE".
I'M IN THE *ENDORSEMENT* GAME.
I DO OKAY. I COULD DO BETTER. I *WILL* DO BETTER!
I'M WARM, GENTLE, AND CARING.
AND AM I CUDDLY!?!
TESTED AT *SEVEN POINT EIGHT DECICUDDLES* ON THE SHANE-HUGHES CONTACT SCALE.
CERTIFIED!
CUDDLINESS CERTIFICATE
7.8
I'M *NOT* LOOKING FOR THRILLS. YOU DON'T NEED TO BE A HUBBA-HUBBA SEXPOT.
NOT THAT I DISCRIMINATE AGAINST SEXPOTS, OF COURSE!
WHAT I REALLY NEED IS COMPATIBILITY IN LONG-TERM GOALS, AND BY THAT I MEAN –
– *OFF-SPRING!*

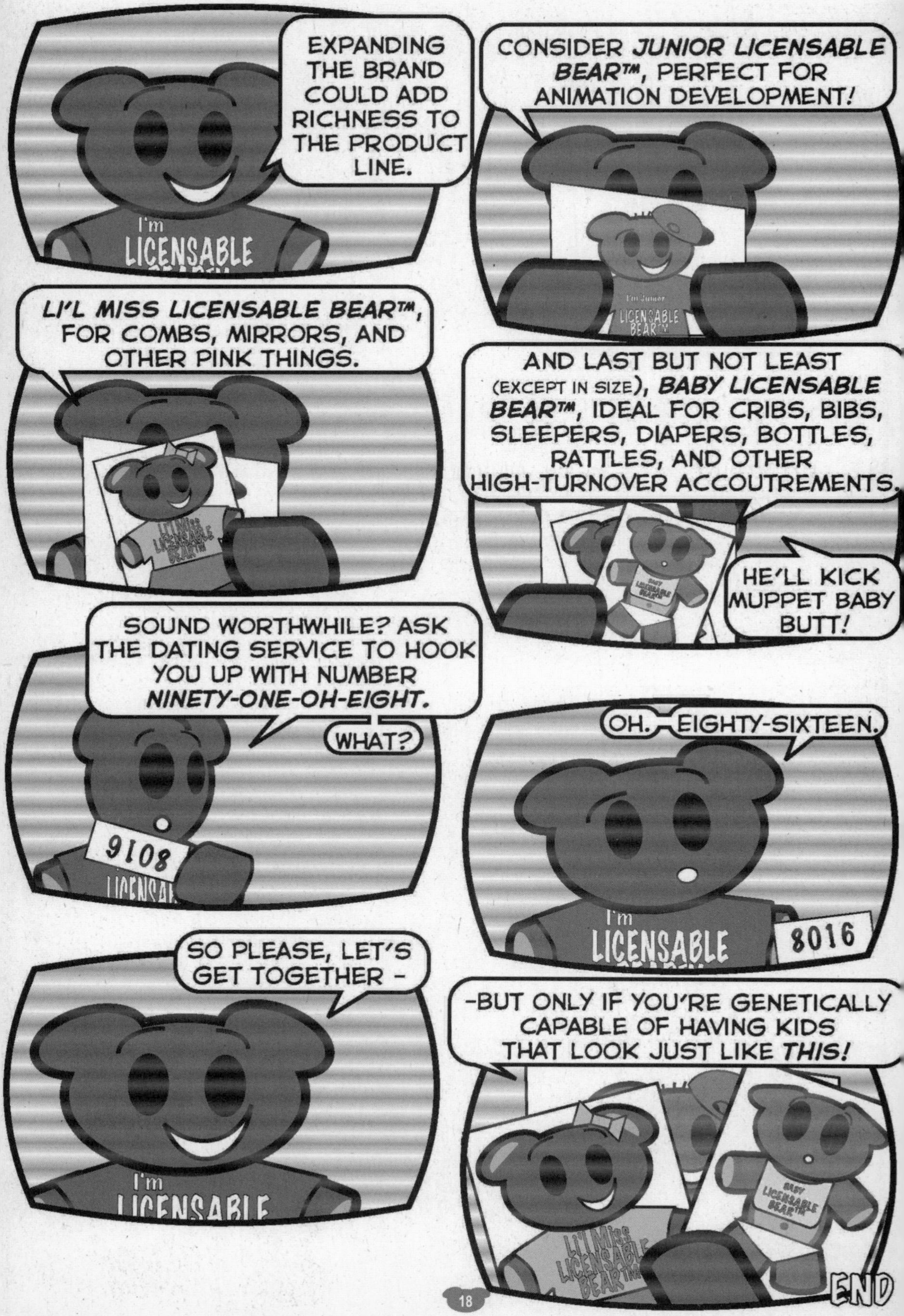
EXPANDING THE BRAND COULD ADD RICHNESS TO THE PRODUCT LINE.
I'm LICENSABLE
CONSIDER *JUNIOR LICENSABLE BEAR™*, PERFECT FOR ANIMATION DEVELOPMENT!
LICENSABLE BEAR™
LI'L MISS LICENSABLE BEAR™, FOR COMBS, MIRRORS, AND OTHER PINK THINGS.
AND LAST BUT NOT LEAST (EXCEPT IN SIZE), *BABY LICENSABLE BEAR™*, IDEAL FOR CRIBS, BIBS, SLEEPERS, DIAPERS, BOTTLES, RATTLES, AND OTHER HIGH-TURNOVER ACCOUTREMENTS.
HE'LL KICK MUPPET BABY BUTT!
SOUND WORTHWHILE? ASK THE DATING SERVICE TO HOOK YOU UP WITH NUMBER *NINETY-ONE-OH-EIGHT*.
WHAT?
9108
OH. EIGHTY-SIXTEEN.
I'm LICENSABLE
8016
SO PLEASE, LET'S GET TOGETHER –
I'm LICENSABLE
–BUT ONLY IF YOU'RE GENETICALLY CAPABLE OF HAVING KIDS THAT LOOK JUST LIKE *THIS*!
LI'L MISS LICENSABLE BEAR™
BABY LICENSABLE BEAR™
END

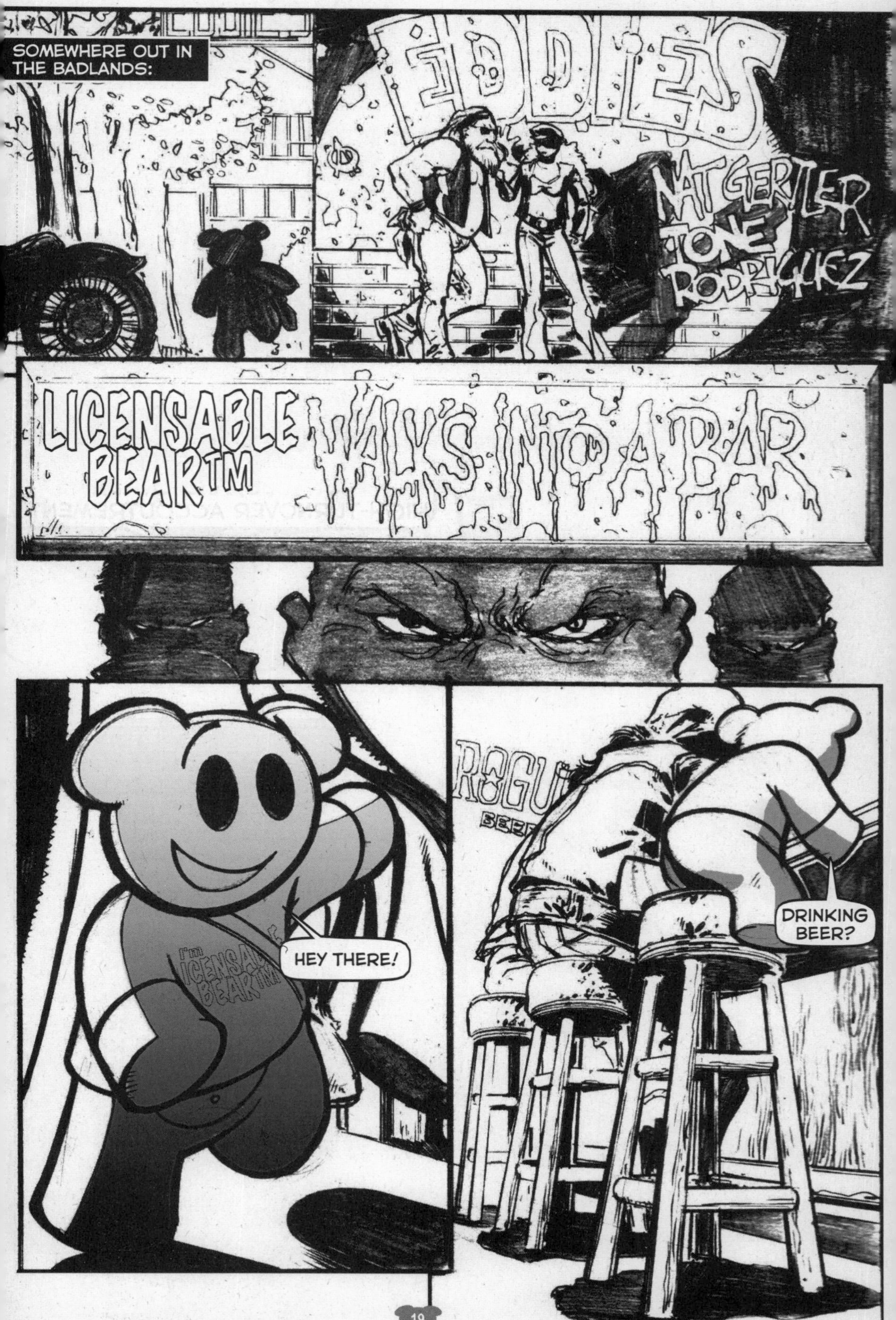

SOMEWHERE OUT IN THE BADLANDS:
EDDIE'S
NAT GERTLER
TONE RODRIGUEZ
LICENSABLE BEAR™
WALKS INTO A BAR
HEY THERE!
I'm LICENSABLE BEAR™
DRINKING BEER?

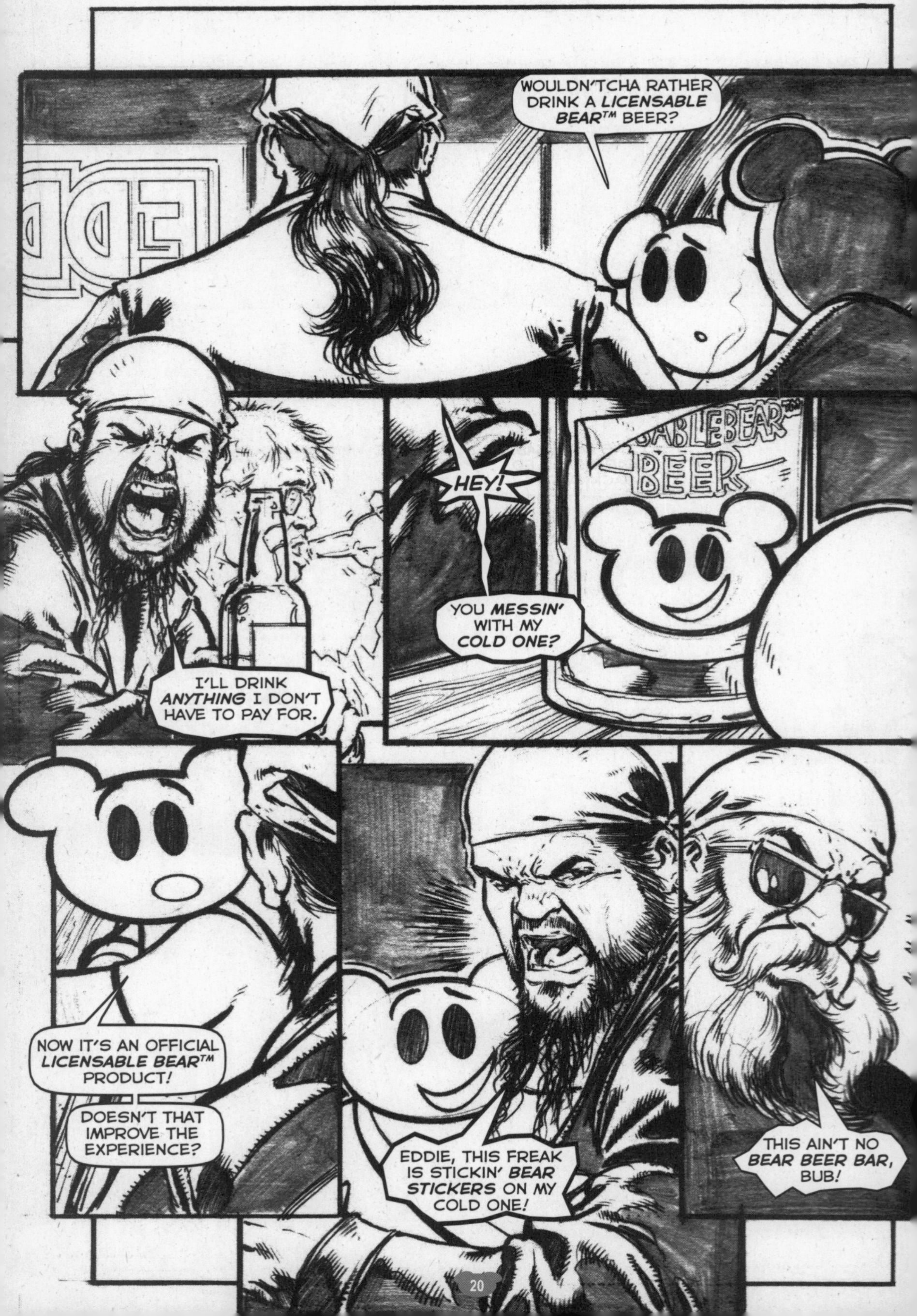

WOULDN'TCHA RATHER DRINK A *LICENSABLE BEAR*™ BEER?
I'LL DRINK *ANYTHING* I DON'T HAVE TO PAY FOR.
HEY!
YOU *MESSIN'* WITH MY *COLD ONE?*
SABLE BEAR™
BEER
NOW IT'S AN OFFICIAL *LICENSABLE BEAR*™ PRODUCT!
DOESN'T THAT IMPROVE THE EXPERIENCE?
EDDIE, THIS FREAK IS STICKIN' *BEAR STICKERS* ON MY COLD ONE!
THIS AIN'T NO *BEAR BEER BAR*, BUB!

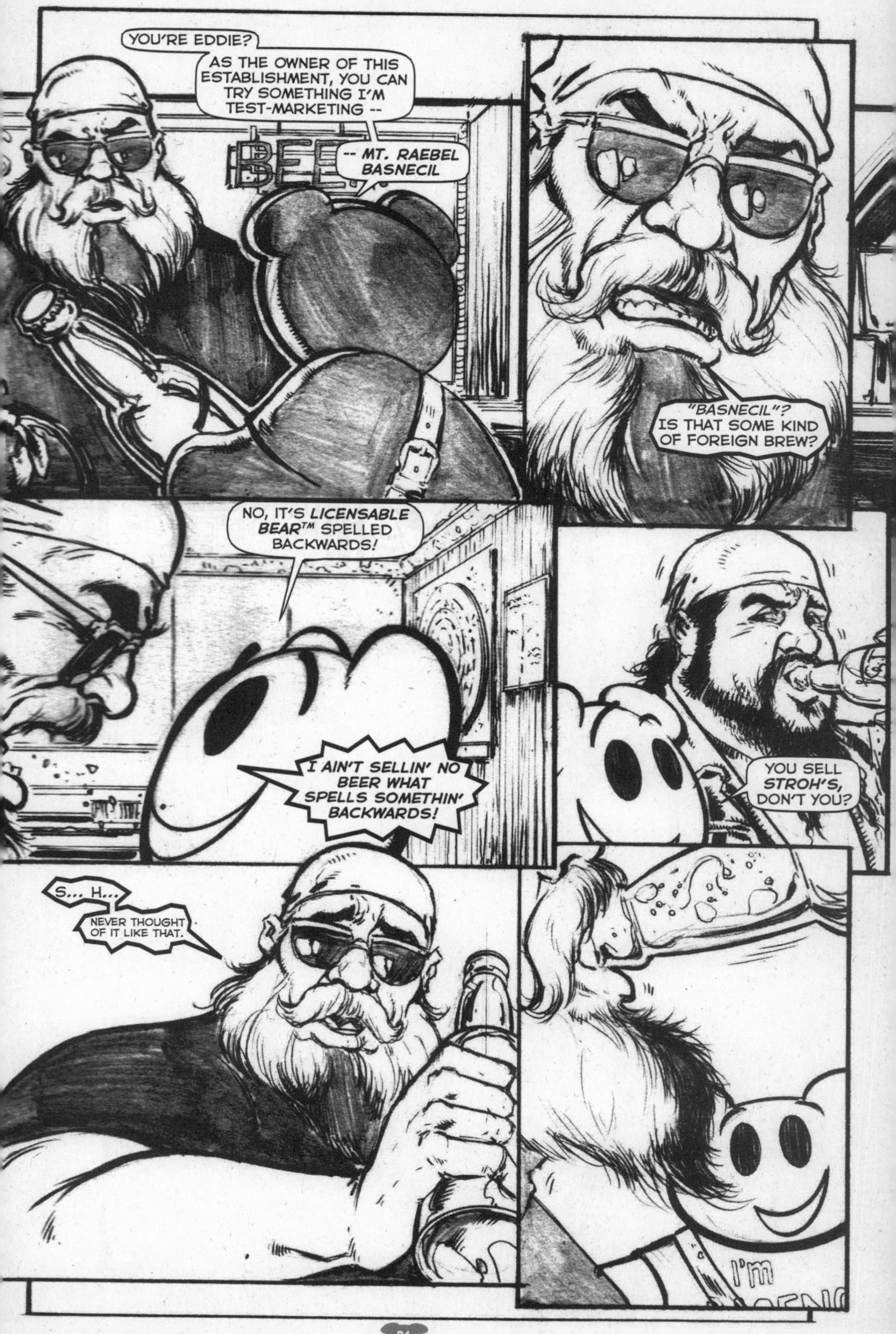

YOU'RE EDDIE?
AS THE OWNER OF THIS ESTABLISHMENT, YOU CAN TRY SOMETHING I'M TEST-MARKETING --
-- MT. RAEBEL BASNECIL
"BASNECIL"? IS THAT SOME KIND OF FOREIGN BREW?
NO, IT'S LICENSABLE BEAR™ SPELLED BACKWARDS!
I AIN'T SELLIN' NO BEER WHAT SPELLS SOMETHIN' BACKWARDS!
YOU SELL STROH'S, DON'T YOU?
S... H...
NEVER THOUGHT OF IT LIKE THAT.
I'm

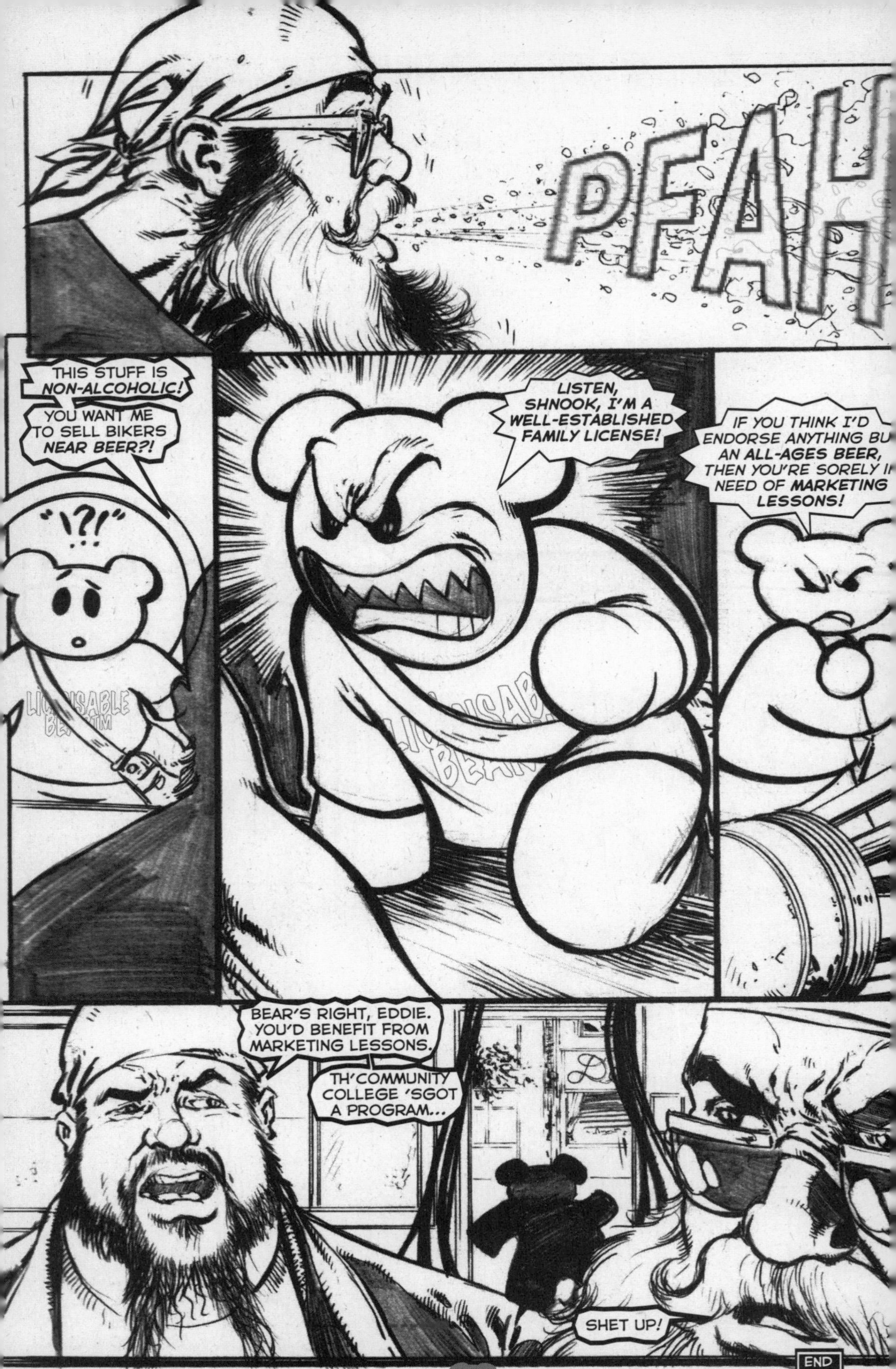

PFAH
THIS STUFF IS NON-ALCOHOLIC!
YOU WANT ME TO SELL BIKERS NEAR BEER?!
"!?!"
LISTEN, SHNOOK, I'M A WELL-ESTABLISHED FAMILY LICENSE!
IF YOU THINK I'D ENDORSE ANYTHING BU AN ALL-AGES BEER, THEN YOU'RE SORELY I NEED OF MARKETING LESSONS!
BEAR'S RIGHT, EDDIE. YOU'D BENEFIT FROM MARKETING LESSONS.
TH'COMMUNITY COLLEGE 'SGOT A PROGRAM...
SHET UP!
END

LICENSABLE BEAR™ INFILTRATES

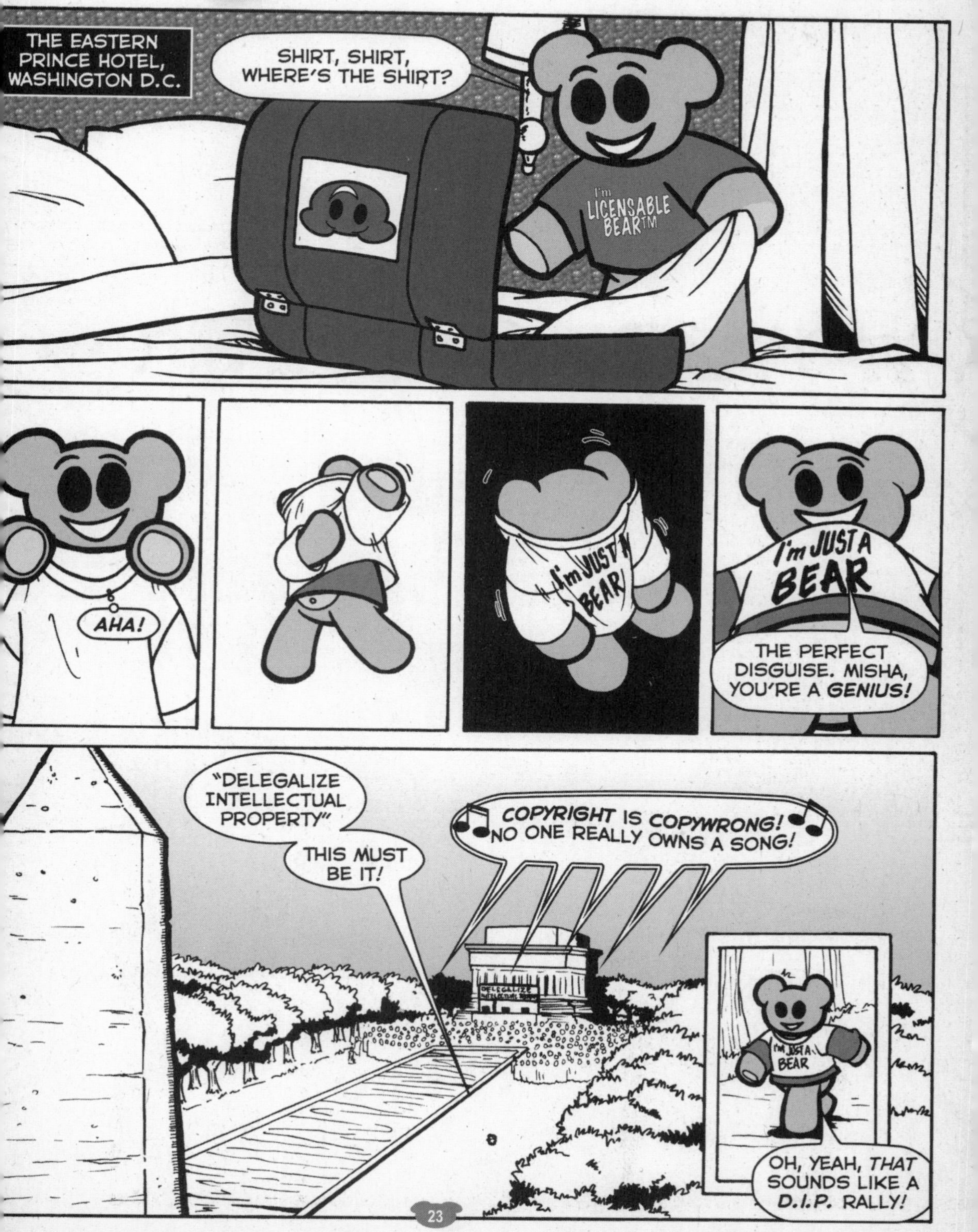
THE EASTERN PRINCE HOTEL, WASHINGTON D.C.
SHIRT, SHIRT, WHERE'S THE SHIRT?
I'm LICENSABLE BEAR™
AHA!
I'm JUST A BEAR
THE PERFECT DISGUISE. MISHA, YOU'RE A *GENIUS!*
"DELEGALIZE INTELLECTUAL PROPERTY"
THIS MUST BE IT!
COPYRIGHT IS *COPYWRONG!* NO ONE REALLY OWNS A SONG!
I'm JUST A BEAR
OH, YEAH, *THAT* SOUNDS LIKE A *D.I.P.* RALLY!

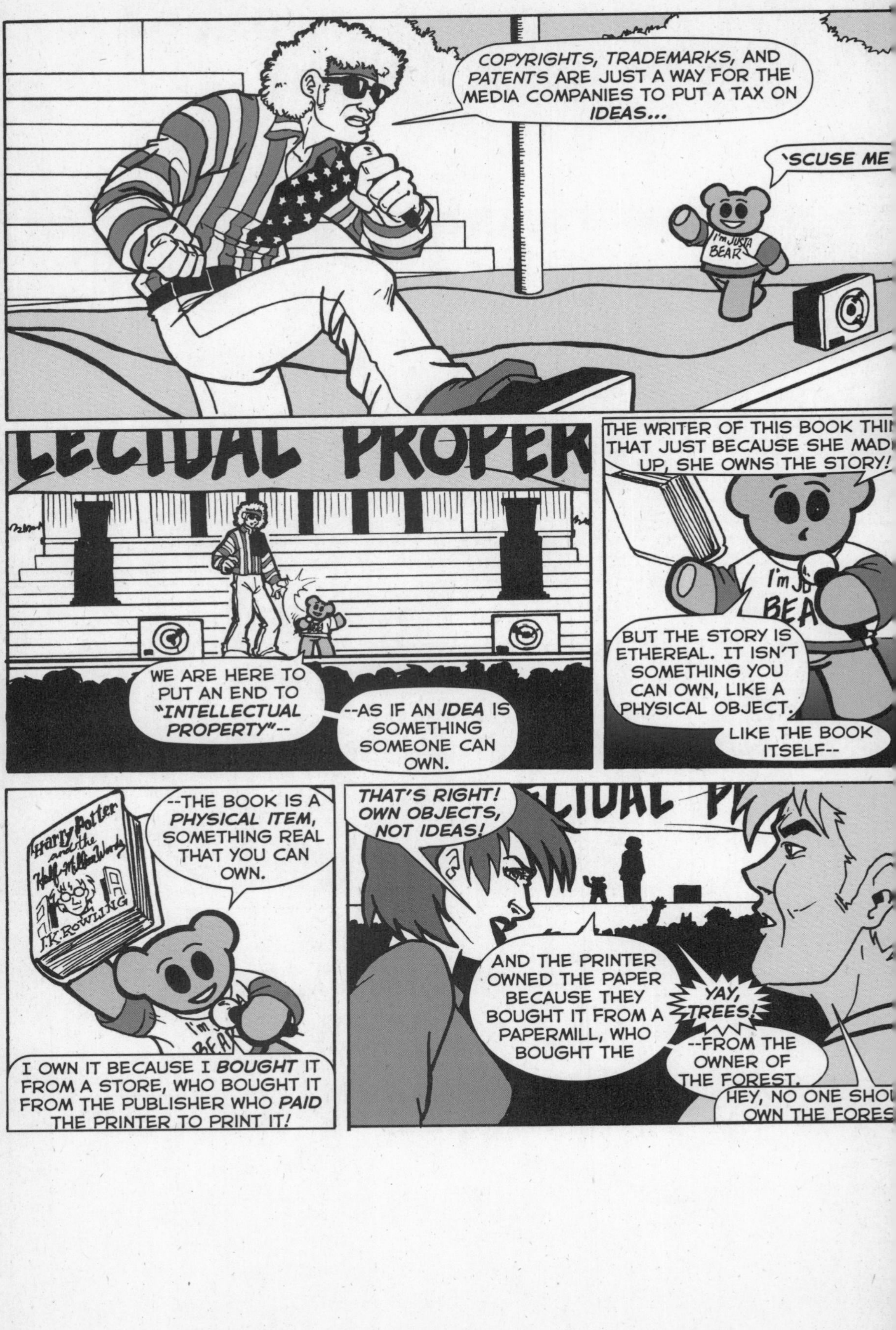
COPYRIGHTS, TRADEMARKS, AND PATENTS ARE JUST A WAY FOR THE MEDIA COMPANIES TO PUT A TAX ON IDEAS...
'SCUSE ME
I'm JUST A BEAR
THE WRITER OF THIS BOOK THI THAT JUST BECAUSE SHE MAD UP, SHE OWNS THE STORY!
WE ARE HERE TO PUT AN END TO "INTELLECTUAL PROPERTY"--
--AS IF AN IDEA IS SOMETHING SOMEONE CAN OWN.
BUT THE STORY IS ETHEREAL. IT ISN'T SOMETHING YOU CAN OWN, LIKE A PHYSICAL OBJECT.
LIKE THE BOOK ITSELF--
--THE BOOK IS A PHYSICAL ITEM, SOMETHING REAL THAT YOU CAN OWN.
Harry Potter and the Half-Million Words
J.K. ROWLING
I OWN IT BECAUSE I BOUGHT IT FROM A STORE, WHO BOUGHT IT FROM THE PUBLISHER WHO PAID THE PRINTER TO PRINT IT!
THAT'S RIGHT! OWN OBJECTS, NOT IDEAS!
AND THE PRINTER OWNED THE PAPER BECAUSE THEY BOUGHT IT FROM A PAPERMILL, WHO BOUGHT THE
YAY, TREES!
--FROM THE OWNER OF THE FOREST.
HEY, NO ONE SHO OWN THE FORES

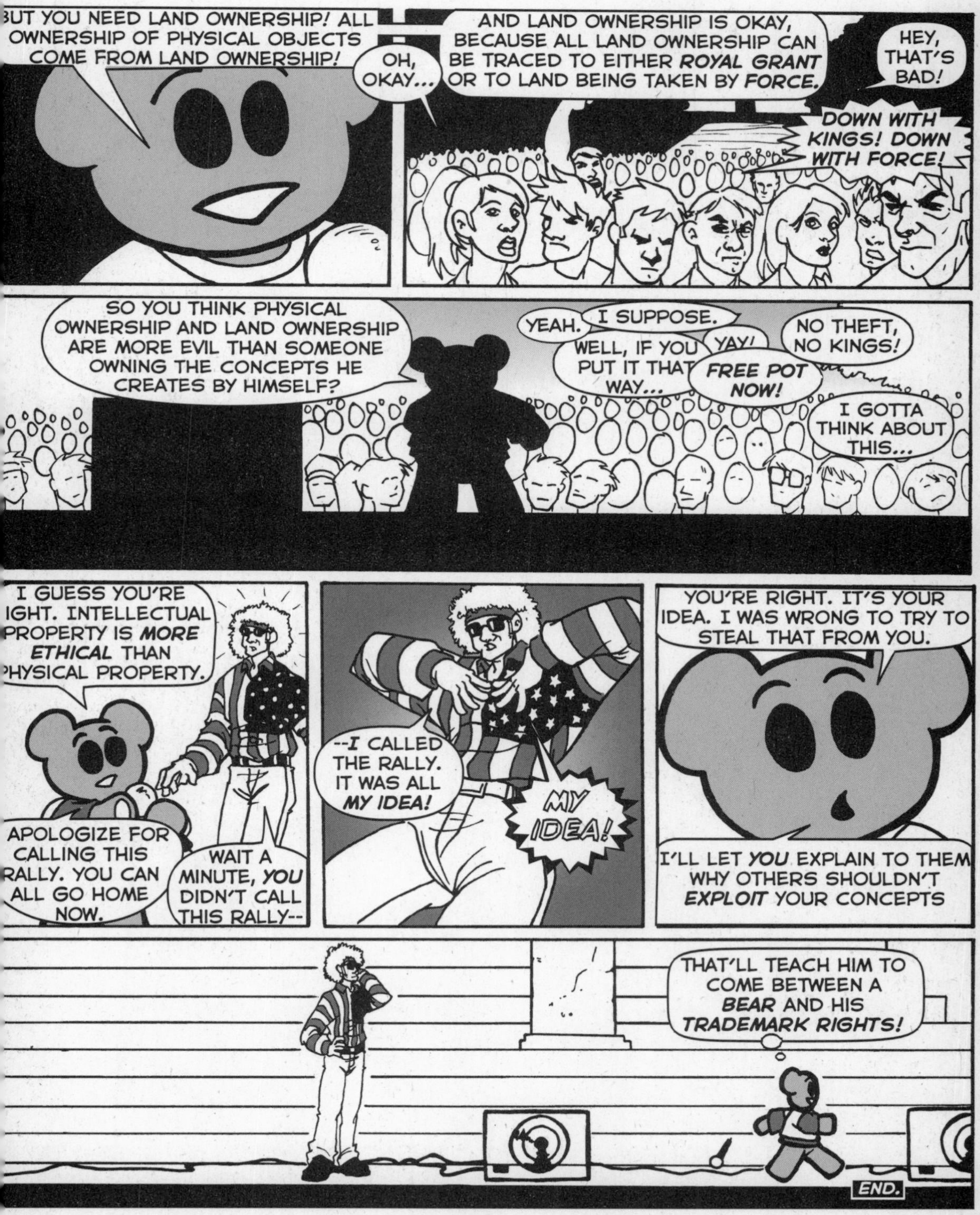
BUT YOU NEED LAND OWNERSHIP! ALL OWNERSHIP OF PHYSICAL OBJECTS COME FROM LAND OWNERSHIP!
OH, OKAY...
AND LAND OWNERSHIP IS OKAY, BECAUSE ALL LAND OWNERSHIP CAN BE TRACED TO EITHER ROYAL GRANT OR TO LAND BEING TAKEN BY FORCE.
HEY, THAT'S BAD!
DOWN WITH KINGS! DOWN WITH FORCE!
SO YOU THINK PHYSICAL OWNERSHIP AND LAND OWNERSHIP ARE MORE EVIL THAN SOMEONE OWNING THE CONCEPTS HE CREATES BY HIMSELF?
YEAH.
I SUPPOSE.
WELL, IF YOU PUT IT THAT WAY...
YAY!
FREE POT NOW!
NO THEFT, NO KINGS!
I GOTTA THINK ABOUT THIS...
I GUESS YOU'RE RIGHT. INTELLECTUAL PROPERTY IS MORE ETHICAL THAN PHYSICAL PROPERTY.
APOLOGIZE FOR CALLING THIS RALLY. YOU CAN ALL GO HOME NOW.
WAIT A MINUTE, YOU DIDN'T CALL THIS RALLY--
--I CALLED THE RALLY. IT WAS ALL MY IDEA!
MY IDEA!
YOU'RE RIGHT. IT'S YOUR IDEA. I WAS WRONG TO TRY TO STEAL THAT FROM YOU.
I'LL LET YOU EXPLAIN TO THEM WHY OTHERS SHOULDN'T EXPLOIT YOUR CONCEPTS
THAT'LL TEACH HIM TO COME BETWEEN A BEAR AND HIS TRADEMARK RIGHTS!
END.

The Licensable Bear™ Family of products Album

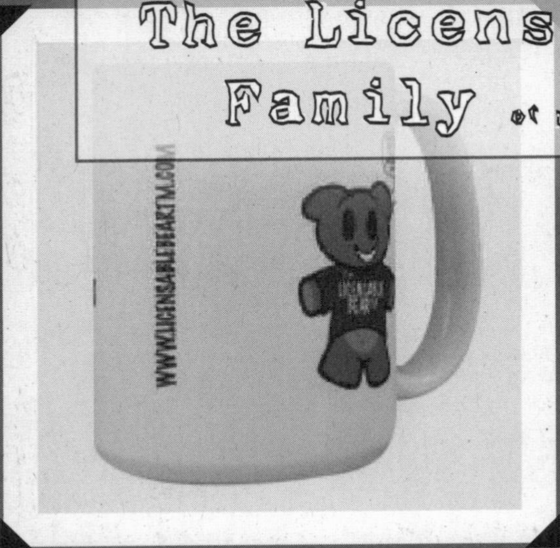
WWW.LICENSABLEBEARTM.COM
LICENSABLE BEAR

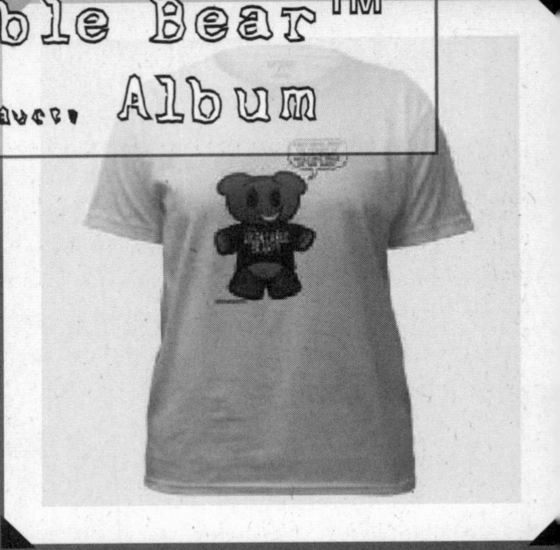

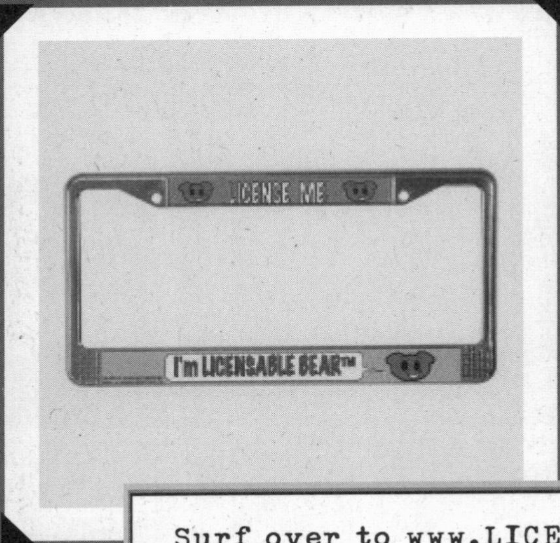
LICENSE ME
I'm LICENSABLE BEAR™

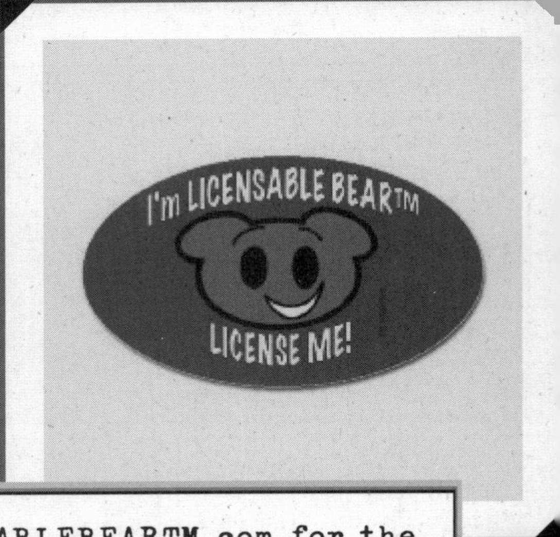
I'm LICENSABLE BEAR™
LICENSE ME!

Surf over to www.LICENSABLEBEARTM.com for the latest Licensable Bear™ goods, news, and notes!

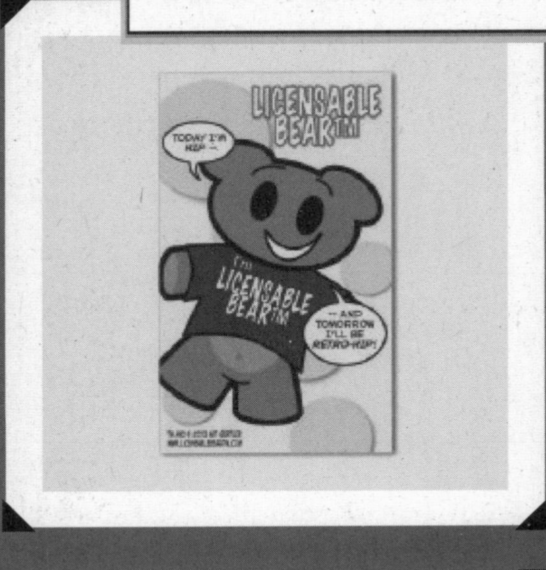
LICENSABLE BEAR™
TODAY I'M HIP —
I'm LICENSABLE BEAR™
— AND TOMORROW I'LL BE RETRO-HIP!

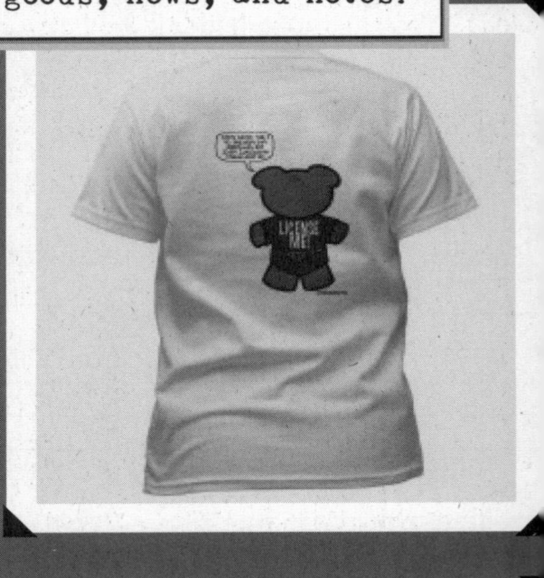
LICENSE ME!

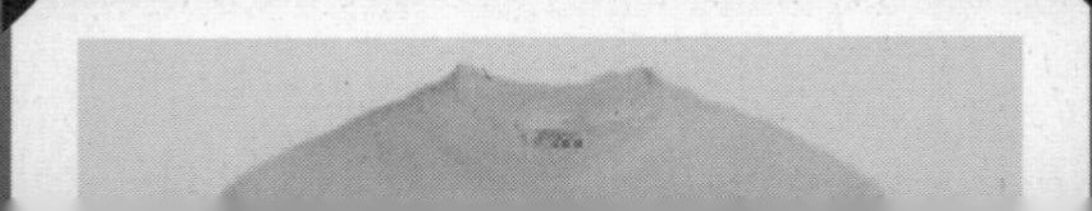

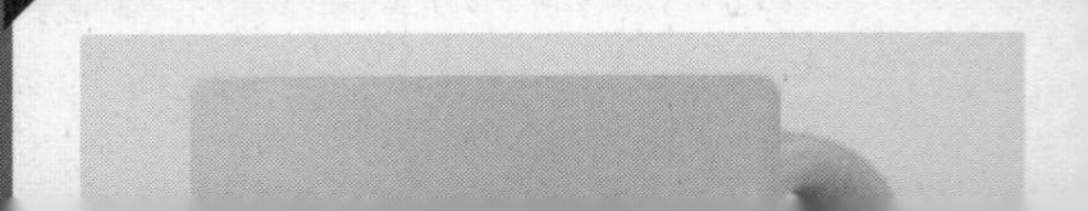

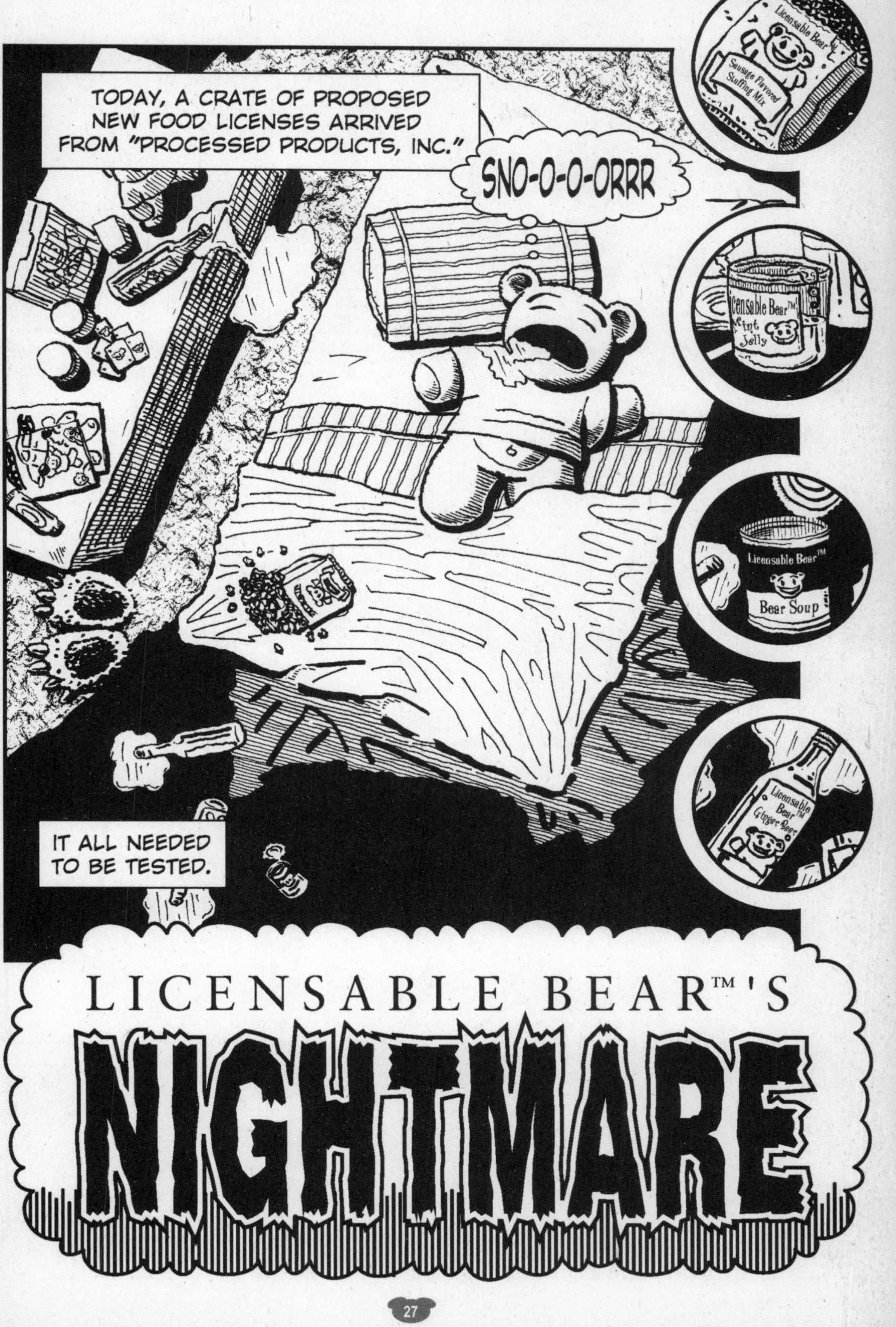
TODAY, A CRATE OF PROPOSED NEW FOOD LICENSES ARRIVED FROM "PROCESSED PRODUCTS, INC."
SNO-O-O-ORRR
Licensable Bear™
Sausage Flavored Stuffing Mix
icensable Bear™
Mint Jelly
Licensable Bear™
Bear Soup
Licensable Bear™
Ginger Beer
IT ALL NEEDED TO BE TESTED.
LICENSABLE BEAR™'S
NIGHTMARE

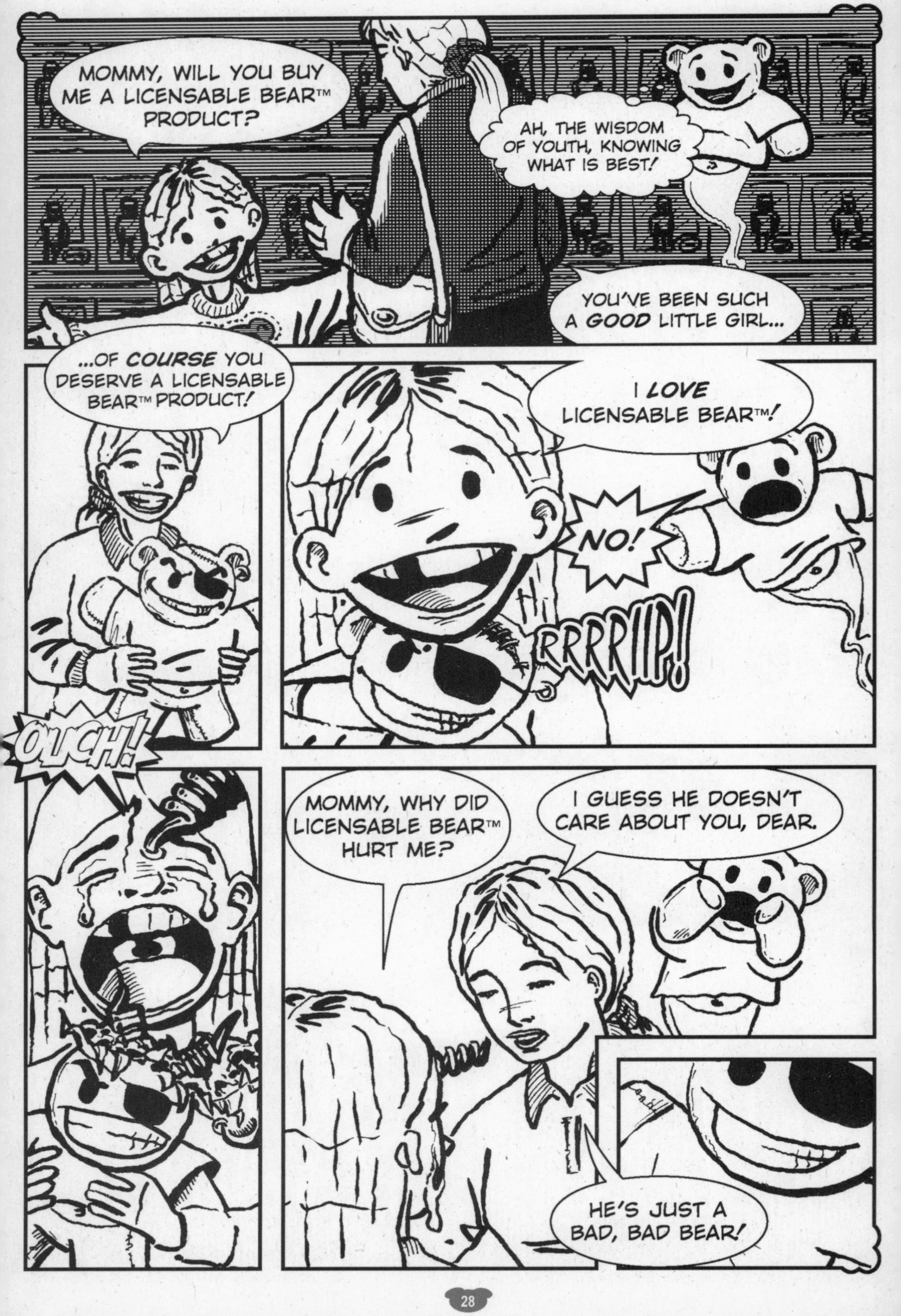

MOMMY, WILL YOU BUY ME A LICENSABLE BEAR™ PRODUCT?
AH, THE WISDOM OF YOUTH, KNOWING WHAT IS BEST!
YOU'VE BEEN SUCH A GOOD LITTLE GIRL...
...OF COURSE YOU DESERVE A LICENSABLE BEAR™ PRODUCT!
I LOVE LICENSABLE BEAR™!
NO!
RRRRIIP!
OUCH!
MOMMY, WHY DID LICENSABLE BEAR™ HURT ME?
I GUESS HE DOESN'T CARE ABOUT YOU, DEAR.
HE'S JUST A BAD, BAD BEAR!

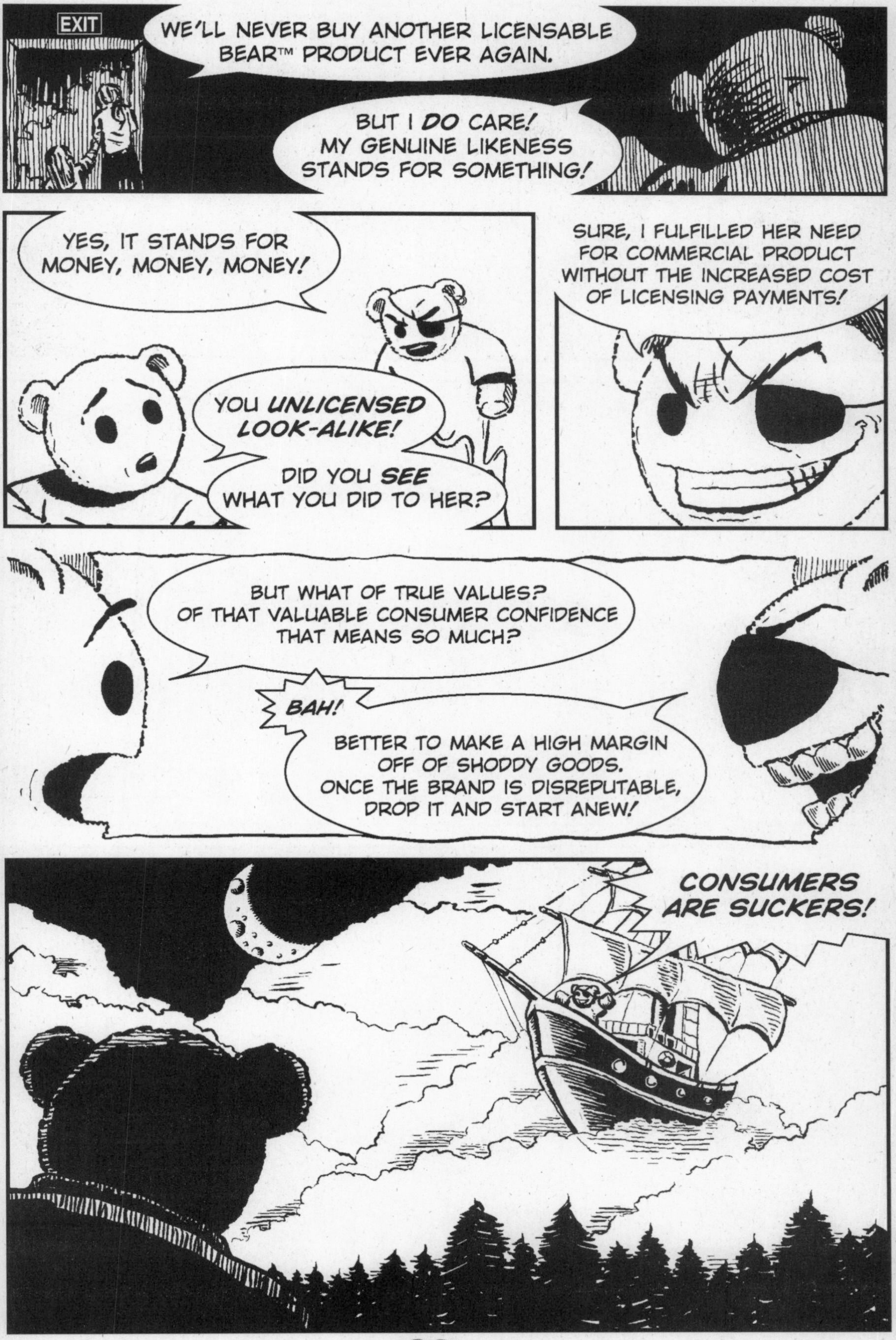
EXIT
WE'LL NEVER BUY ANOTHER LICENSABLE BEAR™ PRODUCT EVER AGAIN.
BUT I DO CARE! MY GENUINE LIKENESS STANDS FOR SOMETHING!
YES, IT STANDS FOR MONEY, MONEY, MONEY!
YOU UNLICENSED LOOK-ALIKE!
DID YOU SEE WHAT YOU DID TO HER?
SURE, I FULFILLED HER NEED FOR COMMERCIAL PRODUCT WITHOUT THE INCREASED COST OF LICENSING PAYMENTS!
BUT WHAT OF TRUE VALUES? OF THAT VALUABLE CONSUMER CONFIDENCE THAT MEANS SO MUCH?
BAH!
BETTER TO MAKE A HIGH MARGIN OFF OF SHODDY GOODS. ONCE THE BRAND IS DISREPUTABLE, DROP IT AND START ANEW!
CONSUMERS ARE SUCKERS!

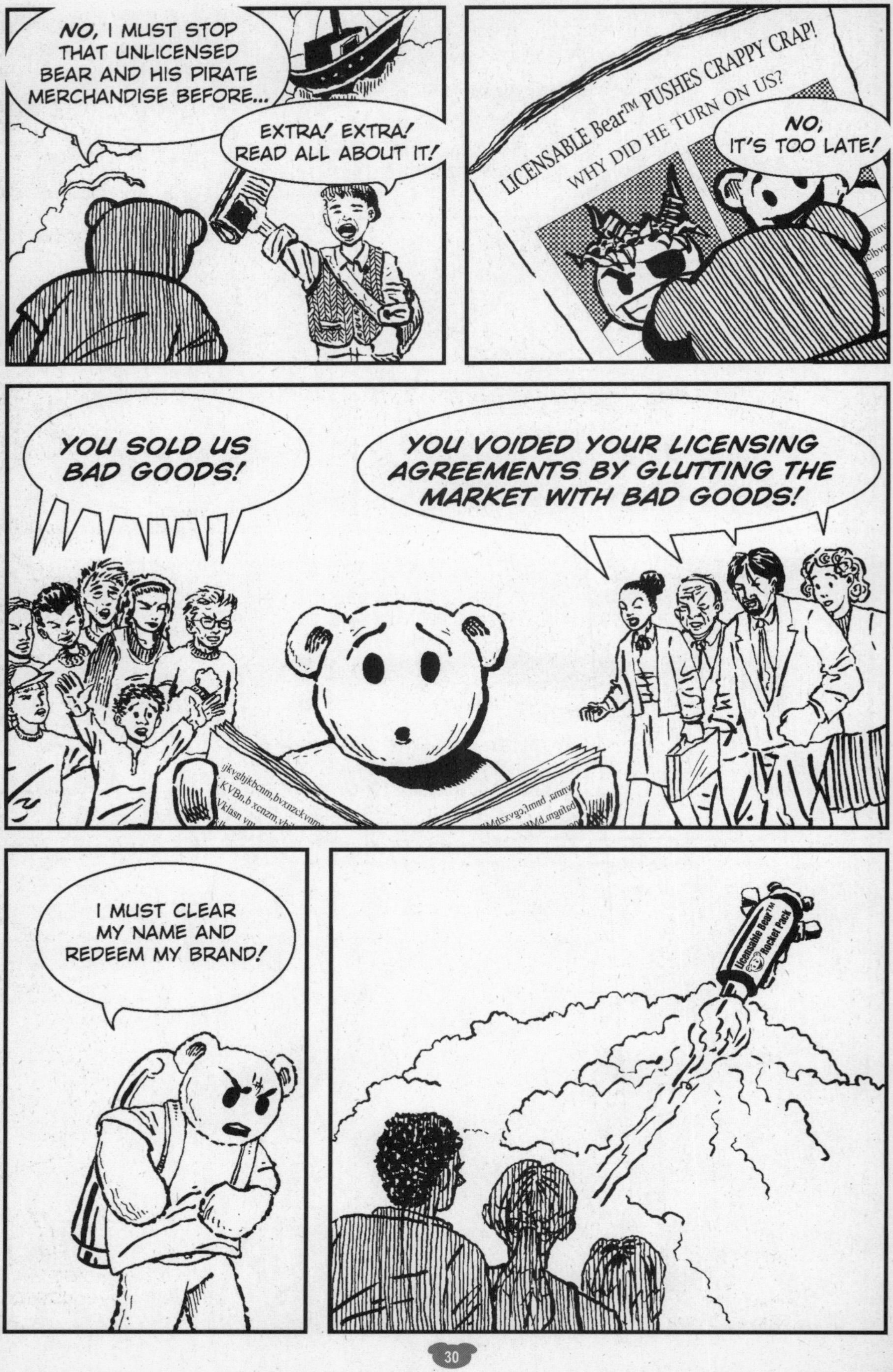
NO, I MUST STOP THAT UNLICENSED BEAR AND HIS PIRATE MERCHANDISE BEFORE...
EXTRA! EXTRA! READ ALL ABOUT IT!
LICENSABLE Bear™ PUSHES CRAPPY CRAP!
WHY DID HE TURN ON US?
NO, IT'S TOO LATE!
YOU SOLD US BAD GOODS!
YOU VOIDED YOUR LICENSING AGREEMENTS BY GLUTTING THE MARKET WITH BAD GOODS!
I MUST CLEAR MY NAME AND REDEEM MY BRAND!
Licensable Bear™ Rocket Pack

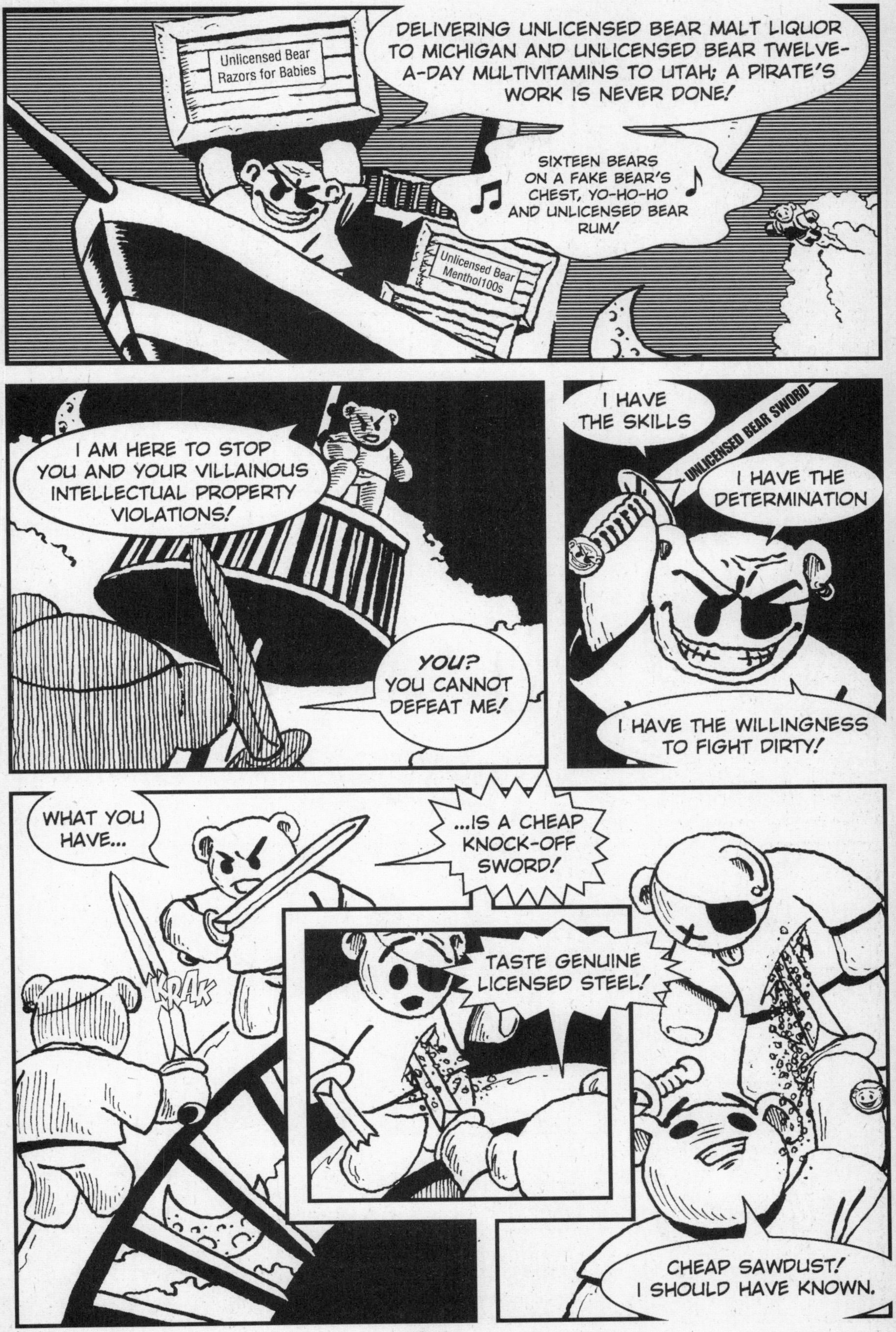

Unlicensed Bear Razors for Babies
DELIVERING UNLICENSED BEAR MALT LIQUOR TO MICHIGAN AND UNLICENSED BEAR TWELVE-A-DAY MULTIVITAMINS TO UTAH; A PIRATE'S WORK IS NEVER DONE!
SIXTEEN BEARS ON A FAKE BEAR'S CHEST, YO-HO-HO AND UNLICENSED BEAR RUM!
Unlicensed Bear Menthol100s
I AM HERE TO STOP YOU AND YOUR VILLAINOUS INTELLECTUAL PROPERTY VIOLATIONS!
YOU? YOU CANNOT DEFEAT ME!
I HAVE THE SKILLS
UNLICENSED BEAR SWORD
I HAVE THE DETERMINATION
I HAVE THE WILLINGNESS TO FIGHT DIRTY!
WHAT YOU HAVE...
...IS A CHEAP KNOCK-OFF SWORD!
KRAK
TASTE GENUINE LICENSED STEEL!
CHEAP SAWDUST! I SHOULD HAVE KNOWN.

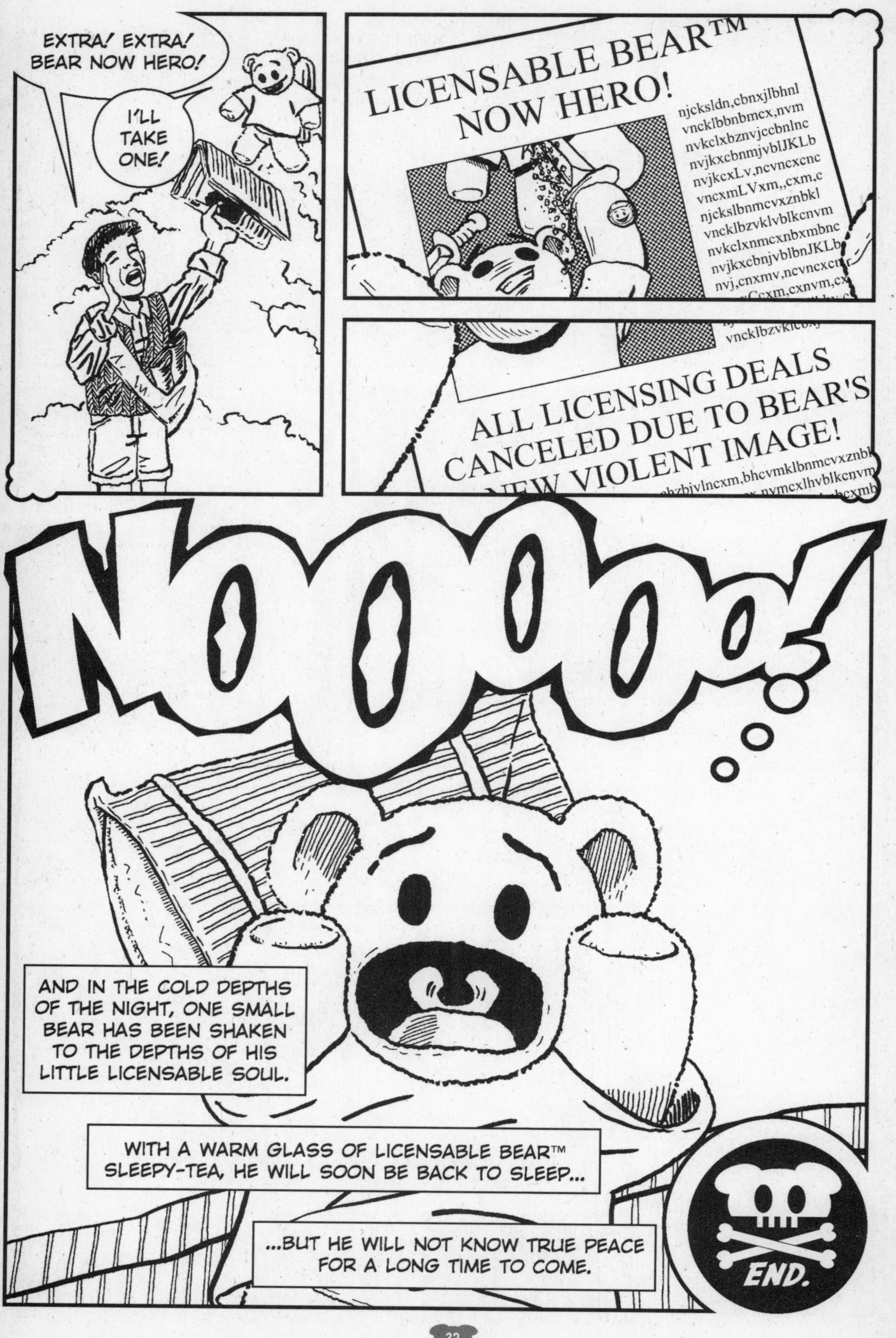
EXTRA! EXTRA! BEAR NOW HERO!
I'LL TAKE ONE!
LICENSABLE BEAR™ NOW HERO!
ALL LICENSING DEALS CANCELED DUE TO BEAR'S NEW VIOLENT IMAGE!
NOOOoo!
AND IN THE COLD DEPTHS OF THE NIGHT, ONE SMALL BEAR HAS BEEN SHAKEN TO THE DEPTHS OF HIS LITTLE LICENSABLE SOUL.
WITH A WARM GLASS OF LICENSABLE BEAR™ SLEEPY-TEA, HE WILL SOON BE BACK TO SLEEP...
...BUT HE WILL NOT KNOW TRUE PEACE FOR A LONG TIME TO COME.
END.

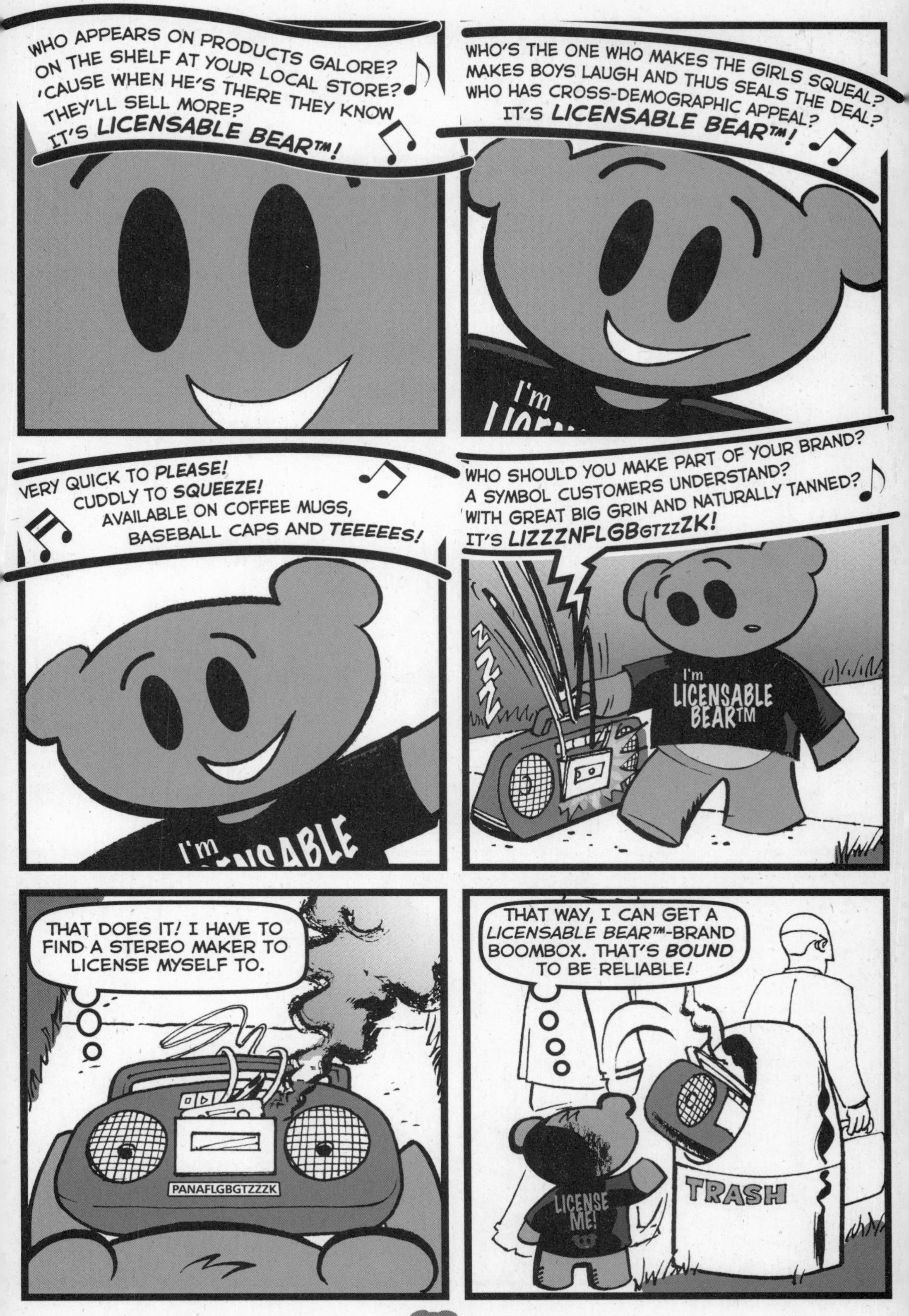

WHO APPEARS ON PRODUCTS GALORE?
ON THE SHELF AT YOUR LOCAL STORE?
'CAUSE WHEN HE'S THERE THEY KNOW
THEY'LL SELL MORE?
IT'S LICENSABLE BEAR™!
WHO'S THE ONE WHO MAKES THE GIRLS SQUEAL?
MAKES BOYS LAUGH AND THUS SEALS THE DEAL?
WHO HAS CROSS-DEMOGRAPHIC APPEAL?
IT'S LICENSABLE BEAR™!
I'm
VERY QUICK TO PLEASE!
CUDDLY TO SQUEEZE!
AVAILABLE ON COFFEE MUGS,
BASEBALL CAPS AND TEEEEES!
I'm
WHO SHOULD YOU MAKE PART OF YOUR BRAND?
A SYMBOL CUSTOMERS UNDERSTAND?
WITH GREAT BIG GRIN AND NATURALLY TANNED?
IT'S LIZZZNFLGBGTZZZK!
NNN
I'm LICENSABLE BEAR™
THAT DOES IT! I HAVE TO FIND A STEREO MAKER TO LICENSE MYSELF TO.
PANAFLGBGTZZZK
THAT WAY, I CAN GET A LICENSABLE BEAR™-BRAND BOOMBOX. THAT'S BOUND TO BE RELIABLE!
LICENSE ME!
TRASH

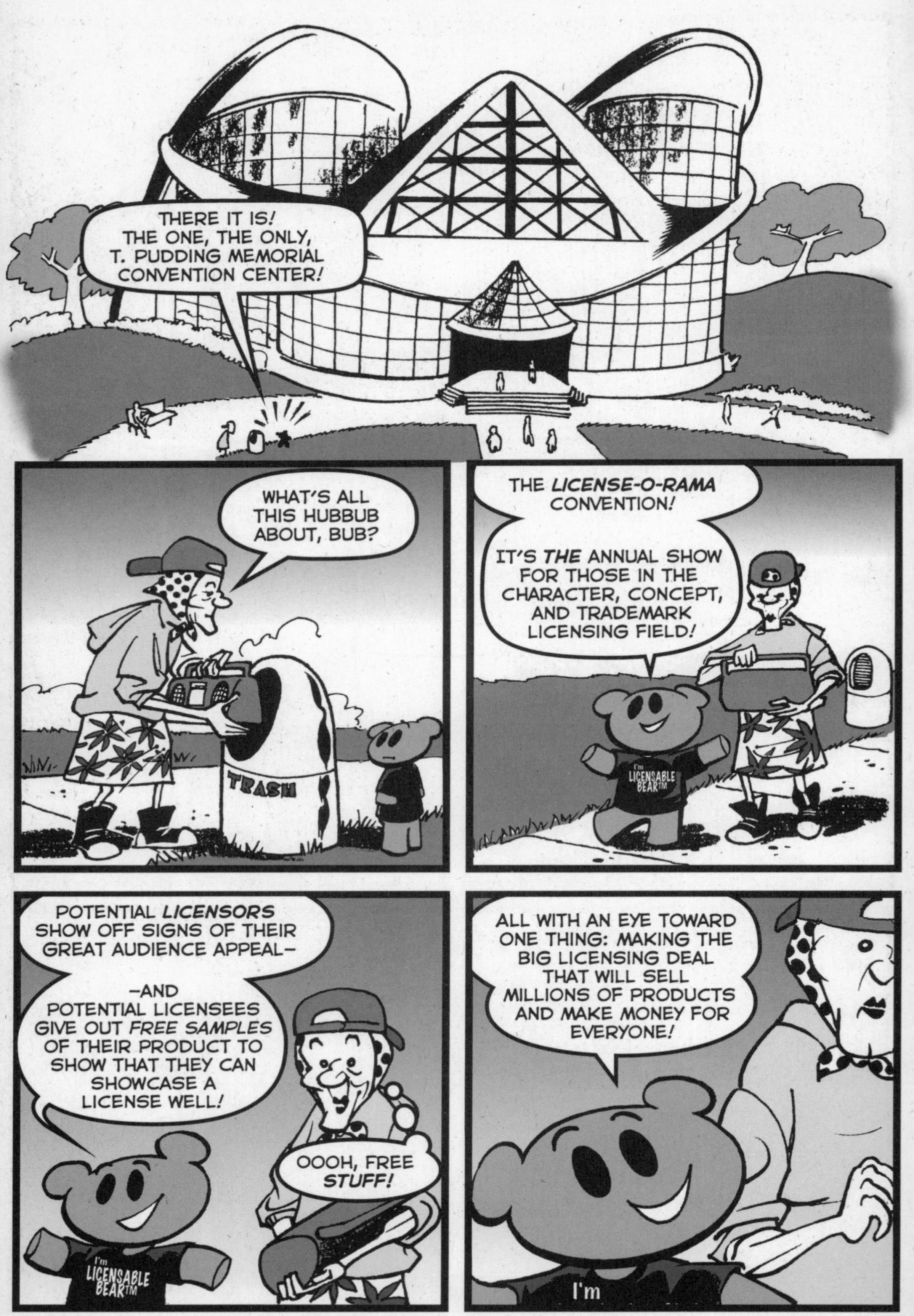
THERE IT IS! THE ONE, THE ONLY, T. PUDDING MEMORIAL CONVENTION CENTER!
WHAT'S ALL THIS HUBBUB ABOUT, BUB?
TRASH
THE LICENSE-O-RAMA CONVENTION!
IT'S THE ANNUAL SHOW FOR THOSE IN THE CHARACTER, CONCEPT, AND TRADEMARK LICENSING FIELD!
I'm LICENSABLE BEAR™
POTENTIAL LICENSORS SHOW OFF SIGNS OF THEIR GREAT AUDIENCE APPEAL–
–AND POTENTIAL LICENSEES GIVE OUT FREE SAMPLES OF THEIR PRODUCT TO SHOW THAT THEY CAN SHOWCASE A LICENSE WELL!
OOOH, FREE STUFF!
I'm LICENSABLE BEAR™
ALL WITH AN EYE TOWARD ONE THING: MAKING THE BIG LICENSING DEAL THAT WILL SELL MILLIONS OF PRODUCTS AND MAKE MONEY FOR EVERYONE!
I'm

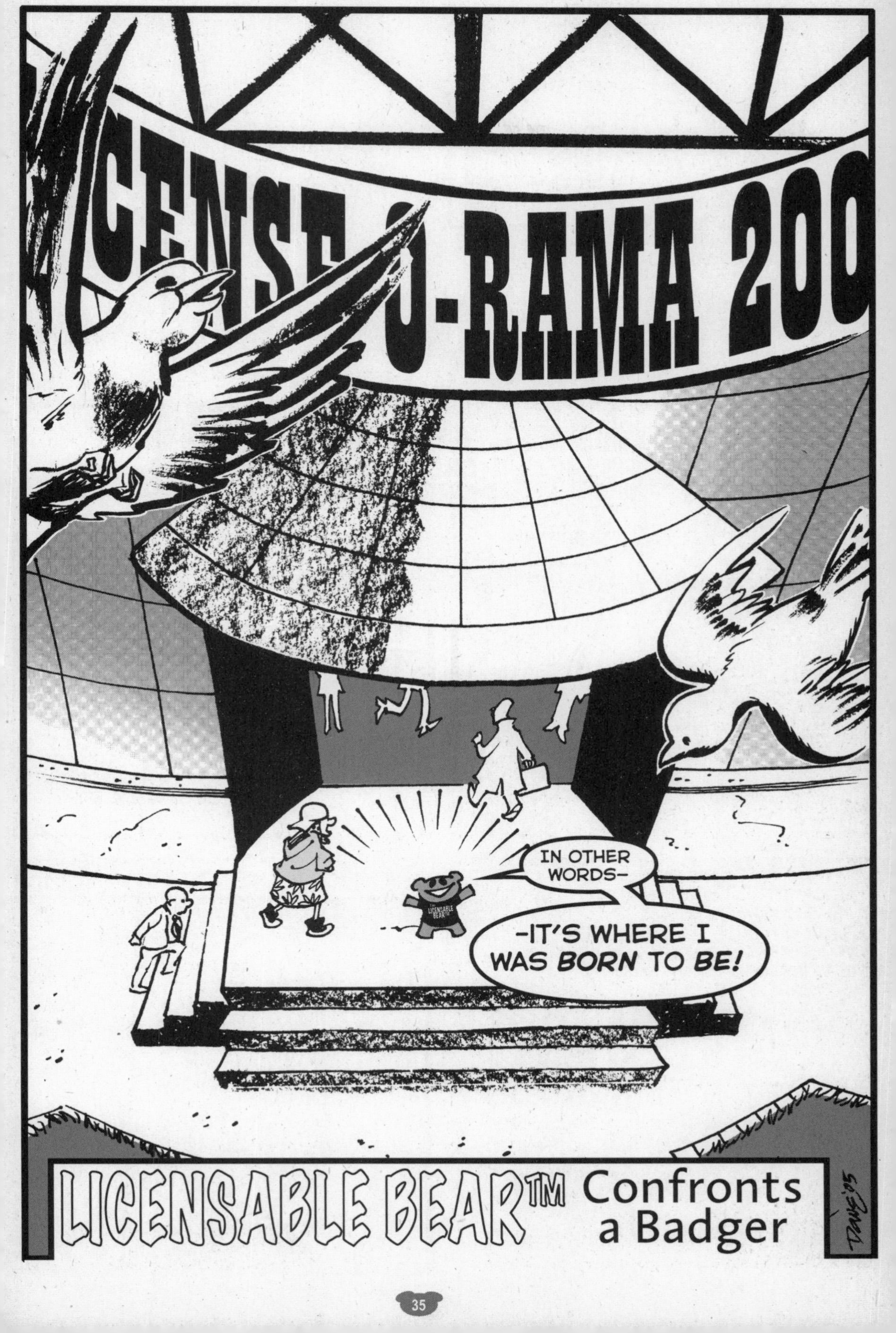
CENSE O-RAMA 200
IN OTHER WORDS–
–IT'S WHERE I WAS BORN TO BE!
LICENSABLE BEAR™ Confronts a Badger

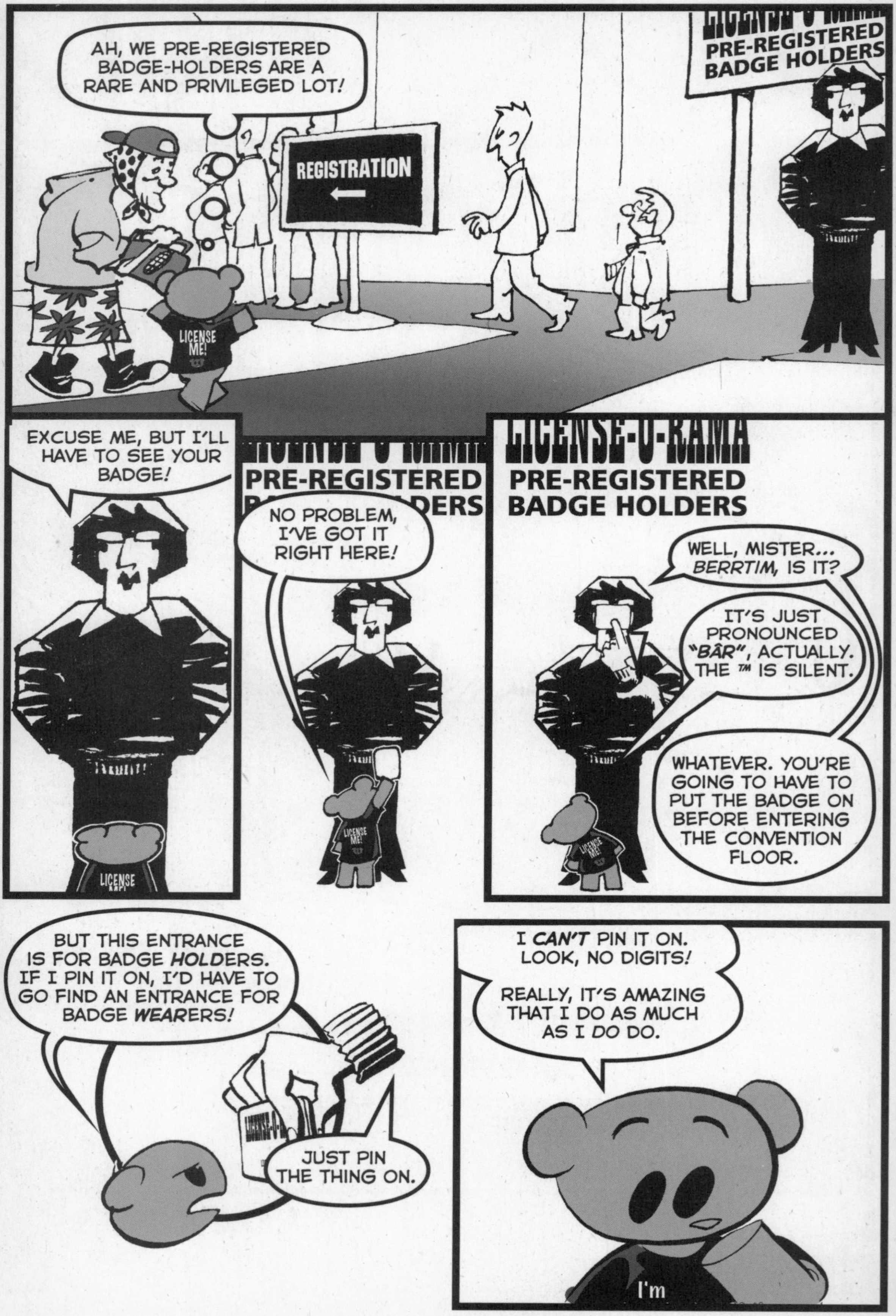
PRE-REGISTERED BADGE HOLDERS
AH, WE PRE-REGISTERED BADGE-HOLDERS ARE A RARE AND PRIVILEGED LOT!
REGISTRATION
LICENSE ME!
EXCUSE ME, BUT I'LL HAVE TO SEE YOUR BADGE!
PRE-REGISTERED
NO PROBLEM, I'VE GOT IT RIGHT HERE!
LICENSE ME!
LICENSE-O-RAMA
PRE-REGISTERED BADGE HOLDERS
WELL, MISTER... *BERRTIM*, IS IT?
IT'S JUST PRONOUNCED *"BÂR"*, ACTUALLY. THE ™ IS SILENT.
WHATEVER. YOU'RE GOING TO HAVE TO PUT THE BADGE ON BEFORE ENTERING THE CONVENTION FLOOR.
BUT THIS ENTRANCE IS FOR BADGE *HOLD*ERS. IF I PIN IT ON, I'D HAVE TO GO FIND AN ENTRANCE FOR BADGE *WEAR*ERS!
JUST PIN THE THING ON.
I *CAN'T* PIN IT ON. LOOK, NO DIGITS!
REALLY, IT'S AMAZING THAT I DO AS MUCH AS I *DO* DO.
I'm

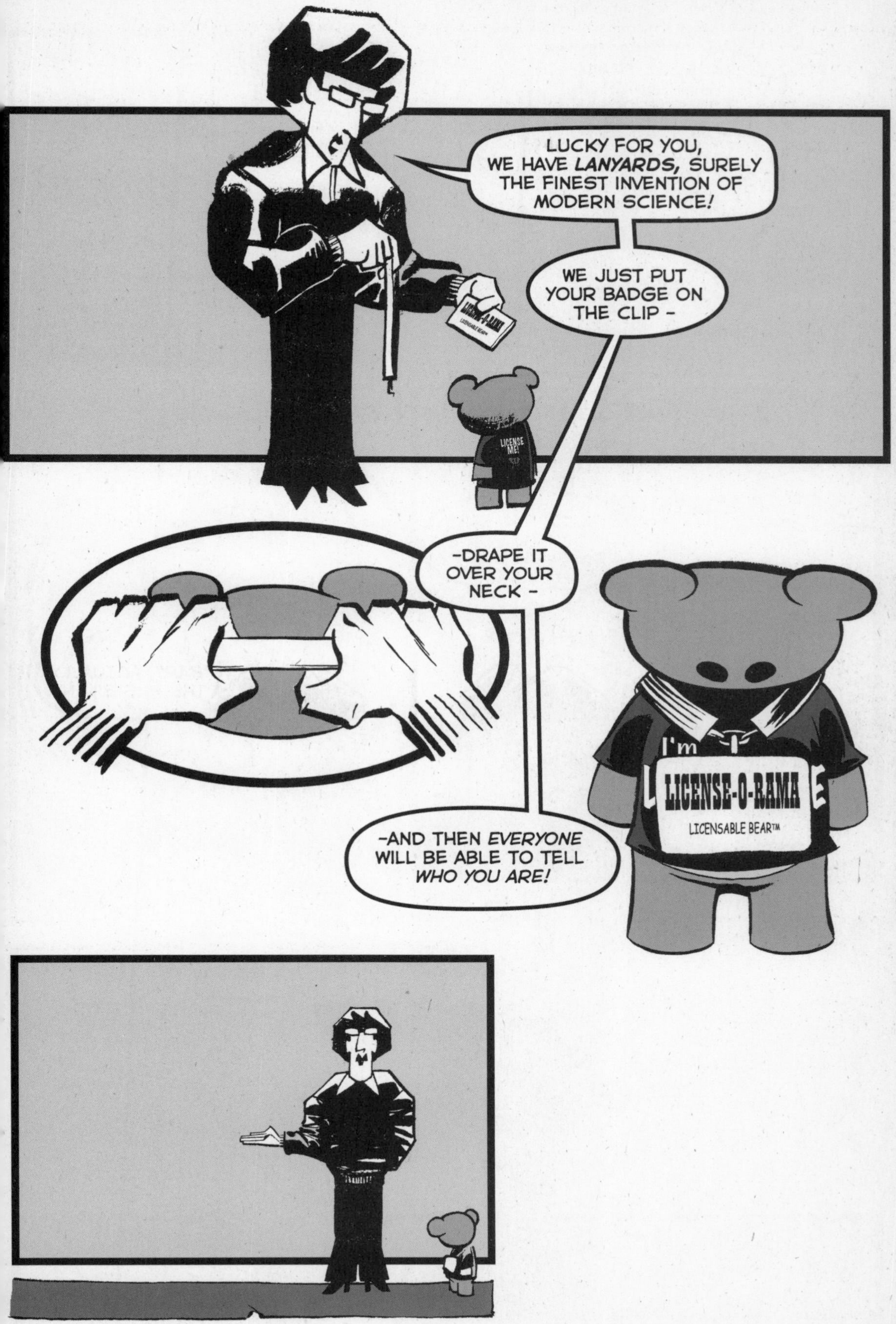

LUCKY FOR YOU, WE HAVE *LANYARDS,* SURELY THE FINEST INVENTION OF MODERN SCIENCE!
LICENSE-O-RAMA
LICENSABLE BEAR™
WE JUST PUT YOUR BADGE ON THE CLIP -
LICENSE ME!
-DRAPE IT OVER YOUR NECK -
-AND THEN *EVERYONE* WILL BE ABLE TO TELL *WHO YOU ARE!*
I'm
LICENSE-O-RAMA
LICENSABLE BEAR™

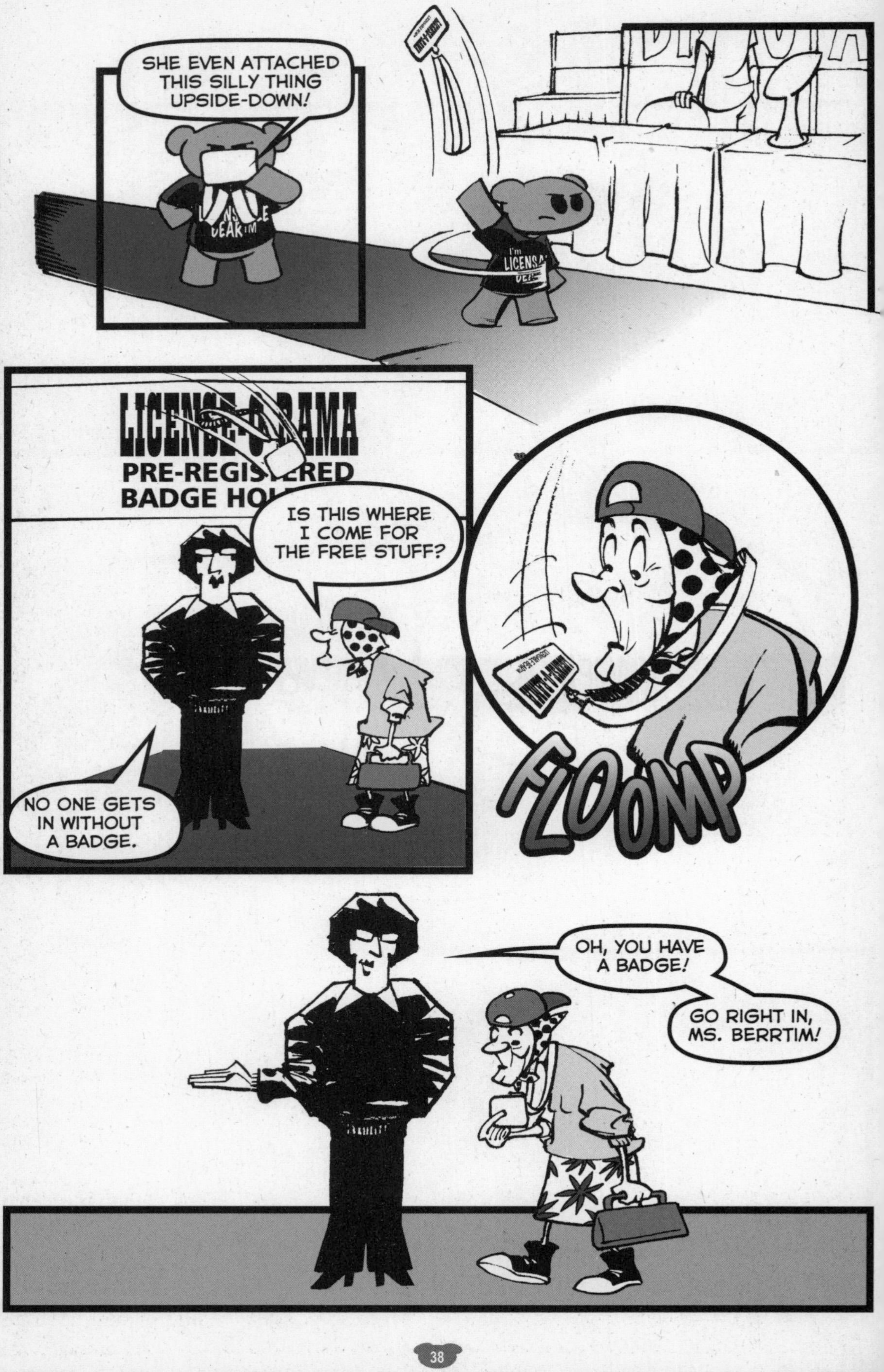
SHE EVEN ATTACHED THIS SILLY THING UPSIDE-DOWN!
LICENSE-O-RAMA
PRE-REGISTERED BADGE HOL
IS THIS WHERE I COME FOR THE FREE STUFF?
NO ONE GETS IN WITHOUT A BADGE.
FLOOMP
OH, YOU HAVE A BADGE!
GO RIGHT IN, MS. BERRTIM!

LICENSABLE BEAR™, Finder of Lost Consumers

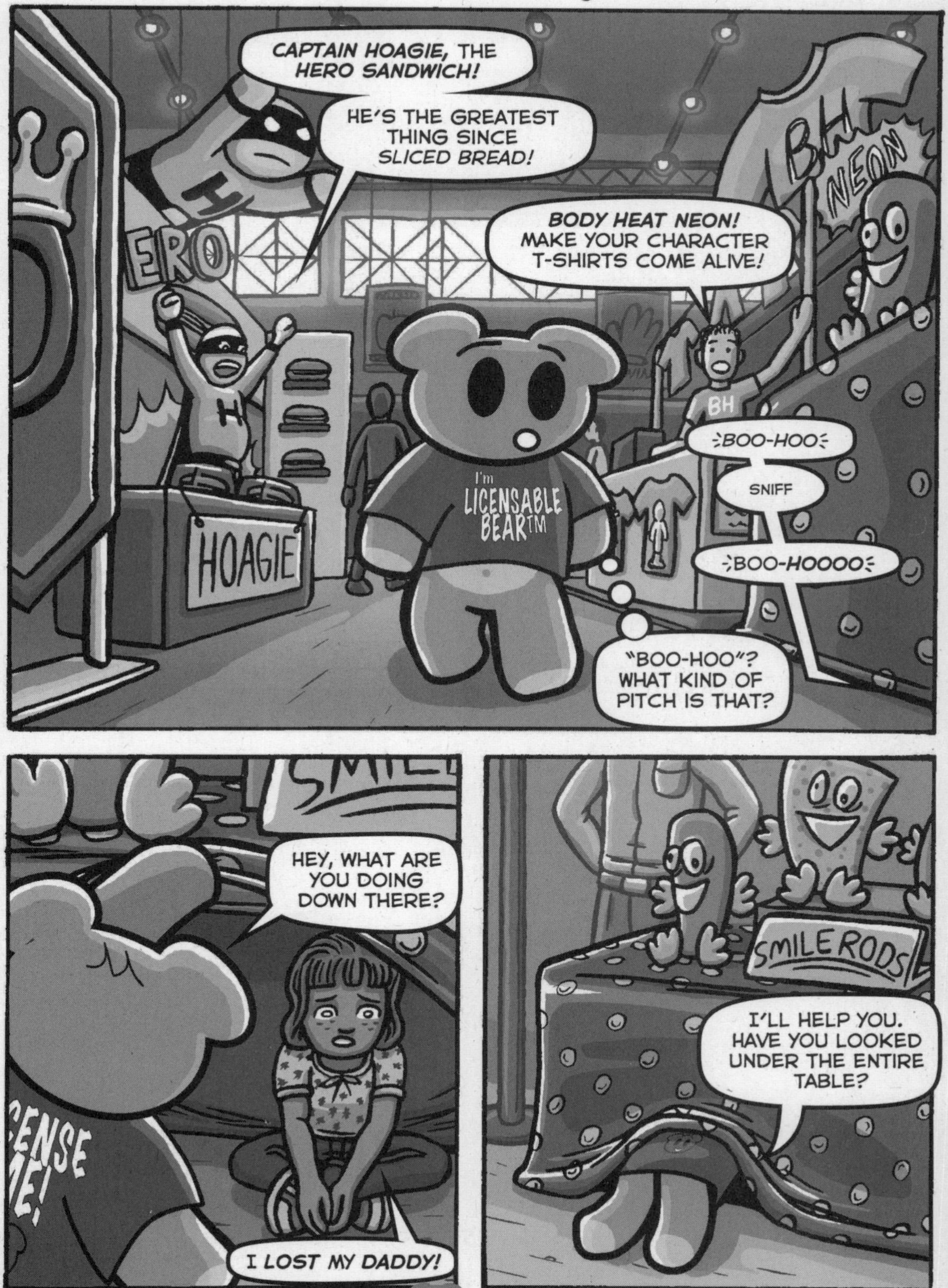
CAPTAIN HOAGIE, THE HERO SANDWICH!
HE'S THE GREATEST THING SINCE SLICED BREAD!
HERO
HOAGIE
BODY HEAT NEON! MAKE YOUR CHARACTER T-SHIRTS COME ALIVE!
BH
NEON
I'm LICENSABLE BEAR™
BOO-HOO
SNIFF
BOO-HOOOO
"BOO-HOO"? WHAT KIND OF PITCH IS THAT?
HEY, WHAT ARE YOU DOING DOWN THERE?
I LOST MY DADDY!
SMILE RODS
I'LL HELP YOU. HAVE YOU LOOKED UNDER THE ENTIRE TABLE?

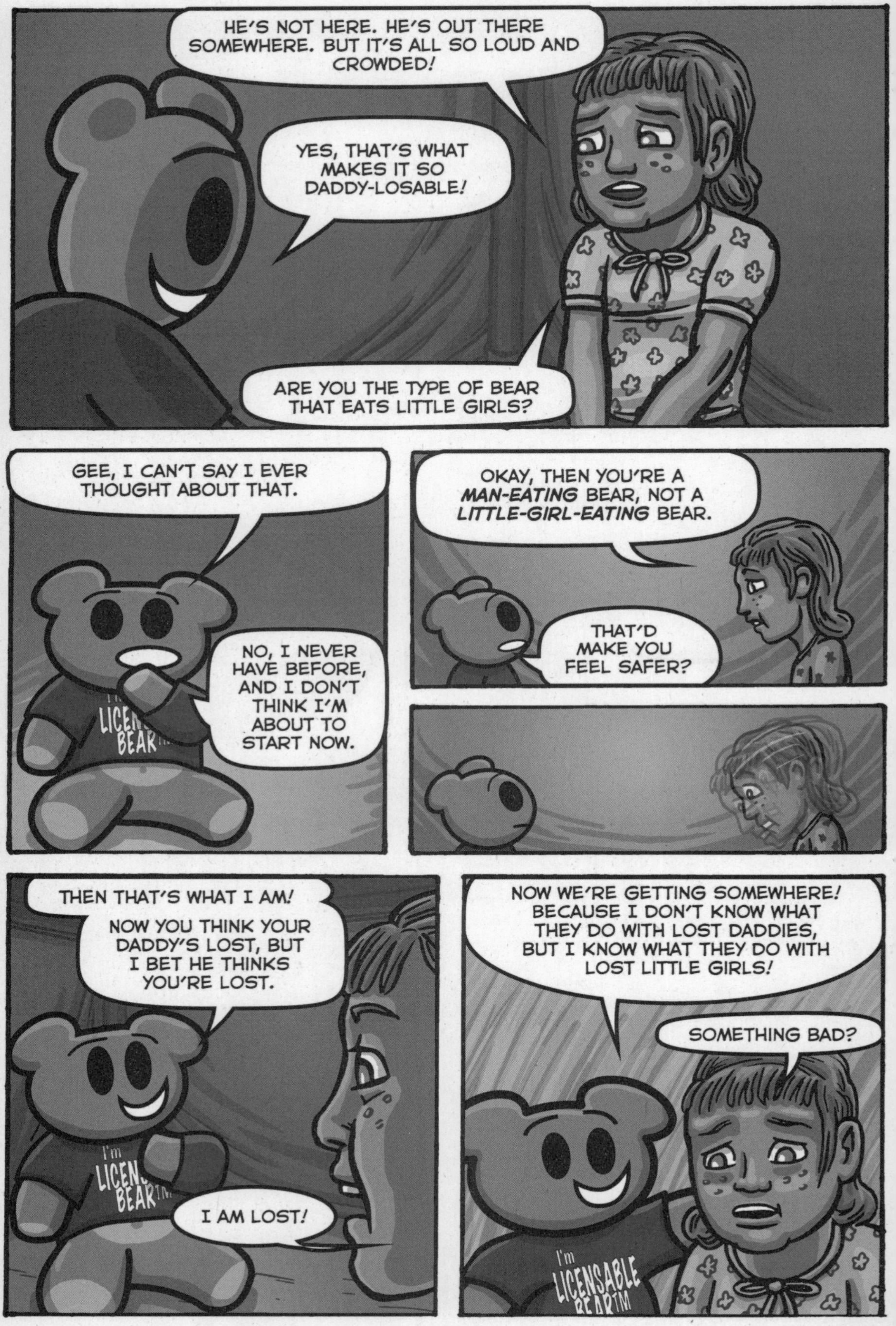
HE'S NOT HERE. HE'S OUT THERE SOMEWHERE. BUT IT'S ALL SO LOUD AND CROWDED!
YES, THAT'S WHAT MAKES IT SO DADDY-LOSABLE!
ARE YOU THE TYPE OF BEAR THAT EATS LITTLE GIRLS?
GEE, I CAN'T SAY I EVER THOUGHT ABOUT THAT.
NO, I NEVER HAVE BEFORE, AND I DON'T THINK I'M ABOUT TO START NOW.
OKAY, THEN YOU'RE A *MAN-EATING* BEAR, NOT A *LITTLE-GIRL-EATING* BEAR.
THAT'D MAKE YOU FEEL SAFER?
THEN THAT'S WHAT I AM!
NOW YOU THINK YOUR DADDY'S LOST, BUT I BET HE THINKS YOU'RE LOST.
I AM LOST!
NOW WE'RE GETTING SOMEWHERE! BECAUSE I DON'T KNOW WHAT THEY DO WITH LOST DADDIES, BUT I KNOW WHAT THEY DO WITH LOST LITTLE GIRLS!
SOMETHING BAD?
I'm LICENSABLE BEAR™

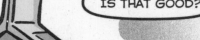

NO! THEY PUT THEIR PICTURES ON THE SIDE OF MILK CARTONS!

IS THAT GOOD?

YOU BET IT IS! I MEAN, I GET MY FACE ON A LOT OF PRODUCTS, AND IT'S WONDERFUL. BUT *MILK?* YOU CAN'T BEAT MILK!

I *LIKE* MILK!

OPEN

HAVE YOU SEEN THIS CUTE LI'L GIRL?

LOTS OF PEOPLE LIKE MILK.

AND I DON'T KNOW HOW MUCH MONEY KIDS GET FOR LICENSING THEIR PICTURES FOR THE CARTON, BUT EVEN A *SMALL PER-UNIT FEE* WOULD MEAN SIZABLE RESIDUAL INCOME ON SUCH A COMMODITY.

NOT TO MENTION THE SECONDARY BRANDING POSSIBILITIES!

I'm LICENSABLE BEAR™

WHAT'S SECETARY BANDING POSABILITY?

MONEY!

LICENSE ME!

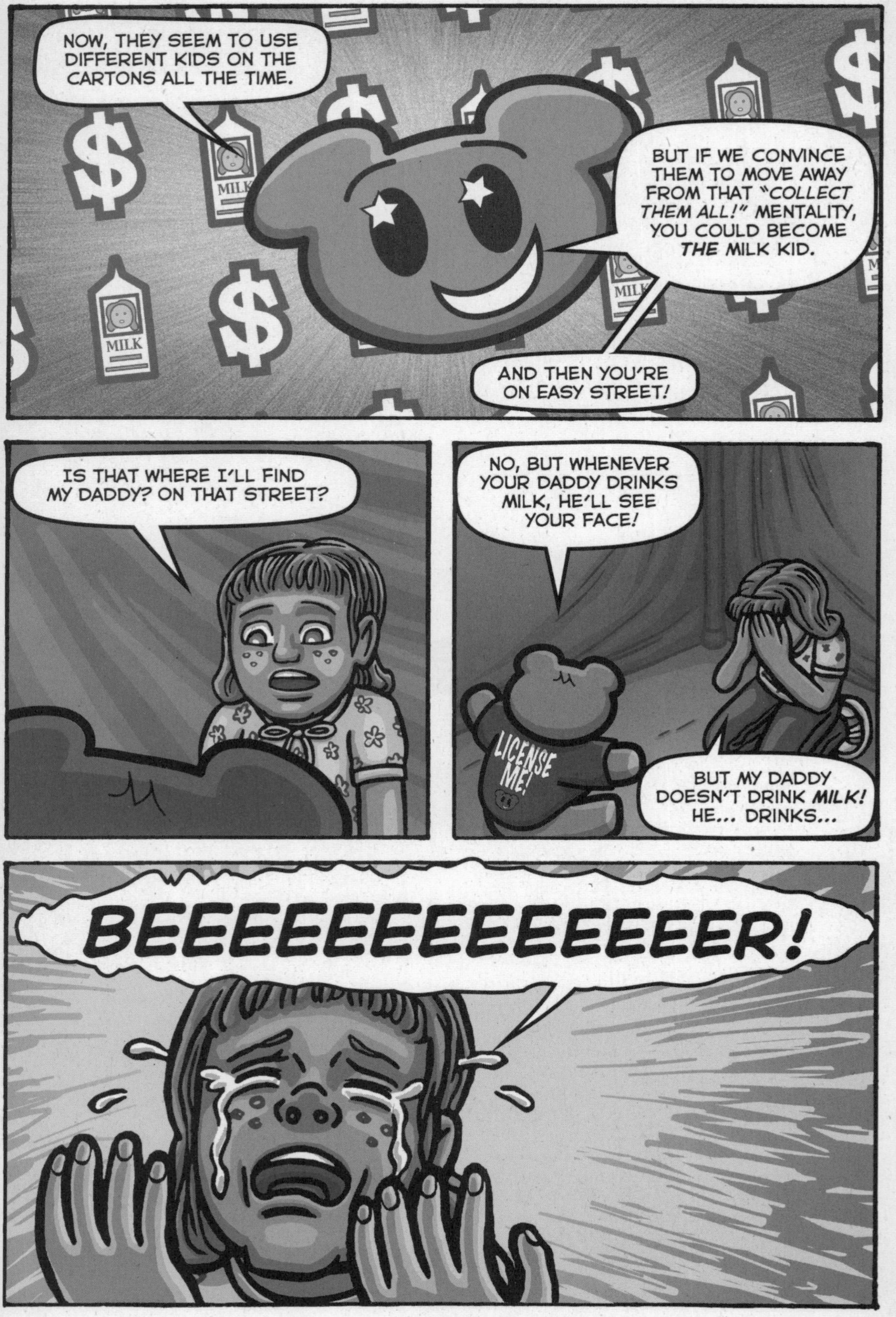

NOW, THEY SEEM TO USE DIFFERENT KIDS ON THE CARTONS ALL THE TIME.
MILK
BUT IF WE CONVINCE THEM TO MOVE AWAY FROM THAT "COLLECT THEM ALL!" MENTALITY, YOU COULD BECOME THE MILK KID.
AND THEN YOU'RE ON EASY STREET!
IS THAT WHERE I'LL FIND MY DADDY? ON THAT STREET?
NO, BUT WHENEVER YOUR DADDY DRINKS MILK, HE'LL SEE YOUR FACE!
LICENSE ME!
BUT MY DADDY DOESN'T DRINK MILK! HE... DRINKS...
BEEEEEEEEEEEEEER!

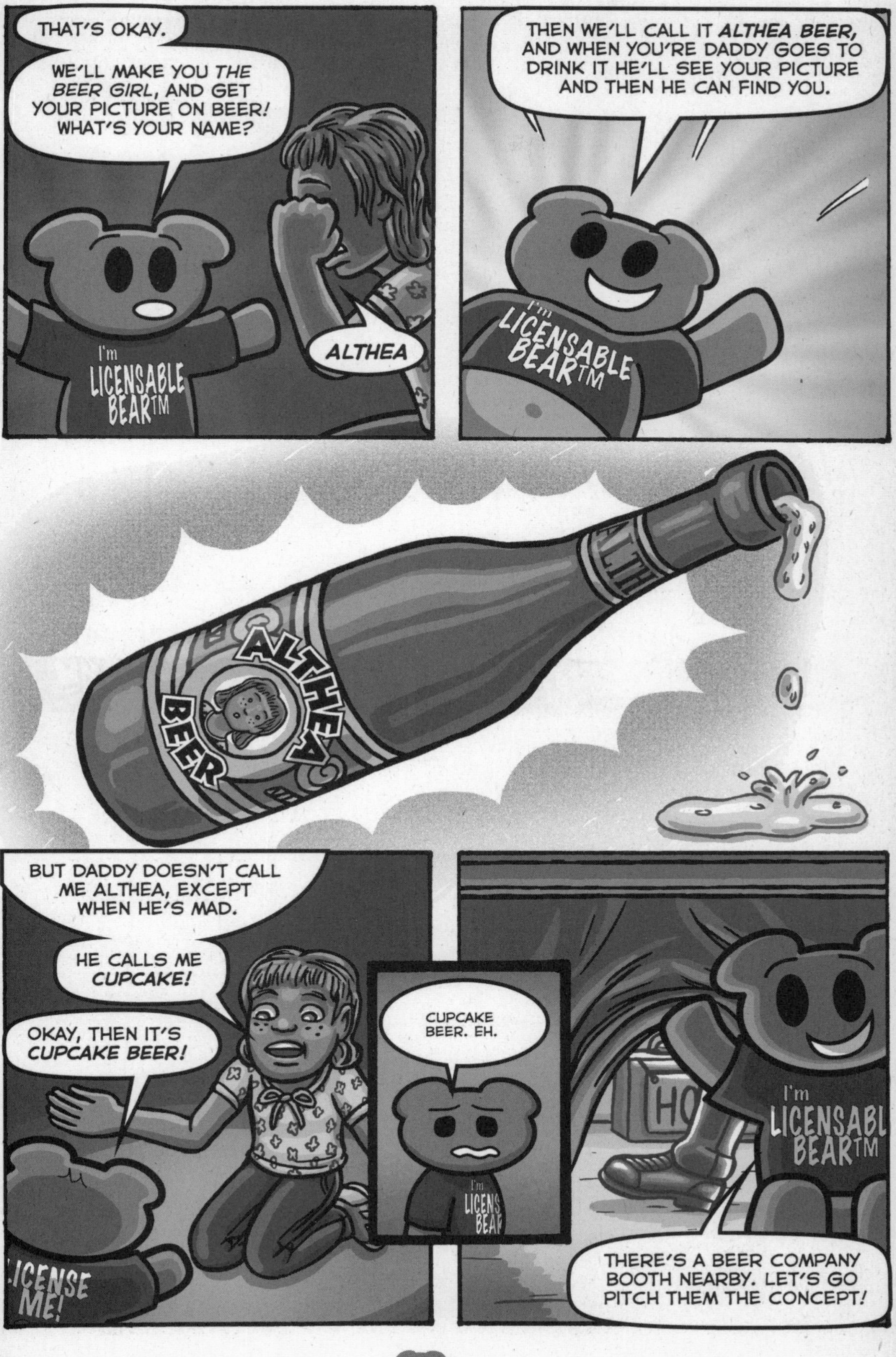
THAT'S OKAY.
WE'LL MAKE YOU *THE BEER GIRL*, AND GET YOUR PICTURE ON BEER! WHAT'S YOUR NAME?
ALTHEA
I'm LICENSABLE BEAR™
THEN WE'LL CALL IT *ALTHEA BEER,* AND WHEN YOU'RE DADDY GOES TO DRINK IT HE'LL SEE YOUR PICTURE AND THEN HE CAN FIND YOU.
I'm LICENSABLE BEAR™
ALTHEA BEER
BUT DADDY DOESN'T CALL ME ALTHEA, EXCEPT WHEN HE'S MAD.
HE CALLS ME *CUPCAKE!*
OKAY, THEN IT'S *CUPCAKE BEER!*
LICENSE ME!
CUPCAKE BEER. EH.
I'm LICENSABLE BEAR™
THERE'S A BEER COMPANY BOOTH NEARBY. LET'S GO PITCH THEM THE CONCEPT!

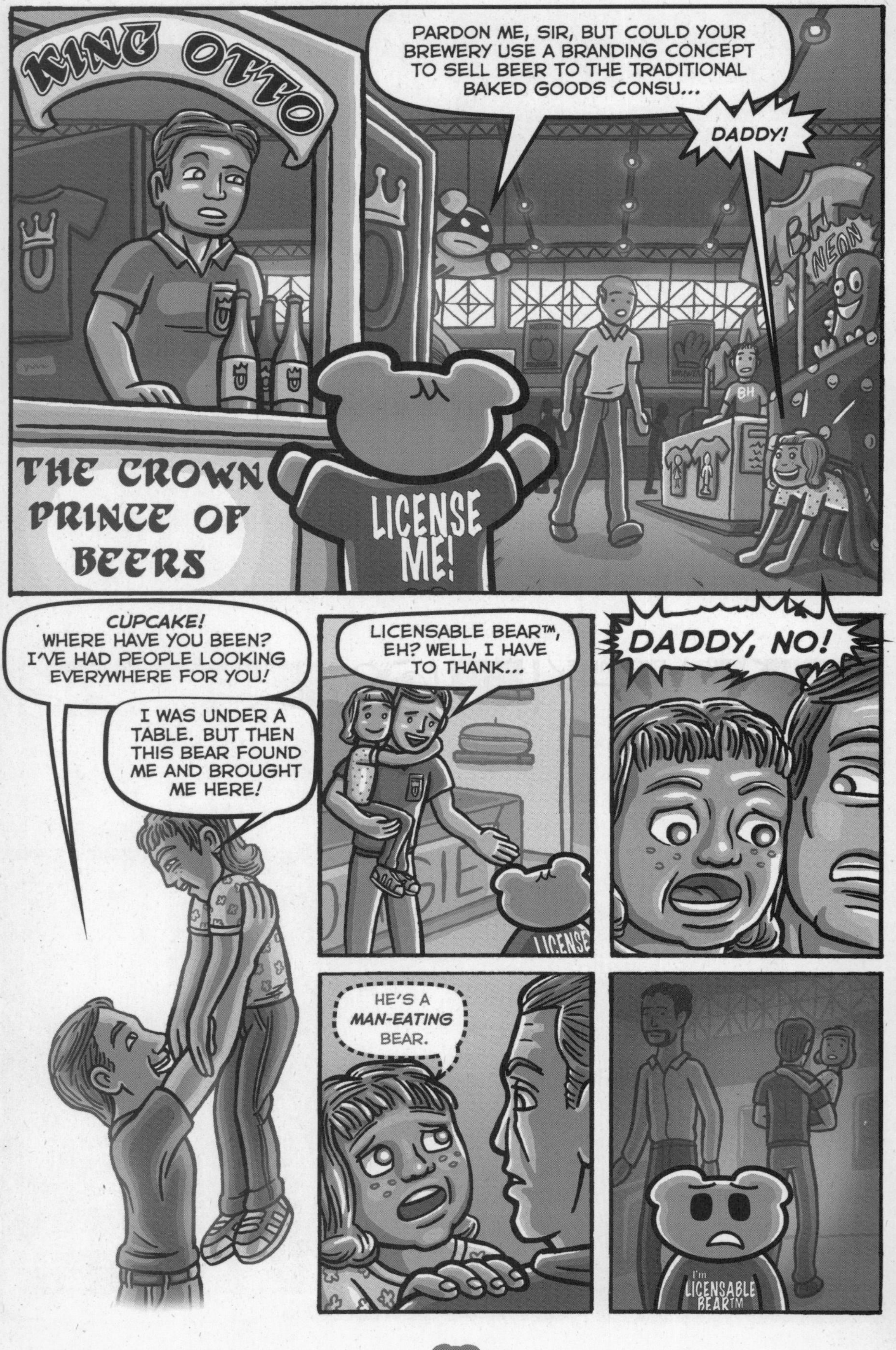
KING OTTO
PARDON ME, SIR, BUT COULD YOUR BREWERY USE A BRANDING CONCEPT TO SELL BEER TO THE TRADITIONAL BAKED GOODS CONSU...
DADDY!
NEON
BH
THE CROWN PRINCE OF BEERS
LICENSE ME!
CUPCAKE! WHERE HAVE YOU BEEN? I'VE HAD PEOPLE LOOKING EVERYWHERE FOR YOU!
I WAS UNDER A TABLE. BUT THEN THIS BEAR FOUND ME AND BROUGHT ME HERE!
LICENSABLE BEAR™, EH? WELL, I HAVE TO THANK...
LICENSE
DADDY, NO!
HE'S A MAN-EATING BEAR.
I'm LICENSABLE BEAR™

LICENSABLE BEAR™ Learns the Truth

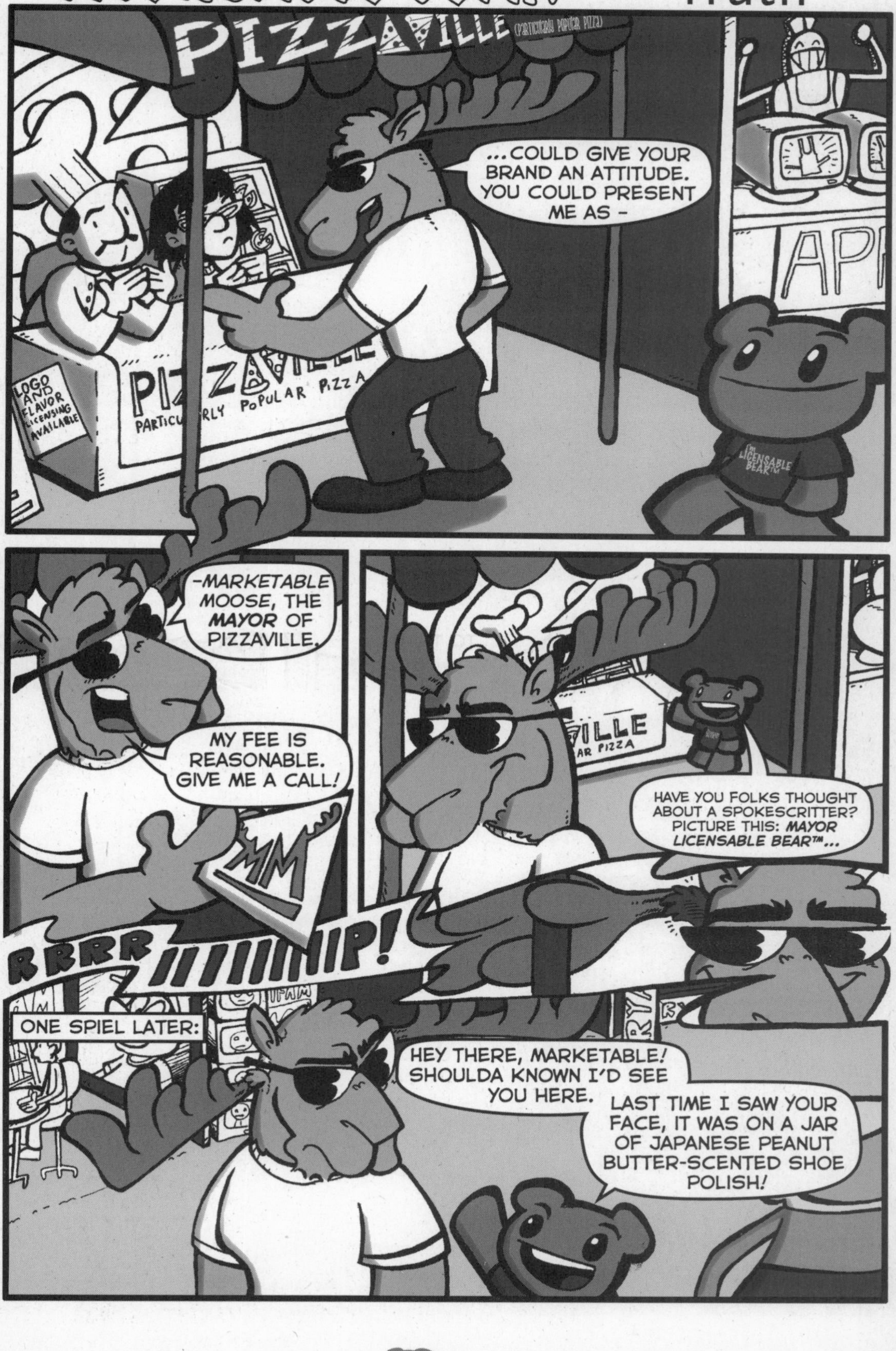

PIZZAVILLE (PARTICULARLY POPULAR PIZZA)
...COULD GIVE YOUR BRAND AN ATTITUDE. YOU COULD PRESENT ME AS –
LOGO AND FLAVOR LICENSING AVAILABLE
PIZZAVILLE PARTICULARLY POPULAR PIZZA
APP
LICENSABLE BEAR™
–MARKETABLE MOOSE, THE MAYOR OF PIZZAVILLE.
MY FEE IS REASONABLE. GIVE ME A CALL!
HAVE YOU FOLKS THOUGHT ABOUT A SPOKESCRITTER? PICTURE THIS: MAYOR LICENSABLE BEAR™...
RRRRIIIIIIIIIP!
ONE SPIEL LATER:
HEY THERE, MARKETABLE! SHOULDA KNOWN I'D SEE YOU HERE.
LAST TIME I SAW YOUR FACE, IT WAS ON A JAR OF JAPANESE PEANUT BUTTER-SCENTED SHOE POLISH!

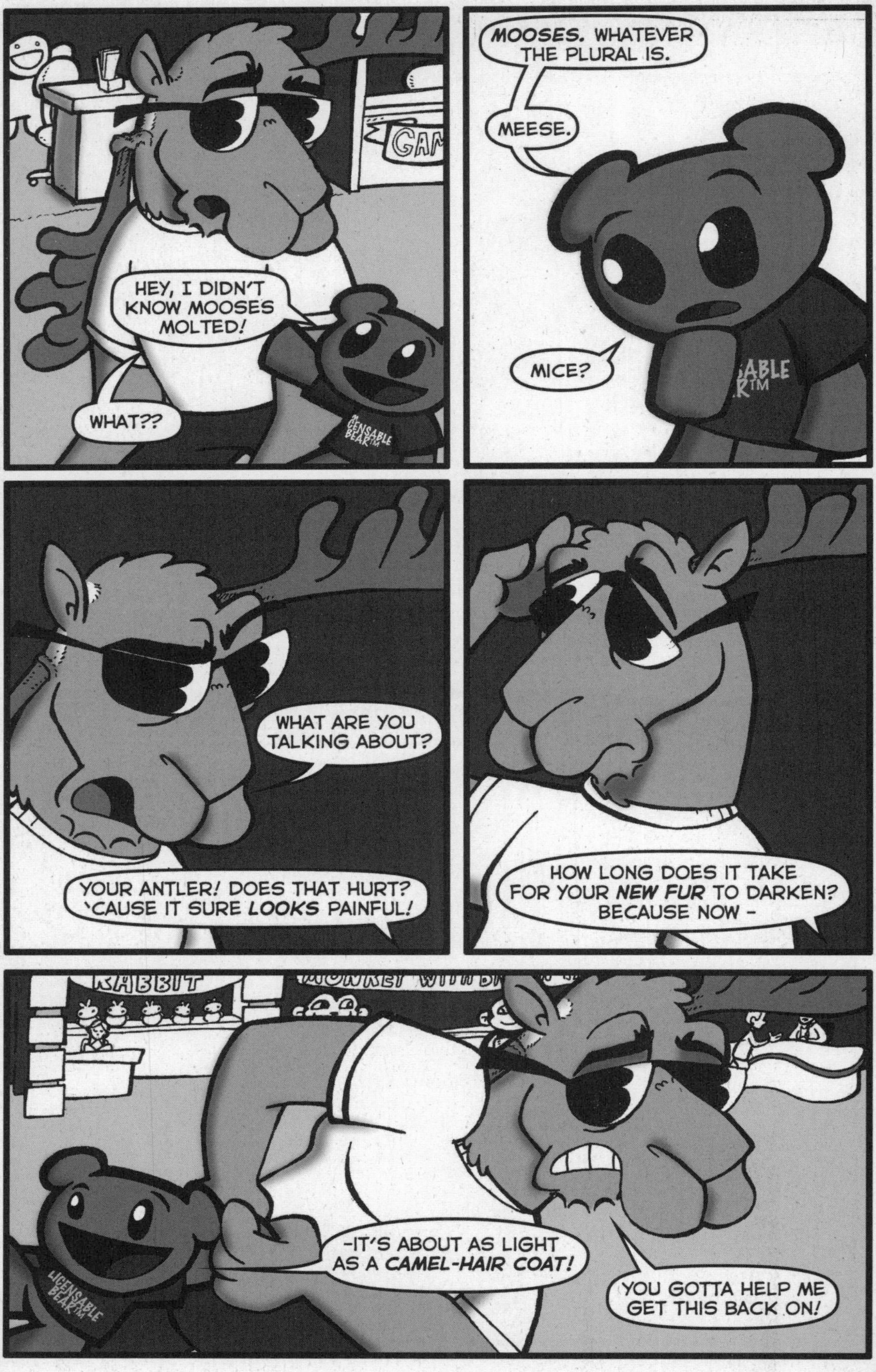

HEY, I DIDN'T KNOW MOOSES MOLTED!
WHAT??
MOOSES. WHATEVER THE PLURAL IS.
MEESE.
MICE?
WHAT ARE YOU TALKING ABOUT?
YOUR ANTLER! DOES THAT HURT? 'CAUSE IT SURE LOOKS PAINFUL!
HOW LONG DOES IT TAKE FOR YOUR NEW FUR TO DARKEN? BECAUSE NOW -
-IT'S ABOUT AS LIGHT AS A CAMEL-HAIR COAT!
YOU GOTTA HELP ME GET THIS BACK ON!
LICENSABLE BEAR™

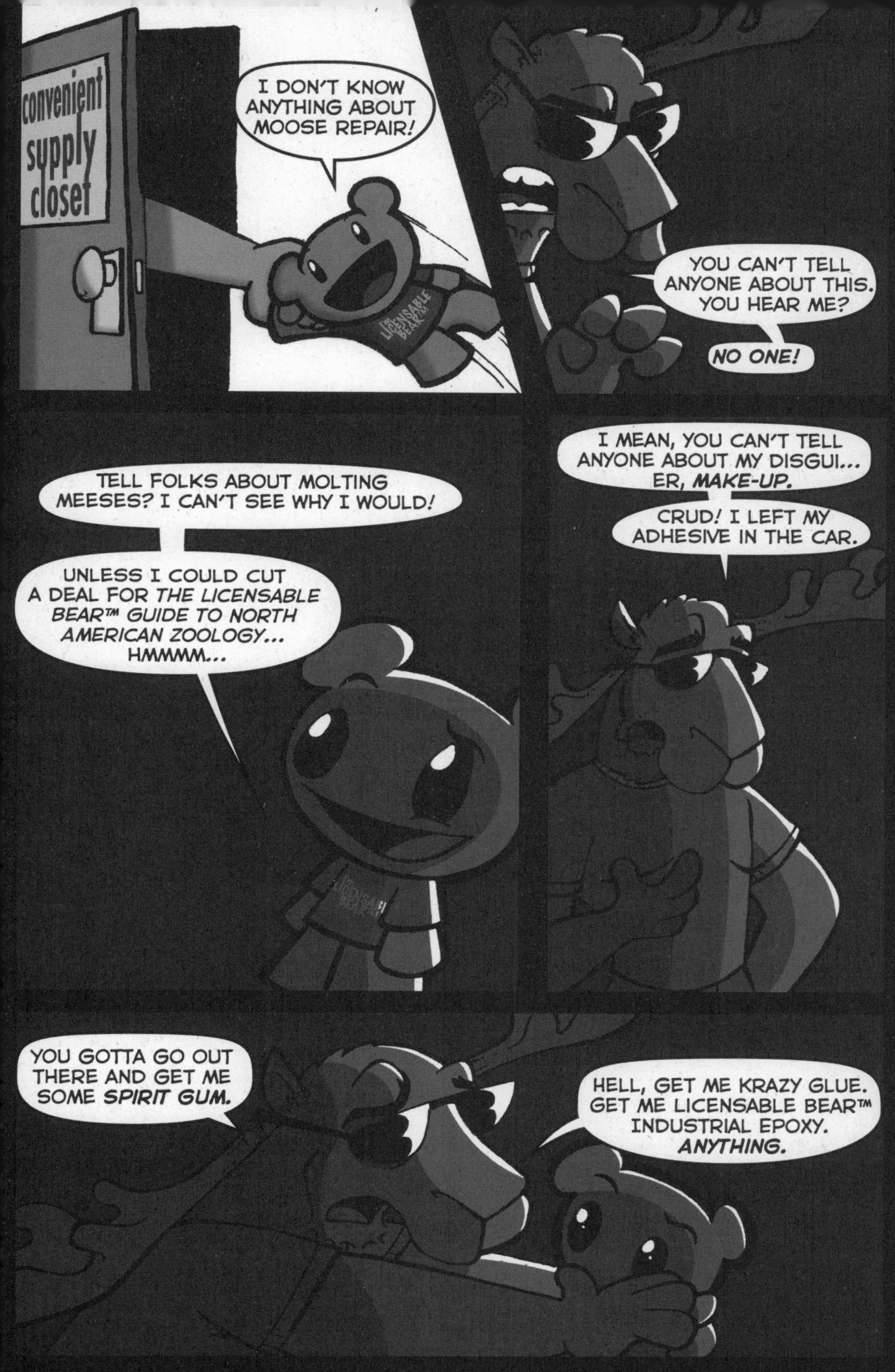
convenient supply closet
I DON'T KNOW ANYTHING ABOUT MOOSE REPAIR!
I'M LICENSABLE BEAR™
YOU CAN'T TELL ANYONE ABOUT THIS. YOU HEAR ME?
NO ONE!
TELL FOLKS ABOUT MOLTING MEESES? I CAN'T SEE WHY I WOULD!
UNLESS I COULD CUT A DEAL FOR THE LICENSABLE BEAR™ GUIDE TO NORTH AMERICAN ZOOLOGY... HMMMM...
I MEAN, YOU CAN'T TELL ANYONE ABOUT MY DISGUI... ER, MAKE-UP.
CRUD! I LEFT MY ADHESIVE IN THE CAR.
YOU GOTTA GO OUT THERE AND GET ME SOME SPIRIT GUM.
HELL, GET ME KRAZY GLUE. GET ME LICENSABLE BEAR™ INDUSTRIAL EPOXY. ANYTHING.

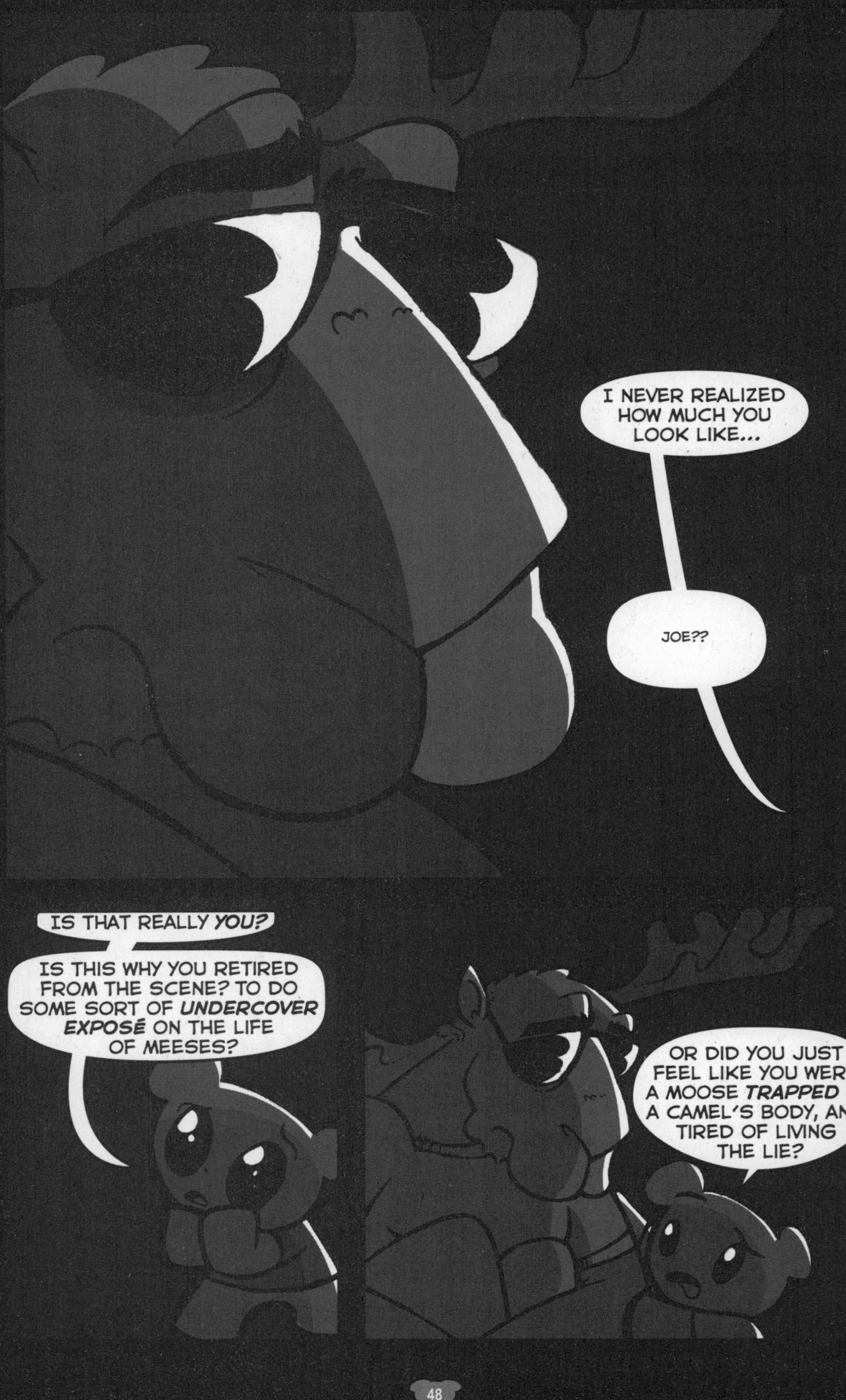
I NEVER REALIZED HOW MUCH YOU LOOK LIKE...
JOE??
IS THAT REALLY YOU?
IS THIS WHY YOU RETIRED FROM THE SCENE? TO DO SOME SORT OF UNDERCOVER EXPOSÉ ON THE LIFE OF MEESES?
OR DID YOU JUST FEEL LIKE YOU WERE A MOOSE TRAPPED IN A CAMEL'S BODY, AND TIRED OF LIVING THE LIE?

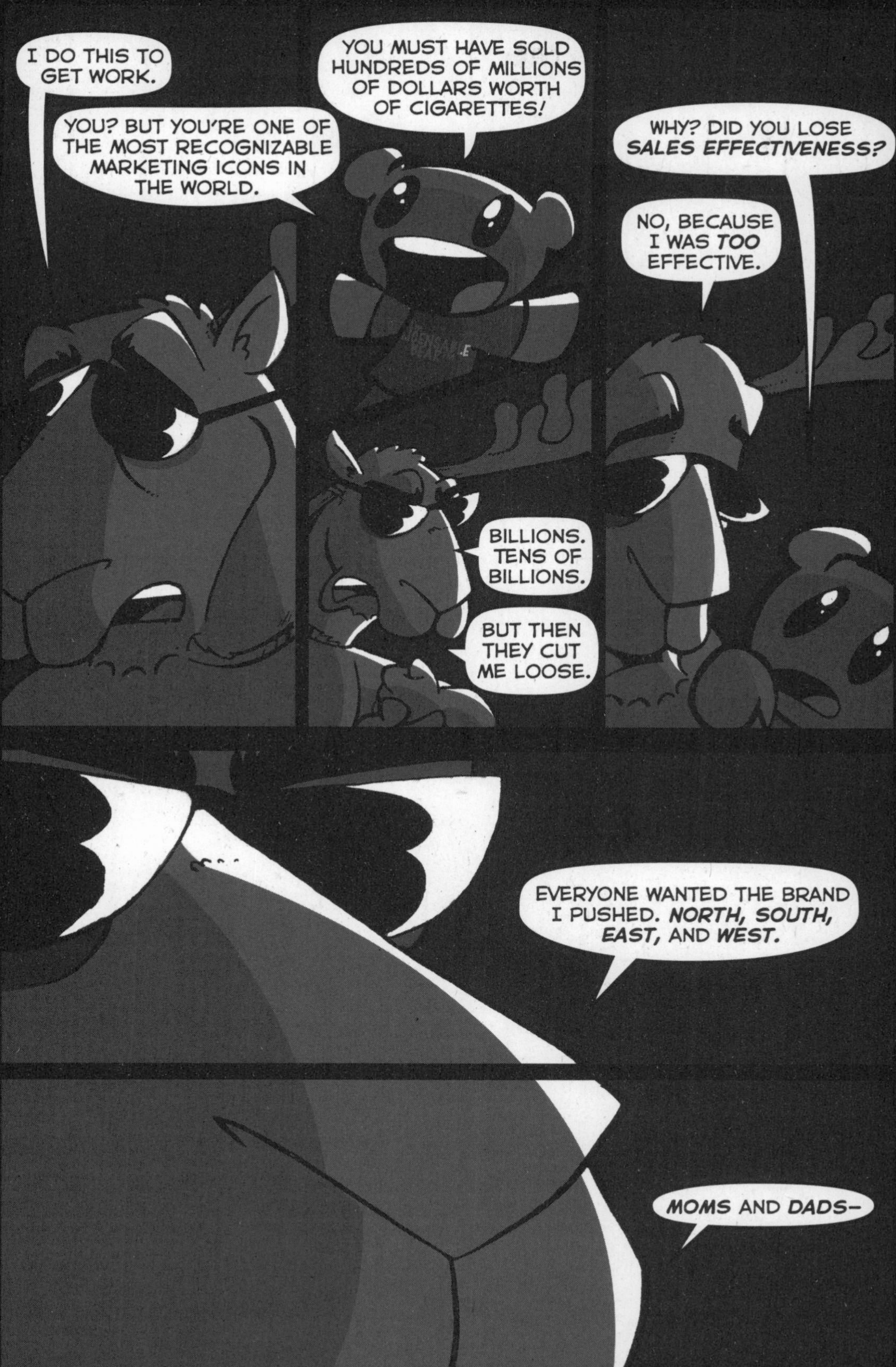
I DO THIS TO GET WORK.
YOU? BUT YOU'RE ONE OF THE MOST RECOGNIZABLE MARKETING ICONS IN THE WORLD.
YOU MUST HAVE SOLD HUNDREDS OF MILLIONS OF DOLLARS WORTH OF CIGARETTES!
BILLIONS. TENS OF BILLIONS.
BUT THEN THEY CUT ME LOOSE.
WHY? DID YOU LOSE *SALES EFFECTIVENESS?*
NO, BECAUSE I WAS *TOO* EFFECTIVE.
EVERYONE WANTED THE BRAND I PUSHED. *NORTH, SOUTH, EAST,* AND *WEST.*
MOMS AND *DADS*–

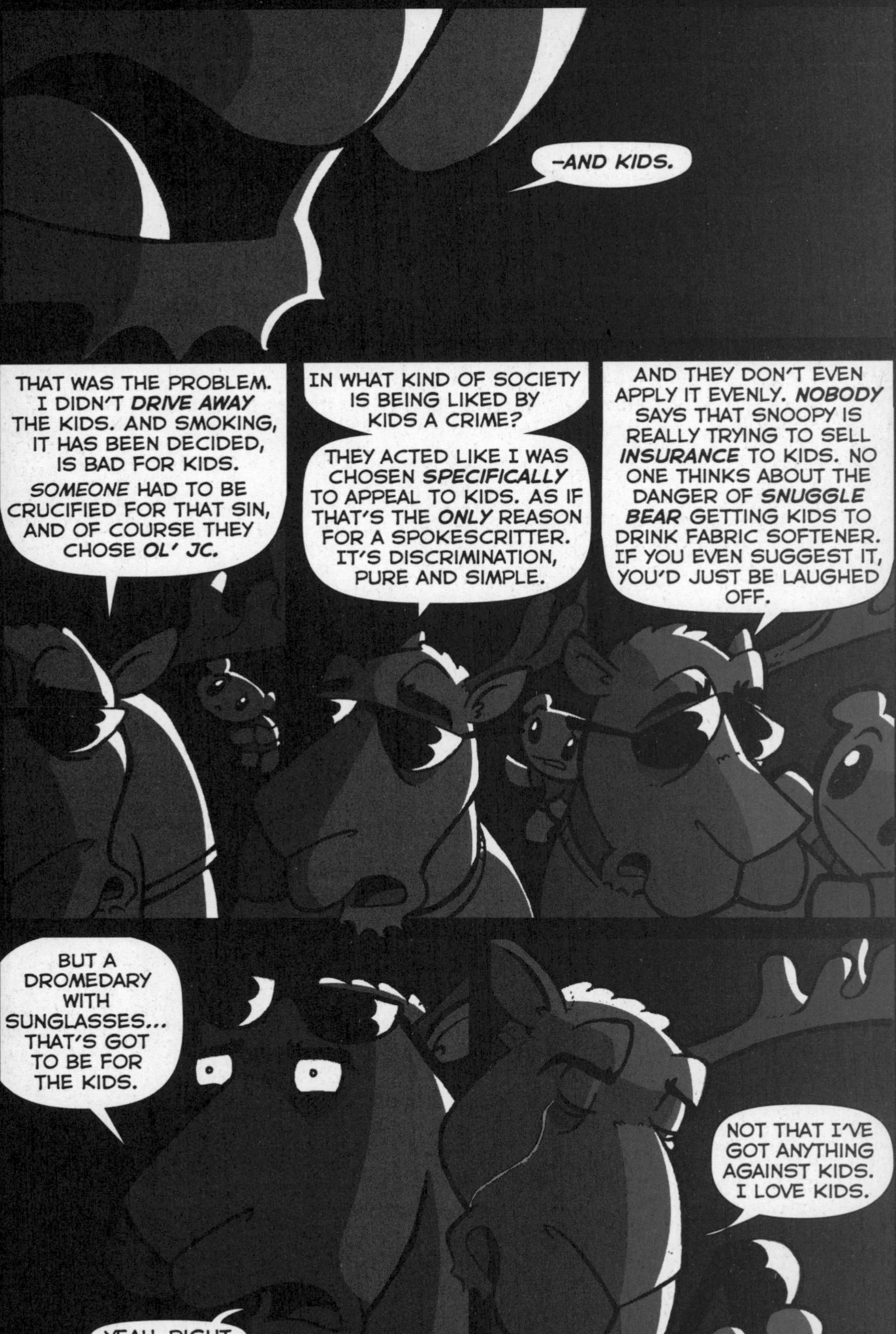
–AND KIDS.
THAT WAS THE PROBLEM. I DIDN'T *DRIVE AWAY* THE KIDS. AND SMOKING, IT HAS BEEN DECIDED, IS BAD FOR KIDS.
SOMEONE HAD TO BE CRUCIFIED FOR THAT SIN, AND OF COURSE THEY CHOSE *OL' JC.*
IN WHAT KIND OF SOCIETY IS BEING LIKED BY KIDS A CRIME?
THEY ACTED LIKE I WAS CHOSEN *SPECIFICALLY* TO APPEAL TO KIDS. AS IF THAT'S THE *ONLY* REASON FOR A SPOKESCRITTER. IT'S DISCRIMINATION, PURE AND SIMPLE.
AND THEY DON'T EVEN APPLY IT EVENLY. *NOBODY* SAYS THAT SNOOPY IS REALLY TRYING TO SELL *INSURANCE* TO KIDS. NO ONE THINKS ABOUT THE DANGER OF *SNUGGLE BEAR* GETTING KIDS TO DRINK FABRIC SOFTENER. IF YOU EVEN SUGGEST IT, YOU'D JUST BE LAUGHED OFF.
BUT A DROMEDARY WITH SUNGLASSES... THAT'S GOT TO BE FOR THE KIDS.
NOT THAT I'VE GOT ANYTHING AGAINST KIDS. I LOVE KIDS.
YEAH, RIGHT.

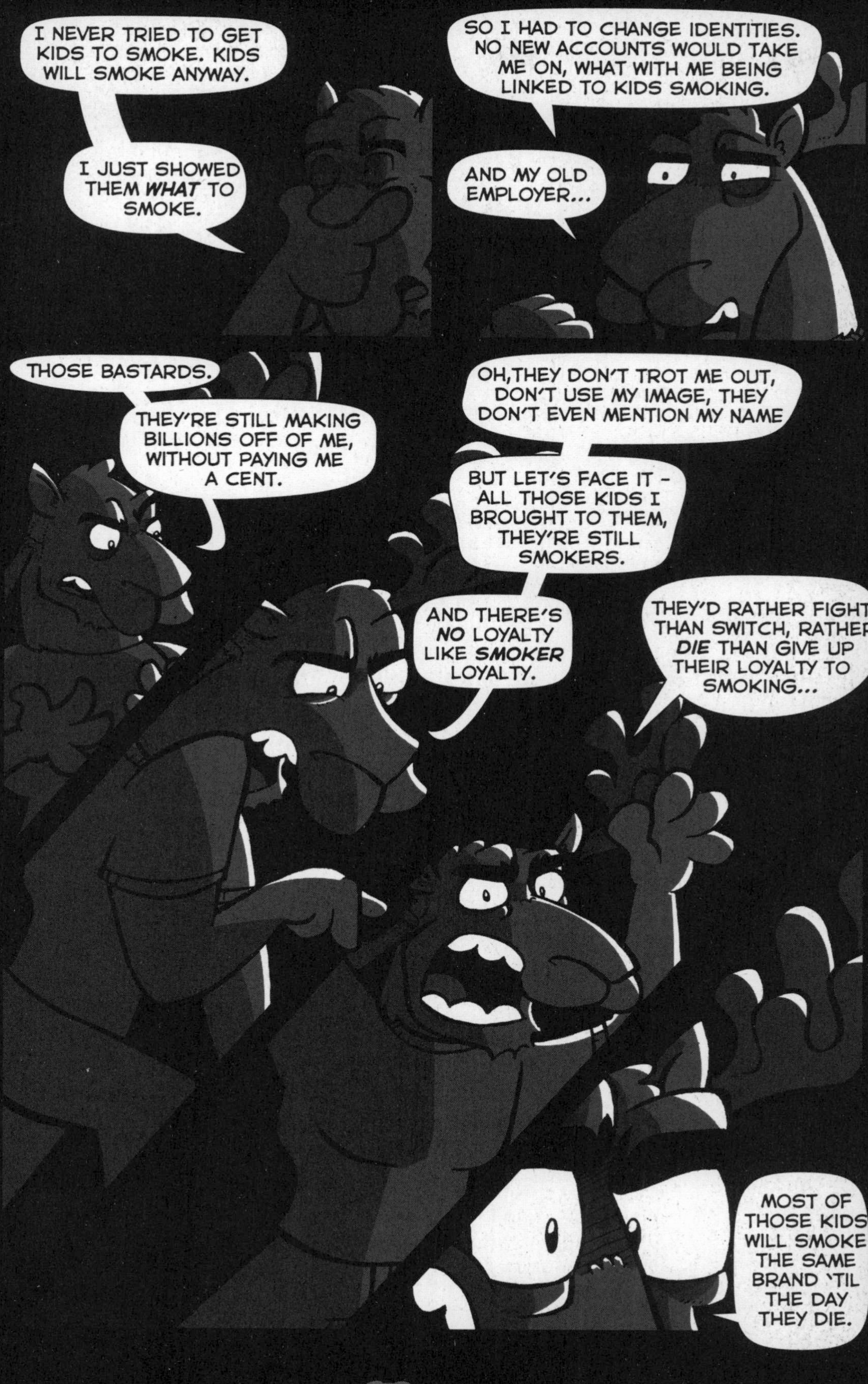
I NEVER TRIED TO GET KIDS TO SMOKE. KIDS WILL SMOKE ANYWAY.
I JUST SHOWED THEM *WHAT* TO SMOKE.
SO I HAD TO CHANGE IDENTITIES. NO NEW ACCOUNTS WOULD TAKE ME ON, WHAT WITH ME BEING LINKED TO KIDS SMOKING.
AND MY OLD EMPLOYER...
THOSE BASTARDS.
THEY'RE STILL MAKING BILLIONS OFF OF ME, WITHOUT PAYING ME A CENT.
OH,THEY DON'T TROT ME OUT, DON'T USE MY IMAGE, THEY DON'T EVEN MENTION MY NAME
BUT LET'S FACE IT - ALL THOSE KIDS I BROUGHT TO THEM, THEY'RE STILL SMOKERS.
AND THERE'S *NO* LOYALTY LIKE *SMOKER* LOYALTY.
THEY'D RATHER FIGHT THAN SWITCH, RATHER *DIE* THAN GIVE UP THEIR LOYALTY TO SMOKING...
MOST OF THOSE KIDS WILL SMOKE THE SAME BRAND 'TIL THE DAY THEY DIE.

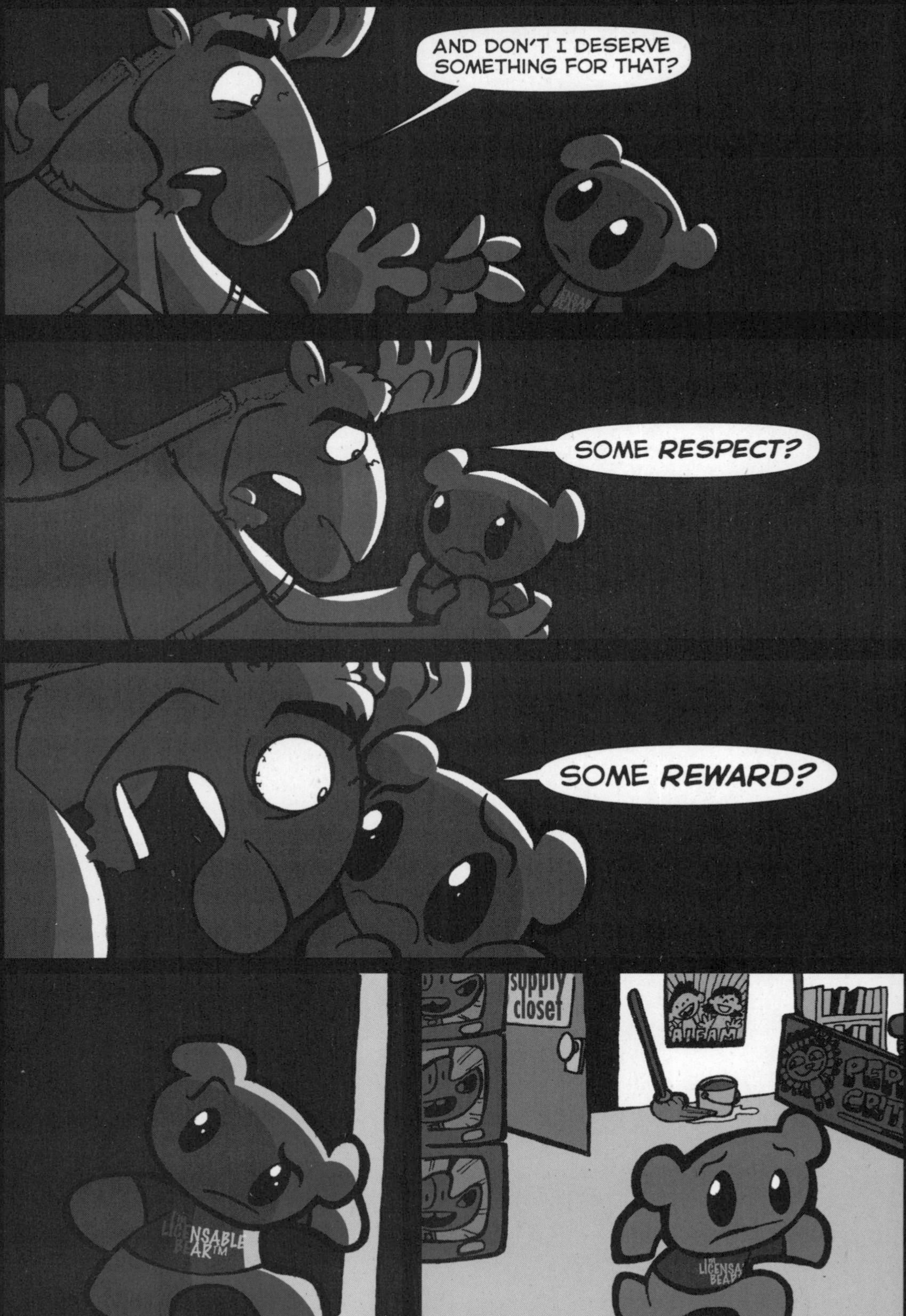
AND DON'T I DESERVE SOMETHING FOR THAT?
SOME *RESPECT?*
SOME *REWARD?*
THE LICENSABLE BEAR™
supply closet

LICENSABLE BEAR™ Discusses a Deal

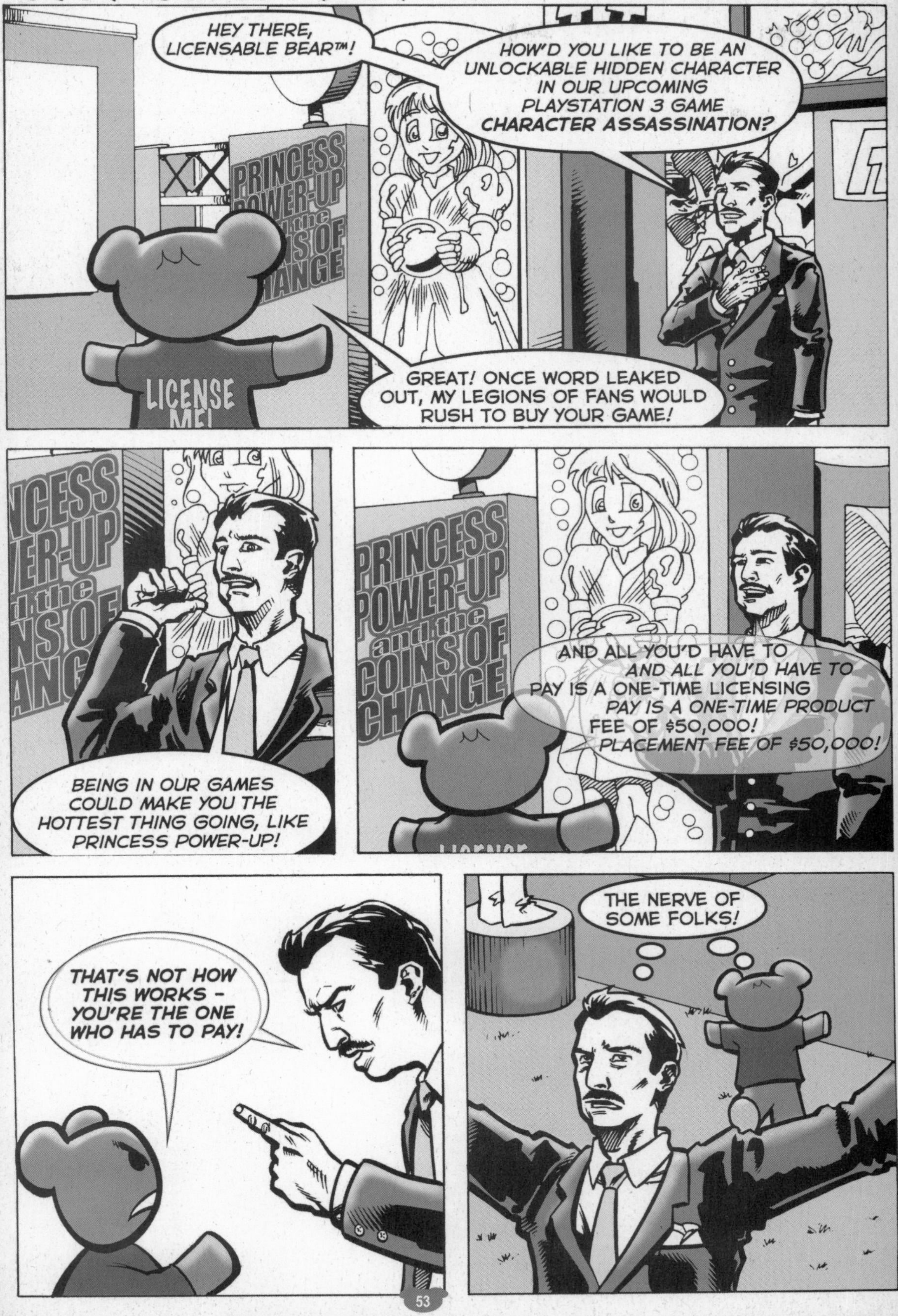
HEY THERE, LICENSABLE BEAR™!
HOW'D YOU LIKE TO BE AN UNLOCKABLE HIDDEN CHARACTER IN OUR UPCOMING PLAYSTATION 3 GAME CHARACTER ASSASSINATION?
PRINCESS POWER-UP and the COINS OF CHANGE
GREAT! ONCE WORD LEAKED OUT, MY LEGIONS OF FANS WOULD RUSH TO BUY YOUR GAME!
LICENSE ME!
BEING IN OUR GAMES COULD MAKE YOU THE HOTTEST THING GOING, LIKE PRINCESS POWER-UP!
AND ALL YOU'D HAVE TO PAY IS A ONE-TIME LICENSING FEE OF $50,000!
AND ALL YOU'D HAVE TO PAY IS A ONE-TIME PRODUCT PLACEMENT FEE OF $50,000!
THAT'S NOT HOW THIS WORKS - YOU'RE THE ONE WHO HAS TO PAY!
THE NERVE OF SOME FOLKS!

LICENSABLE BEAR™ Walks the Floor

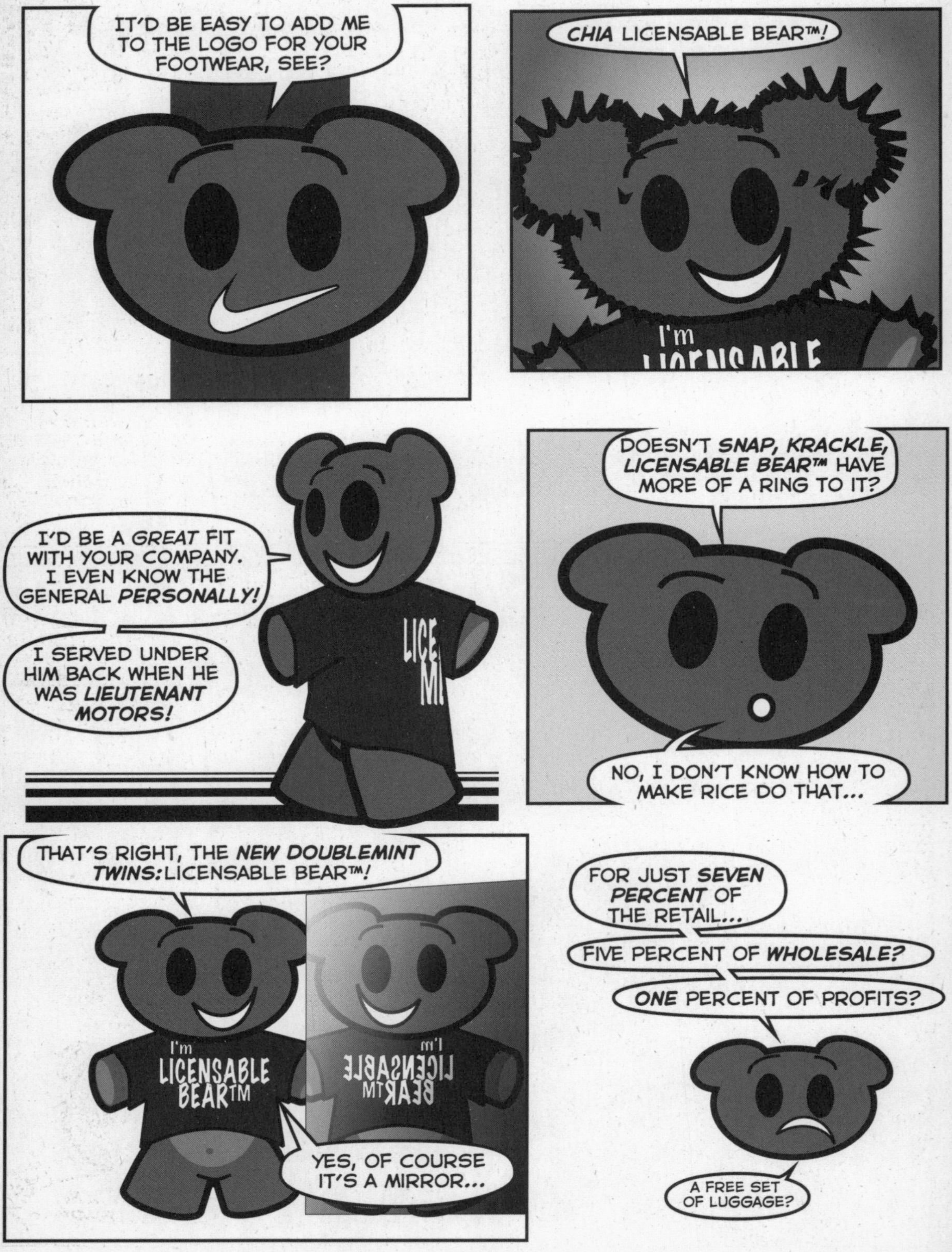
IT'D BE EASY TO ADD ME TO THE LOGO FOR YOUR FOOTWEAR, SEE?
CHIA LICENSABLE BEAR™!
I'm
I'D BE A GREAT FIT WITH YOUR COMPANY. I EVEN KNOW THE GENERAL PERSONALLY!
I SERVED UNDER HIM BACK WHEN HE WAS LIEUTENANT MOTORS!
DOESN'T SNAP, KRACKLE, LICENSABLE BEAR™ HAVE MORE OF A RING TO IT?
NO, I DON'T KNOW HOW TO MAKE RICE DO THAT...
THAT'S RIGHT, THE NEW DOUBLEMINT TWINS: LICENSABLE BEAR™!
I'm LICENSABLE BEAR™
YES, OF COURSE IT'S A MIRROR...
FOR JUST SEVEN PERCENT OF THE RETAIL...
FIVE PERCENT OF WHOLESALE?
ONE PERCENT OF PROFITS?
A FREE SET OF LUGGAGE?

LICENSABLE BEAR™ Gets Duplicated

HEY, IF IT ISN'T MY LITTLE LICENSABLE FRIEND! LONG TIME, NO SEE!

HOW'S IT GOING?

IT'S STEWGURT!

THE WORLD'S ONLY MEAT-BASED YOGURT!

THOSE CARDS THAT FALL OUT OF MAGAZINES.com

BunnyBikiniteam.com

MISTER U.S. MAC N' CHEEZSICLES SHAPED LIKE MISTER U.S.!

★ The Man...

MISTER U.S.

...the Brand! ★

BEEN BETTER.

THIS SHOULD BE MY ELEMENT, I SHOULD BE DOING GREAT HERE. BUT I'VE BEEN HERE ALL DAY, AND NOT A DEAL IN SIGHT!

AND YOU?

THE SUPERHEROING IS GOING GREAT, BUT THE *LICENSING*...

SEEMS THE WORLD DOESN'T WANT A HEROIC SYMBOL OF ALL-AMERICAN *BUTT-KICKING* AT THE MOMENT.

I CAN'T HELP BEING WHO I AM, BUT IT'S GOTTEN SO BAD, I ALMOST ASKED IF I COULD BECOME *MISTER PIZZAVILLE*...

YOU GOTTA JUST KEEP BEING WHO YOU ARE, AND WAIT FOR YOUR TIME TO COME.

TRY TO BE ALL THINGS TO ALL PEOPLE, AND YOU END UP BEING SPECIAL TO NO ONE!

I GET INVOLVED IN DIFFERENT THINGS, BUT AT CORE I'M ALWAYS THE ONE, UNIQUE ME!

HEY THERE! I'M *LICENSABLE BEAR™* —

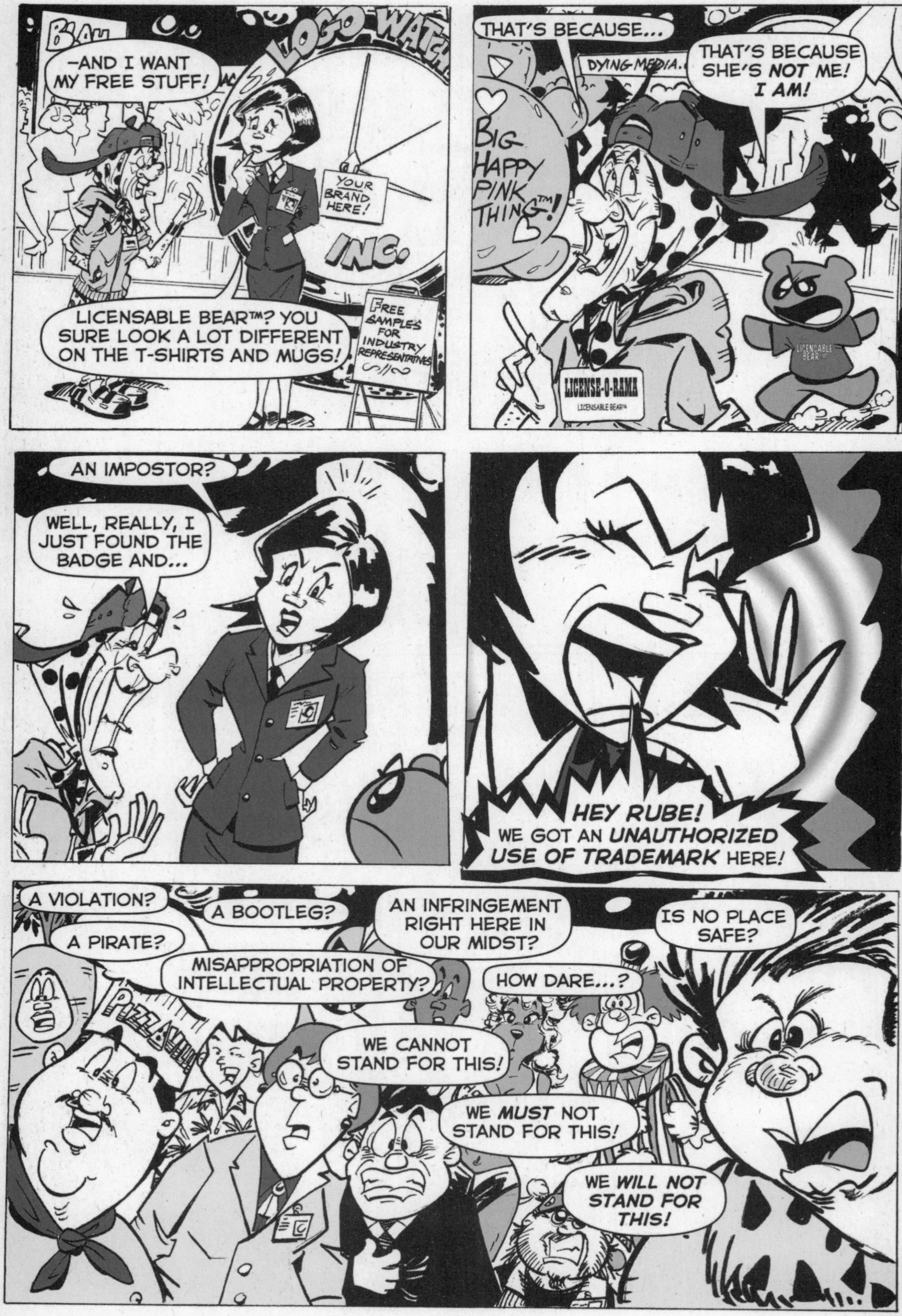
LOGO WATCH
–AND I WANT MY FREE STUFF!
YOUR BRAND HERE!
INC.
FREE SAMPLES FOR INDUSTRY REPRESENTATIVES
LICENSABLE BEAR™? YOU SURE LOOK A LOT DIFFERENT ON THE T-SHIRTS AND MUGS!
THAT'S BECAUSE...
DYING MEDIA...
THAT'S BECAUSE SHE'S *NOT* ME! *I AM!*
BIG HAPPY PINK THING™!
LICENSE-O-RAMA
LICENSABLE BEAR™
AN IMPOSTOR?
WELL, REALLY, I JUST FOUND THE BADGE AND...
HEY RUBE! WE GOT AN *UNAUTHORIZED USE OF TRADEMARK* HERE!
A VIOLATION?
A PIRATE?
A BOOTLEG?
AN INFRINGEMENT RIGHT HERE IN OUR MIDST?
IS NO PLACE SAFE?
MISAPPROPRIATION OF INTELLECTUAL PROPERTY?
HOW DARE...?
WE CANNOT STAND FOR THIS!
WE *MUST* NOT STAND FOR THIS!
WE *WILL NOT* STAND FOR THIS!

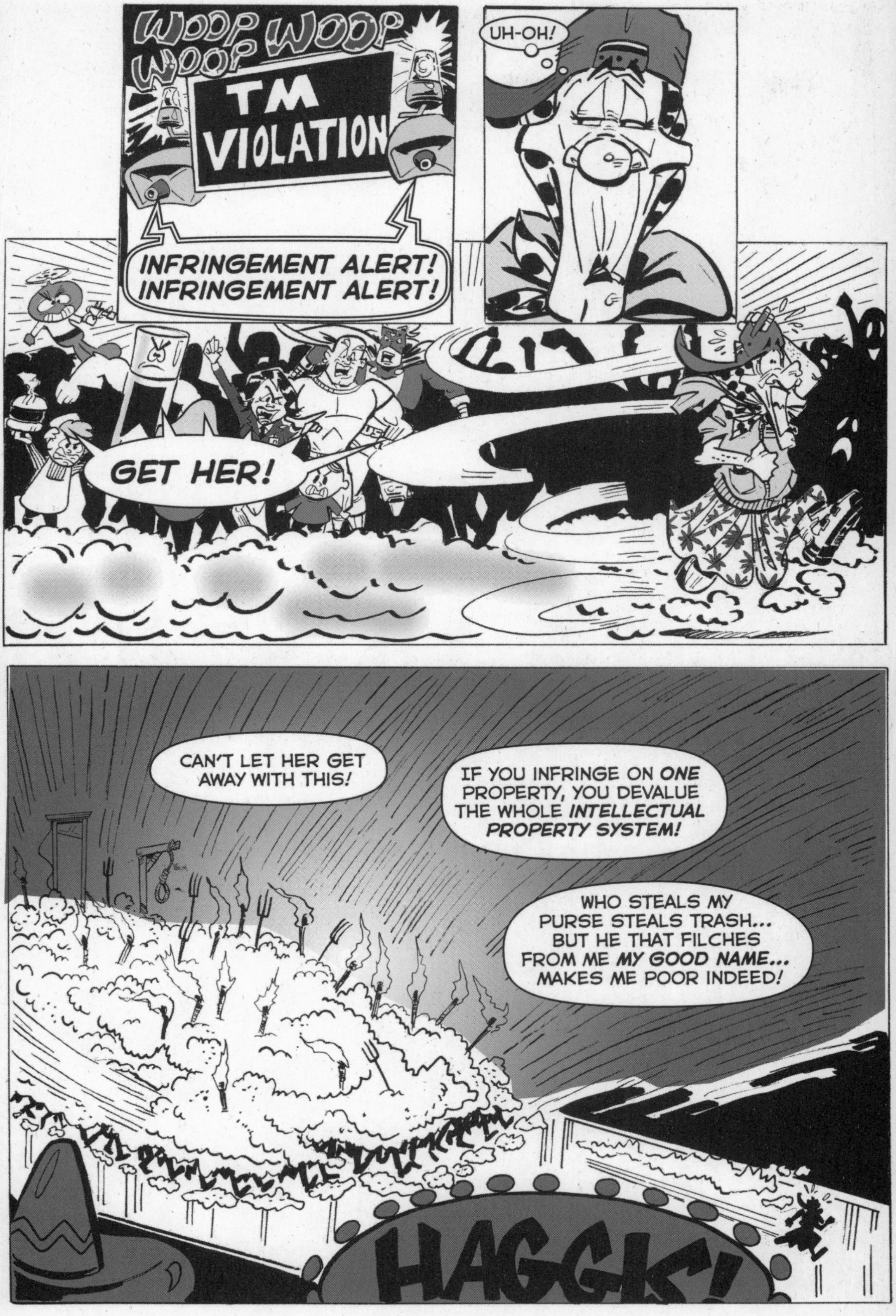
WOOP WOOP WOOP
TM VIOLATION
INFRINGEMENT ALERT! INFRINGEMENT ALERT!
UH-OH!
GET HER!
CAN'T LET HER GET AWAY WITH THIS!
IF YOU INFRINGE ON ONE PROPERTY, YOU DEVALUE THE WHOLE INTELLECTUAL PROPERTY SYSTEM!
WHO STEALS MY PURSE STEALS TRASH... BUT HE THAT FILCHES FROM ME MY GOOD NAME... MAKES ME POOR INDEED!
HAGGK!

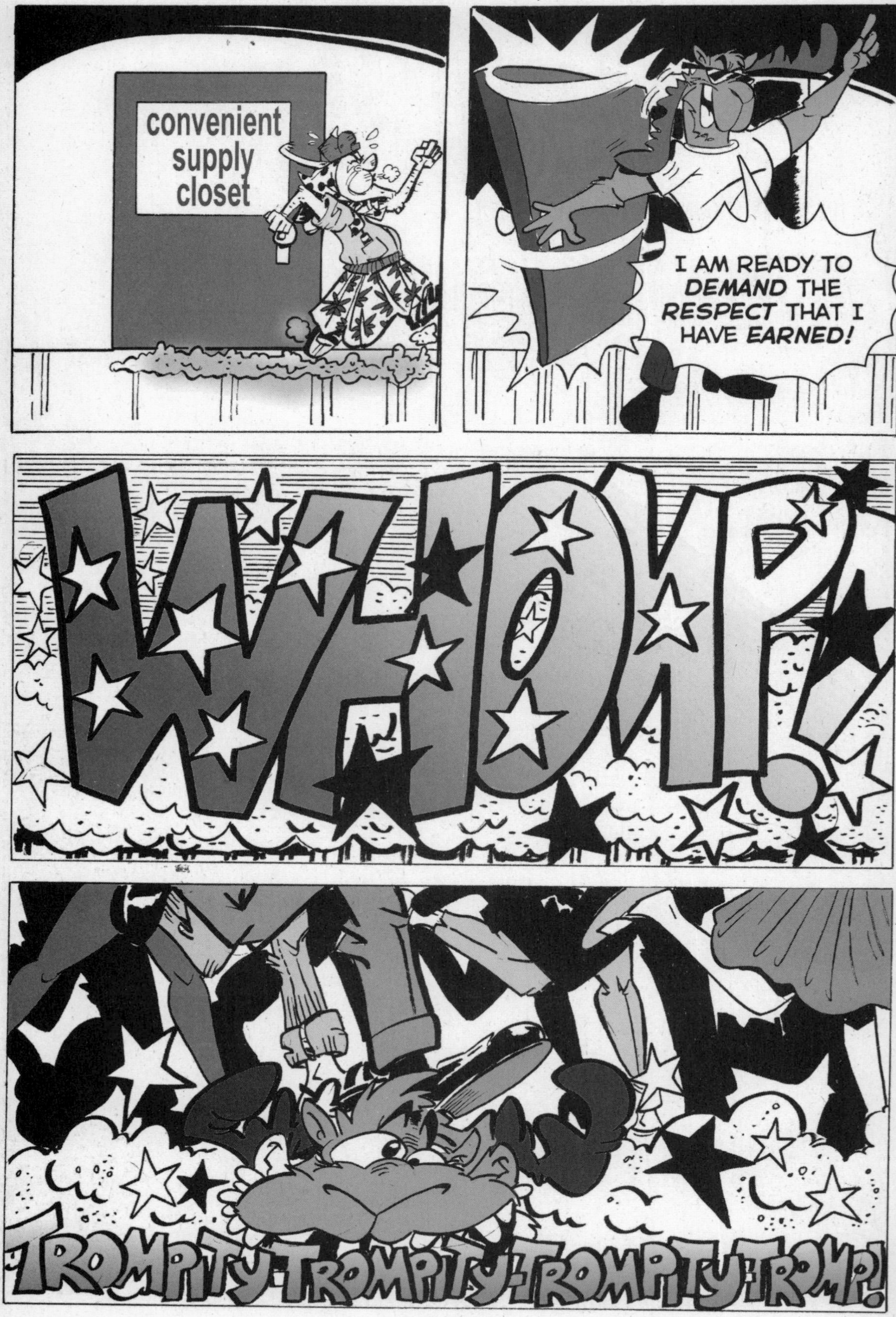
convenient supply closet
I AM READY TO *DEMAND* THE *RESPECT* THAT I HAVE *EARNED!*
WHOMP!
TROMPITY-TROMPITY-TROMPITY-TROMP!

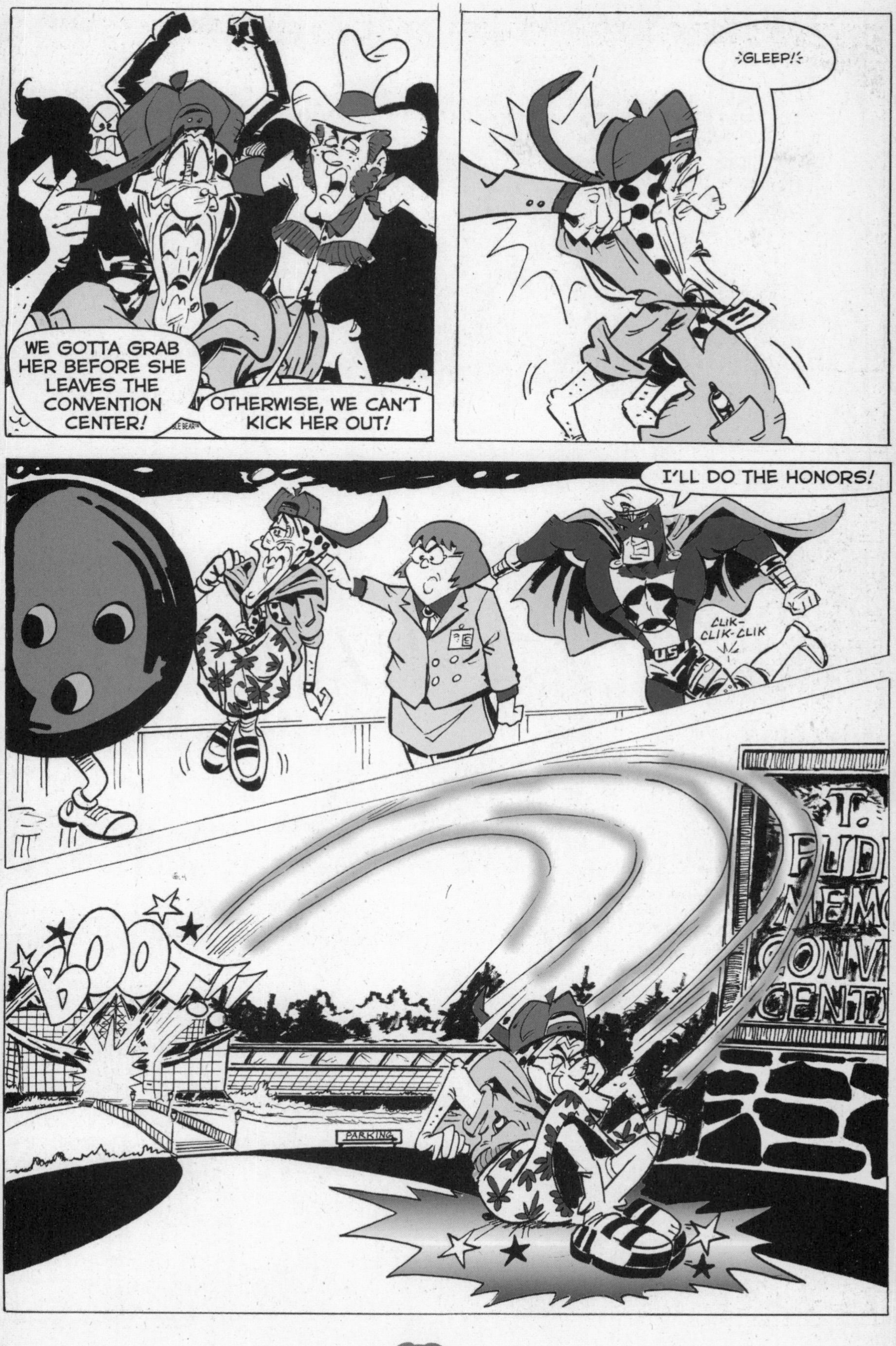
WE GOTTA GRAB HER BEFORE SHE LEAVES THE CONVENTION CENTER!
OTHERWISE, WE CAN'T KICK HER OUT!
GLEEP!
I'LL DO THE HONORS!
CLIK-CLIK-CLIK
US
BOOT!
PARKING

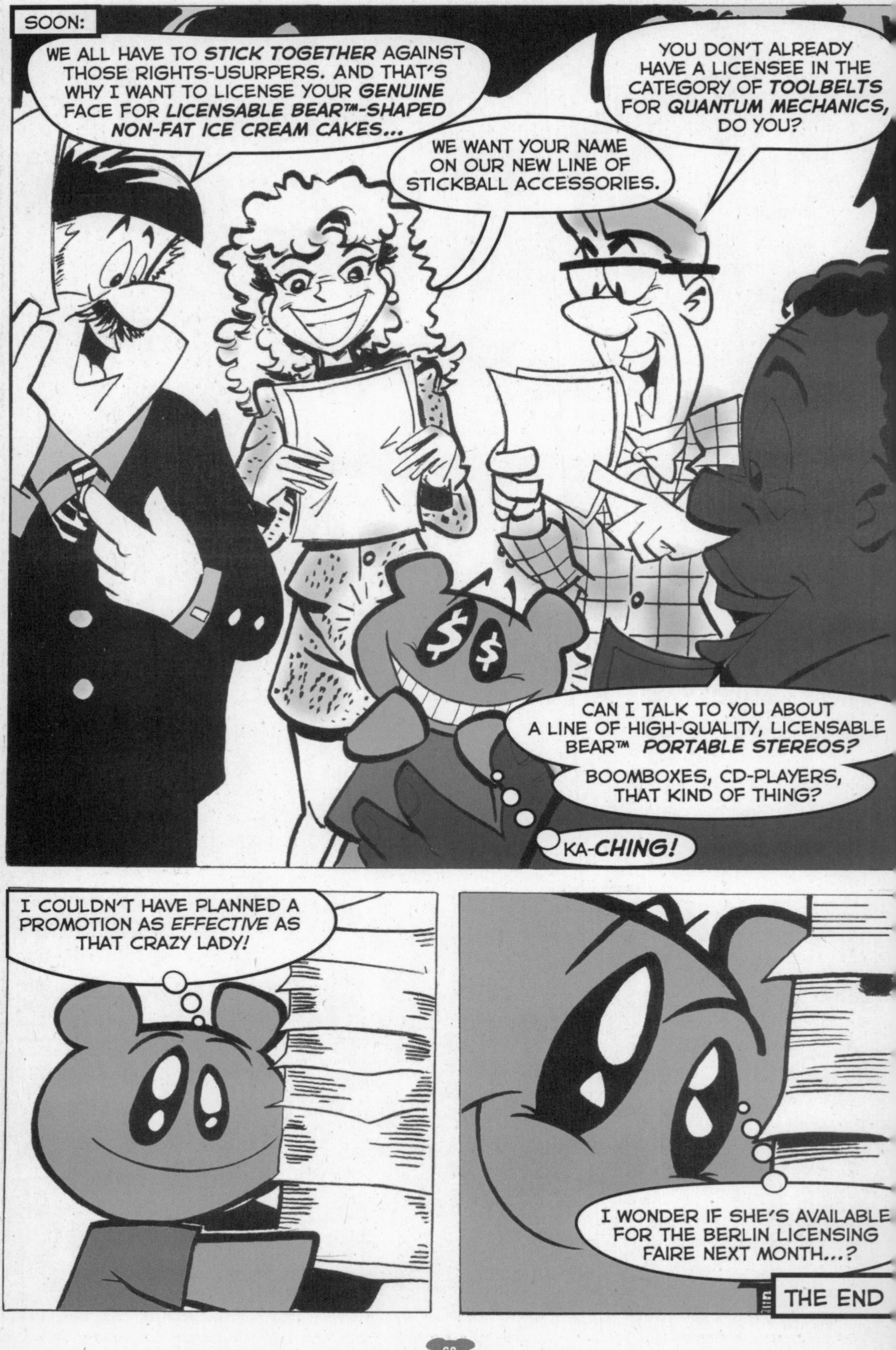
SOON:
WE ALL HAVE TO STICK TOGETHER AGAINST THOSE RIGHTS-USURPERS. AND THAT'S WHY I WANT TO LICENSE YOUR GENUINE FACE FOR LICENSABLE BEAR™-SHAPED NON-FAT ICE CREAM CAKES...
WE WANT YOUR NAME ON OUR NEW LINE OF STICKBALL ACCESSORIES.
YOU DON'T ALREADY HAVE A LICENSEE IN THE CATEGORY OF TOOLBELTS FOR QUANTUM MECHANICS, DO YOU?
CAN I TALK TO YOU ABOUT A LINE OF HIGH-QUALITY, LICENSABLE BEAR™ PORTABLE STEREOS?
BOOMBOXES, CD-PLAYERS, THAT KIND OF THING?
KA-CHING!
I COULDN'T HAVE PLANNED A PROMOTION AS EFFECTIVE AS THAT CRAZY LADY!
I WONDER IF SHE'S AVAILABLE FOR THE BERLIN LICENSING FAIRE NEXT MONTH...?
THE END

Licensable Bear™'s intellectual property insights

The trademark is the longest-lasting form of intellectual property. Unlike patents or copyrights, a trademark has no built-in expiration date; so long as the trademark is used, the rights are maintained. This is because trademarks do not exist for the benefit of the trademark holder. No, they exist to protect the consumer, to keep the consumer from being confused or misled into thinking they are getting a better brand of product than they are.

QUAKER
CAP'N CRUNCH
Crunch-a-tize Me Cap'n!™
NET WT 16 OZ (1 LB) • 453 g

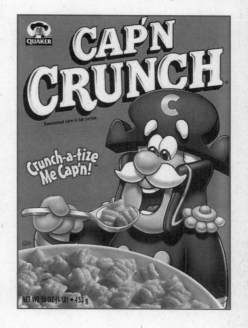

For example, consider the trademark "Crunch-a-tize Me Cap'n", which you might find on a box of Cap'n Crunch breakfast cereal. This trademark is owned by Quaker Oats, who can protect the trademark by making sure that it is only associated with quality products and thus become a sign of quality product. It is very important that they own and protect this trademark, so that it becomes meaningful to the consumer. If every cereal manufacturer could put "Crunch-a-tize Me Cap'n" on their product, then it would be meaningless when Quaker put it on canisters of their fine instant oatmeal.

It should also be noted that trademark protection only inherently covers other products in the same class. The protection that the trademark offers protects the consumer from non-Quaker-approved Crunch-a-tize Me Cap'n Bananas, as they would also be foodstuffs. The need to provide the consumer with such protection is why the fine folks at Quaker were moved to claim trademark status on the phrase. However, in itself the trademark cannot stop Crunch-a-tize Me Cap'n Perfume, nor will it force the grounding of Crunch-a-tize Me Cap'n Airlines.

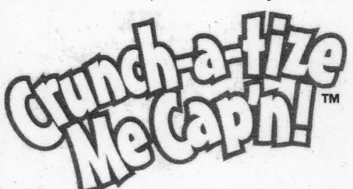

Licensable Bear™ is a freelance marketing icon and is not a trained attorney. Please do not name your new airline "Crunch-a-tize Me Cap'n Airlines" or take similar steps until consulting with a whole bevy of rights attorneys. Remember, your lawyer is your friend; it's other people's lawyers who are the enemy.

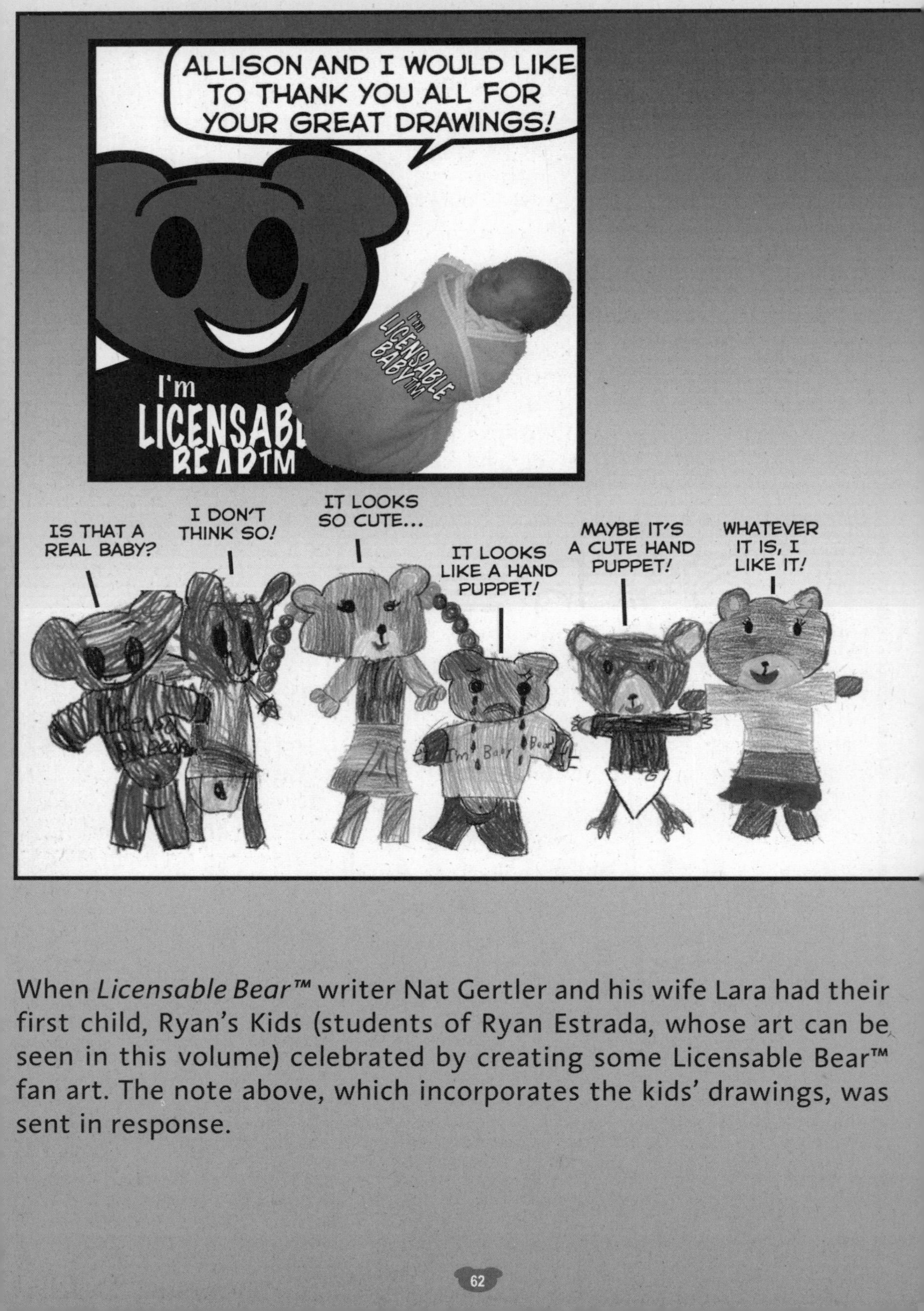
ALLISON AND I WOULD LIKE TO THANK YOU ALL FOR YOUR GREAT DRAWINGS!
I'm LICENSABLE BEAR™
I'm LICENSABLE BABY™
IS THAT A REAL BABY?
I DON'T THINK SO!
IT LOOKS SO CUTE...
IT LOOKS LIKE A HAND PUPPET!
MAYBE IT'S A CUTE HAND PUPPET!
WHATEVER IT IS, I LIKE IT!

When *Licensable Bear™* writer Nat Gertler and his wife Lara had their first child, Ryan's Kids (students of Ryan Estrada, whose art can be seen in this volume) celebrated by creating some Licensable Bear™ fan art. The note above, which incorporates the kids' drawings, was sent in response.

LICENSABLE BEAR™ Perpetuates Freedom

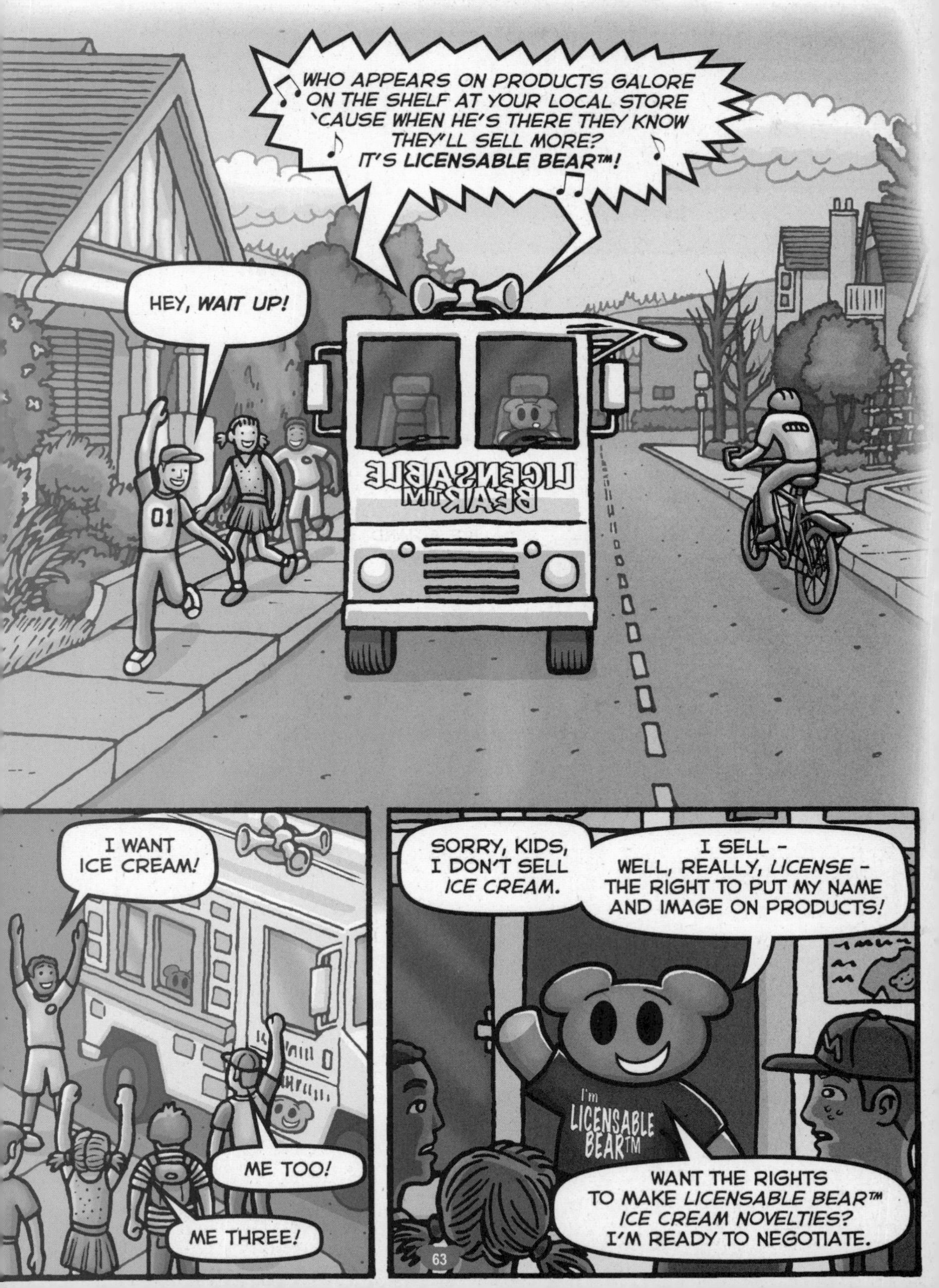

WHO APPEARS ON PRODUCTS GALORE ON THE SHELF AT YOUR LOCAL STORE 'CAUSE WHEN HE'S THERE THEY KNOW THEY'LL SELL MORE? IT'S LICENSABLE BEAR™!
HEY, *WAIT UP!*
01
I WANT ICE CREAM!
ME TOO!
ME THREE!
SORRY, KIDS, I DON'T SELL *ICE CREAM.*
I SELL - WELL, REALLY, *LICENSE* - THE RIGHT TO PUT MY NAME AND IMAGE ON PRODUCTS!
I'm LICENSABLE BEAR™
WANT THE RIGHTS TO MAKE *LICENSABLE BEAR™ ICE CREAM NOVELTIES?* I'M READY TO NEGOTIATE.

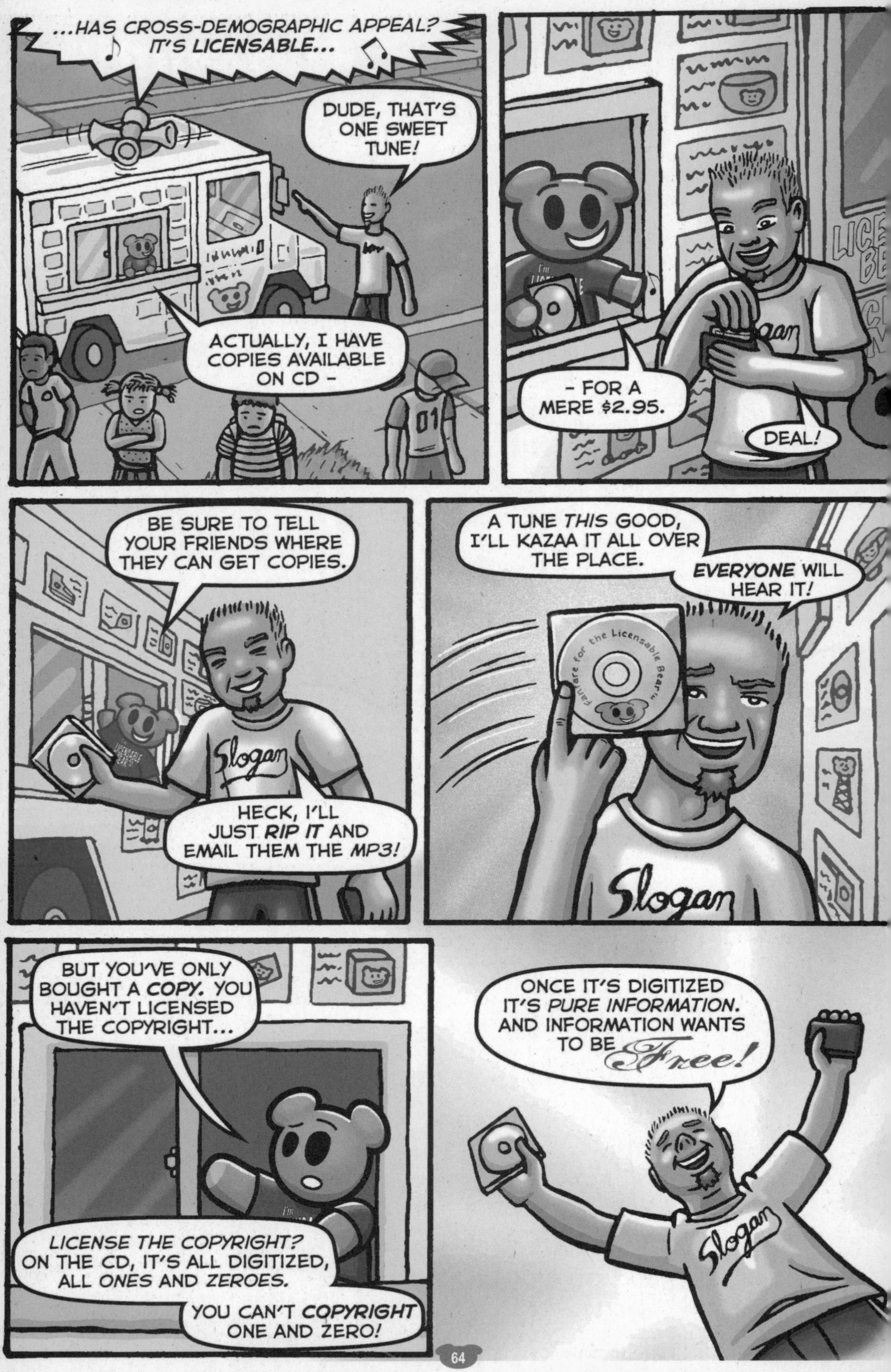
...HAS CROSS-DEMOGRAPHIC APPEAL? IT'S LICENSABLE...
DUDE, THAT'S ONE SWEET TUNE!
ACTUALLY, I HAVE COPIES AVAILABLE ON CD –
– FOR A MERE $2.95.
DEAL!
BE SURE TO TELL YOUR FRIENDS WHERE THEY CAN GET COPIES.
HECK, I'LL JUST RIP IT AND EMAIL THEM THE MP3!
A TUNE THIS GOOD, I'LL KAZAA IT ALL OVER THE PLACE.
EVERYONE WILL HEAR IT!
Fanfare for the Licensable Bear™
Slogan
BUT YOU'VE ONLY BOUGHT A COPY. YOU HAVEN'T LICENSED THE COPYRIGHT...
LICENSE THE COPYRIGHT? ON THE CD, IT'S ALL DIGITIZED, ALL ONES AND ZEROES.
YOU CAN'T COPYRIGHT ONE AND ZERO!
ONCE IT'S DIGITIZED IT'S PURE INFORMATION. AND INFORMATION WANTS TO BE Free!

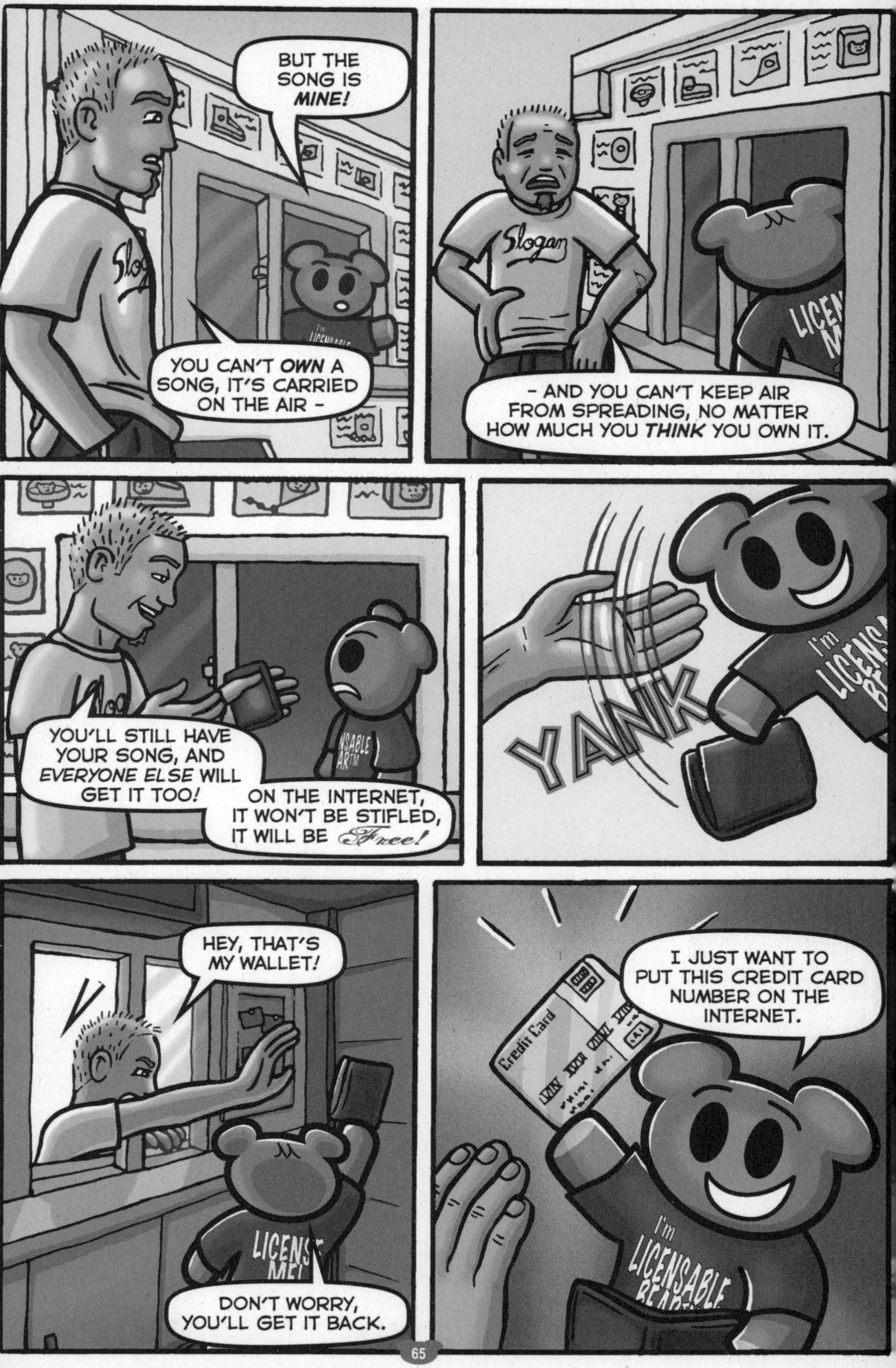
BUT THE SONG IS *MINE!*
YOU CAN'T *OWN* A SONG, IT'S CARRIED ON THE AIR -
Slogan
I'm LICENSABLE
- AND YOU CAN'T KEEP AIR FROM SPREADING, NO MATTER HOW MUCH YOU *THINK* YOU OWN IT.
YOU'LL STILL HAVE YOUR SONG, AND *EVERYONE ELSE* WILL GET IT TOO!
ON THE INTERNET, IT WON'T BE STIFLED, IT WILL BE *Free!*
YANK
HEY, THAT'S MY WALLET!
DON'T WORRY, YOU'LL GET IT BACK.
I JUST WANT TO PUT THIS CREDIT CARD NUMBER ON THE INTERNET.
Credit Card
I'm LICENSABLE

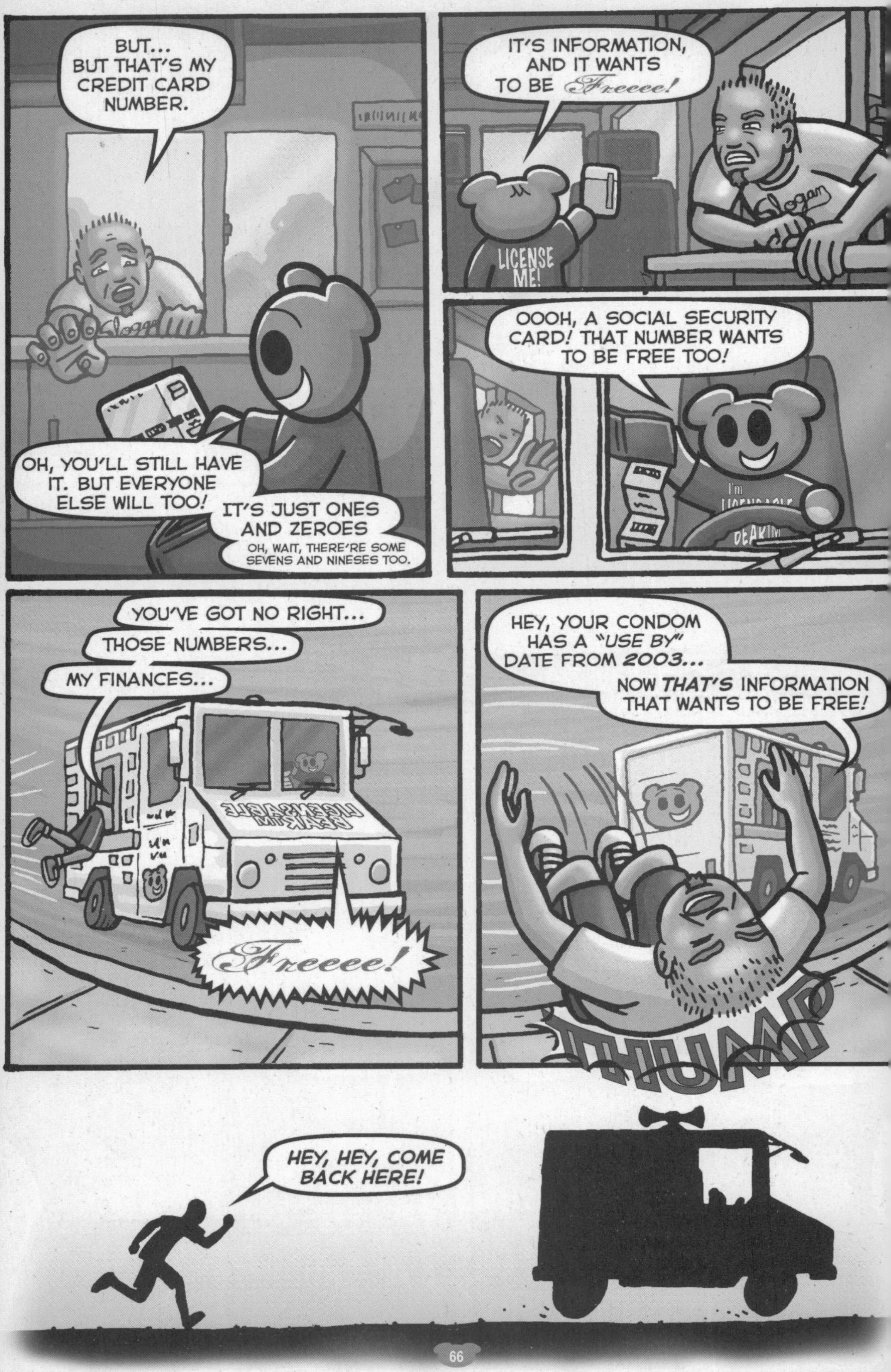
BUT... BUT THAT'S MY CREDIT CARD NUMBER.
OH, YOU'LL STILL HAVE IT. BUT EVERYONE ELSE WILL TOO!
IT'S JUST ONES AND ZEROES
OH, WAIT, THERE'RE SOME SEVENS AND NINESES TOO.
IT'S INFORMATION, AND IT WANTS TO BE Freeee!
LICENSE ME!
OOOH, A SOCIAL SECURITY CARD! THAT NUMBER WANTS TO BE FREE TOO!
YOU'VE GOT NO RIGHT...
THOSE NUMBERS...
MY FINANCES...
Freeee!
HEY, YOUR CONDOM HAS A "USE BY" DATE FROM 2003...
NOW THAT'S INFORMATION THAT WANTS TO BE FREE!
THUMP
HEY, HEY, COME BACK HERE!

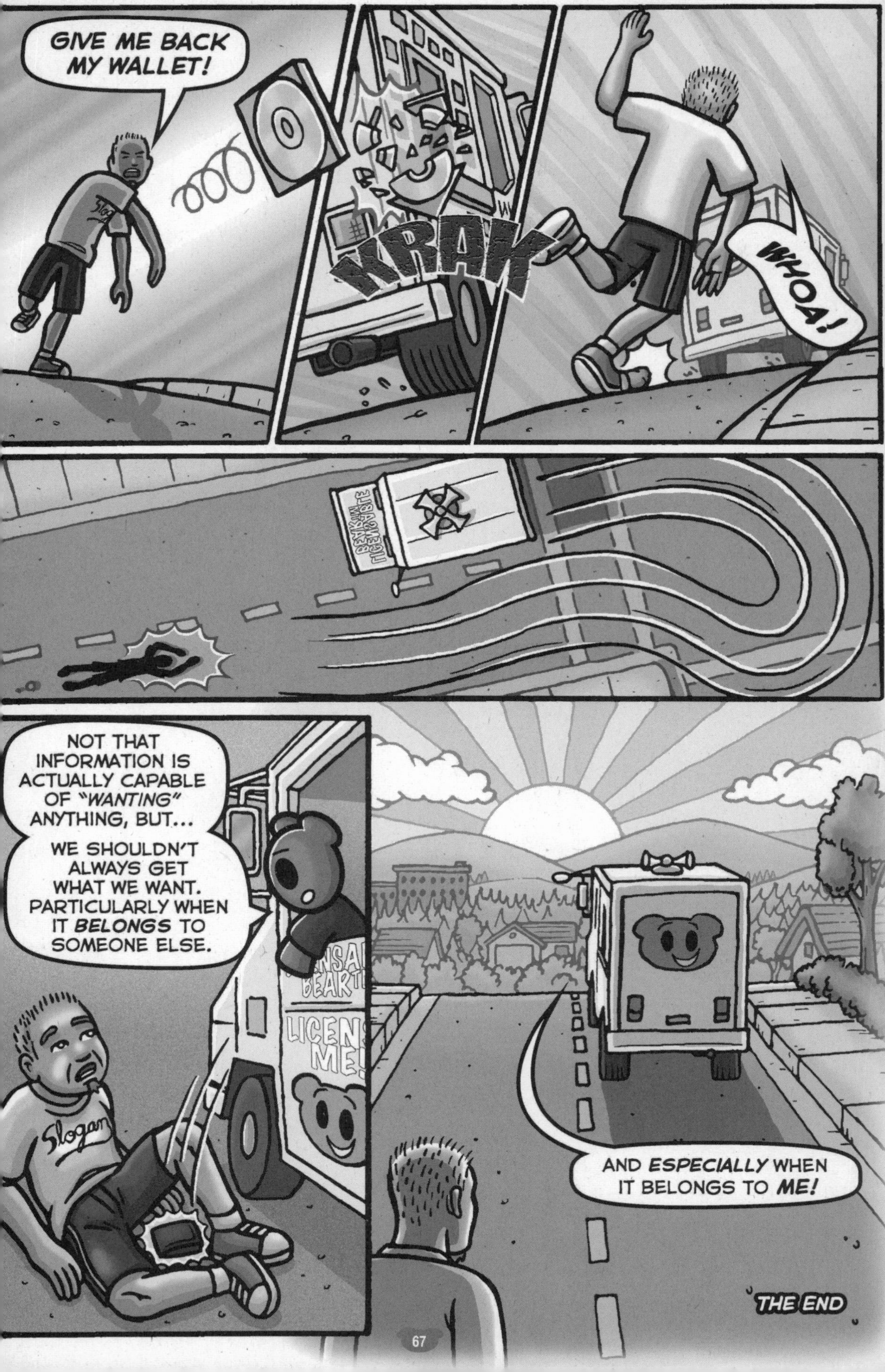
GIVE ME BACK MY WALLET!
KRAK
WHOA!
NOT THAT INFORMATION IS ACTUALLY CAPABLE OF "WANTING" ANYTHING, BUT...
WE SHOULDN'T ALWAYS GET WHAT WE WANT. PARTICULARLY WHEN IT BELONGS TO SOMEONE ELSE.
Slogan
AND ESPECIALLY WHEN IT BELONGS TO ME!
THE END

LICENSABLE BEAR™ uses Free Weekend Minutes

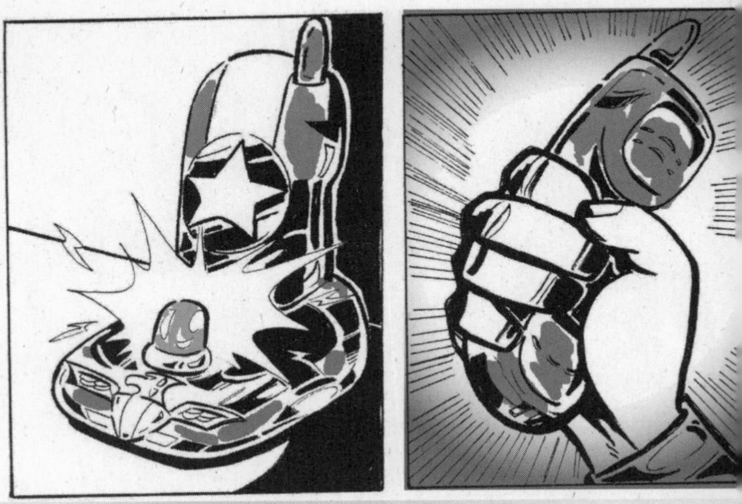

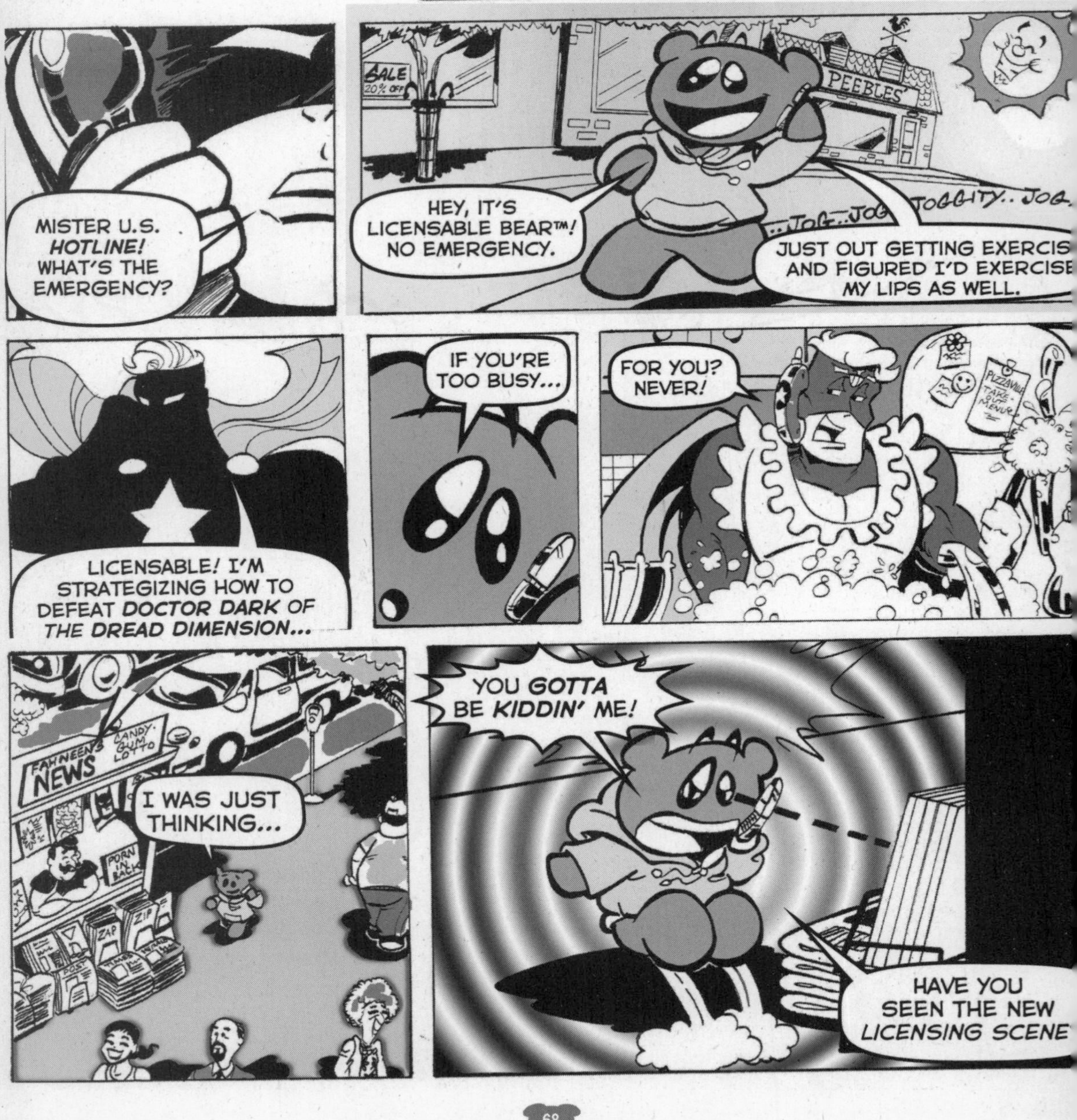
MISTER U.S. *HOTLINE!* WHAT'S THE EMERGENCY?
SALE 20% OFF
PEEBLES'
HEY, IT'S LICENSABLE BEAR™! NO EMERGENCY.
JOG..JOG JOGGITY.. JOG..
JUST OUT GETTING EXERCIS AND FIGURED I'D EXERCISE MY LIPS AS WELL.
LICENSABLE! I'M STRATEGIZING HOW TO DEFEAT *DOCTOR DARK* OF *THE DREAD DIMENSION...*
IF YOU'RE TOO BUSY...
FOR YOU? NEVER!
PIZZAVILLE TAKE-OUT MENU
FAHNEEN'S NEWS
CANDY GUM LOTTO
I WAS JUST THINKING...
PORN IN BACK
ZAP
ZIP
YOU *GOTTA* BE *KIDDIN'* ME!
HAVE YOU SEEN THE NEW *LICENSING SCENE*

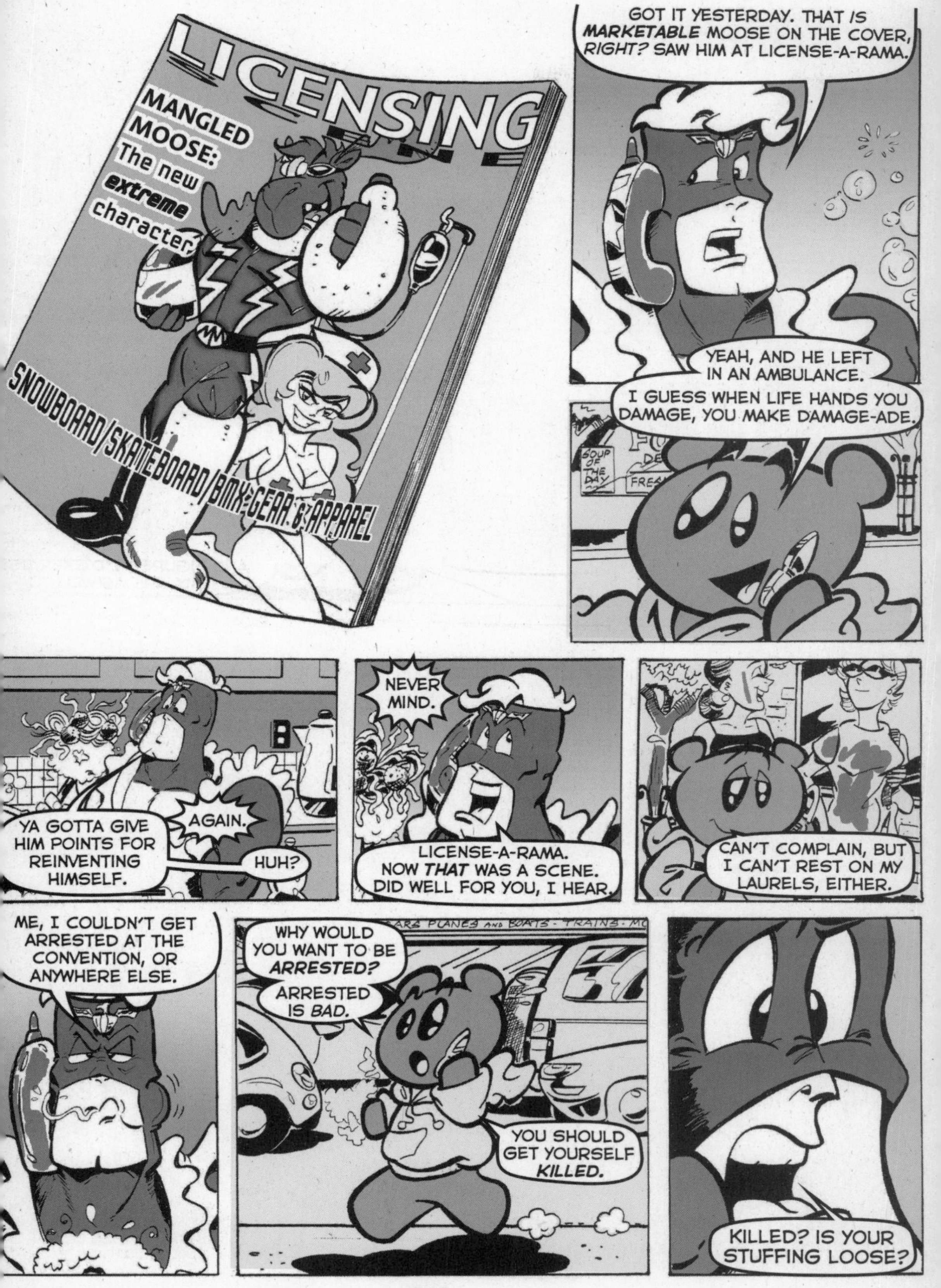
LICENSING
MANGLED MOOSE: The new extreme character.
SNOWBOARD/SKATEBOARD/BMX GEAR & APPAREL
GOT IT YESTERDAY. THAT IS MARKETABLE MOOSE ON THE COVER, RIGHT? SAW HIM AT LICENSE-A-RAMA.
YEAH, AND HE LEFT IN AN AMBULANCE.
I GUESS WHEN LIFE HANDS YOU DAMAGE, YOU MAKE DAMAGE-ADE.
SOUP OF THE DAY
YA GOTTA GIVE HIM POINTS FOR REINVENTING HIMSELF.
AGAIN.
HUH?
NEVER MIND.
LICENSE-A-RAMA. NOW THAT WAS A SCENE. DID WELL FOR YOU, I HEAR.
CAN'T COMPLAIN, BUT I CAN'T REST ON MY LAURELS, EITHER.
ME, I COULDN'T GET ARRESTED AT THE CONVENTION, OR ANYWHERE ELSE.
CARS PLANES AND BOATS - TRAINS
WHY WOULD YOU WANT TO BE ARRESTED?
ARRESTED IS BAD.
YOU SHOULD GET YOURSELF KILLED.
KILLED? IS YOUR STUFFING LOOSE?

NO, NO, THINK ABOUT IT – ELVIS, MARILYN, AUDREY, CHE, JAMES DEAN... LET'S FACE IT, TO BE A *BIG HIP LICENSE*, IT HELPS TO BE DEAD.

BETTER YET, DEAD *BEFORE YOUR TIME.*

YOU *AREN'T* REALLY HAPPENIN' IF YOU'RE *STILL HAPPENIN'.*

BUT ISN'T THAT A BIT... EXTREME?

I ADMIT THAT IN DARK MOMENTS, I THINK ABOUT GOING THAT ROUTE. BUT FOR ME, IT WOULD BE THE END. FOR YOU?

YOU SUPER-TYPES DIE ALL THE TIME. 'FESS UP, YOU DIED YOURSELF ONCE, DIDN'T YOU?

WELL, NO. NOT *ONCE*.

A COUPL[E] TIMES

SO YOU KNOW THE DANCE. SUDDENLY, EVERYBODY DECLARES THEY LOVE YOU, MISS YOU, HOW YOU WERE THE REAL DEAL—

—AND A FEW MONTHS LATER, *BAM!* YOU'RE BACK AMONG THE LIVING.

YOU'RE *RIGHTING THE BUCKET,*

SELLING THE FARM,

PUSHING *DOWN* THE DAISIES.

YEAH. PEOPLE ACT REAL NICE TO YOU WHEN THAT HAPPENS.

SURE THEY DO. SO STEP 1: GET YOUR LICENSING HOUSE IN ORDER. STEP 2: GET KILLED

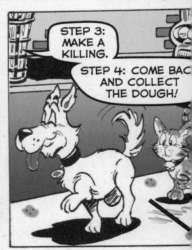

STEP 3: MAKE A KILLING.

STEP 4: COME BAC[K] AND COLLECT THE DOUGH!

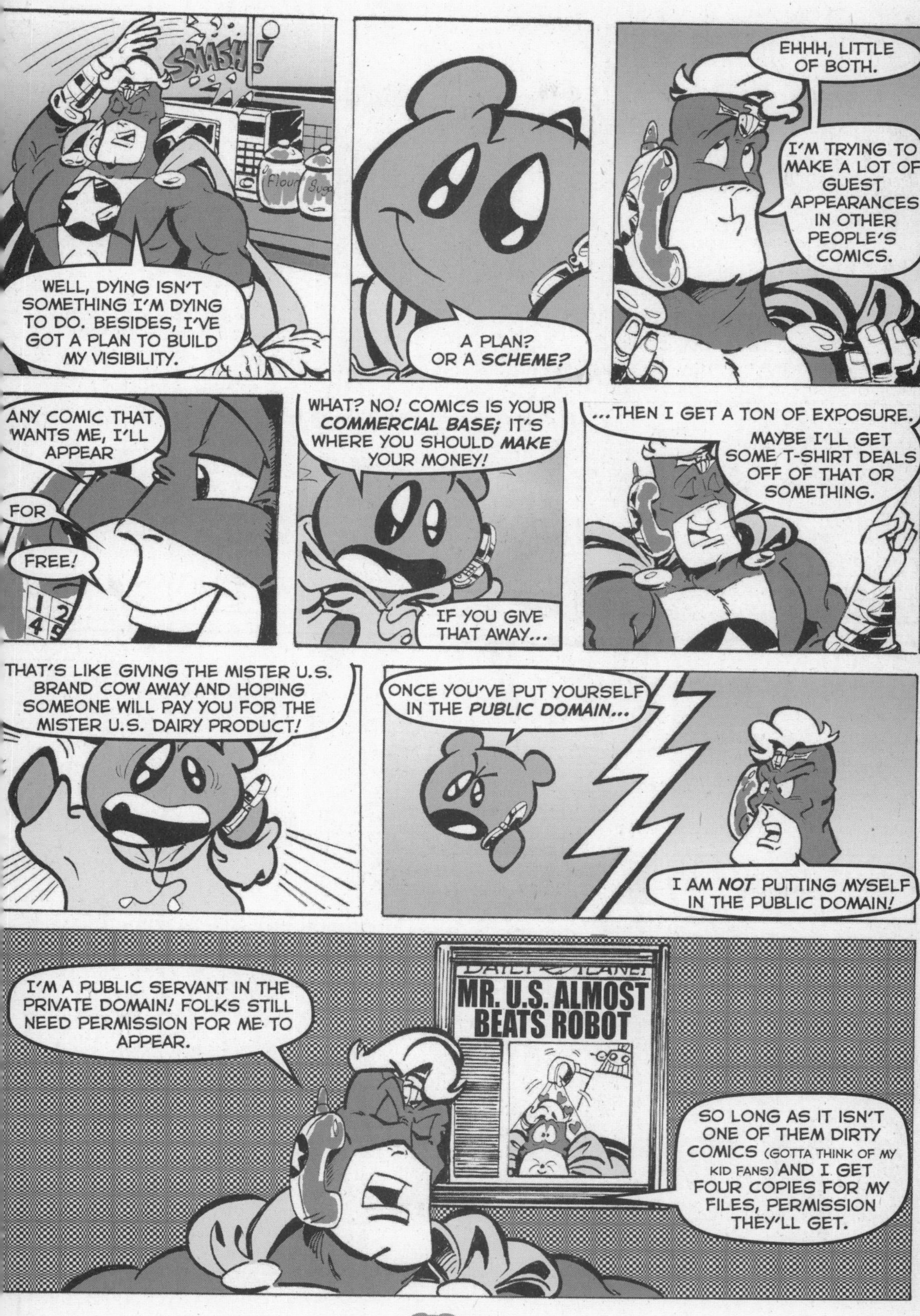

SMASH!
Flour
WELL, DYING ISN'T SOMETHING I'M DYING TO DO. BESIDES, I'VE GOT A PLAN TO BUILD MY VISIBILITY.
A PLAN? OR A *SCHEME?*
EHHH, LITTLE OF BOTH.
I'M TRYING TO MAKE A LOT OF GUEST APPEARANCES IN OTHER PEOPLE'S COMICS.
ANY COMIC THAT WANTS ME, I'LL APPEAR
FOR
FREE!
WHAT? NO! COMICS IS YOUR *COMMERCIAL BASE;* IT'S WHERE YOU SHOULD *MAKE* YOUR MONEY!
IF YOU GIVE THAT AWAY...
...THEN I GET A TON OF EXPOSURE.
MAYBE I'LL GET SOME T-SHIRT DEALS OFF OF THAT OR SOMETHING.
THAT'S LIKE GIVING THE MISTER U.S. BRAND COW AWAY AND HOPING SOMEONE WILL PAY YOU FOR THE MISTER U.S. DAIRY PRODUCT!
ONCE YOU'VE PUT YOURSELF IN THE *PUBLIC DOMAIN...*
I AM *NOT* PUTTING MYSELF IN THE PUBLIC DOMAIN!
I'M A PUBLIC SERVANT IN THE PRIVATE DOMAIN! FOLKS STILL NEED PERMISSION FOR ME TO APPEAR.
DAILY PLANET
MR. U.S. ALMOST BEATS ROBOT
SO LONG AS IT ISN'T ONE OF THEM DIRTY COMICS (GOTTA THINK OF MY KID FANS) AND I GET FOUR COPIES FOR MY FILES, PERMISSION THEY'LL GET.

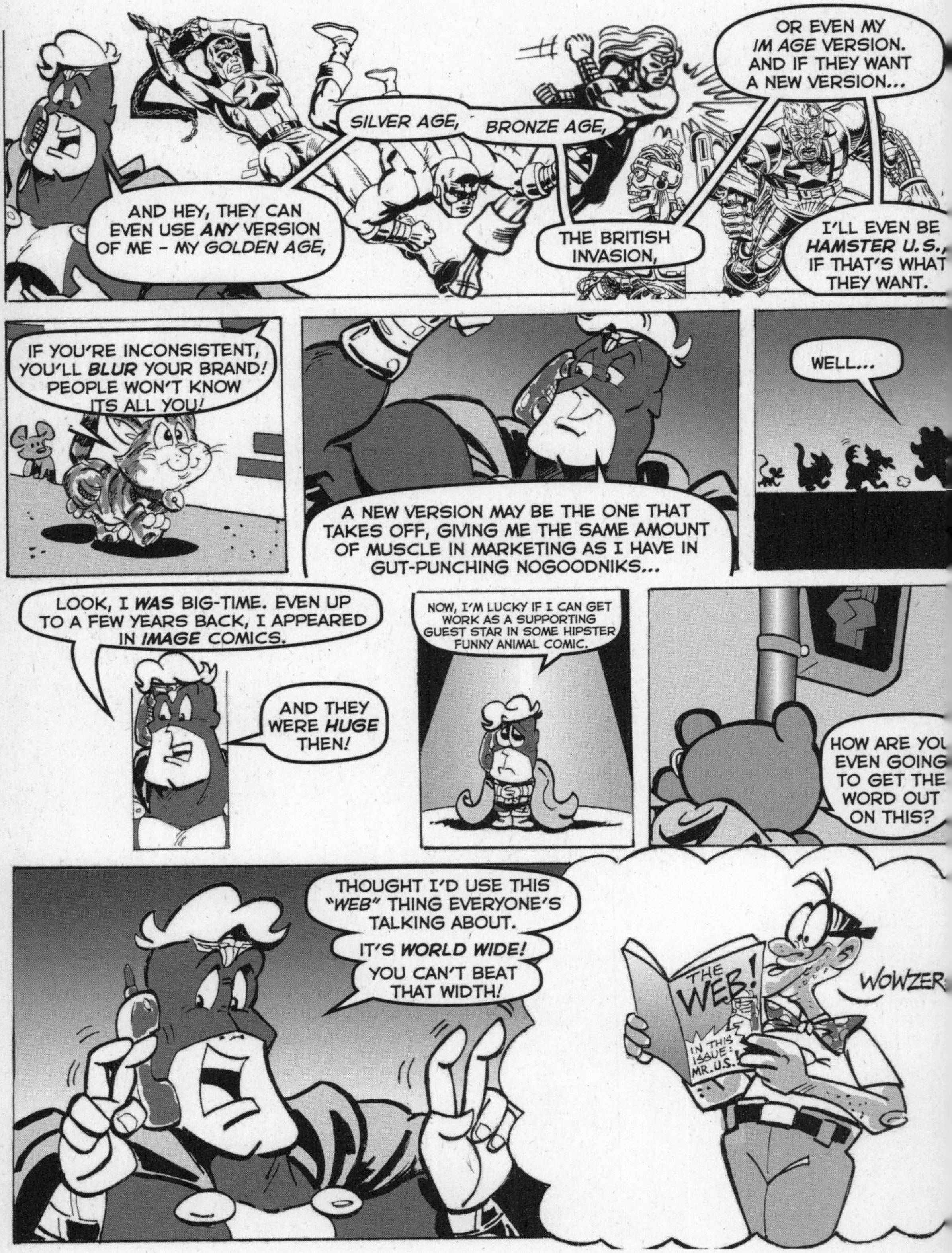
AND HEY, THEY CAN EVEN USE ANY VERSION OF ME - MY GOLDEN AGE,
SILVER AGE,
BRONZE AGE,
THE BRITISH INVASION,
OR EVEN MY IM AGE VERSION. AND IF THEY WANT A NEW VERSION...
I'LL EVEN BE HAMSTER U.S., IF THAT'S WHAT THEY WANT.
IF YOU'RE INCONSISTENT, YOU'LL BLUR YOUR BRAND! PEOPLE WON'T KNOW ITS ALL YOU!
A NEW VERSION MAY BE THE ONE THAT TAKES OFF, GIVING ME THE SAME AMOUNT OF MUSCLE IN MARKETING AS I HAVE IN GUT-PUNCHING NOGOODNIKS...
WELL...
LOOK, I WAS BIG-TIME. EVEN UP TO A FEW YEARS BACK, I APPEARED IN IMAGE COMICS.
AND THEY WERE HUGE THEN!
NOW, I'M LUCKY IF I CAN GET WORK AS A SUPPORTING GUEST STAR IN SOME HIPSTER FUNNY ANIMAL COMIC.
HOW ARE YOU EVEN GOING TO GET THE WORD OUT ON THIS?
THOUGHT I'D USE THIS "WEB" THING EVERYONE'S TALKING ABOUT.
IT'S WORLD WIDE!
YOU CAN'T BEAT THAT WIDTH!
THE WEB!
IN THIS ISSUE: MR. U.S.
WOWZER

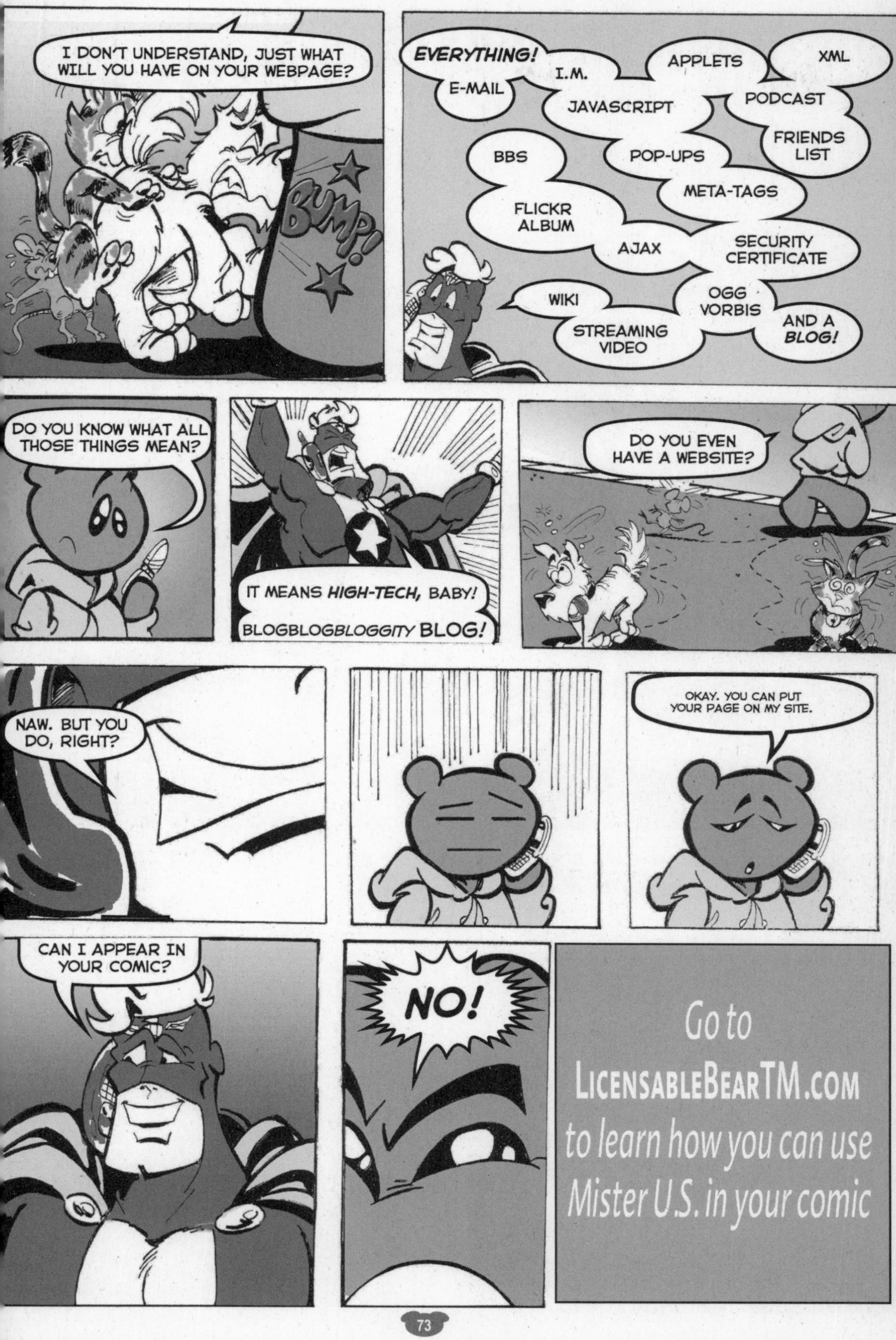

I DON'T UNDERSTAND, JUST WHAT WILL YOU HAVE ON YOUR WEBPAGE?
BUMP!
EVERYTHING!
E-MAIL
I.M.
APPLETS
XML
JAVASCRIPT
PODCAST
FRIENDS LIST
BBS
POP-UPS
META-TAGS
FLICKR ALBUM
AJAX
SECURITY CERTIFICATE
WIKI
OGG VORBIS
STREAMING VIDEO
AND A BLOG!
DO YOU KNOW WHAT ALL THOSE THINGS MEAN?
IT MEANS HIGH-TECH, BABY!
BLOGBLOGBLOGGITY BLOG!
DO YOU EVEN HAVE A WEBSITE?
NAW. BUT YOU DO, RIGHT?
OKAY. YOU CAN PUT YOUR PAGE ON MY SITE.
CAN I APPEAR IN YOUR COMIC?
NO!
Go to
LicensableBearTM.com
to learn how you can use
Mister U.S. in your comic

LICENSABLE BEAR™ Presses a Sui

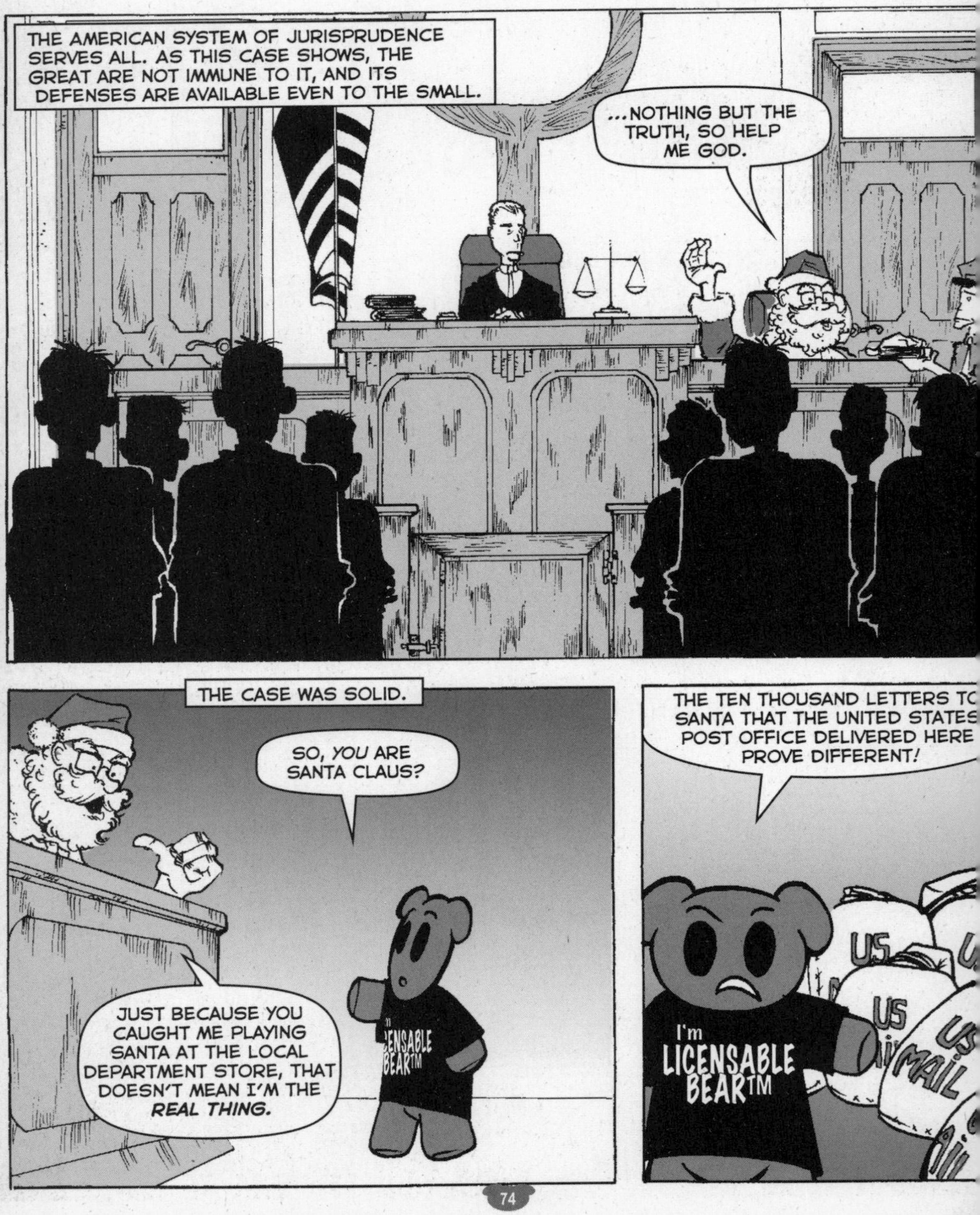
THE AMERICAN SYSTEM OF JURISPRUDENCE SERVES ALL. AS THIS CASE SHOWS, THE GREAT ARE NOT IMMUNE TO IT, AND ITS DEFENSES ARE AVAILABLE EVEN TO THE SMALL.
...NOTHING BUT THE TRUTH, SO HELP ME GOD.
THE CASE WAS SOLID.
SO, *YOU* ARE SANTA CLAUS?
JUST BECAUSE YOU CAUGHT ME PLAYING SANTA AT THE LOCAL DEPARTMENT STORE, THAT DOESN'T MEAN I'M THE *REAL THING.*
I'm LICENSABLE BEAR™
THE TEN THOUSAND LETTERS TO SANTA THAT THE UNITED STATES POST OFFICE DELIVERED HERE PROVE DIFFERENT!
I'm LICENSABLE BEAR™
US
US
US MAIL

THE CRIME WAS NEFARIOUS.

YOUR ELVES MAKE ALL THE TOYS YOU DISTRIBUTE... INCLUDING LICENSABLE BEAR™ DOLLS AND PLAYSETS. HAVE YOU LICENSED THE RIGHT TO MAKE THEM?

UMMM...

NO, YOU HAVEN'T!

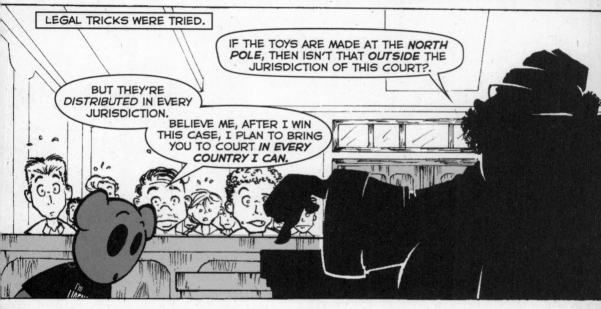

LEGAL TRICKS WERE TRIED.

IF THE TOYS ARE MADE AT THE *NORTH POLE*, THEN ISN'T THAT *OUTSIDE* THE JURISDICTION OF THIS COURT?

BUT THEY'RE *DISTRIBUTED* IN EVERY JURISDICTION.

BELIEVE ME, AFTER I WIN THIS CASE, I PLAN TO BRING YOU TO COURT *IN EVERY COUNTRY I CAN.*

EXPERT TESTIMONY WAS GIVEN.

TO THE BEST OF OUR UNDERSTANDING, MISTER CLAUS TRAVELS BY AIR FROM HOUSE TO HOUSE, COVERING THE ENTIRE WORLD BETWEEN SUNSET OF DECEMBER TWENTY-FOUR AND SUNRISE THE FOLLOWING DAY.

SO IN YOUR EXPERT OPINION—

REPUTATIONS WERE UNDERMINED.

-- SANTA RUNS A FLY-BY-NIGHT OPERATION!

I'm LICENSABLE

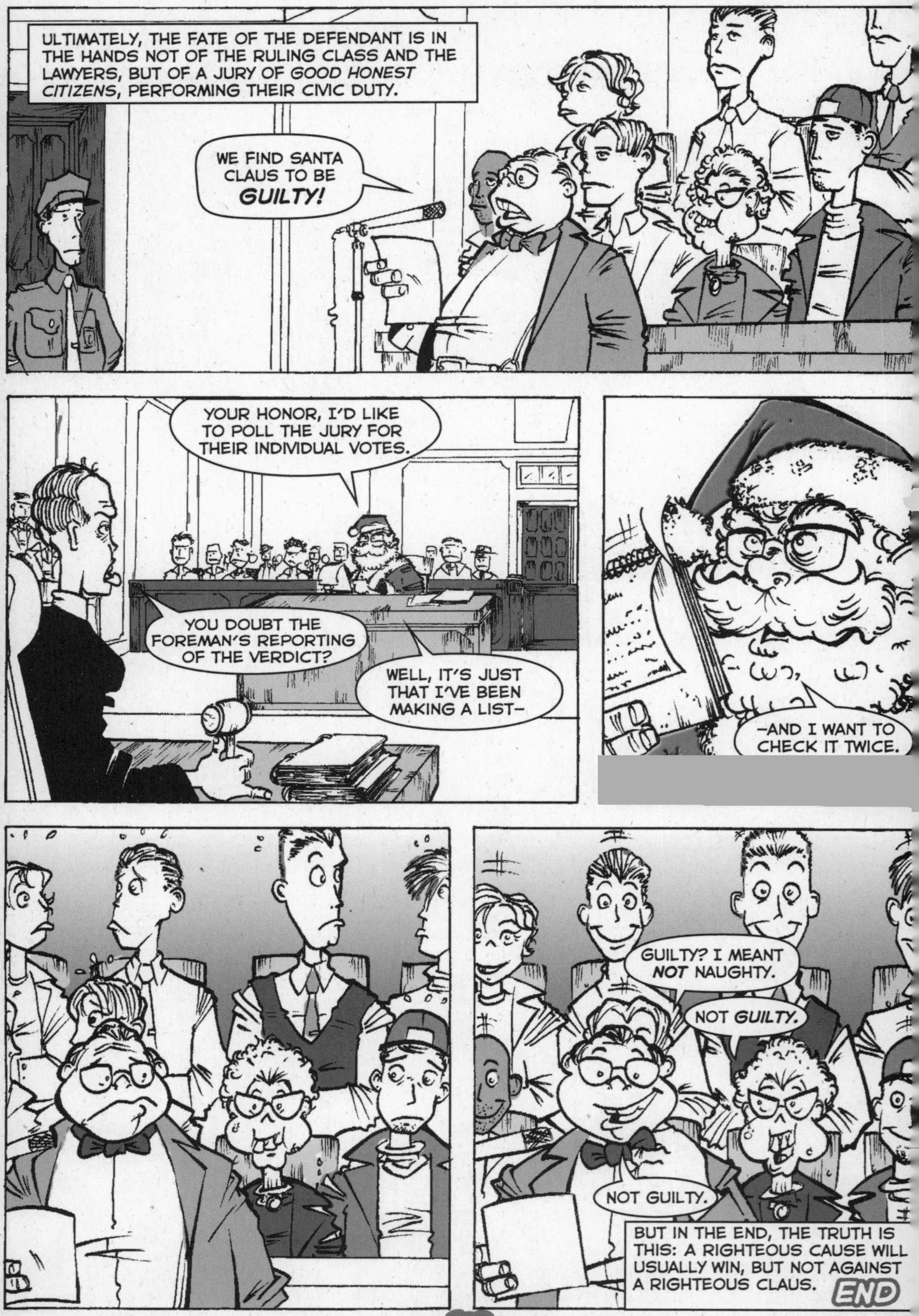
ULTIMATELY, THE FATE OF THE DEFENDANT IS IN THE HANDS NOT OF THE RULING CLASS AND THE LAWYERS, BUT OF A JURY OF *GOOD HONEST CITIZENS*, PERFORMING THEIR CIVIC DUTY.
WE FIND SANTA CLAUS TO BE ***GUILTY!***
YOUR HONOR, I'D LIKE TO POLL THE JURY FOR THEIR INDIVIDUAL VOTES.
YOU DOUBT THE FOREMAN'S REPORTING OF THE VERDICT?
WELL, IT'S JUST THAT I'VE BEEN MAKING A LIST–
–AND I WANT TO CHECK IT TWICE.
GUILTY? I MEANT ***NOT*** NAUGHTY.
NOT ***GUILTY.***
NOT GUILTY.
BUT IN THE END, THE TRUTH IS THIS: A RIGHTEOUS CAUSE WILL USUALLY WIN, BUT NOT AGAINST A RIGHTEOUS CLAUS.
END

LICENSABLE BEAR™ Recommends Another

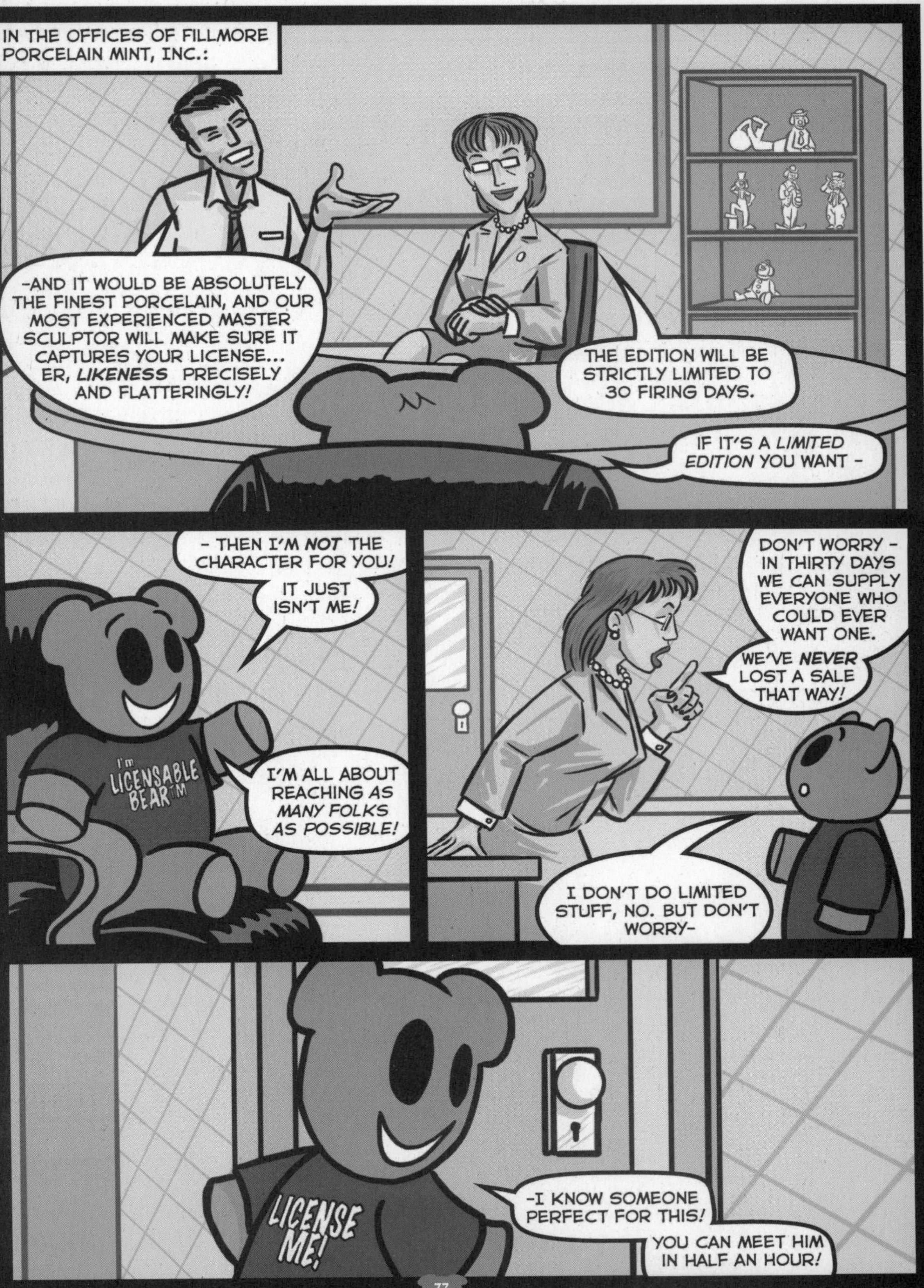

IN THE OFFICES OF FILLMORE PORCELAIN MINT, INC.:
-AND IT WOULD BE ABSOLUTELY THE FINEST PORCELAIN, AND OUR MOST EXPERIENCED MASTER SCULPTOR WILL MAKE SURE IT CAPTURES YOUR LICENSE... ER, *LIKENESS* PRECISELY AND FLATTERINGLY!
THE EDITION WILL BE STRICTLY LIMITED TO 30 FIRING DAYS.
IF IT'S A *LIMITED EDITION* YOU WANT -
- THEN I'M ***NOT*** THE CHARACTER FOR YOU!
IT JUST ISN'T ME!
I'm LICENSABLE BEAR™
I'M ALL ABOUT REACHING AS *MANY FOLKS* AS *POSSIBLE!*
DON'T WORRY - IN THIRTY DAYS WE CAN SUPPLY EVERYONE WHO COULD EVER WANT ONE.
WE'VE ***NEVER*** LOST A SALE THAT WAY!
I DON'T DO LIMITED STUFF, NO. BUT DON'T WORRY-
LICENSE ME!
-I KNOW SOMEONE PERFECT FOR THIS!
YOU CAN MEET HIM IN HALF AN HOUR!

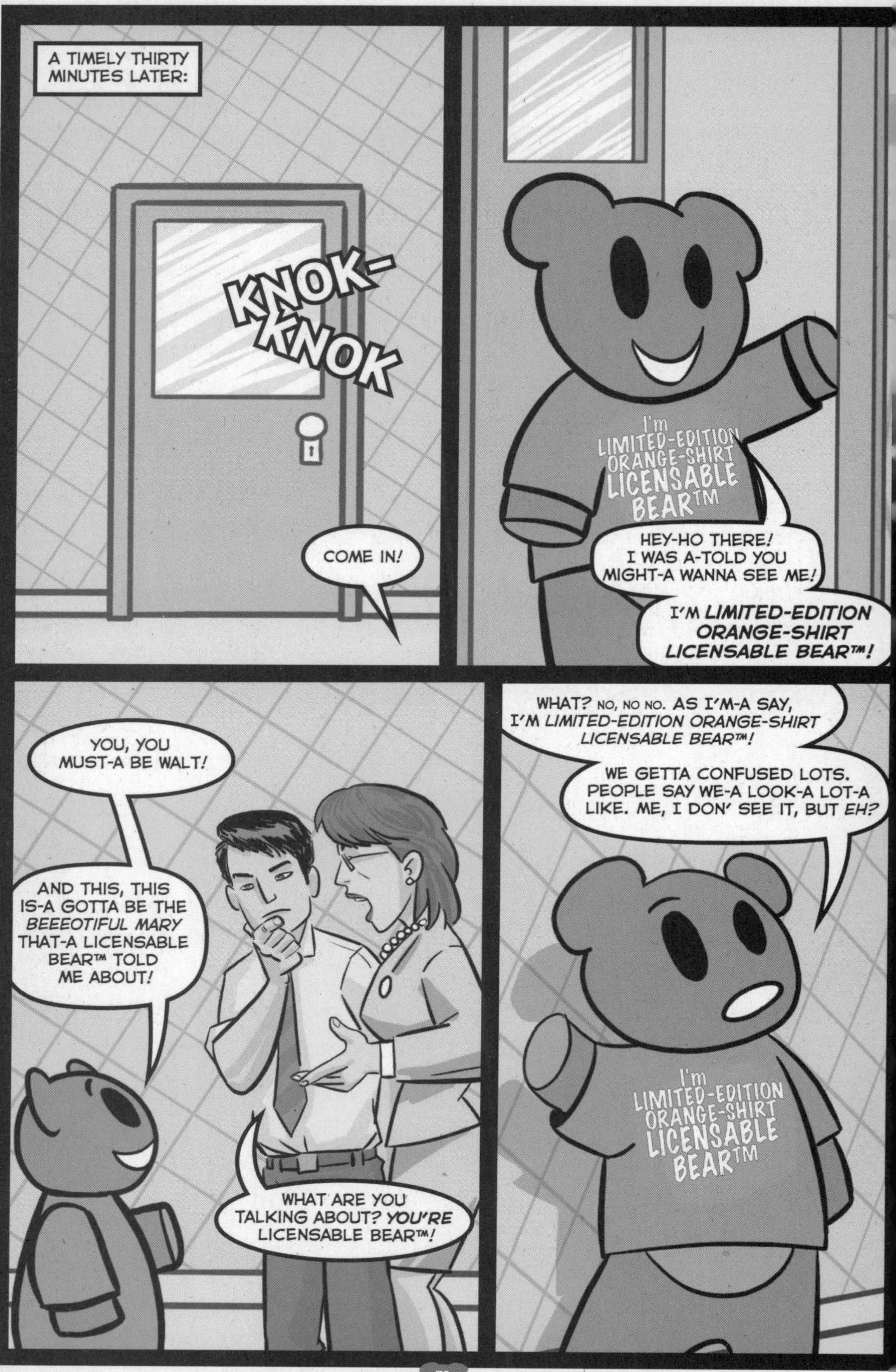
A TIMELY THIRTY MINUTES LATER:
KNOK-KNOK
COME IN!
I'm LIMITED-EDITION ORANGE-SHIRT LICENSABLE BEAR™
HEY-HO THERE! I WAS A-TOLD YOU MIGHT-A WANNA SEE ME!
I'M *LIMITED-EDITION ORANGE-SHIRT LICENSABLE BEAR™!*
YOU, YOU MUST-A BE WALT!
AND THIS, THIS IS-A GOTTA BE THE *BEEEOTIFUL MARY* THAT-A LICENSABLE BEAR™ TOLD ME ABOUT!
WHAT ARE YOU TALKING ABOUT? *YOU'RE* LICENSABLE BEAR™!
WHAT? NO, NO NO. AS I'M-A SAY, I'M *LIMITED-EDITION ORANGE-SHIRT LICENSABLE BEAR™!*
WE GETTA CONFUSED LOTS. PEOPLE SAY WE-A LOOK-A LOT-A LIKE. ME, I DON' SEE IT, BUT *EH?*
I'm LIMITED-EDITION ORANGE-SHIRT LICENSABLE BEAR™

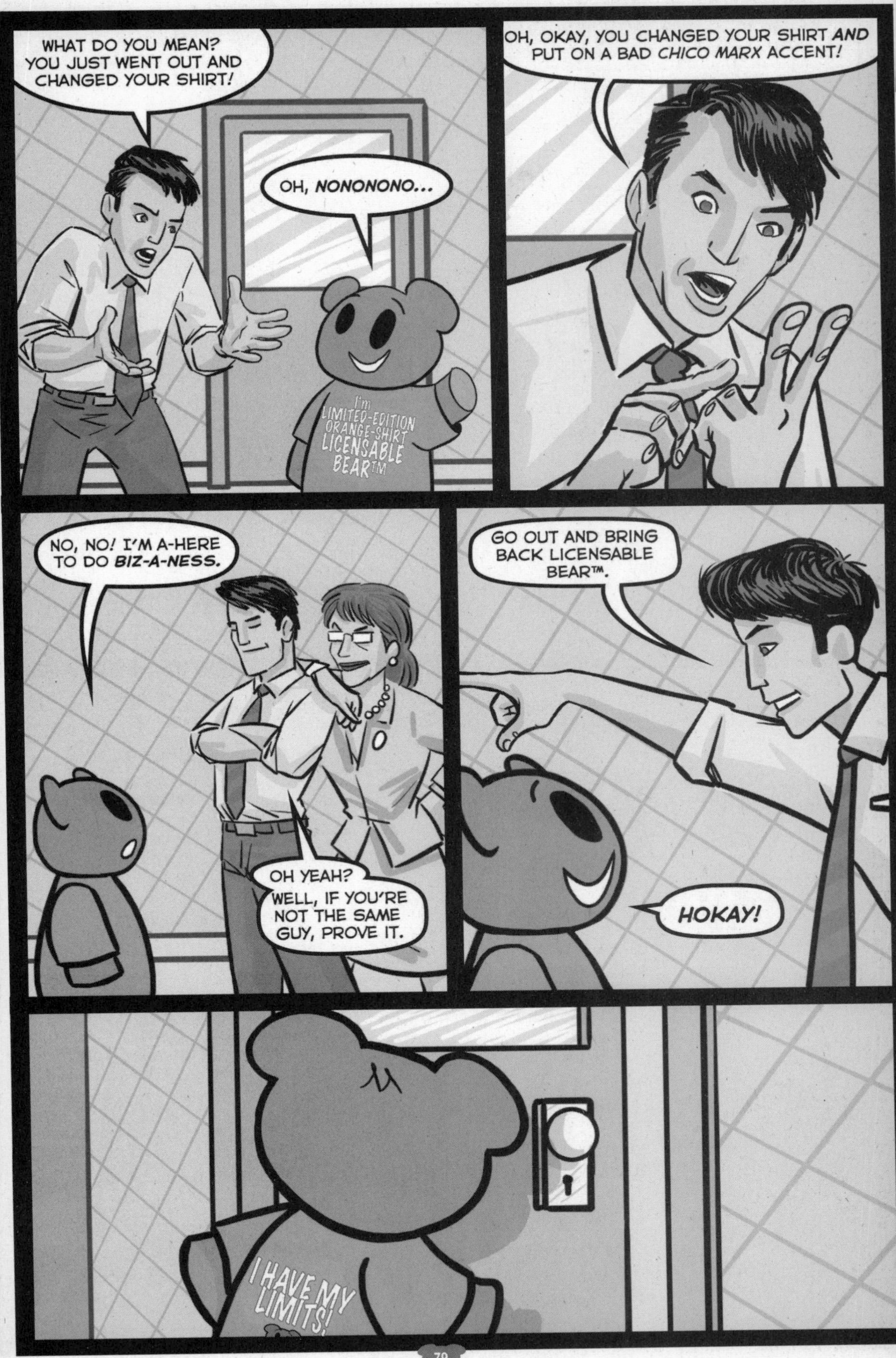
WHAT DO YOU MEAN? YOU JUST WENT OUT AND CHANGED YOUR SHIRT!
OH, NONONONO...
I'm LIMITED-EDITION ORANGE-SHIRT LICENSABLE BEAR™
OH, OKAY, YOU CHANGED YOUR SHIRT AND PUT ON A BAD CHICO MARX ACCENT!
NO, NO! I'M A-HERE TO DO BIZ-A-NESS.
OH YEAH? WELL, IF YOU'RE NOT THE SAME GUY, PROVE IT.
GO OUT AND BRING BACK LICENSABLE BEAR™.
HOKAY!
I HAVE MY LIMITS!

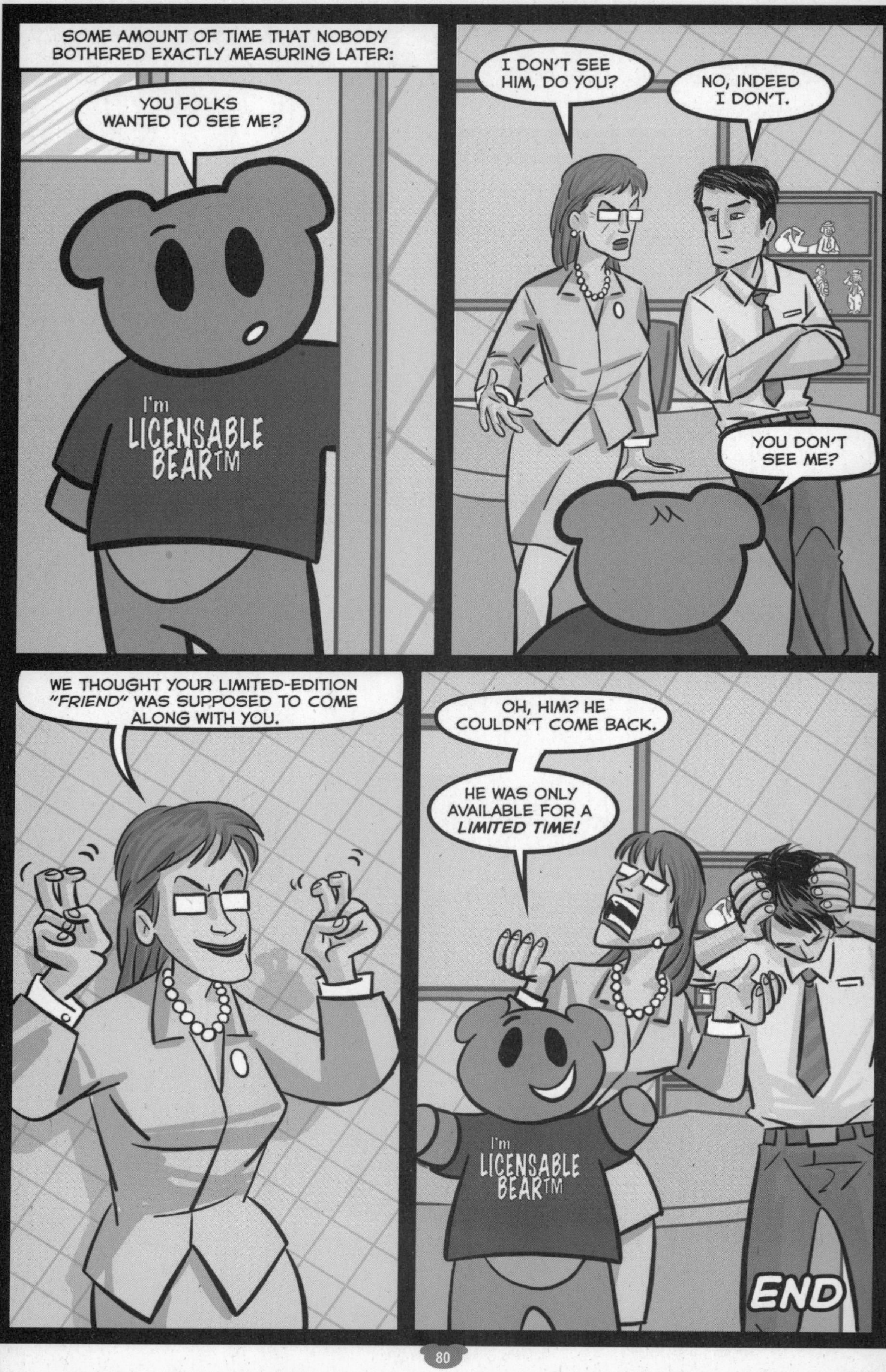
SOME AMOUNT OF TIME THAT NOBODY BOTHERED EXACTLY MEASURING LATER:
YOU FOLKS WANTED TO SEE ME?
I'm LICENSABLE BEAR™
I DON'T SEE HIM, DO YOU?
NO, INDEED I DON'T.
YOU DON'T SEE ME?
WE THOUGHT YOUR LIMITED-EDITION *"FRIEND"* WAS SUPPOSED TO COME ALONG WITH YOU.
OH, HIM? HE COULDN'T COME BACK.
HE WAS ONLY AVAILABLE FOR A *LIMITED TIME!*
I'm LICENSABLE BEAR™
END

LICENSABLE BEAR™ Meets the Press

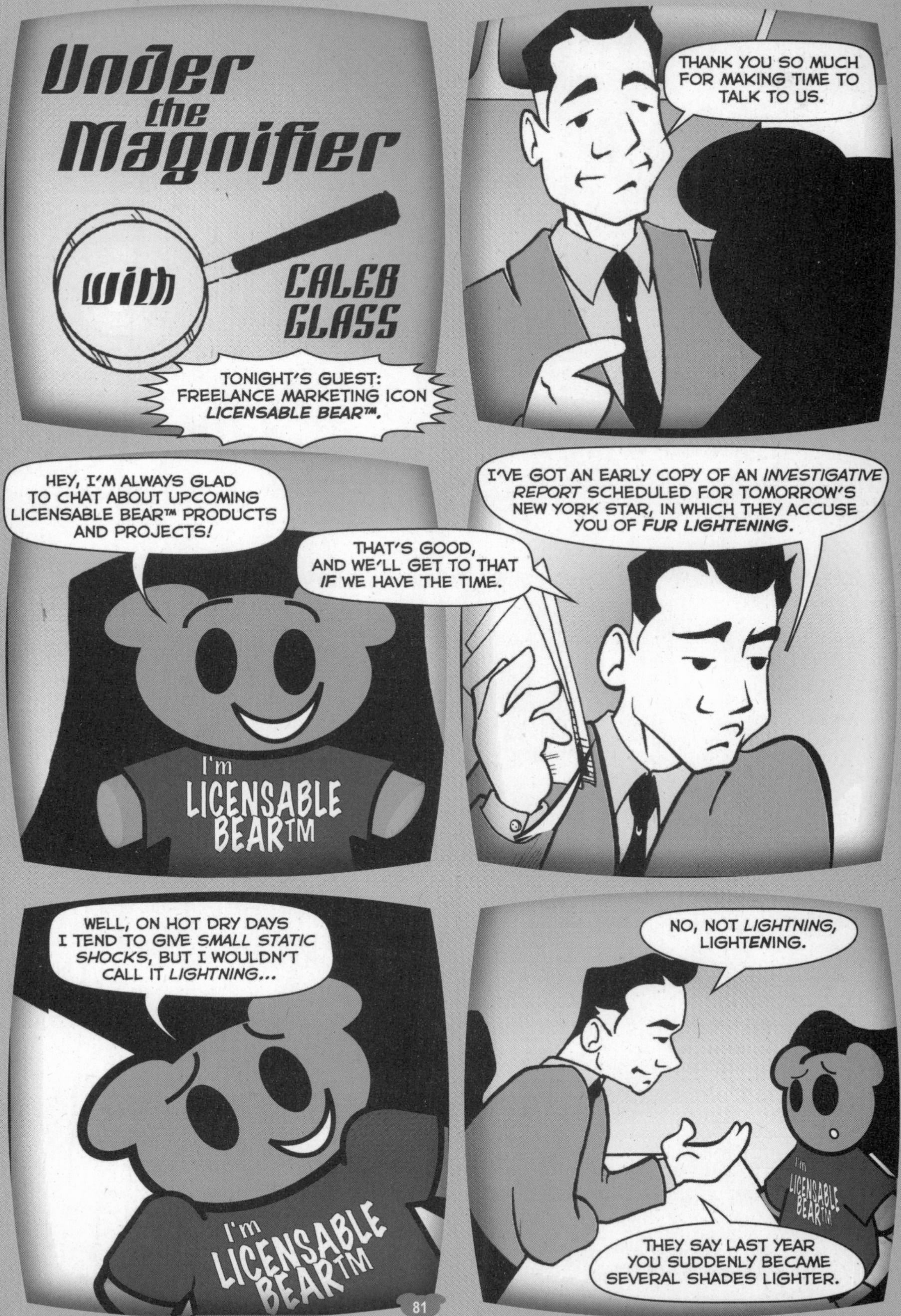

Under the Magnifier
with
CALEB GLASS
TONIGHT'S GUEST: FREELANCE MARKETING ICON *LICENSABLE BEAR™.*
THANK YOU SO MUCH FOR MAKING TIME TO TALK TO US.
HEY, I'M ALWAYS GLAD TO CHAT ABOUT UPCOMING LICENSABLE BEAR™ PRODUCTS AND PROJECTS!
THAT'S GOOD, AND WE'LL GET TO THAT *IF* WE HAVE THE TIME.
I'm LICENSABLE BEAR™
I'VE GOT AN EARLY COPY OF AN *INVESTIGATIVE REPORT* SCHEDULED FOR TOMORROW'S NEW YORK STAR, IN WHICH THEY ACCUSE YOU OF *FUR LIGHTENING*.
WELL, ON HOT DRY DAYS I TEND TO GIVE *SMALL STATIC SHOCKS*, BUT I WOULDN'T CALL IT *LIGHTNING...*
I'm LICENSABLE BEAR™
NO, NOT *LIGHTNING*, LIGHTENING.
I'm LICENSABLE BEAR™
THEY SAY LAST YEAR YOU SUDDENLY BECAME SEVERAL SHADES LIGHTER.

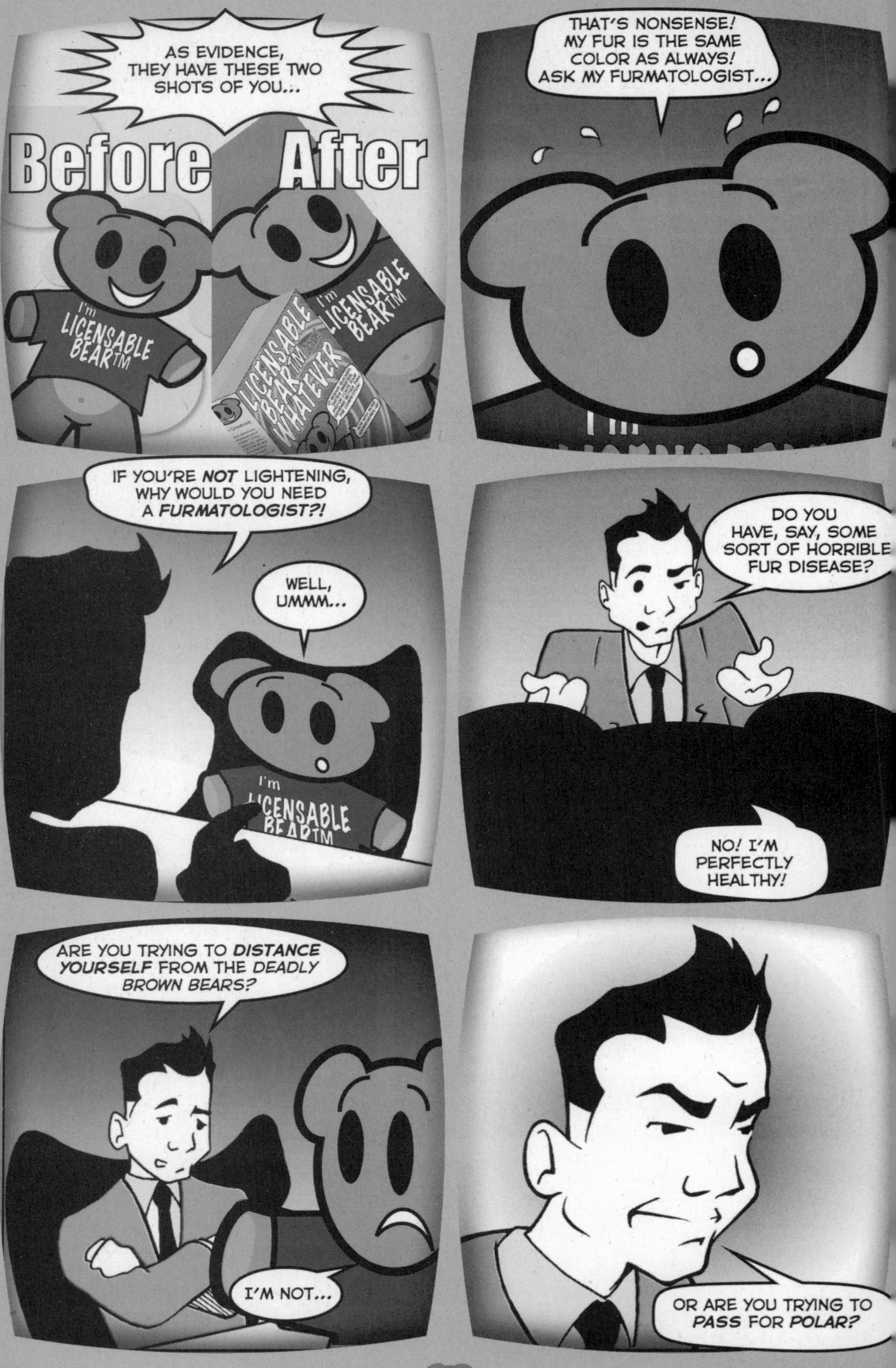
AS EVIDENCE, THEY HAVE THESE TWO SHOTS OF YOU...
Before
After
I'm LICENSABLE BEAR™
I'm LICENSABLE BEAR™
LICENSABLE BEAR™ and WHATEVER
THAT'S NONSENSE! MY FUR IS THE SAME COLOR AS ALWAYS! ASK MY FURMATOLOGIST...
IF YOU'RE *NOT* LIGHTENING, WHY WOULD YOU NEED A *FURMATOLOGIST?!*
WELL, UMMM...
DO YOU HAVE, SAY, SOME SORT OF HORRIBLE FUR DISEASE?
NO! I'M PERFECTLY HEALTHY!
ARE YOU TRYING TO *DISTANCE YOURSELF* FROM THE *DEADLY BROWN BEARS?*
I'M NOT...
OR ARE YOU TRYING TO *PASS* FOR *POLAR?*

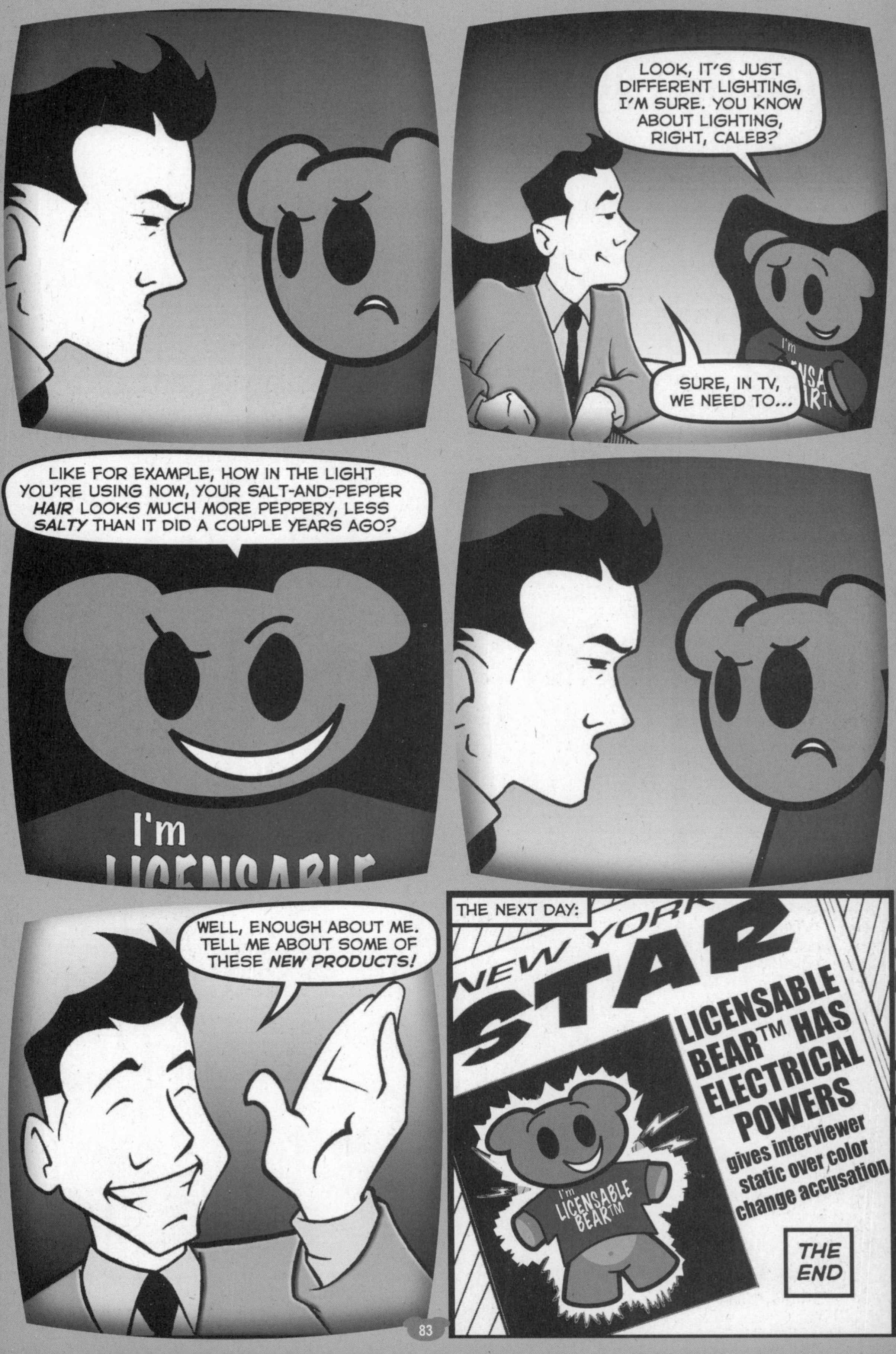
LOOK, IT'S JUST DIFFERENT LIGHTING, I'M SURE. YOU KNOW ABOUT LIGHTING, RIGHT, CALEB?
SURE, IN TV, WE NEED TO...
LIKE FOR EXAMPLE, HOW IN THE LIGHT YOU'RE USING NOW, YOUR SALT-AND-PEPPER *HAIR* LOOKS MUCH MORE PEPPERY, LESS *SALTY* THAN IT DID A COUPLE YEARS AGO?
I'm
WELL, ENOUGH ABOUT ME. TELL ME ABOUT SOME OF THESE *NEW PRODUCTS!*
THE NEXT DAY:
NEW YORK STAR
LICENSABLE BEAR™ HAS ELECTRICAL POWERS
gives interviewer static over color change accusation
I'm LICENSABLE BEAR™
THE END

LICENSABLE BEAR™ Forms a Union

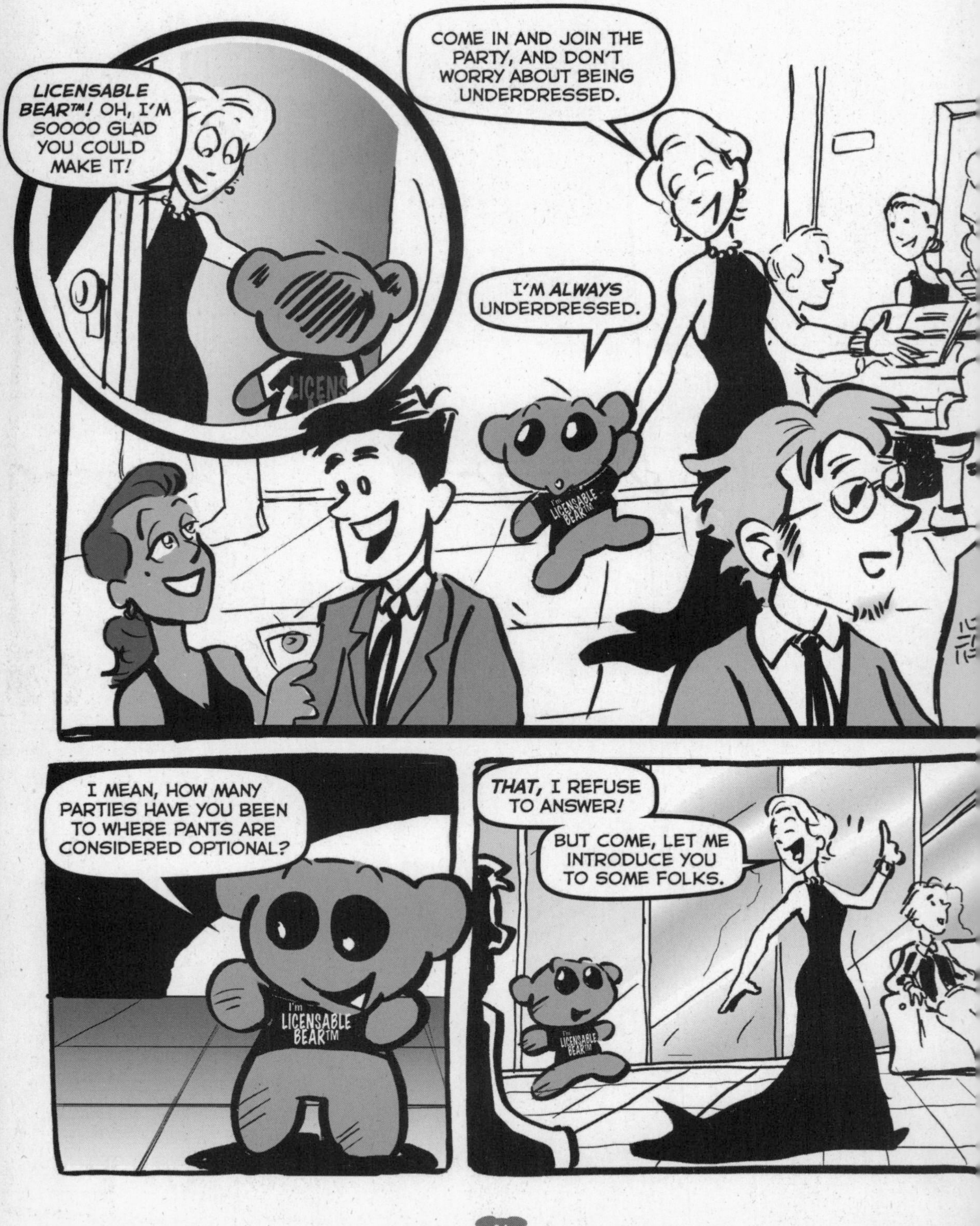
LICENSABLE BEAR™! OH, I'M SOOOO GLAD YOU COULD MAKE IT!
COME IN AND JOIN THE PARTY, AND DON'T WORRY ABOUT BEING UNDERDRESSED.
I'M ALWAYS UNDERDRESSED.
I'm LICENSABLE BEAR™
I MEAN, HOW MANY PARTIES HAVE YOU BEEN TO WHERE PANTS ARE CONSIDERED OPTIONAL?
I'm LICENSABLE BEAR™
THAT, I REFUSE TO ANSWER!
BUT COME, LET ME INTRODUCE YOU TO SOME FOLKS.
I'm LICENSABLE BEAR™

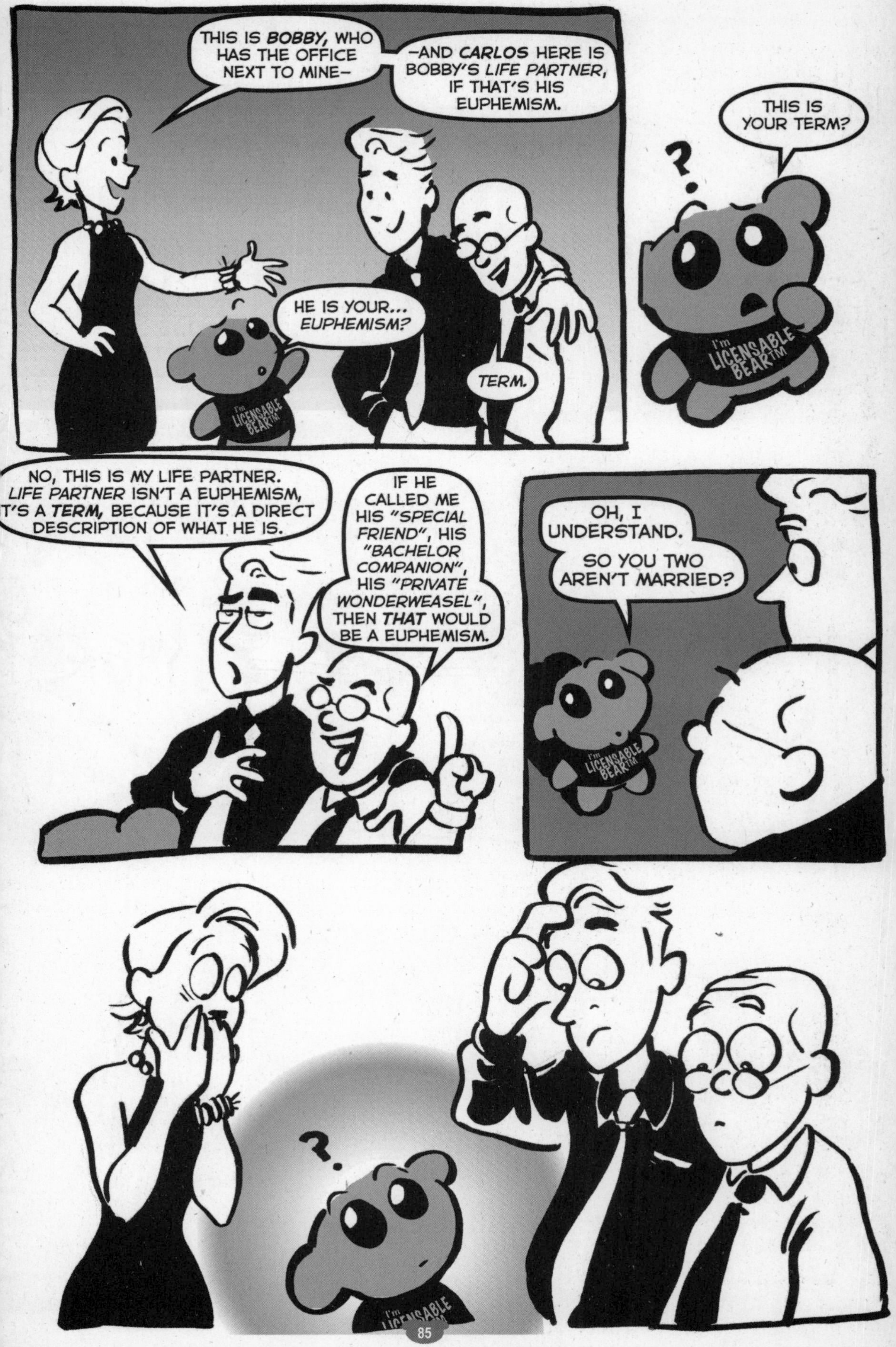
THIS IS *BOBBY,* WHO HAS THE OFFICE NEXT TO MINE–
–AND *CARLOS* HERE IS BOBBY'S *LIFE PARTNER,* IF THAT'S HIS EUPHEMISM.
HE IS YOUR... *EUPHEMISM?*
TERM.
I'm LICENSABLE BEAR™
THIS IS YOUR TERM?
?
I'm LICENSABLE BEAR™
NO, THIS IS MY LIFE PARTNER. *LIFE PARTNER* ISN'T A EUPHEMISM, IT'S A ***TERM,*** BECAUSE IT'S A DIRECT DESCRIPTION OF WHAT HE IS.
IF HE CALLED ME HIS *"SPECIAL FRIEND"*, HIS *"BACHELOR COMPANION"*, HIS *"PRIVATE WONDERWEASEL"*, THEN ***THAT*** WOULD BE A EUPHEMISM.
OH, I UNDERSTAND.
SO YOU TWO AREN'T MARRIED?
I'm LICENSABLE BEAR™
?
I'm LICENSABLE

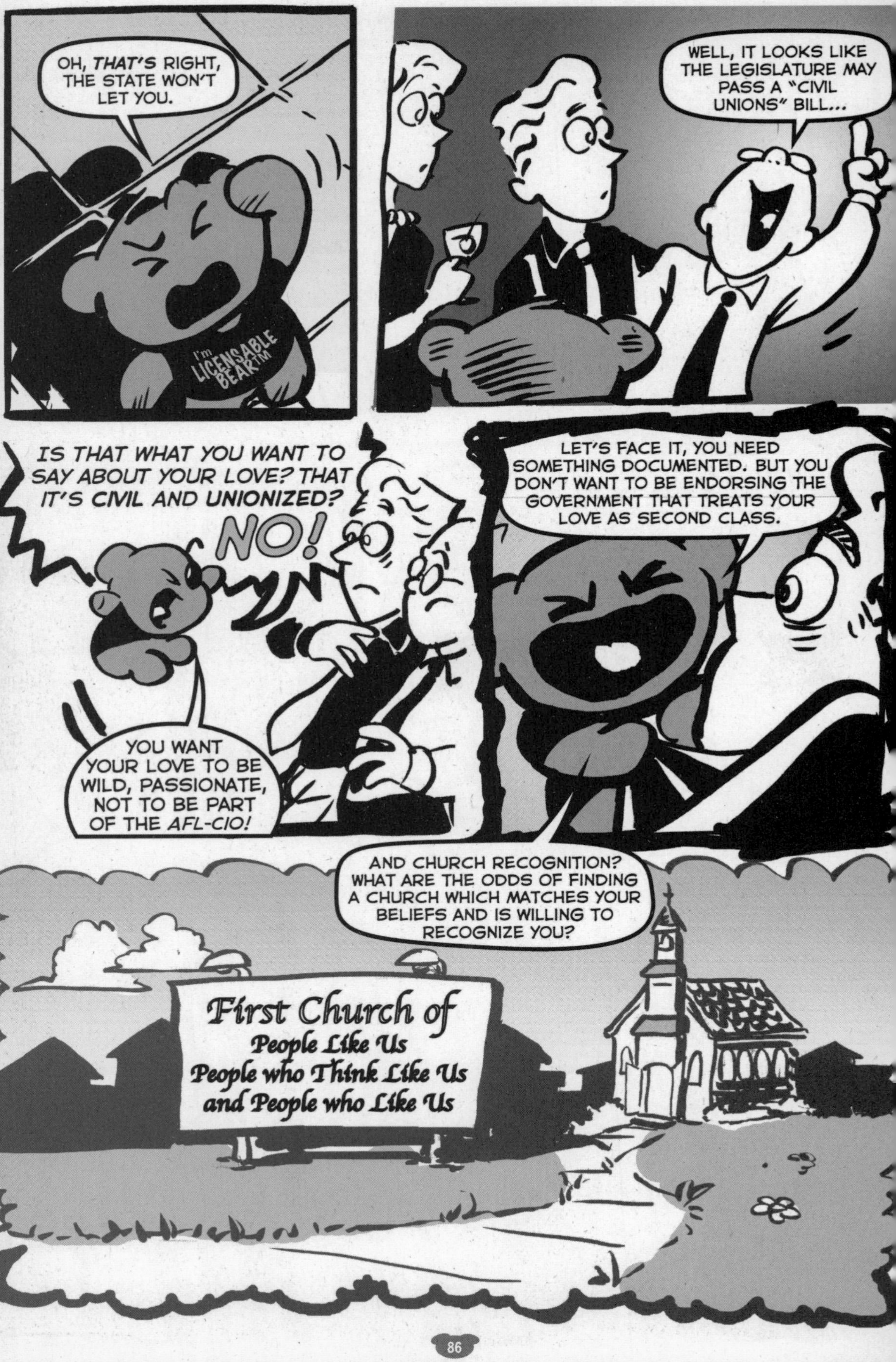

OH, THAT'S RIGHT, THE STATE WON'T LET YOU.
I'm LICENSABLE BEAR™
WELL, IT LOOKS LIKE THE LEGISLATURE MAY PASS A "CIVIL UNIONS" BILL...
IS THAT WHAT YOU WANT TO SAY ABOUT YOUR LOVE? THAT IT'S CIVIL AND UNIONIZED?
NO!
YOU WANT YOUR LOVE TO BE WILD, PASSIONATE, NOT TO BE PART OF THE AFL-CIO!
LET'S FACE IT, YOU NEED SOMETHING DOCUMENTED. BUT YOU DON'T WANT TO BE ENDORSING THE GOVERNMENT THAT TREATS YOUR LOVE AS SECOND CLASS.
AND CHURCH RECOGNITION? WHAT ARE THE ODDS OF FINDING A CHURCH WHICH MATCHES YOUR BELIEFS AND IS WILLING TO RECOGNIZE YOU?
First Church of
People Like Us
People who Think Like Us
and People who Like Us

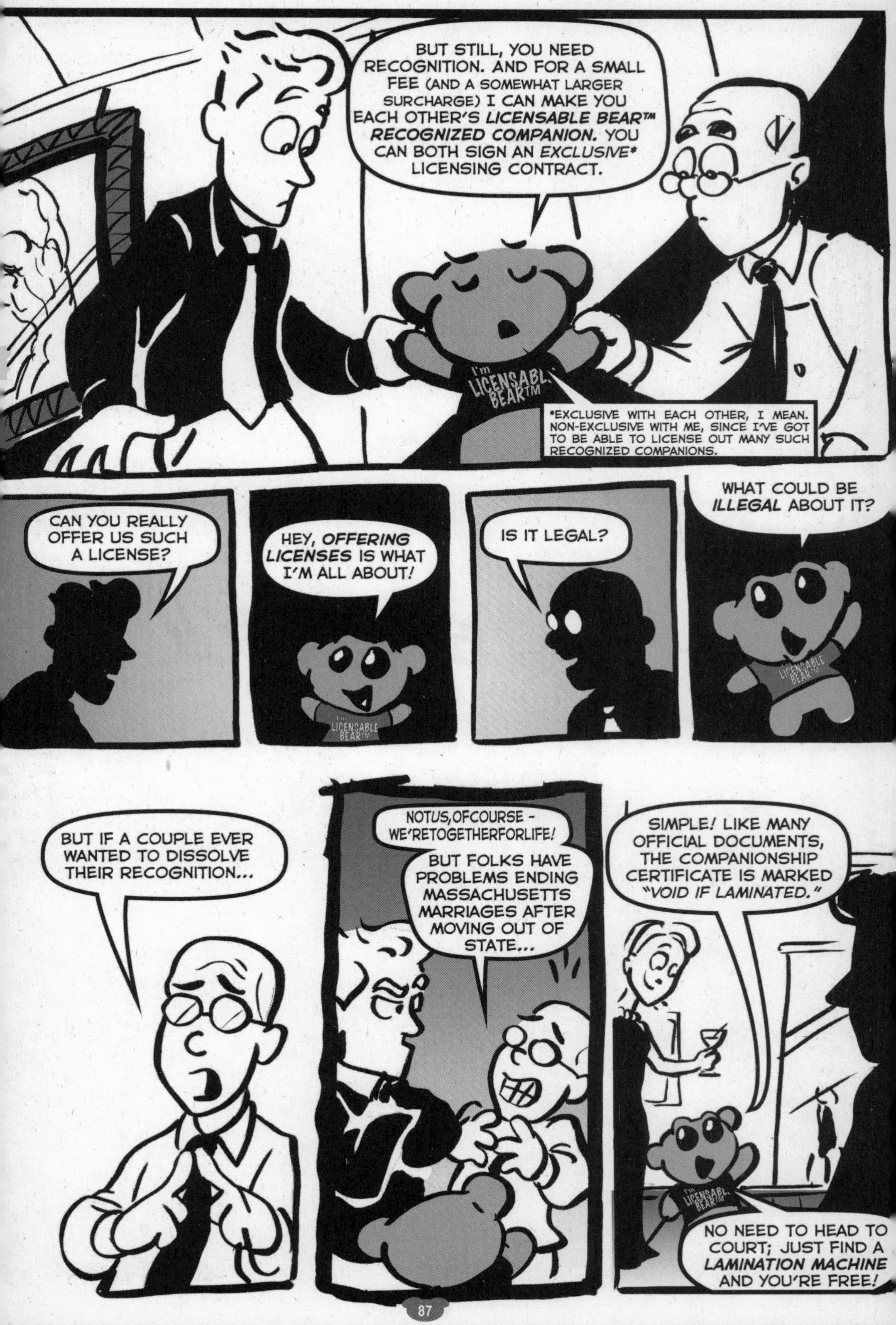

BUT STILL, YOU NEED RECOGNITION. AND FOR A SMALL FEE (AND A SOMEWHAT LARGER SURCHARGE) I CAN MAKE YOU EACH OTHER'S LICENSABLE BEAR™ RECOGNIZED COMPANION. YOU CAN BOTH SIGN AN EXCLUSIVE* LICENSING CONTRACT.
I'm LICENSABLE BEAR™
*EXCLUSIVE WITH EACH OTHER, I MEAN. NON-EXCLUSIVE WITH ME, SINCE I'VE GOT TO BE ABLE TO LICENSE OUT MANY SUCH RECOGNIZED COMPANIONS.
CAN YOU REALLY OFFER US SUCH A LICENSE?
HEY, OFFERING LICENSES IS WHAT I'M ALL ABOUT!
I'm LICENSABLE BEAR™
IS IT LEGAL?
WHAT COULD BE ILLEGAL ABOUT IT?
BUT IF A COUPLE EVER WANTED TO DISSOLVE THEIR RECOGNITION...
NOTUS,OFCOURSE - WE'RETOGETHERFORLIFE!
BUT FOLKS HAVE PROBLEMS ENDING MASSACHUSETTS MARRIAGES AFTER MOVING OUT OF STATE...
SIMPLE! LIKE MANY OFFICIAL DOCUMENTS, THE COMPANIONSHIP CERTIFICATE IS MARKED "VOID IF LAMINATED."
I'm LICENSABLE BEAR™
NO NEED TO HEAD TO COURT; JUST FIND A LAMINATION MACHINE AND YOU'RE FREE!

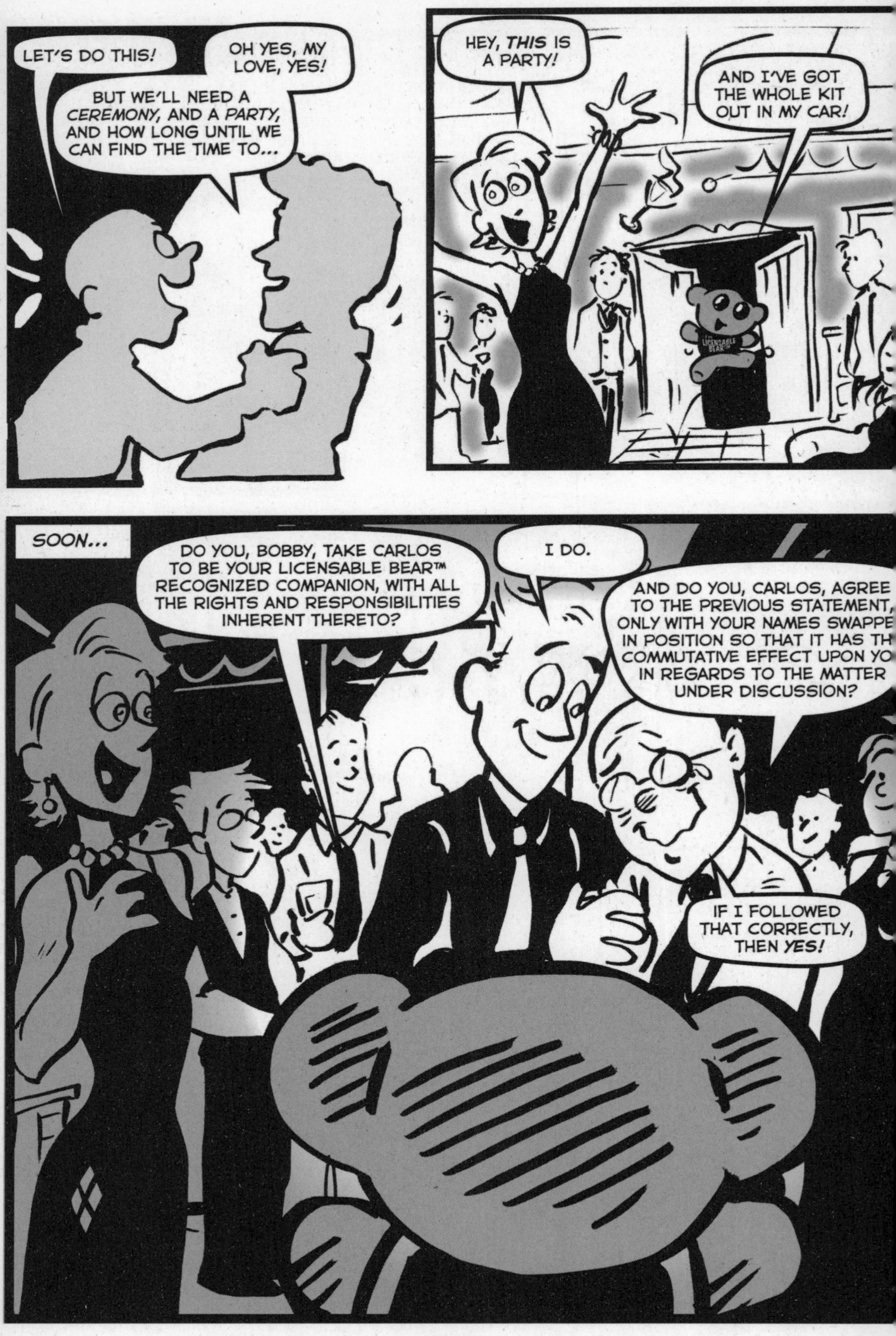
LET'S DO THIS!
OH YES, MY LOVE, YES!
BUT WE'LL NEED A *CEREMONY*, AND A *PARTY*, AND HOW LONG UNTIL WE CAN FIND THE TIME TO...
HEY, *THIS* IS A PARTY!
AND I'VE GOT THE WHOLE KIT OUT IN MY CAR!
SOON...
DO YOU, BOBBY, TAKE CARLOS TO BE YOUR LICENSABLE BEAR™ RECOGNIZED COMPANION, WITH ALL THE RIGHTS AND RESPONSIBILITIES INHERENT THERETO?
I DO.
AND DO YOU, CARLOS, AGREE TO THE PREVIOUS STATEMENT, ONLY WITH YOUR NAMES SWAPPE IN POSITION SO THAT IT HAS TH COMMUTATIVE EFFECT UPON YO IN REGARDS TO THE MATTER UNDER DISCUSSION?
IF I FOLLOWED THAT CORRECTLY, THEN *YES!*

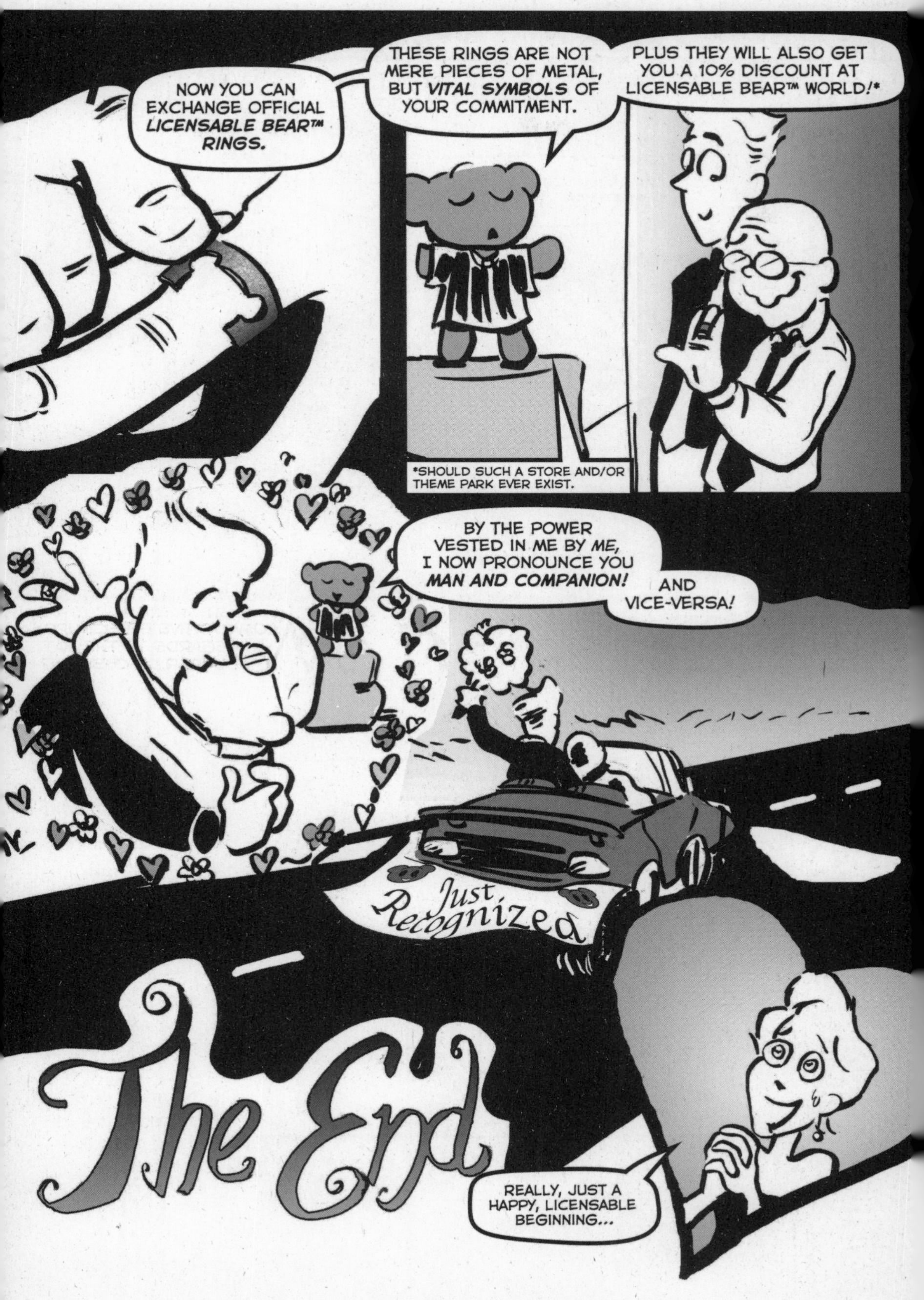

NOW YOU CAN EXCHANGE OFFICIAL *LICENSABLE BEAR™ RINGS.*
THESE RINGS ARE NOT MERE PIECES OF METAL, BUT *VITAL SYMBOLS* OF YOUR COMMITMENT.
PLUS THEY WILL ALSO GET YOU A 10% DISCOUNT AT LICENSABLE BEAR™ WORLD!*
*SHOULD SUCH A STORE AND/OR THEME PARK EVER EXIST.
BY THE POWER VESTED IN ME BY *ME*, I NOW PRONOUNCE YOU ***MAN AND COMPANION!***
AND VICE-VERSA!
Just Recognized
The End
REALLY, JUST A HAPPY, LICENSABLE BEGINNING...

LICENSABLE BEAR™ Works at a Street Fair

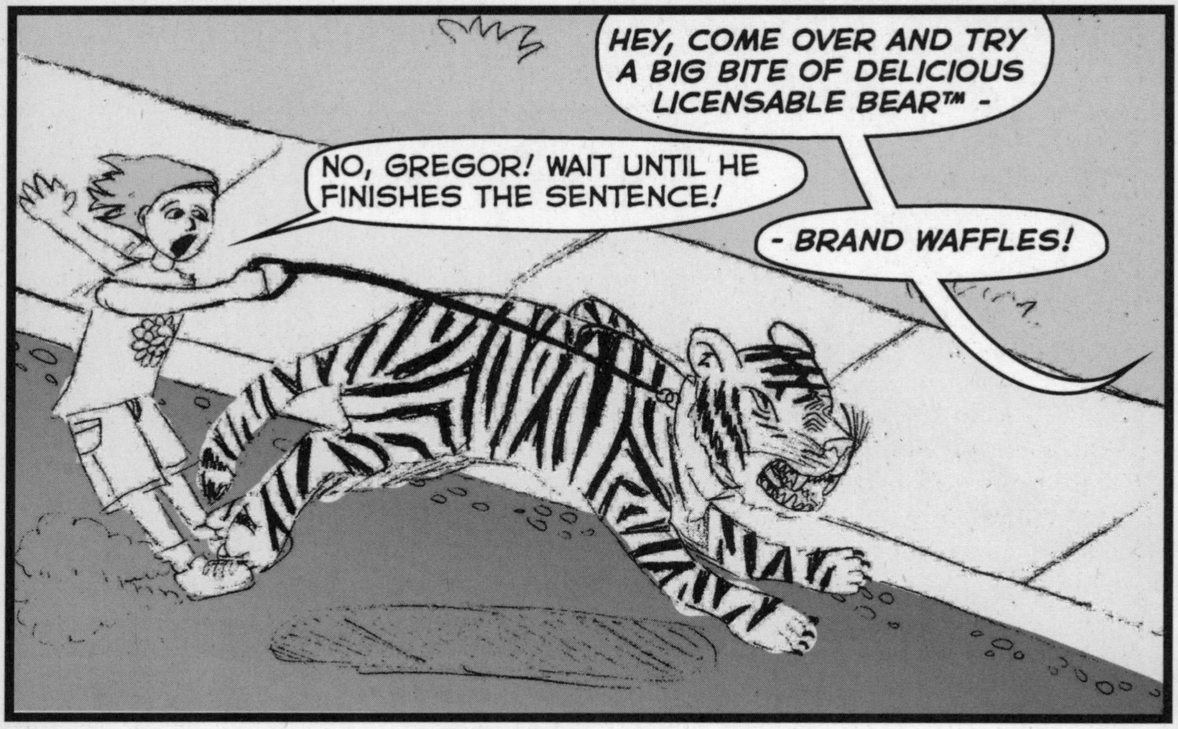
HEY, COME OVER AND TRY A BIG BITE OF DELICIOUS LICENSABLE BEAR™ -
NO, GREGOR! WAIT UNTIL HE FINISHES THE SENTENCE!
- BRAND WAFFLES!

SU-DO-LICENSABLE BEAR™

3	2	4	7	1				
1	9			4			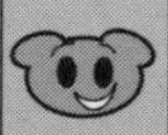	
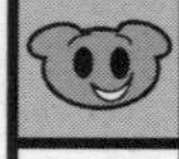			5					
			4				1	
2		6				3		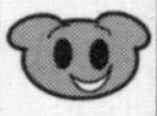
	5				6			
					3			4
	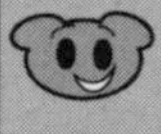			7			3	6
				6	4	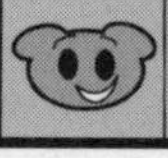	7	9

THE NEW PUZZLE SENSATION, SURE TO SWEEP THE NATION!

To solve the puzzle, fill in the blank squares so that each horizontal row, each vertical column, and each 3x3 section contain the digits 1–7, 9, and a Licensable Bear™ head.

Good luck!

Licensable Bear™'s intellectual property insights

Copyright is the legal grant that allows you control over your creative expression. Despite the name, it is not so much a right to copy as the right to prevent (within limits) others from copying what you have done. As a practical matter, having this right allows you to license the work for publishing and adapting; basically, you're saying "give me some money, and I won't stop you from reproducing this."

Some people claim that the use of copyright inhibits creativity, which is silly. You can create anything new that you want, and in fact copyright gives you incentive for doing so. What it inhibits is *derivativity*, taking someone else's efforts and positing them as your own. As long as you aren't basing your work on someone else's, you're in the clear.

A lot of folks don't seem to realize that, but it's true. Copyright is not exclusive. Two people can have copyright to identical songs, so long as one didn't base their work on the other's. If by some coincidence two songwriters happen to come up with the lyric "I've got a great big waffle in my trousers, and I'm goin' a-lookin' for a big bottle of syrup!" they can each have the copyright on their creation.

Which leads me to the central point of this essay: it's a really good idea to hire an infinite number of monkeys.

Theoreticians talk about how an infinite number of monkeys banging randomly on typewriters will eventually recreate all of the great works of Shakespeare. This points to both why you should hire an infinite number of monkeys and why you should not hire theoreticians. Recreating the works of Shakespeare is pointless. His creations are in the public domain, so you can make all the monkey-free derivative works you want. No, you need monkeys to generate works that just happen to be exactly the same as respected successes like *Gone with the Wind, Tuesdays with Morrie,* or *The Complete Idiot's Guide to Creating a Graphic Novel.* You may not be able to use the same titles, but you can probably market it much the way they market store-brand medicine: "compare to the literary ingredients in *Gone with The Wind*". As long as your monkey has never read *Gone with The Wind*, nor seen the movie, nor read a description of the work, you have just as much legal right to sell this book and license sequel and movie rights as the Margaret Mitchell estate has to their coincidentally similar edition.

Do be sure that the monkeys are actually employees. While there are various financial advantages to paying them as freelancers, you would not end up with the same full set of rights. Only by having the works created by employees are you assured that it is legally monkeywork for hire.

So to sum up, if there's one thing it's important to know about copyright, it's that hiring an infinite number of monkeys is a viable business plan.

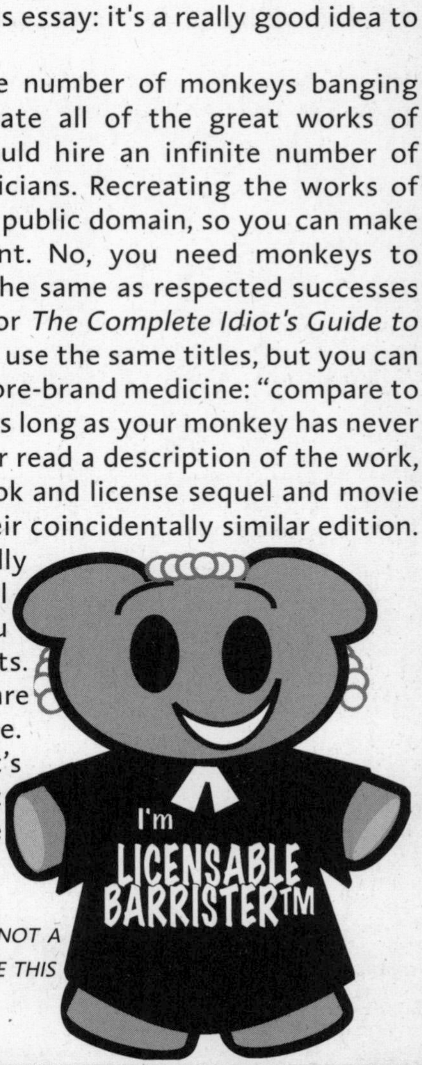
I'm
LICENSABLE BARRISTER™

Licensable Bear™ is a dedicated marketing icon and is not a trained attorney. You couldn't get valuable advice like this from any attorney.

HOW TO DRAW LICENSABLE BEAR™

STEP 1: OPEN UP A NEW DOCUMENT IN ADOBE ILLUSTRATOR.

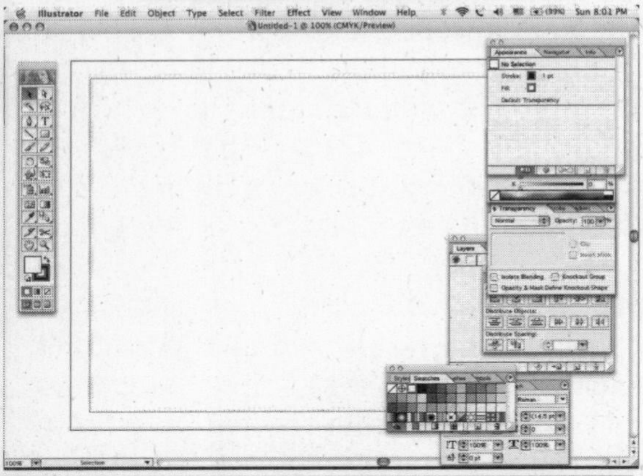

STEP 2: FROM THE *WINDOWS* MENU CHOOSE *SYMBOL LIBRARY* THEN THE SUB-COMMAND *OTHER LIBRARIES*.

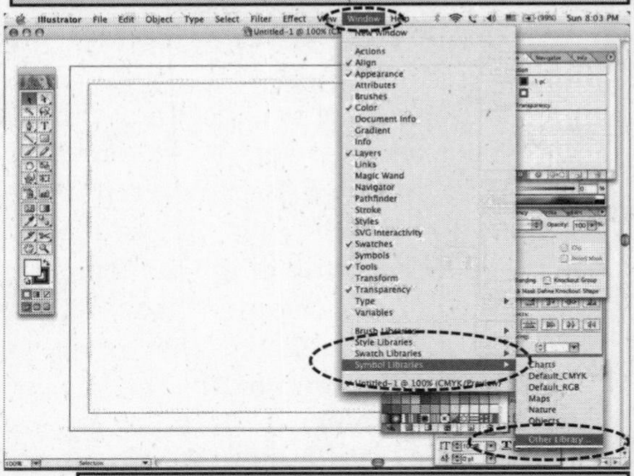

STEP 3: IN THE FILE BROWSER THAT APPEARS, SELECT THE FILE *BEAR SYMBOLS.AI* THEN CLICK *OPEN*.

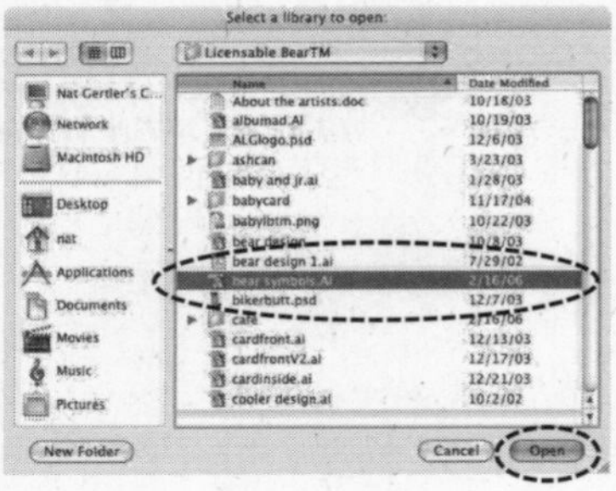
Select a library to open:
Licensable BearTM
Open

STEP 4: FIND THE NEW SYMBOL LIBRARY WINDOW THAT HAS NOW OPENED.

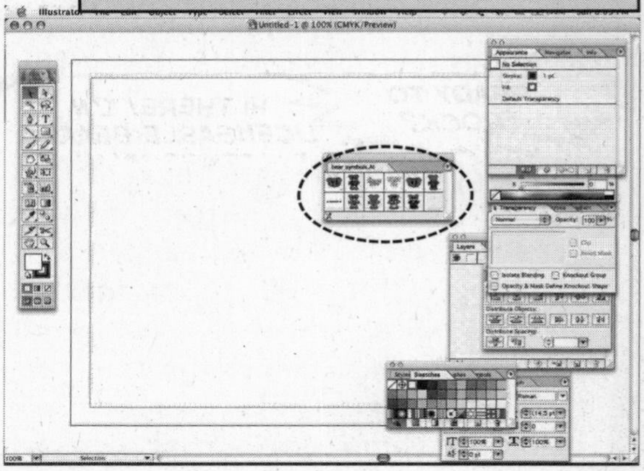

STEP 5: DRAG THE LICENSABLE BEAR™ SYMBOL ONTO YOUR DOCUMENT. VOILÀ!

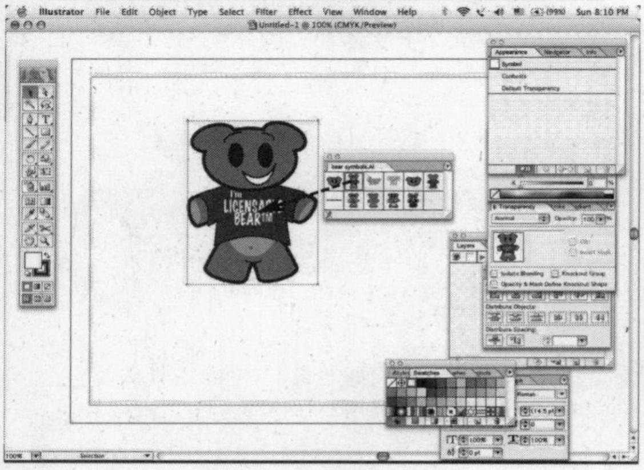

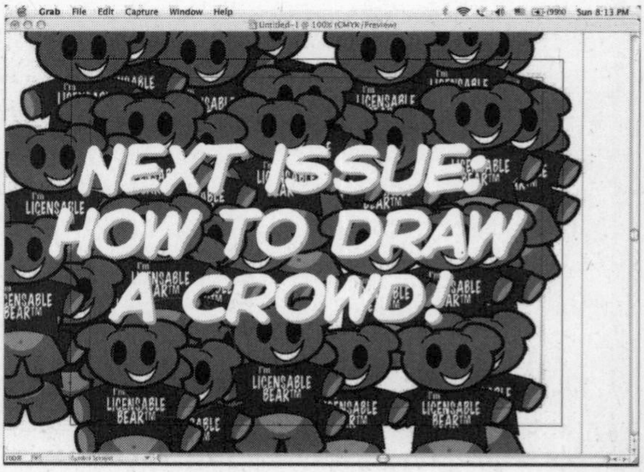
NEXT ISSUE: HOW TO DRAW A CROWD!

LICENSABLE BEAR™ Handles Compulsion

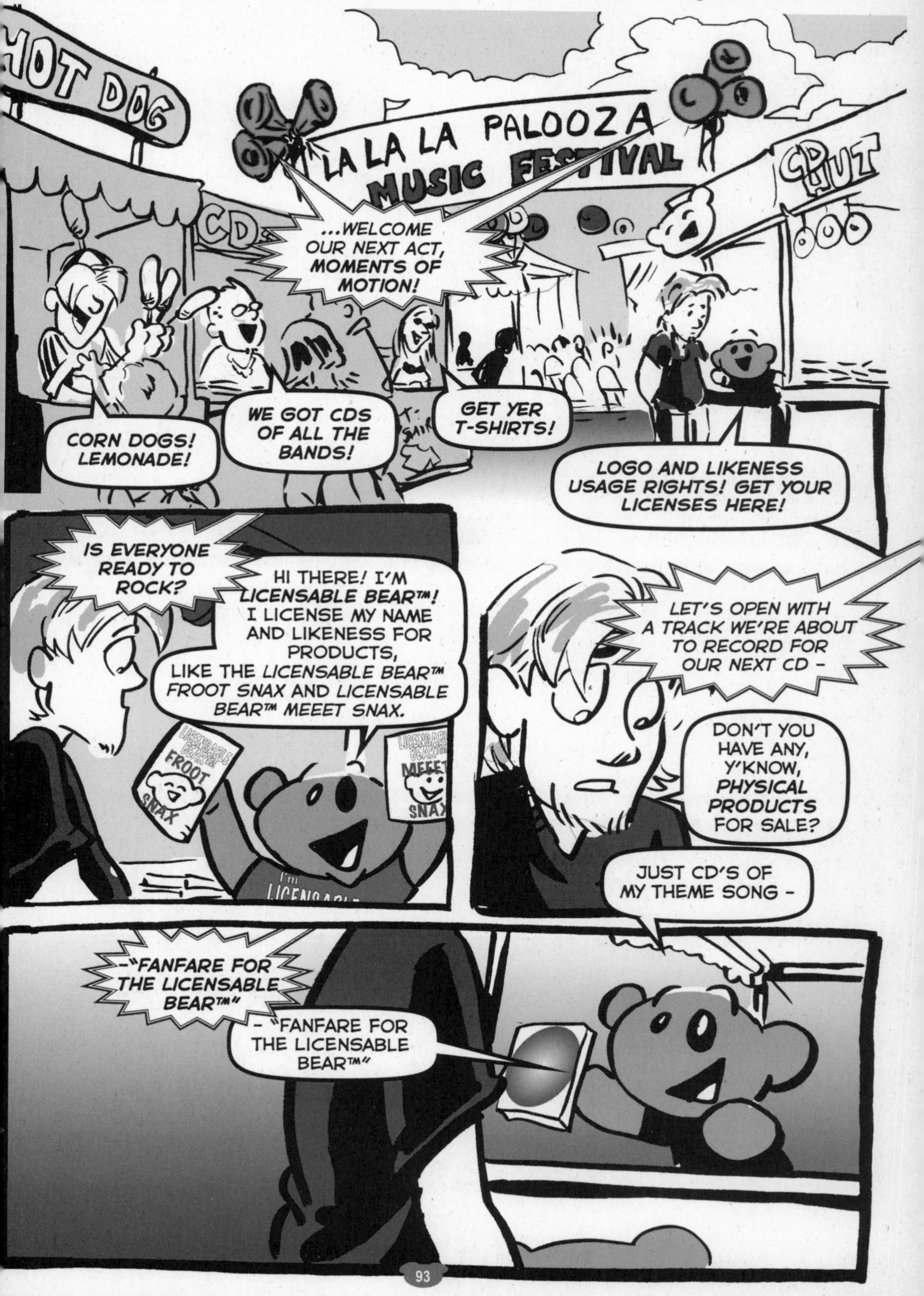
HOT DOG
LA LA LA PALOOZA
MUSIC FESTIVAL
CD
CD HUT
...WELCOME OUR NEXT ACT, MOMENTS OF MOTION!
CORN DOGS! LEMONADE!
WE GOT CDS OF ALL THE BANDS!
GET YER T-SHIRTS!
LOGO AND LIKENESS USAGE RIGHTS! GET YOUR LICENSES HERE!
IS EVERYONE READY TO ROCK?
HI THERE! I'M LICENSABLE BEAR™! I LICENSE MY NAME AND LIKENESS FOR PRODUCTS, LIKE THE LICENSABLE BEAR™ FROOT SNAX AND LICENSABLE BEAR™ MEEET SNAX.
LICENSABLE BEAR™ FROOT SNAX
LICENSABLE BEAR™ MEEET SNAX
LET'S OPEN WITH A TRACK WE'RE ABOUT TO RECORD FOR OUR NEXT CD -
DON'T YOU HAVE ANY, Y'KNOW, PHYSICAL PRODUCTS FOR SALE?
JUST CD'S OF MY THEME SONG -
-"FANFARE FOR THE LICENSABLE BEAR™"
- "FANFARE FOR THE LICENSABLE BEAR™"

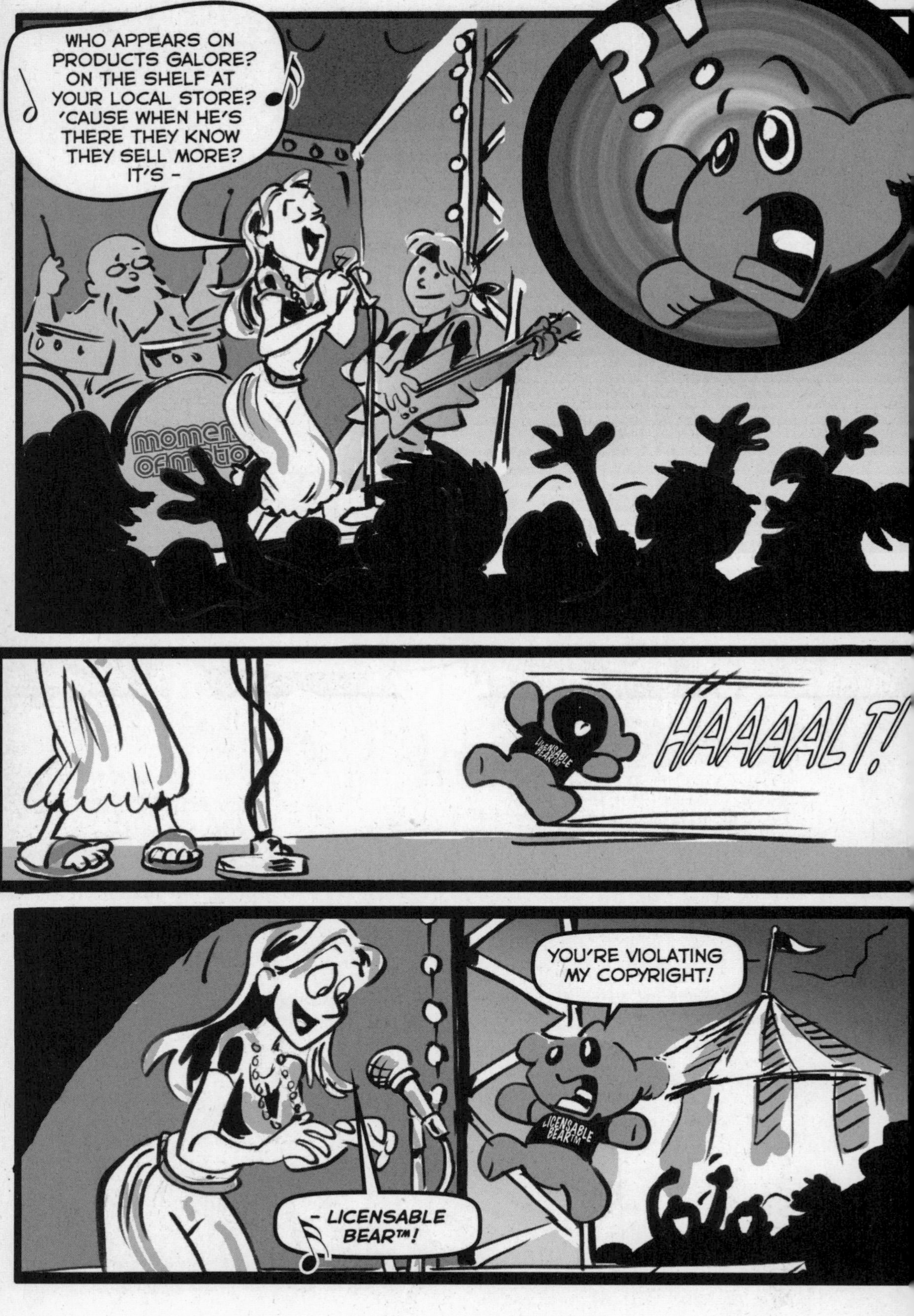
WHO APPEARS ON PRODUCTS GALORE? ON THE SHELF AT YOUR LOCAL STORE? 'CAUSE WHEN HE'S THERE THEY KNOW THEY SELL MORE? IT'S -
?!
HAAAALT!
LICENSABLE BEAR™
YOU'RE VIOLATING MY COPYRIGHT!
- LICENSABLE BEAR™!
LICENSABLE BEAR™

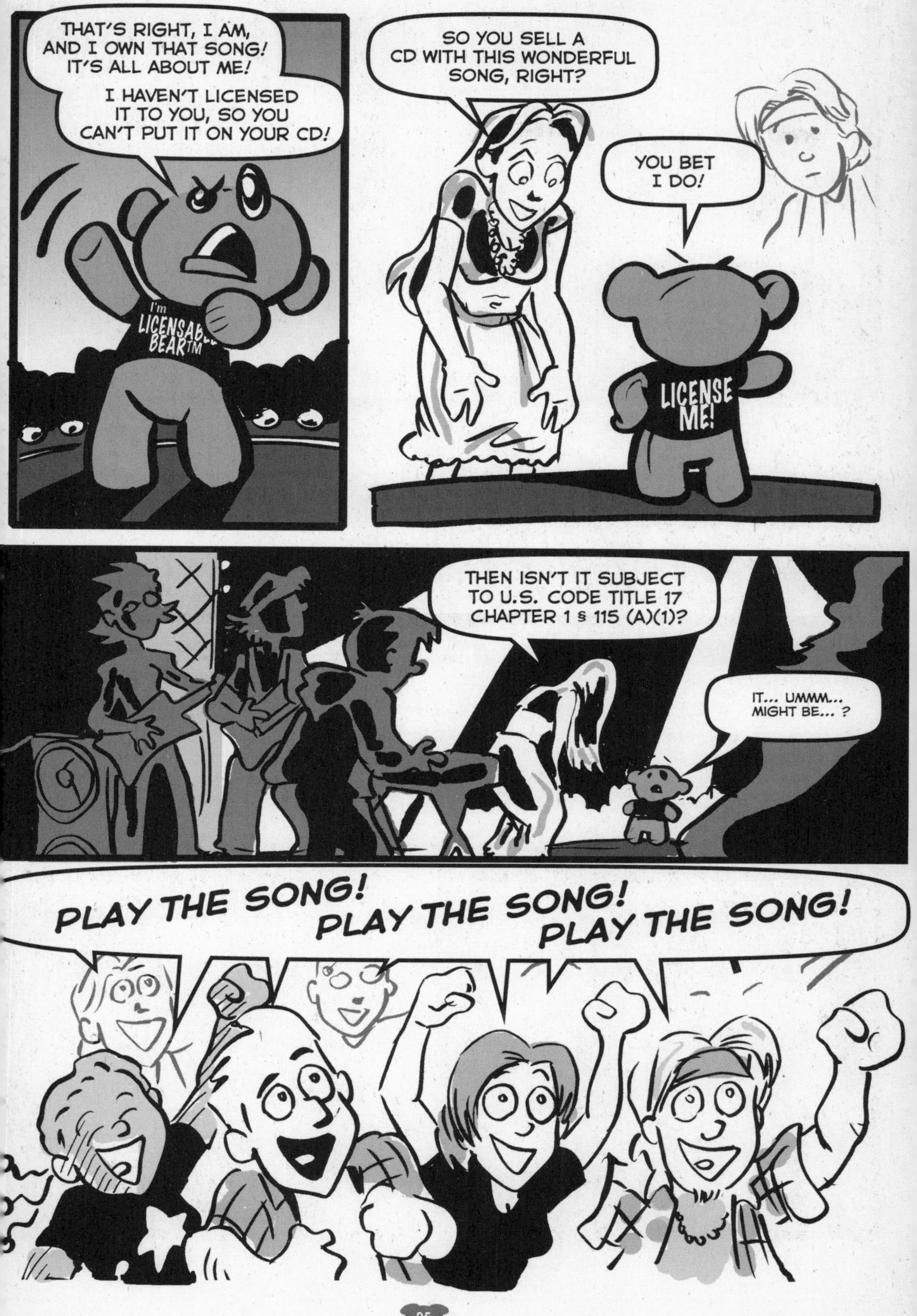
THAT'S RIGHT, I AM, AND I OWN THAT SONG! IT'S ALL ABOUT ME!
I HAVEN'T LICENSED IT TO YOU, SO YOU CAN'T PUT IT ON YOUR CD!
I'm LICENSABLE BEAR™
SO YOU SELL A CD WITH THIS WONDERFUL SONG, RIGHT?
YOU BET I DO!
LICENSE ME!
THEN ISN'T IT SUBJECT TO U.S. CODE TITLE 17 CHAPTER 1 § 115 (A)(1)?
IT... UMMM... MIGHT BE... ?
PLAY THE SONG! PLAY THE SONG! PLAY THE SONG!

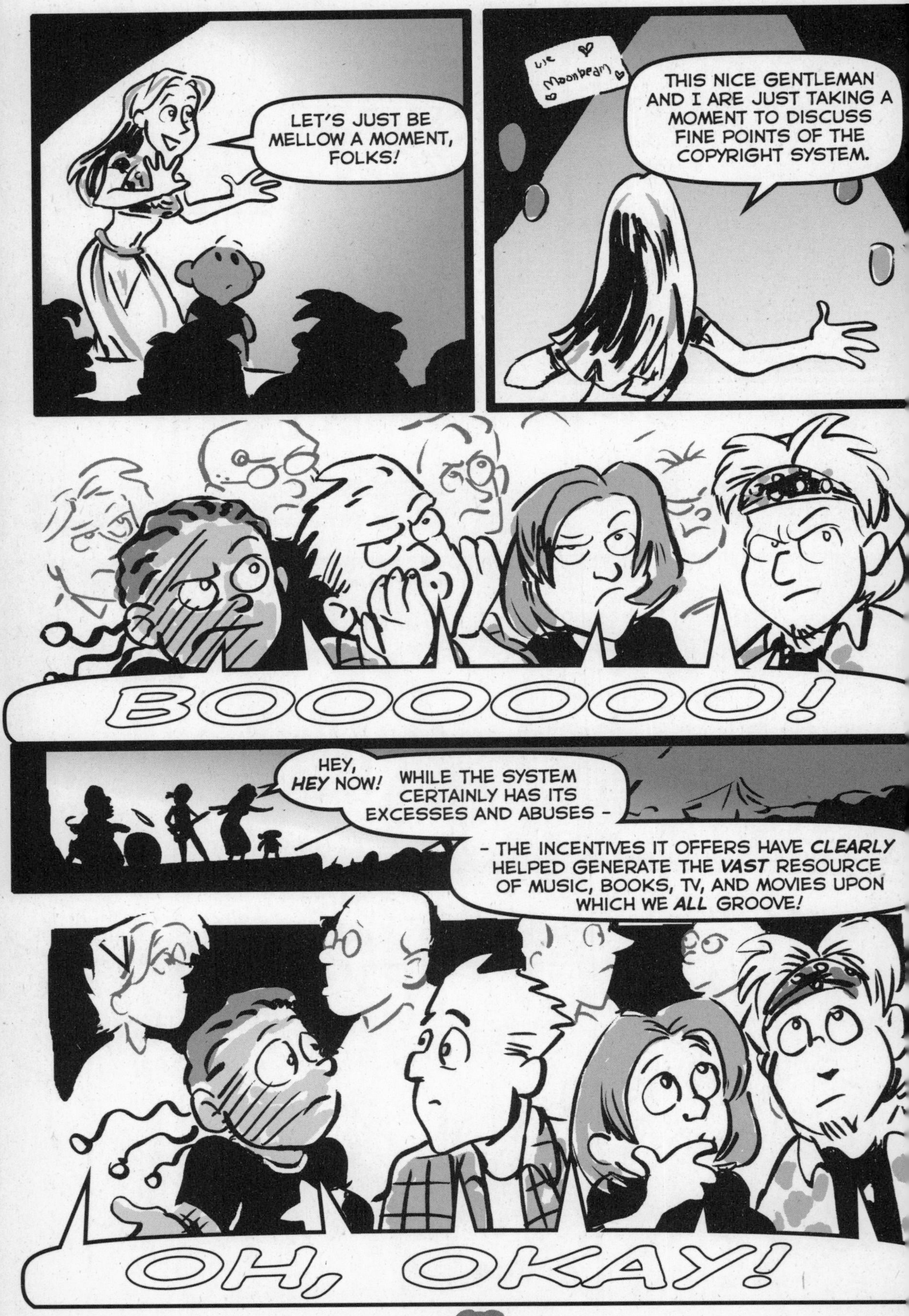
LET'S JUST BE MELLOW A MOMENT, FOLKS!
Moonbeam
THIS NICE GENTLEMAN AND I ARE JUST TAKING A MOMENT TO DISCUSS FINE POINTS OF THE COPYRIGHT SYSTEM.
BOOOOOO!
HEY, HEY NOW! WHILE THE SYSTEM CERTAINLY HAS ITS EXCESSES AND ABUSES -
- THE INCENTIVES IT OFFERS HAVE CLEARLY HELPED GENERATE THE VAST RESOURCE OF MUSIC, BOOKS, TV, AND MOVIES UPON WHICH WE ALL GROOVE!
OH, OKAY!

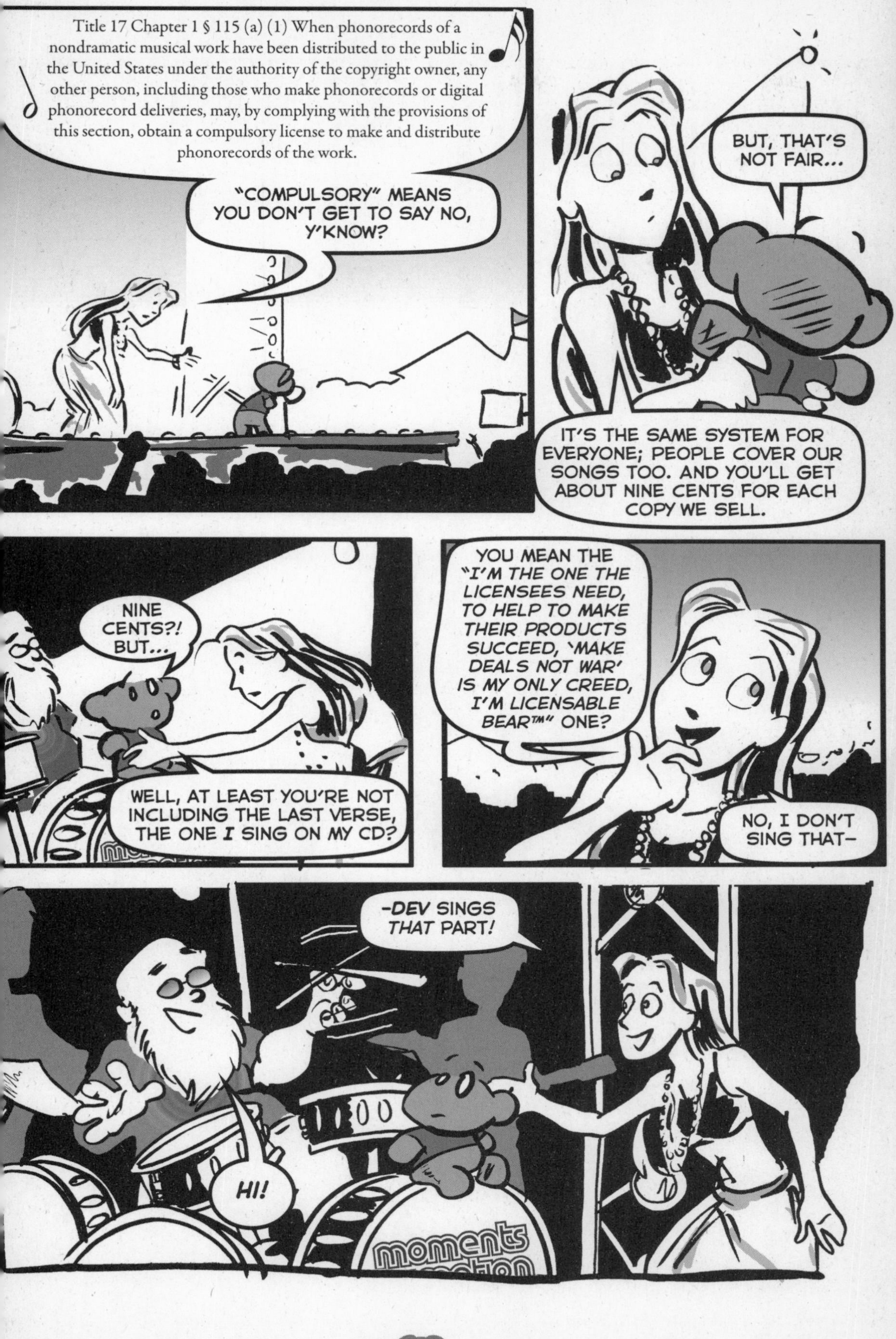

Title 17 Chapter 1 § 115 (a) (1) When phonorecords of a nondramatic musical work have been distributed to the public in the United States under the authority of the copyright owner, any other person, including those who make phonorecords or digital phonorecord deliveries, may, by complying with the provisions of this section, obtain a compulsory license to make and distribute phonorecords of the work.
"COMPULSORY" MEANS YOU DON'T GET TO SAY NO, Y'KNOW?
BUT, THAT'S NOT FAIR...
IT'S THE SAME SYSTEM FOR EVERYONE; PEOPLE COVER OUR SONGS TOO. AND YOU'LL GET ABOUT NINE CENTS FOR EACH COPY WE SELL.
NINE CENTS?! BUT...
WELL, AT LEAST YOU'RE NOT INCLUDING THE LAST VERSE, THE ONE *I* SING ON MY CD?
YOU MEAN THE *"I'M THE ONE THE LICENSEES NEED, TO HELP TO MAKE THEIR PRODUCTS SUCCEED, 'MAKE DEALS NOT WAR' IS MY ONLY CREED, I'M LICENSABLE BEAR™"* ONE?
NO, I DON'T SING THAT–
–*DEV* SINGS *THAT PART!*
HI!
moments

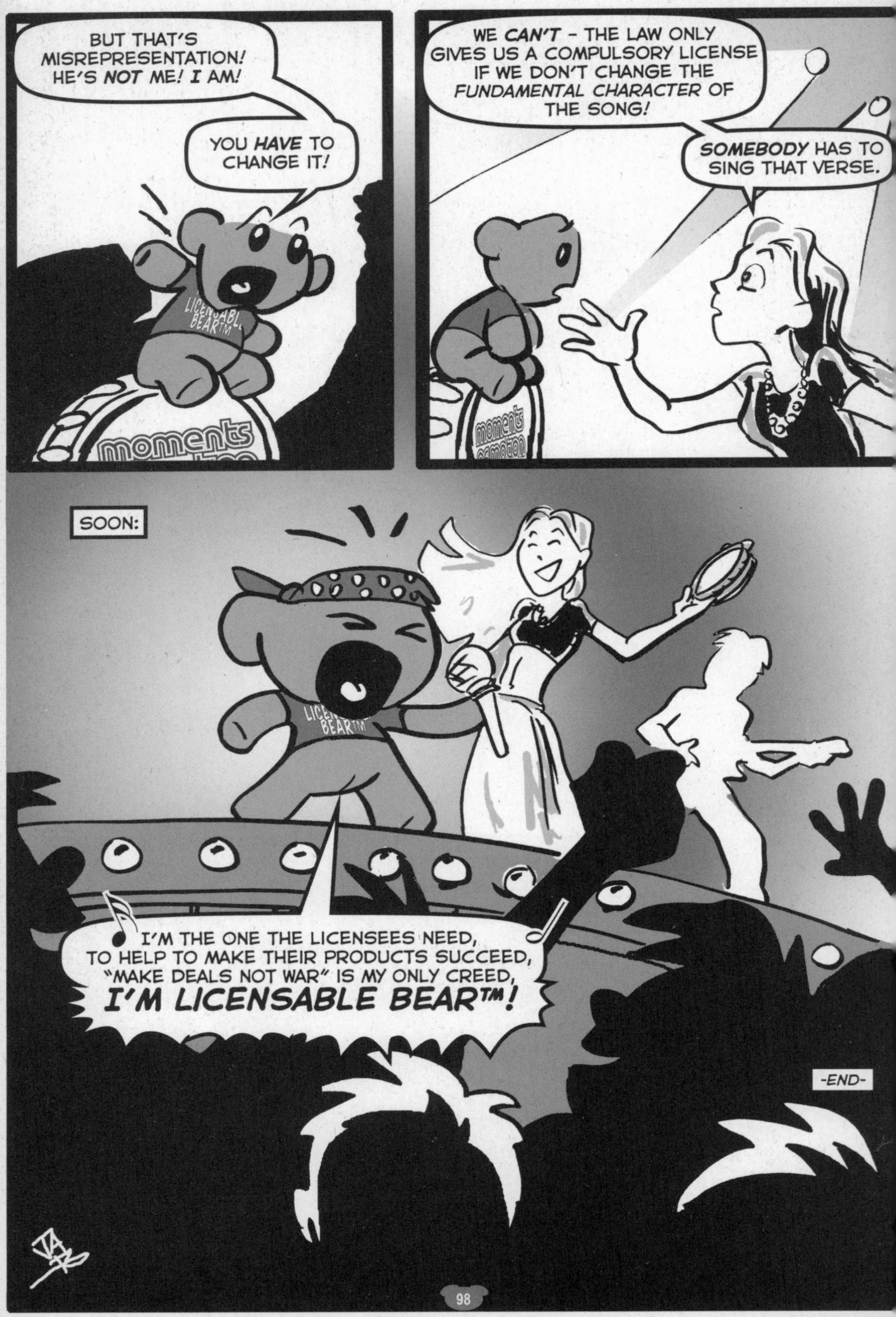
BUT THAT'S MISREPRESENTATION! HE'S NOT ME! I AM!
YOU HAVE TO CHANGE IT!
LICENSABLE BEAR™
moments
WE CAN'T - THE LAW ONLY GIVES US A COMPULSORY LICENSE IF WE DON'T CHANGE THE FUNDAMENTAL CHARACTER OF THE SONG!
SOMEBODY HAS TO SING THAT VERSE.
moments
SOON:
BEAR™
I'M THE ONE THE LICENSEES NEED, TO HELP TO MAKE THEIR PRODUCTS SUCCEED, "MAKE DEALS NOT WAR" IS MY ONLY CREED, I'M LICENSABLE BEAR™!
-END-

What your mother warned you about

High-calorie candy for your ears

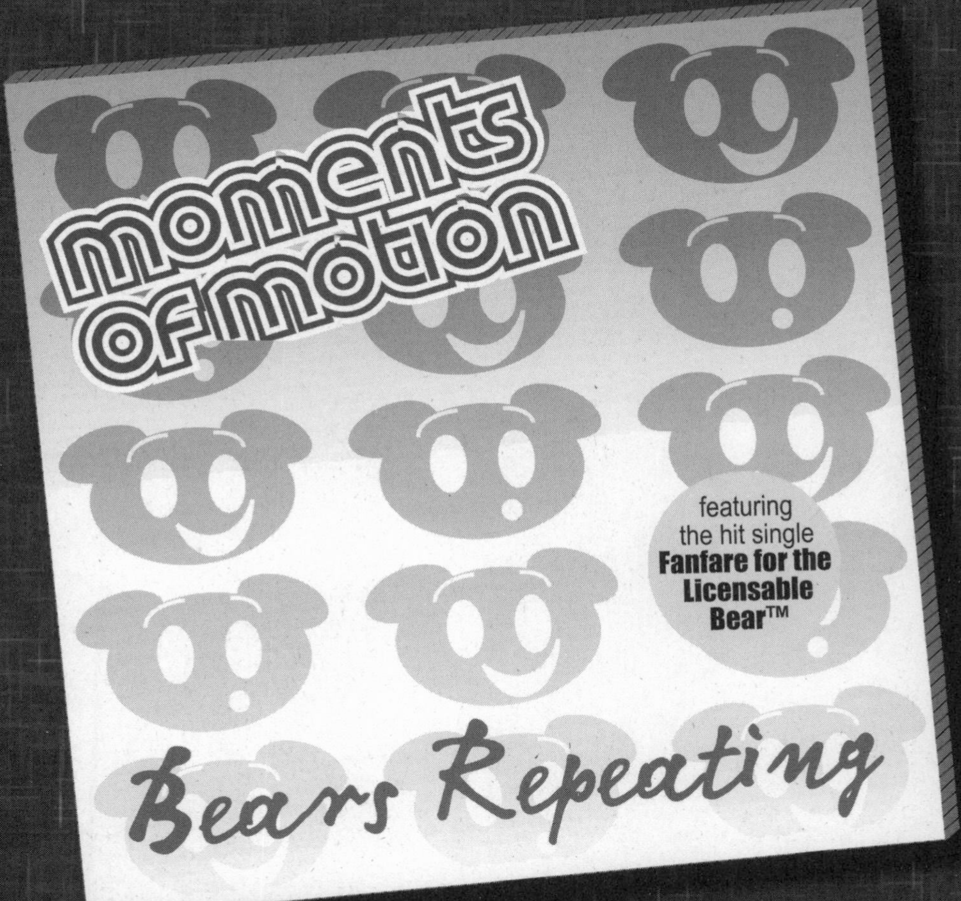

moments of motion
featuring the hit single
Fanfare for the Licensable Bear™
Bears Repeating

vailable at Wal-Buy, Best Mart,
nd other fine musicatoria

ABOUT MUSIC

Share the Joy - Buy the Music™

This message brought to you by the Association of Music-Based Product Processors.

LICENSABLE BEAR™ Gets a Return Visit

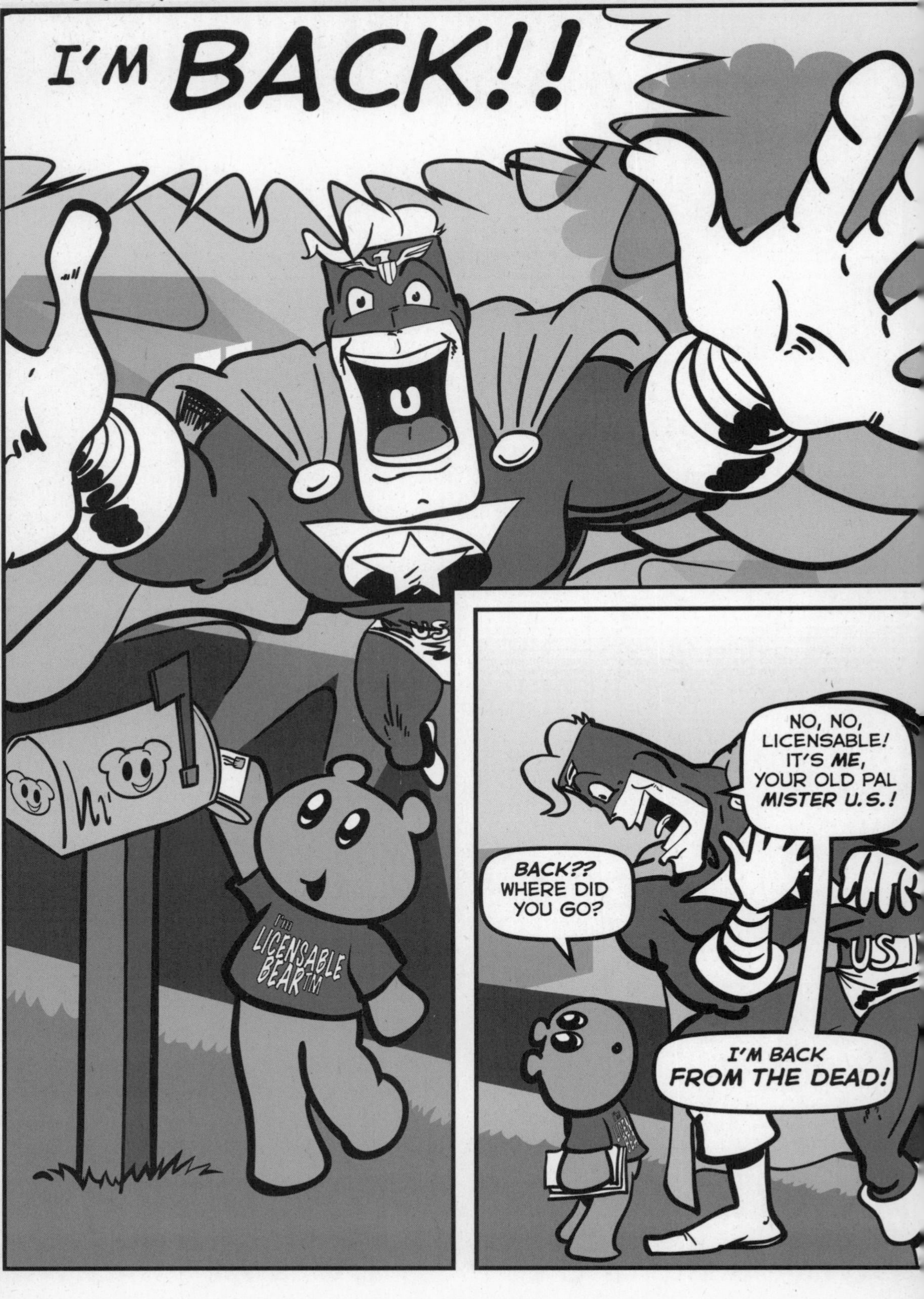
I'M BACK!!
I'M LICENSABLE BEAR™
NO, NO, LICENSABLE! IT'S ME, YOUR OLD PAL MISTER U.S.!
BACK?? WHERE DID YOU GO?
I'M BACK FROM THE DEAD!

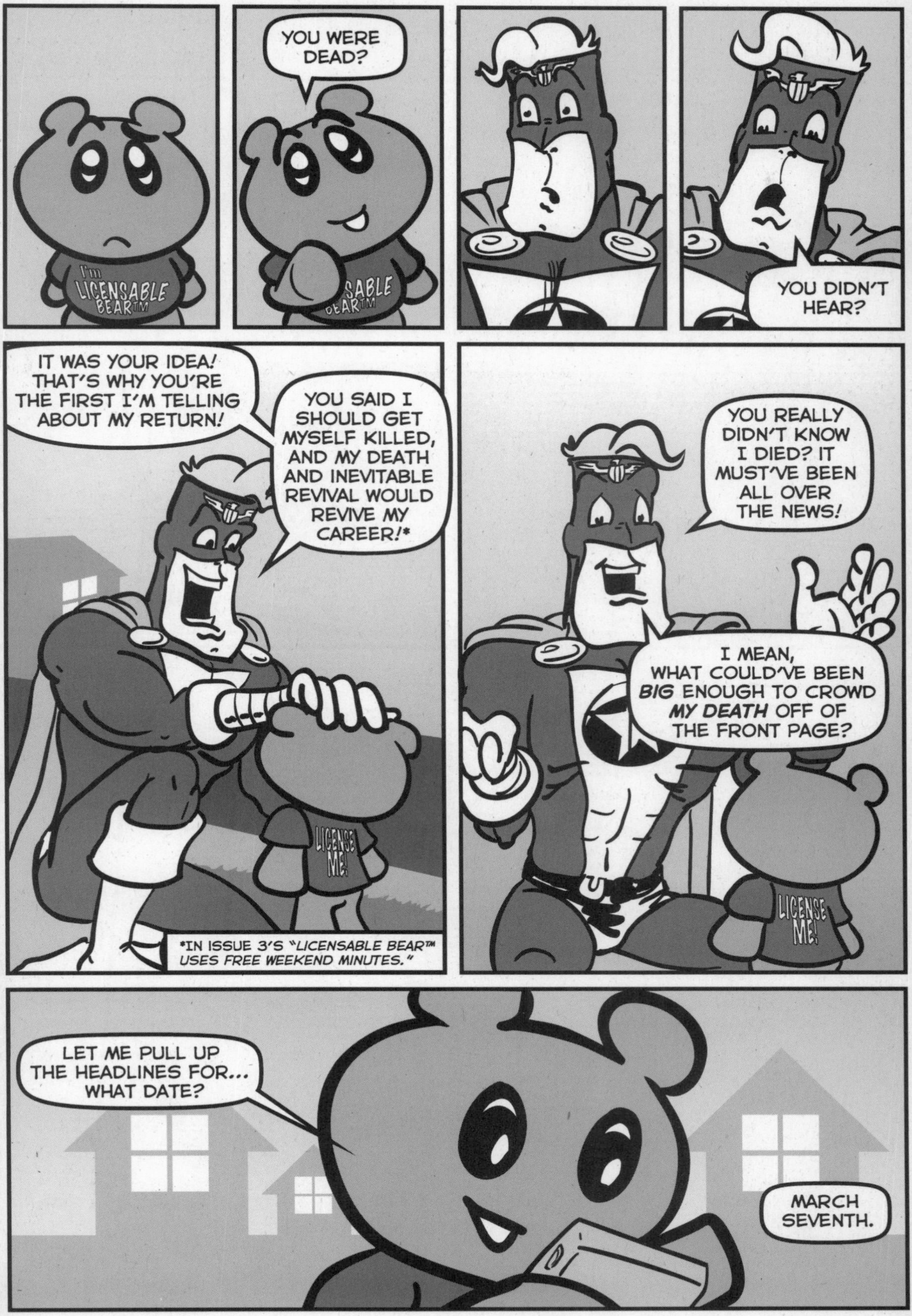

I'm LICENSABLE BEAR™
YOU WERE DEAD?
YOU DIDN'T HEAR?
IT WAS YOUR IDEA! THAT'S WHY YOU'RE THE FIRST I'M TELLING ABOUT MY RETURN!
YOU SAID I SHOULD GET MYSELF KILLED, AND MY DEATH AND INEVITABLE REVIVAL WOULD REVIVE MY CAREER!*
LICENSE ME!
*IN ISSUE 3'S "LICENSABLE BEAR™ USES FREE WEEKEND MINUTES."
YOU REALLY DIDN'T KNOW I DIED? IT MUST'VE BEEN ALL OVER THE NEWS!
I MEAN, WHAT COULD'VE BEEN *BIG* ENOUGH TO CROWD *MY DEATH* OFF OF THE FRONT PAGE?
LICENSE ME!
LET ME PULL UP THE HEADLINES FOR... WHAT DATE?
MARCH SEVENTH.

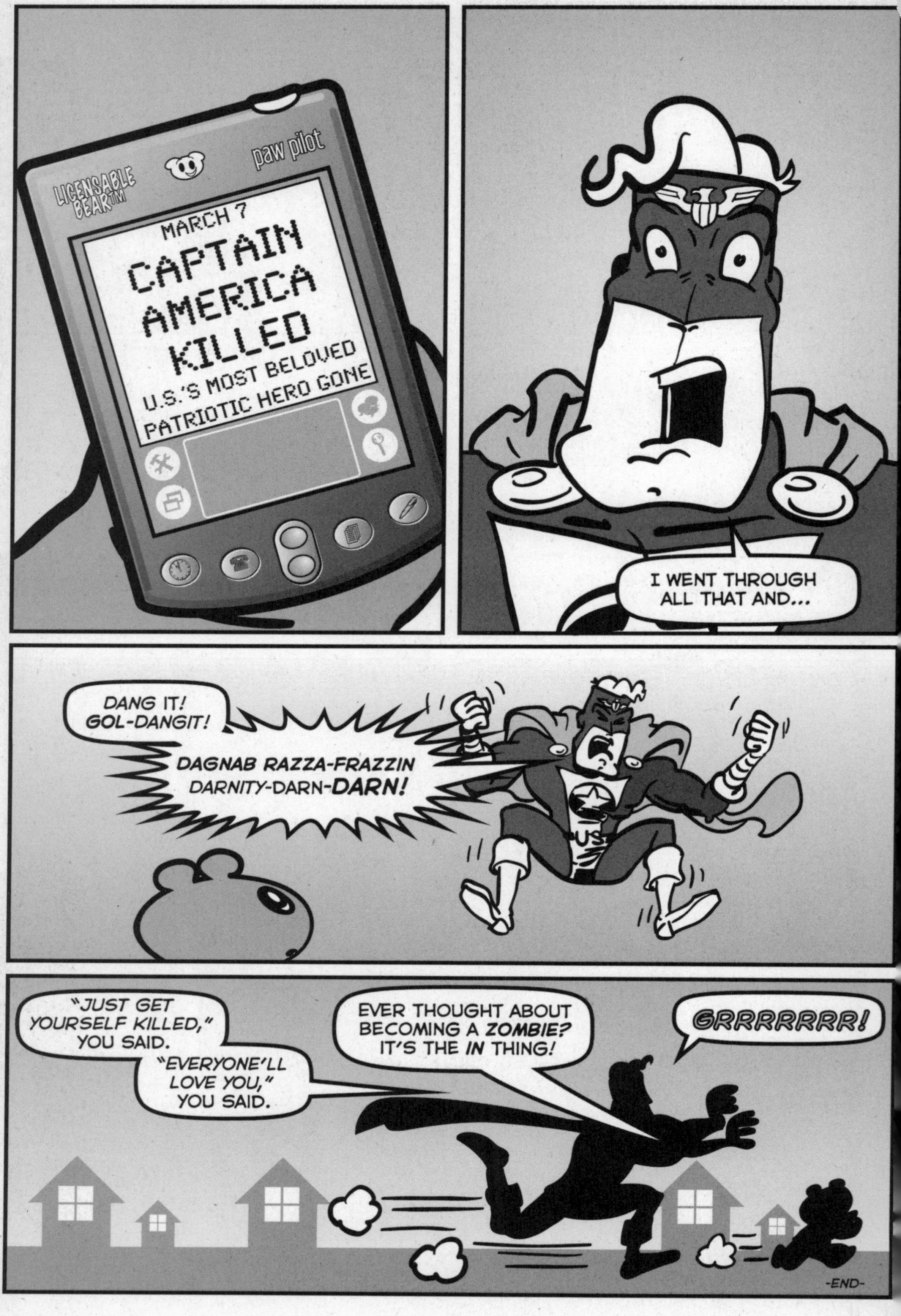
LICENSABLE BEAR TM
paw pilot
MARCH 7
CAPTAIN AMERICA KILLED
U.S.'S MOST BELOVED PATRIOTIC HERO GONE
I WENT THROUGH ALL THAT AND...
DANG IT! GOL-DANGIT!
DAGNAB RAZZA-FRAZZIN DARNITY-DARN-DARN!
"JUST GET YOURSELF KILLED," YOU SAID.
"EVERYONE'LL LOVE YOU," YOU SAID.
EVER THOUGHT ABOUT BECOMING A ZOMBIE? IT'S THE IN THING!
GRRRRRRRR!
-END-

LICENSABLE BEAR™ Enters the Fray

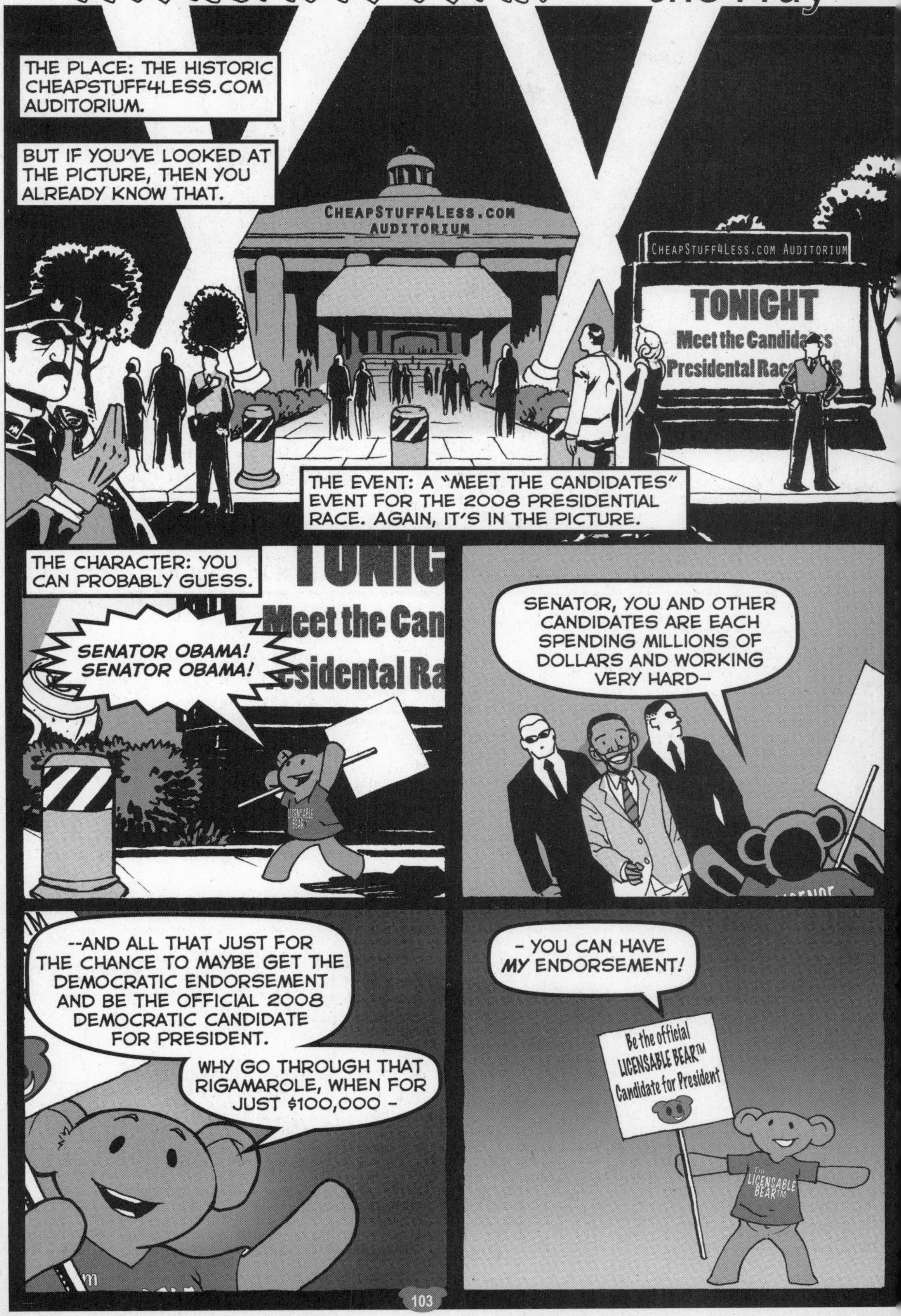
THE PLACE: THE HISTORIC CHEAPSTUFF4LESS.COM AUDITORIUM.
BUT IF YOU'VE LOOKED AT THE PICTURE, THEN YOU ALREADY KNOW THAT.
CheapStuff4Less.com AUDITORIUM
CheapStuff4Less.com Auditorium
TONIGHT
THE EVENT: A "MEET THE CANDIDATES" EVENT FOR THE 2008 PRESIDENTIAL RACE. AGAIN, IT'S IN THE PICTURE.
THE CHARACTER: YOU CAN PROBABLY GUESS.
SENATOR OBAMA! SENATOR OBAMA!
SENATOR, YOU AND OTHER CANDIDATES ARE EACH SPENDING MILLIONS OF DOLLARS AND WORKING VERY HARD–
--AND ALL THAT JUST FOR THE CHANCE TO MAYBE GET THE DEMOCRATIC ENDORSEMENT AND BE THE OFFICIAL 2008 DEMOCRATIC CANDIDATE FOR PRESIDENT.
WHY GO THROUGH THAT RIGAMAROLE, WHEN FOR JUST $100,000 –
– YOU CAN HAVE *MY* ENDORSEMENT!
Be the official LICENSABLE BEAR™ Candidate for President
LICENSABLE BEAR™

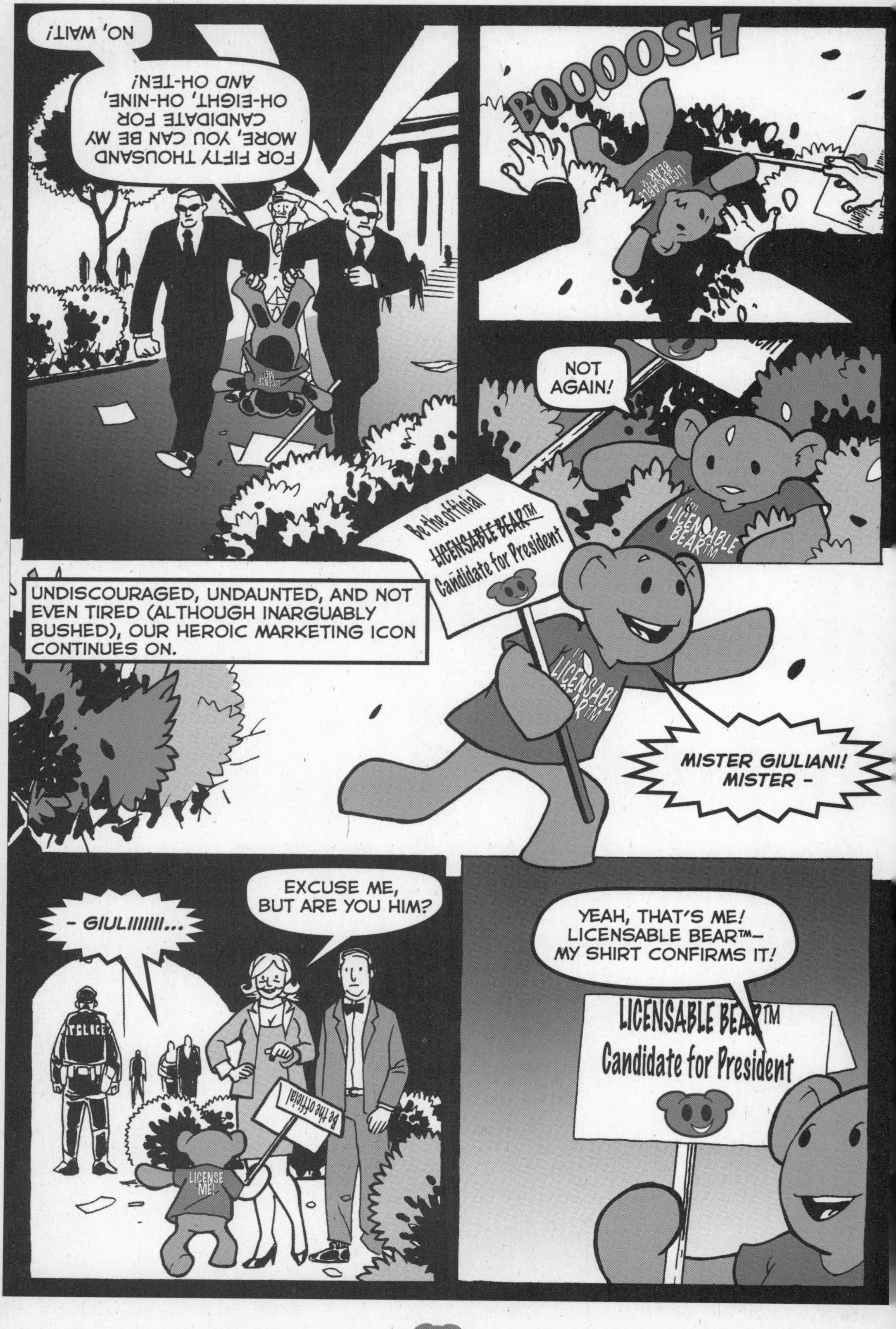
FOR FIFTY THOUSAND MORE, YOU CAN BE MY CANDIDATE FOR OH-EIGHT, OH-NINE, AND OH-TEN!
NO, WAIT!
BOOOOOSH
NOT AGAIN!
Be the official LICENSABLE BEAR™ Candidate for President
UNDISCOURAGED, UNDAUNTED, AND NOT EVEN TIRED (ALTHOUGH INARGUABLY BUSHED), OUR HEROIC MARKETING ICON CONTINUES ON.
MISTER GIULIANI! MISTER -
- GIULIIIIIII...
EXCUSE ME, BUT ARE YOU HIM?
YEAH, THAT'S ME! LICENSABLE BEAR™— MY SHIRT CONFIRMS IT!
LICENSABLE BEAR™ Candidate for President

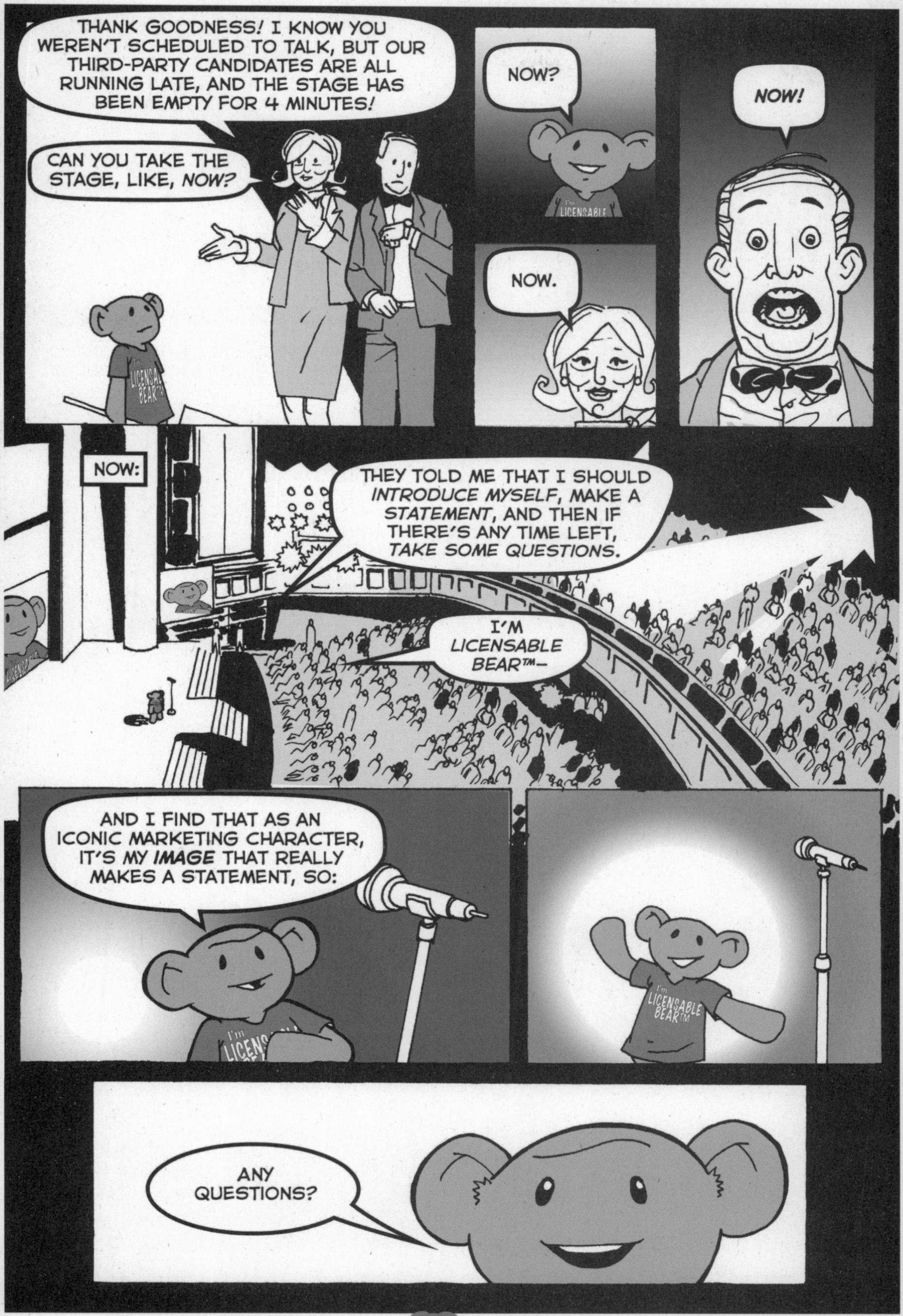
THANK GOODNESS! I KNOW YOU WEREN'T SCHEDULED TO TALK, BUT OUR THIRD-PARTY CANDIDATES ARE ALL RUNNING LATE, AND THE STAGE HAS BEEN EMPTY FOR 4 MINUTES!
CAN YOU TAKE THE STAGE, LIKE, NOW?
I'm LICENSABLE BEAR™
NOW?
I'm LICENSABLE
NOW.
NOW!
NOW:
THEY TOLD ME THAT I SHOULD INTRODUCE MYSELF, MAKE A STATEMENT, AND THEN IF THERE'S ANY TIME LEFT, TAKE SOME QUESTIONS.
I'M LICENSABLE BEAR™—
AND I FIND THAT AS AN ICONIC MARKETING CHARACTER, IT'S MY IMAGE THAT REALLY MAKES A STATEMENT, SO:
I'm LICENSABLE BEAR™
ANY QUESTIONS?

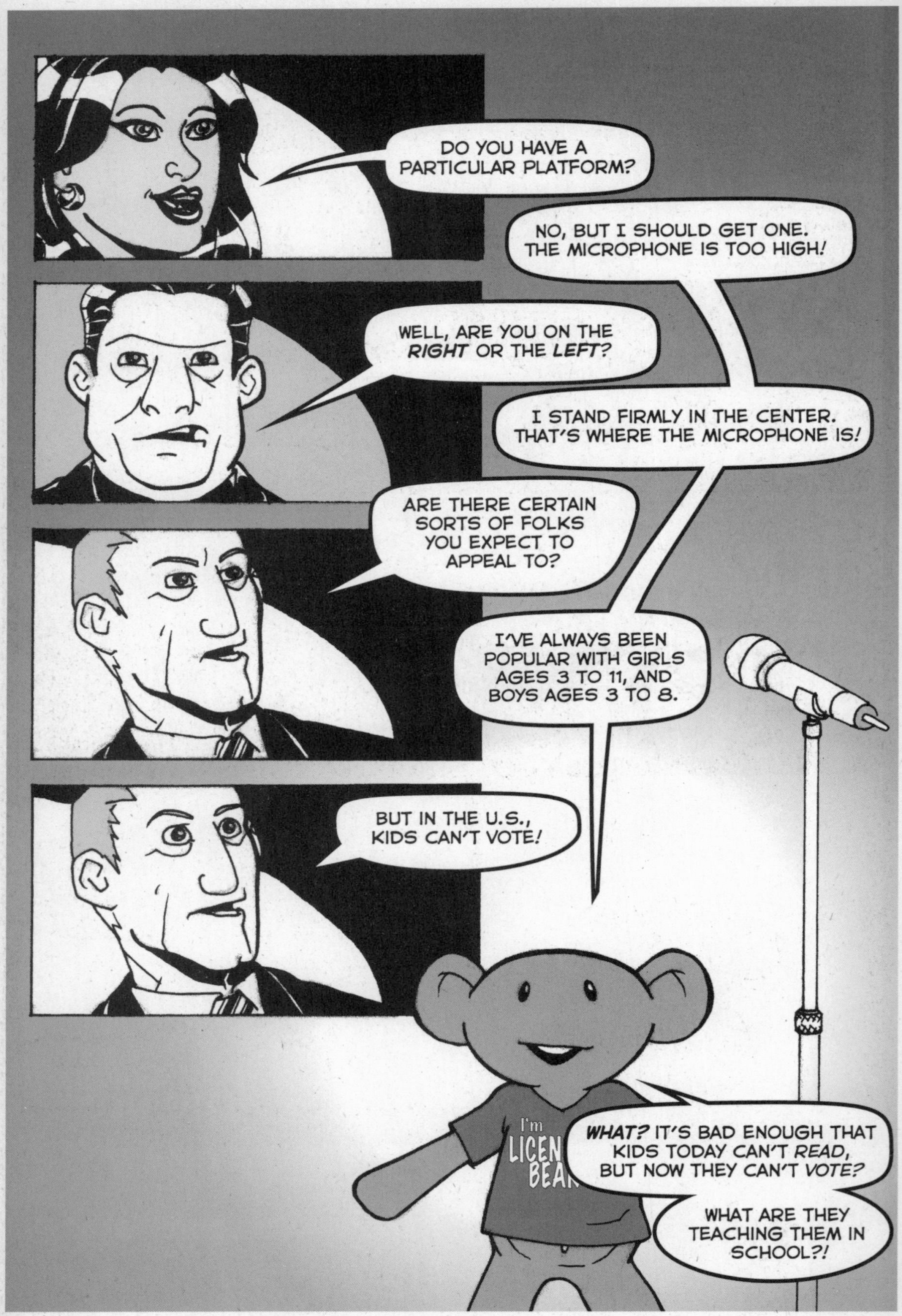
DO YOU HAVE A PARTICULAR PLATFORM?
NO, BUT I SHOULD GET ONE. THE MICROPHONE IS TOO HIGH!
WELL, ARE YOU ON THE *RIGHT* OR THE *LEFT*?
I STAND FIRMLY IN THE CENTER. THAT'S WHERE THE MICROPHONE IS!
ARE THERE CERTAIN SORTS OF FOLKS YOU EXPECT TO APPEAL TO?
I'VE ALWAYS BEEN POPULAR WITH GIRLS AGES 3 TO 11, AND BOYS AGES 3 TO 8.
BUT IN THE U.S., KIDS CAN'T VOTE!
WHAT? IT'S BAD ENOUGH THAT KIDS TODAY CAN'T *READ*, BUT NOW THEY CAN'T *VOTE?*
WHAT ARE THEY TEACHING THEM IN SCHOOL?!

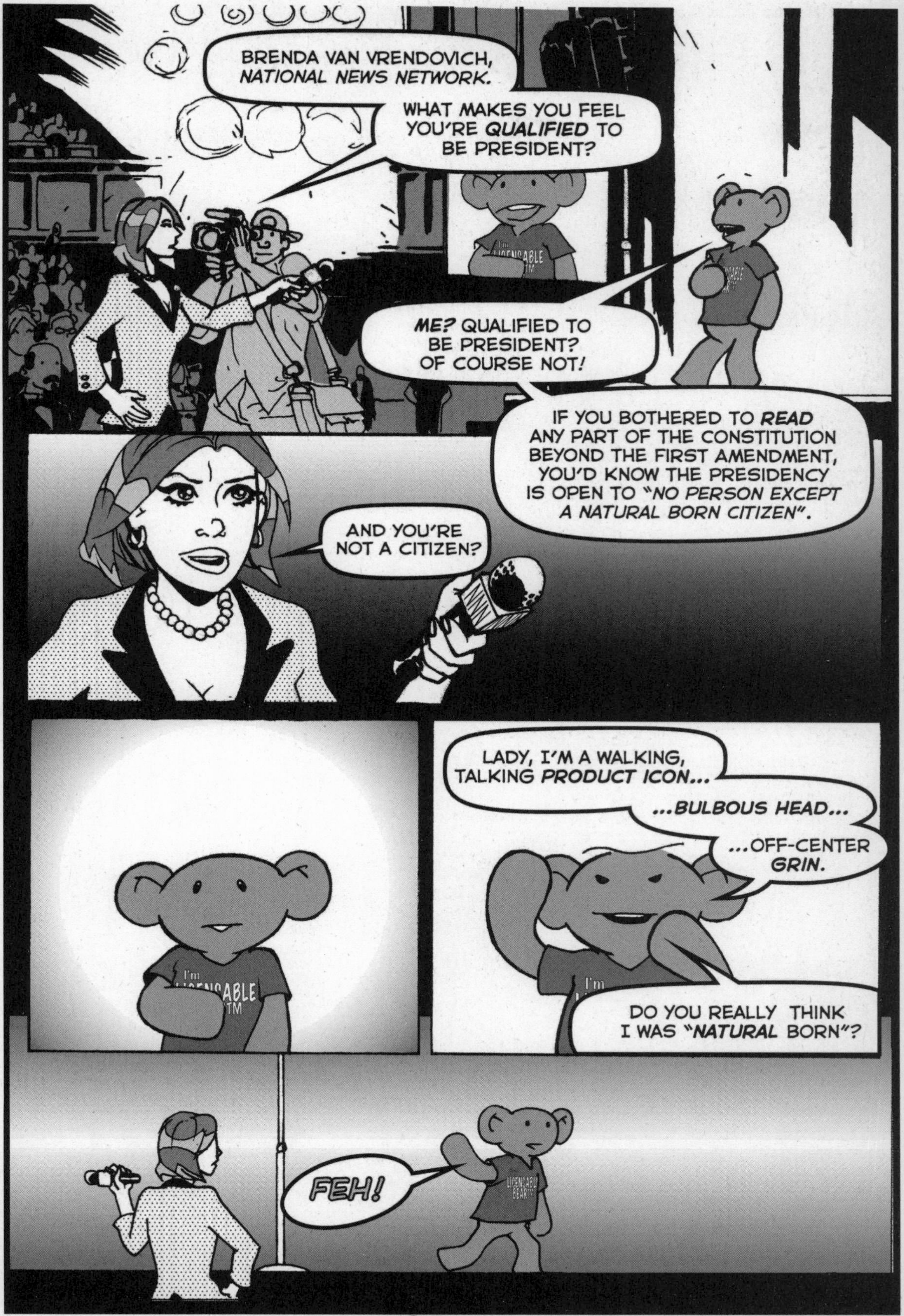
BRENDA VAN VRENDOVICH, NATIONAL NEWS NETWORK.
WHAT MAKES YOU FEEL YOU'RE QUALIFIED TO BE PRESIDENT?
ME? QUALIFIED TO BE PRESIDENT? OF COURSE NOT!
IF YOU BOTHERED TO READ ANY PART OF THE CONSTITUTION BEYOND THE FIRST AMENDMENT, YOU'D KNOW THE PRESIDENCY IS OPEN TO "NO PERSON EXCEPT A NATURAL BORN CITIZEN".
AND YOU'RE NOT A CITIZEN?
LADY, I'M A WALKING, TALKING PRODUCT ICON...
...BULBOUS HEAD...
...OFF-CENTER GRIN.
DO YOU REALLY THINK I WAS "NATURAL BORN"?
FEH!

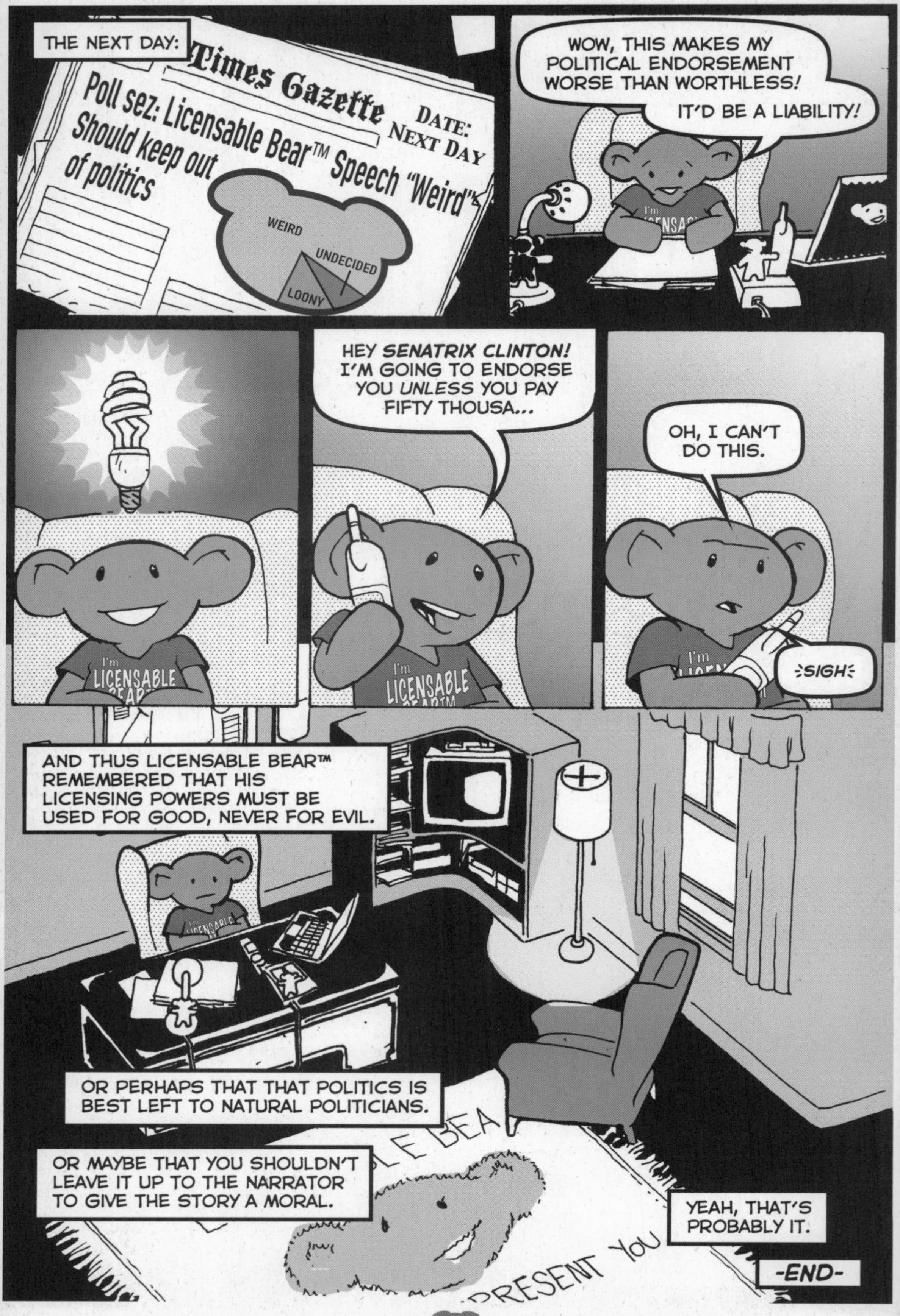
THE NEXT DAY:
Times Gazette
DATE: NEXT DAY
Poll sez: Licensable Bear™ Speech "Weird"
Should keep out of politics
WEIRD
UNDECIDED
LOONY
WOW, THIS MAKES MY POLITICAL ENDORSEMENT WORSE THAN WORTHLESS!
IT'D BE A LIABILITY!
HEY SENATRIX CLINTON! I'M GOING TO ENDORSE YOU UNLESS YOU PAY FIFTY THOUSA...
OH, I CAN'T DO THIS.
SIGH
AND THUS LICENSABLE BEAR™ REMEMBERED THAT HIS LICENSING POWERS MUST BE USED FOR GOOD, NEVER FOR EVIL.
OR PERHAPS THAT THAT POLITICS IS BEST LEFT TO NATURAL POLITICIANS.
OR MAYBE THAT YOU SHOULDN'T LEAVE IT UP TO THE NARRATOR TO GIVE THE STORY A MORAL.
YEAH, THAT'S PROBABLY IT.
-END-

LICENSABLE BEAR™ Checks the Goods

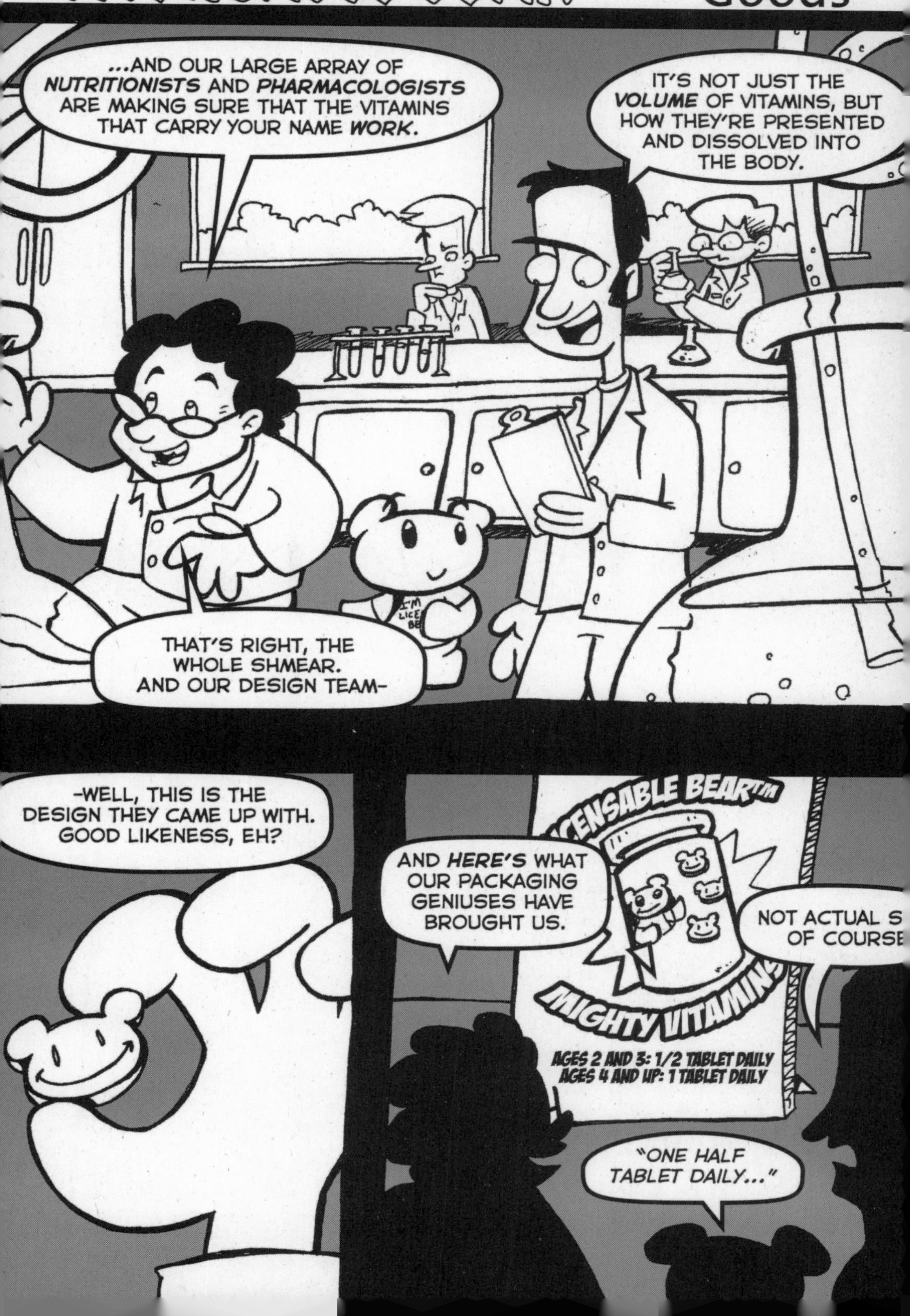
...AND OUR LARGE ARRAY OF NUTRITIONISTS AND PHARMACOLOGISTS ARE MAKING SURE THAT THE VITAMINS THAT CARRY YOUR NAME WORK.
IT'S NOT JUST THE VOLUME OF VITAMINS, BUT HOW THEY'RE PRESENTED AND DISSOLVED INTO THE BODY.
THAT'S RIGHT, THE WHOLE SHMEAR. AND OUR DESIGN TEAM–
–WELL, THIS IS THE DESIGN THEY CAME UP WITH. GOOD LIKENESS, EH?
AND HERE'S WHAT OUR PACKAGING GENIUSES HAVE BROUGHT US.
CENSABLE BEAR™
MIGHTY VITAMIN
AGES 2 AND 3: 1/2 TABLET DAILY
AGES 4 AND UP: 1 TABLET DAILY
NOT ACTUAL S
OF COURSE
"ONE HALF TABLET DAILY..."

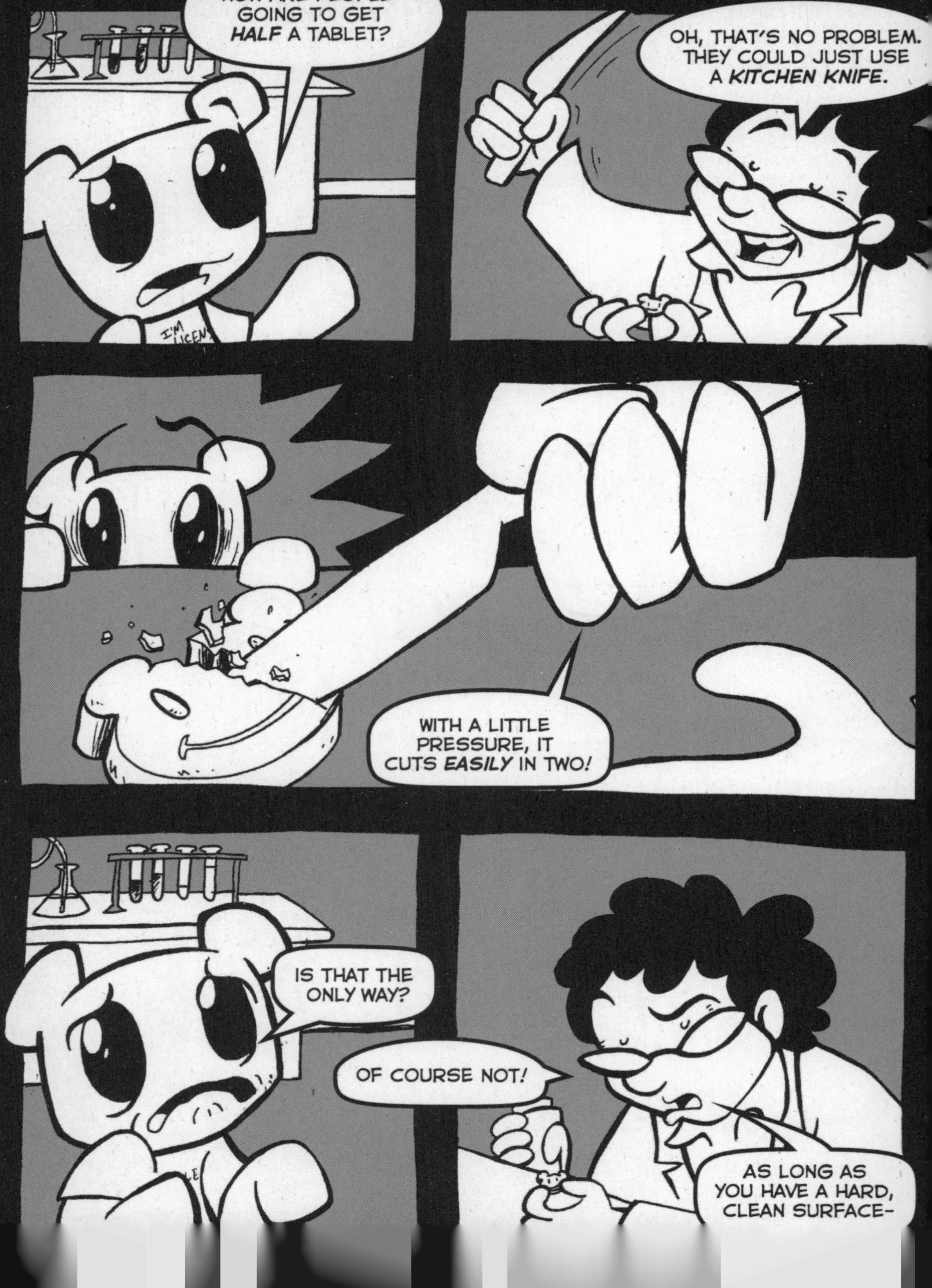
HOW ARE PEOPLE GOING TO GET HALF A TABLET?
OH, THAT'S NO PROBLEM. THEY COULD JUST USE A KITCHEN KNIFE.
WITH A LITTLE PRESSURE, IT CUTS EASILY IN TWO!
IS THAT THE ONLY WAY?
OF COURSE NOT!
AS LONG AS YOU HAVE A HARD, CLEAN SURFACE-

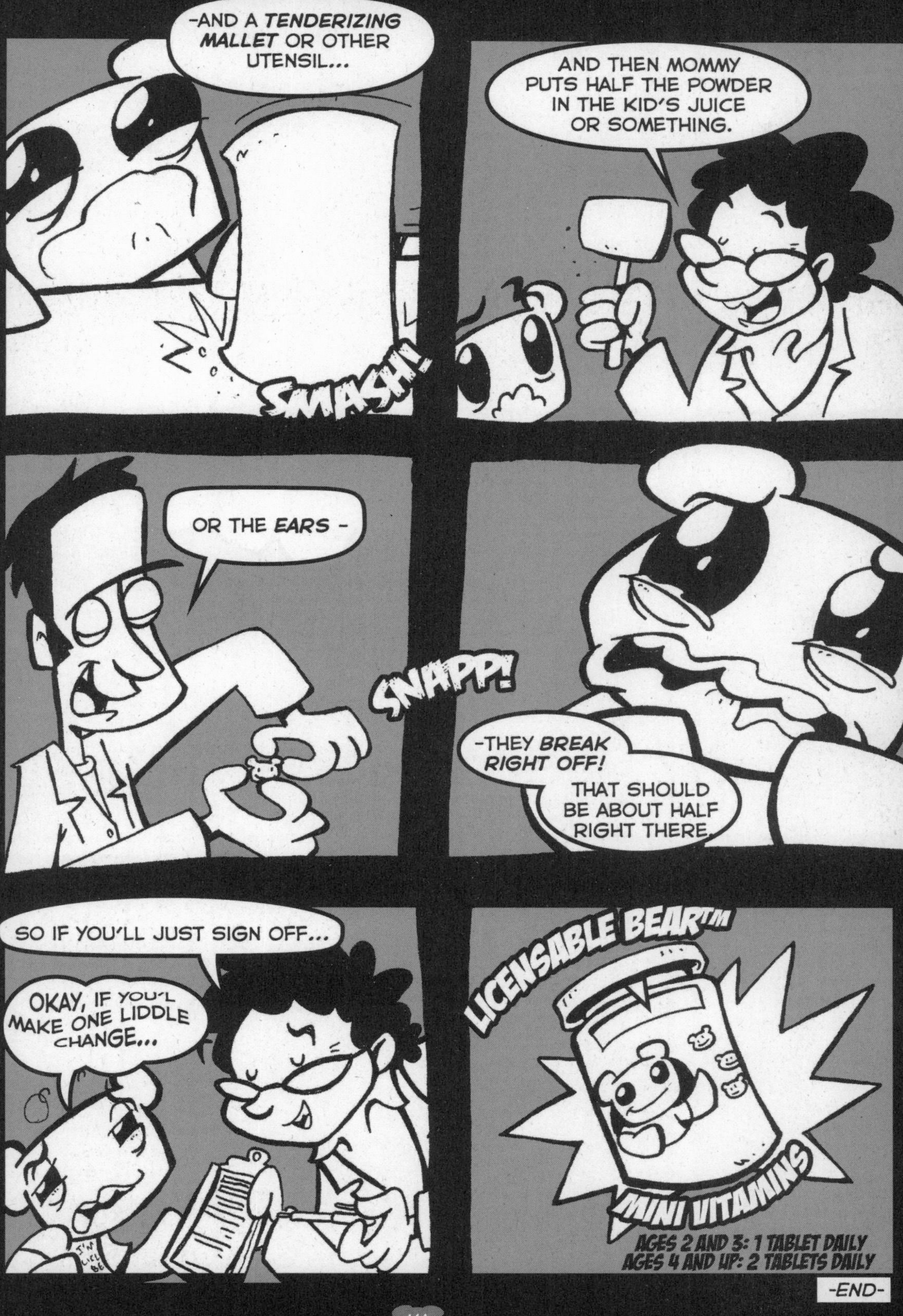
-AND A TENDERIZING MALLET OR OTHER UTENSIL...
SMASH!
AND THEN MOMMY PUTS HALF THE POWDER IN THE KID'S JUICE OR SOMETHING.
OR THE EARS -
SNAPP!
-THEY BREAK RIGHT OFF!
THAT SHOULD BE ABOUT HALF RIGHT THERE.
SO IF YOU'LL JUST SIGN OFF...
OKAY, IF YOU'L MAKE ONE LIDDLE CHANGE...
LICENSABLE BEAR™
MINI VITAMINS
AGES 2 AND 3: 1 TABLET DAILY
AGES 4 AND UP: 2 TABLETS DAILY
-END-

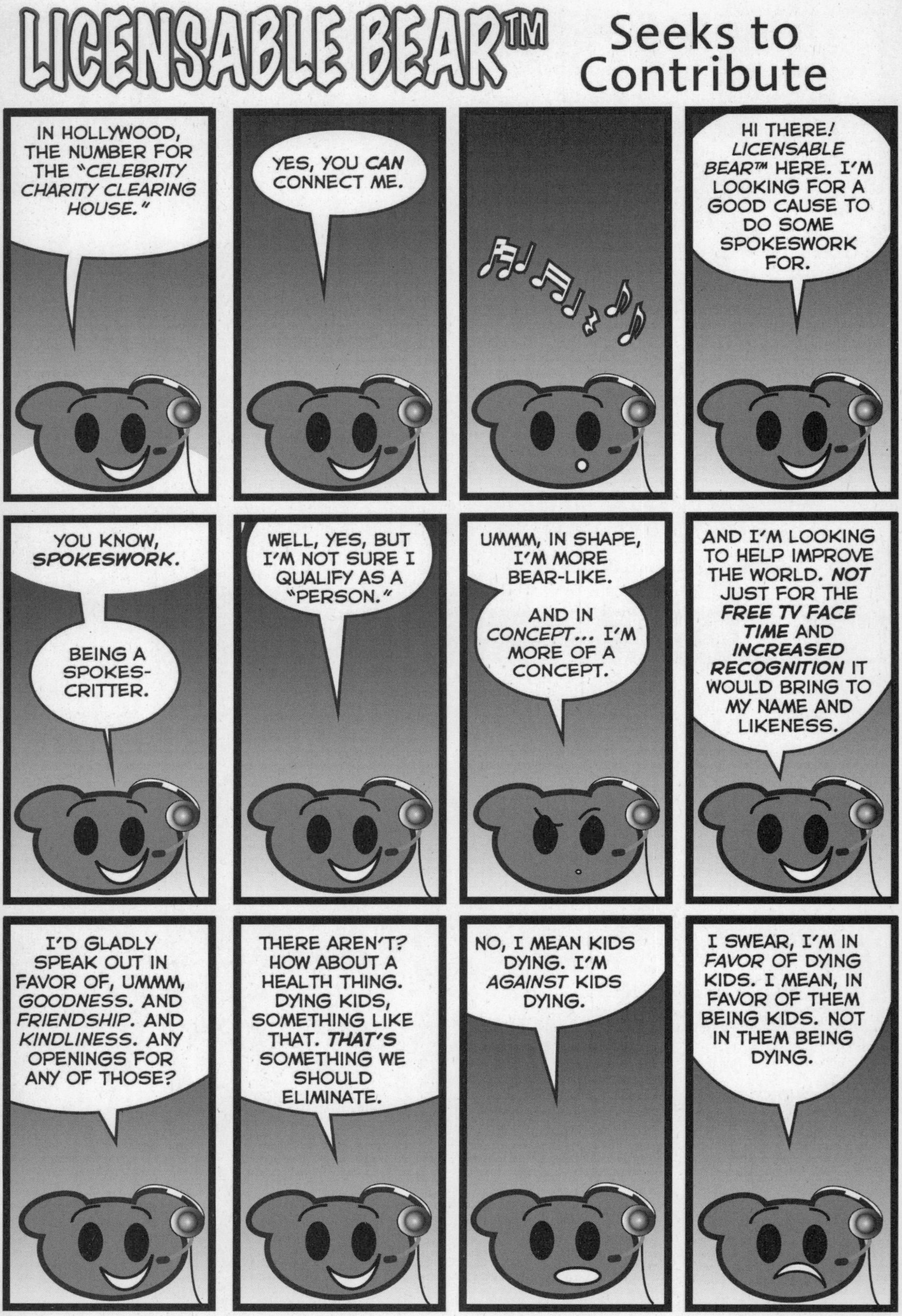
LICENSABLE BEAR™ Seeks to Contribute
IN HOLLYWOOD, THE NUMBER FOR THE "CELEBRITY CHARITY CLEARING HOUSE."
YES, YOU CAN CONNECT ME.
HI THERE! LICENSABLE BEAR™ HERE. I'M LOOKING FOR A GOOD CAUSE TO DO SOME SPOKESWORK FOR.
YOU KNOW, SPOKESWORK.
BEING A SPOKES-CRITTER.
WELL, YES, BUT I'M NOT SURE I QUALIFY AS A "PERSON."
UMMM, IN SHAPE, I'M MORE BEAR-LIKE.
AND IN CONCEPT... I'M MORE OF A CONCEPT.
AND I'M LOOKING TO HELP IMPROVE THE WORLD. NOT JUST FOR THE FREE TV FACE TIME AND INCREASED RECOGNITION IT WOULD BRING TO MY NAME AND LIKENESS.
I'D GLADLY SPEAK OUT IN FAVOR OF, UMMM, GOODNESS. AND FRIENDSHIP. AND KINDLINESS. ANY OPENINGS FOR ANY OF THOSE?
THERE AREN'T? HOW ABOUT A HEALTH THING. DYING KIDS, SOMETHING LIKE THAT. THAT'S SOMETHING WE SHOULD ELIMINATE.
NO, I MEAN KIDS DYING. I'M AGAINST KIDS DYING.
I SWEAR, I'M IN FAVOR OF DYING KIDS. I MEAN, IN FAVOR OF THEM BEING KIDS. NOT IN THEM BEING DYING.

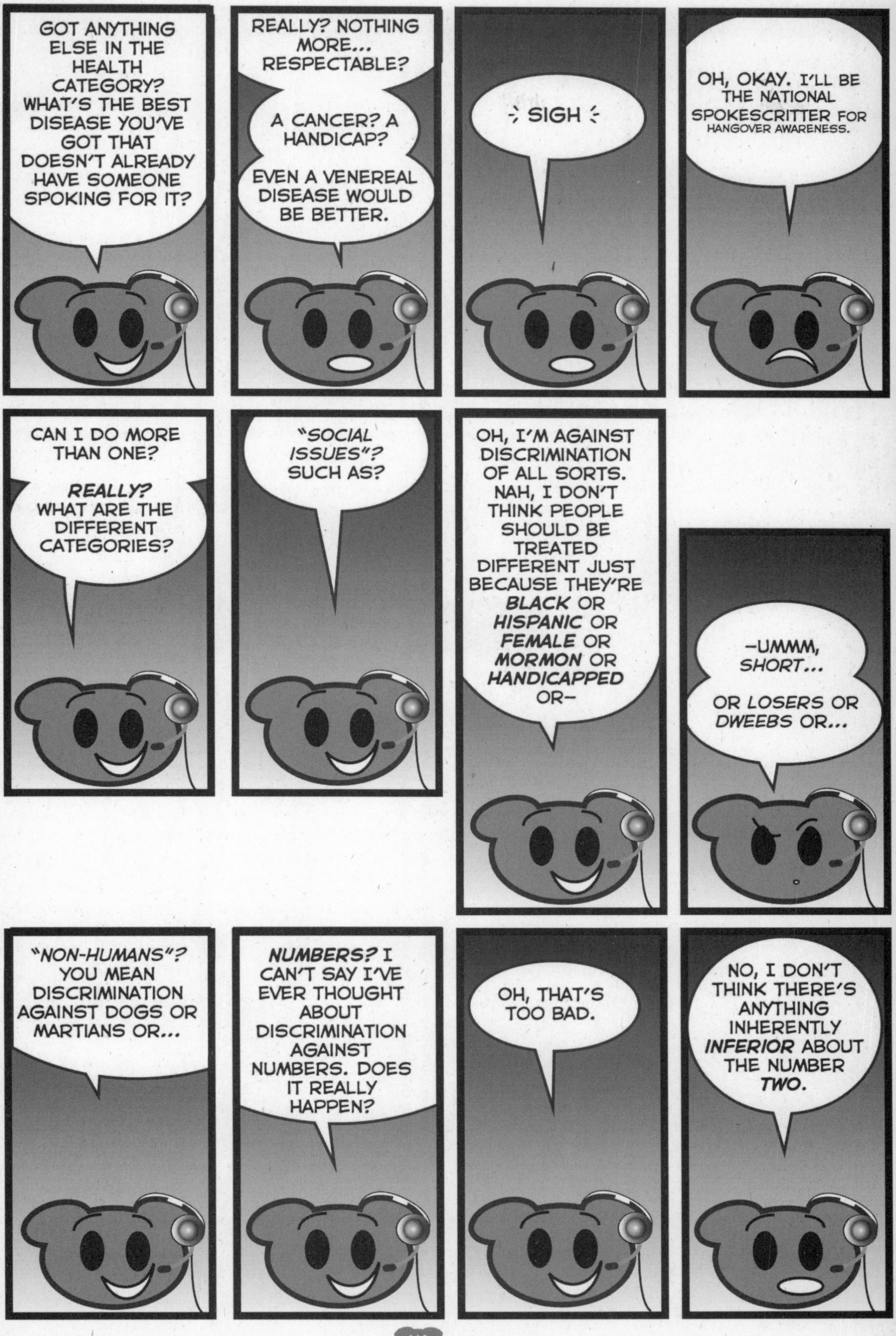
GOT ANYTHING ELSE IN THE HEALTH CATEGORY? WHAT'S THE BEST DISEASE YOU'VE GOT THAT DOESN'T ALREADY HAVE SOMEONE SPOKING FOR IT?
REALLY? NOTHING MORE... RESPECTABLE?
A CANCER? A HANDICAP?
EVEN A VENEREAL DISEASE WOULD BE BETTER.
SIGH
OH, OKAY. I'LL BE THE NATIONAL SPOKESCRITTER FOR HANGOVER AWARENESS.
CAN I DO MORE THAN ONE?
REALLY? WHAT ARE THE DIFFERENT CATEGORIES?
"SOCIAL ISSUES"? SUCH AS?
OH, I'M AGAINST DISCRIMINATION OF ALL SORTS. NAH, I DON'T THINK PEOPLE SHOULD BE TREATED DIFFERENT JUST BECAUSE THEY'RE BLACK OR HISPANIC OR FEMALE OR MORMON OR HANDICAPPED OR–
–UMMM, SHORT...
OR LOSERS OR DWEEBS OR...
"NON-HUMANS"? YOU MEAN DISCRIMINATION AGAINST DOGS OR MARTIANS OR...
NUMBERS? I CAN'T SAY I'VE EVER THOUGHT ABOUT DISCRIMINATION AGAINST NUMBERS. DOES IT REALLY HAPPEN?
OH, THAT'S TOO BAD.
NO, I DON'T THINK THERE'S ANYTHING INHERENTLY INFERIOR ABOUT THE NUMBER TWO.

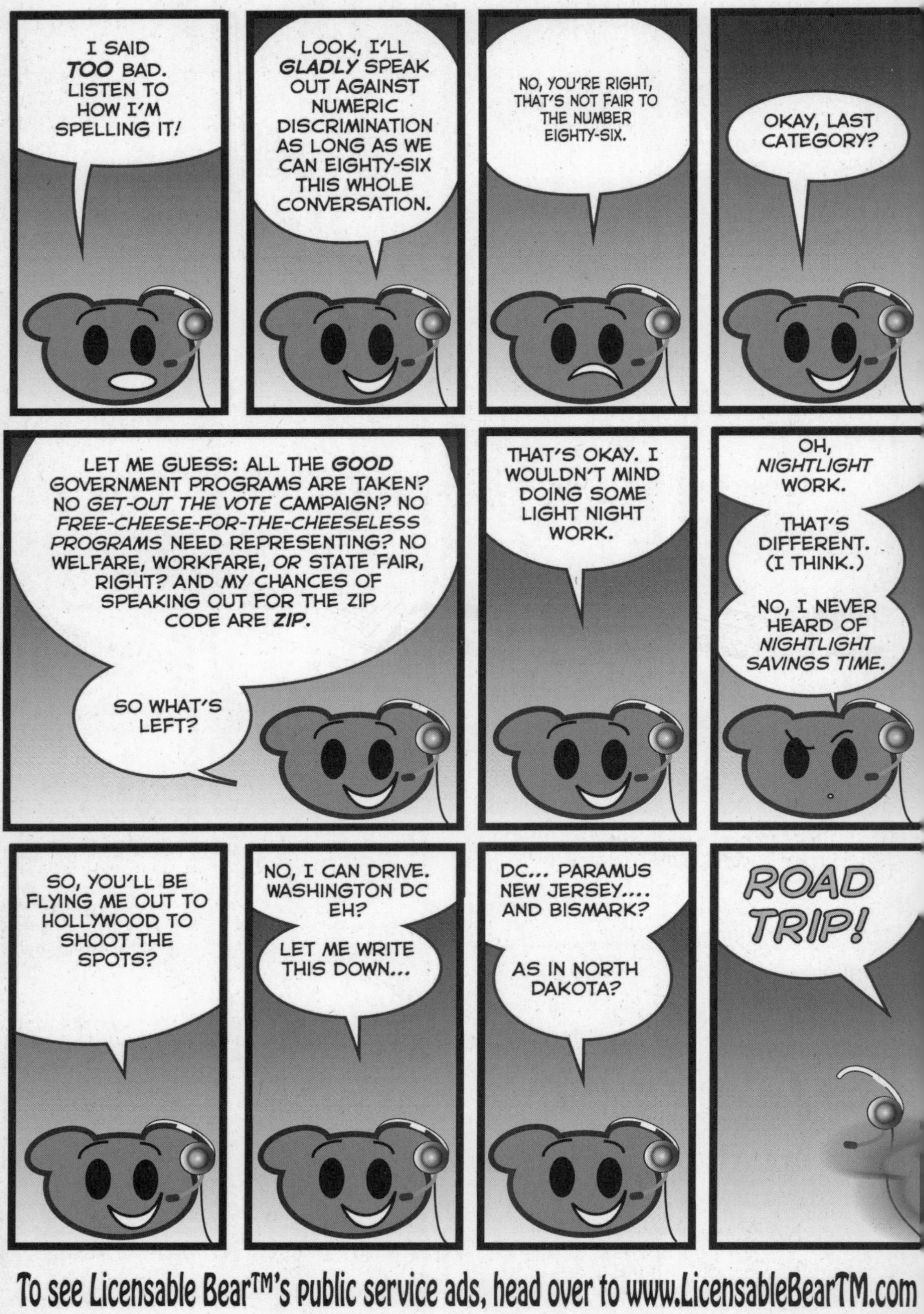
I SAID *TOO* BAD. LISTEN TO HOW I'M SPELLING IT!
LOOK, I'LL *GLADLY* SPEAK OUT AGAINST NUMERIC DISCRIMINATION AS LONG AS WE CAN EIGHTY-SIX THIS WHOLE CONVERSATION.
NO, YOU'RE RIGHT, THAT'S NOT FAIR TO THE NUMBER EIGHTY-SIX.
OKAY, LAST CATEGORY?
LET ME GUESS: ALL THE *GOOD* GOVERNMENT PROGRAMS ARE TAKEN? NO *GET-OUT THE VOTE* CAMPAIGN? NO *FREE-CHEESE-FOR-THE-CHEESELESS PROGRAMS* NEED REPRESENTING? NO WELFARE, WORKFARE, *OR* STATE FAIR, RIGHT? AND MY CHANCES OF SPEAKING OUT FOR THE ZIP CODE ARE *ZIP*.
SO WHAT'S LEFT?
THAT'S OKAY. I WOULDN'T MIND DOING SOME LIGHT NIGHT WORK.
OH, *NIGHTLIGHT* WORK.
THAT'S DIFFERENT. (I THINK.)
NO, I NEVER HEARD OF *NIGHTLIGHT SAVINGS TIME.*
SO, *YOU'LL* BE FLYING ME OUT TO HOLLYWOOD TO SHOOT THE SPOTS?
NO, I CAN DRIVE. WASHINGTON DC EH?
LET ME WRITE THIS DOWN...
DC... PARAMUS NEW JERSEY.... AND BISMARK?
AS IN NORTH DAKOTA?
ROAD TRIP!

To see Licensable Bear™'s public service ads, head over to www.LicensableBearTM.com

LICENSABLE BEAR™ Offers Help

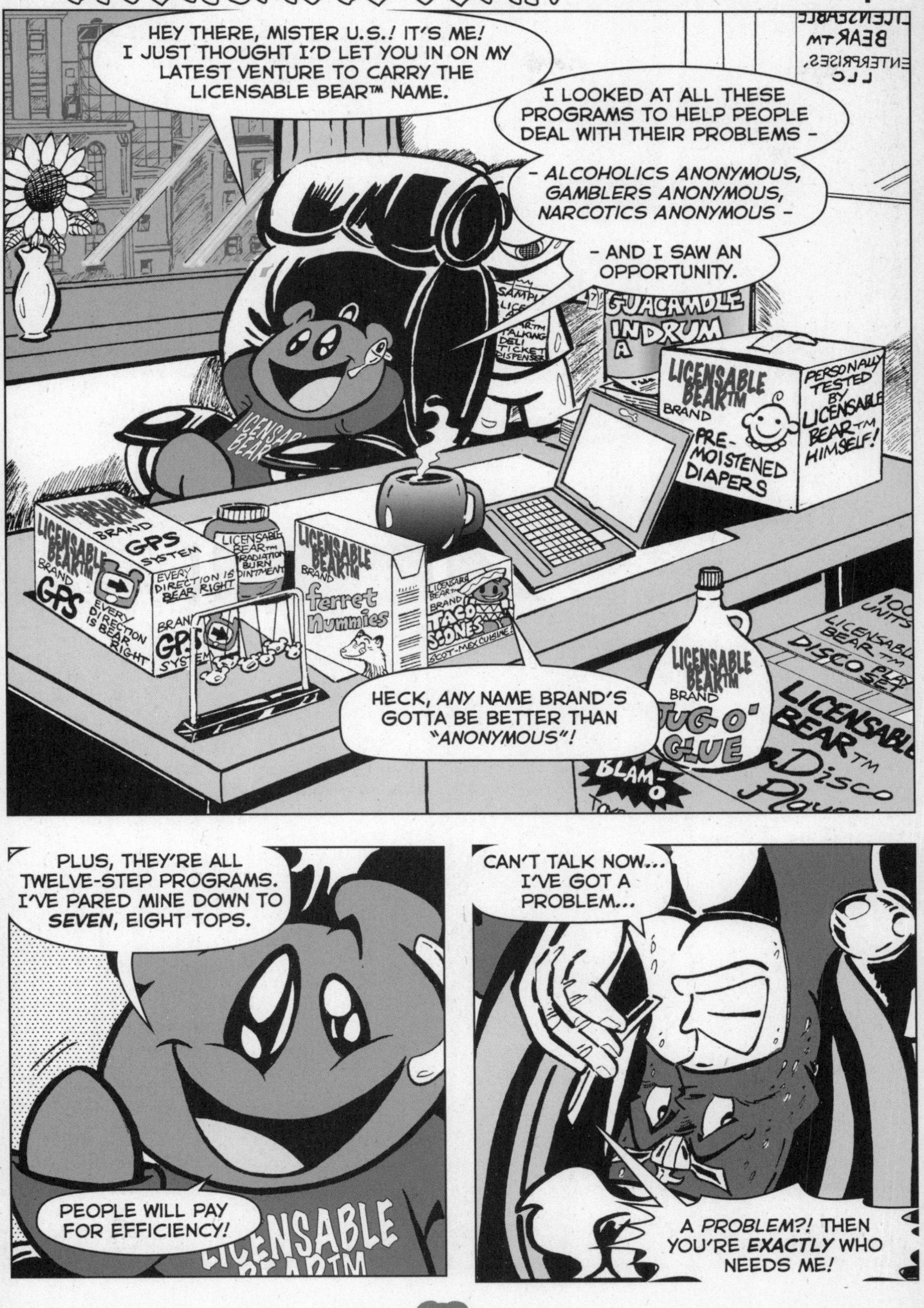
HEY THERE, MISTER U.S.! IT'S ME! I JUST THOUGHT I'D LET YOU IN ON MY LATEST VENTURE TO CARRY THE LICENSABLE BEAR™ NAME.
I LOOKED AT ALL THESE PROGRAMS TO HELP PEOPLE DEAL WITH THEIR PROBLEMS –
– ALCOHOLICS ANONYMOUS, GAMBLERS ANONYMOUS, NARCOTICS ANONYMOUS –
– AND I SAW AN OPPORTUNITY.
HECK, ANY NAME BRAND'S GOTTA BE BETTER THAN "ANONYMOUS"!
LICENSABLE BEAR TM ENTERPRISES, LLC
LICENSABLE BEAR™ BRAND PRE-MOISTENED DIAPERS
PERSONALLY TESTED BY LICENSABLE BEAR™ HIMSELF!
LICENSABLE BEAR™ BRAND GPS SYSTEM
EVERY DIRECTION IS BEAR RIGHT
LICENSABLE BEAR™ RADIATION BURN OINTMENT
LICENSABLE BEAR™ BRAND ferret Nummies
TACO SCONES
SCOT-MEX CUISINE
LICENSABLE BEAR™ BRAND JUG O' GLUE
100 UNITS LICENSABLE BEAR TM DISCO PLAY SET
LICENSABLE BEAR™ Disco
BLAM-O
GUACAMOLE IN A DRUM
PLUS, THEY'RE ALL TWELVE-STEP PROGRAMS. I'VE PARED MINE DOWN TO SEVEN, EIGHT TOPS.
PEOPLE WILL PAY FOR EFFICIENCY!
LICENSABLE BEAR™
CAN'T TALK NOW... I'VE GOT A PROBLEM...
A PROBLEM?! THEN YOU'RE EXACTLY WHO NEEDS ME!

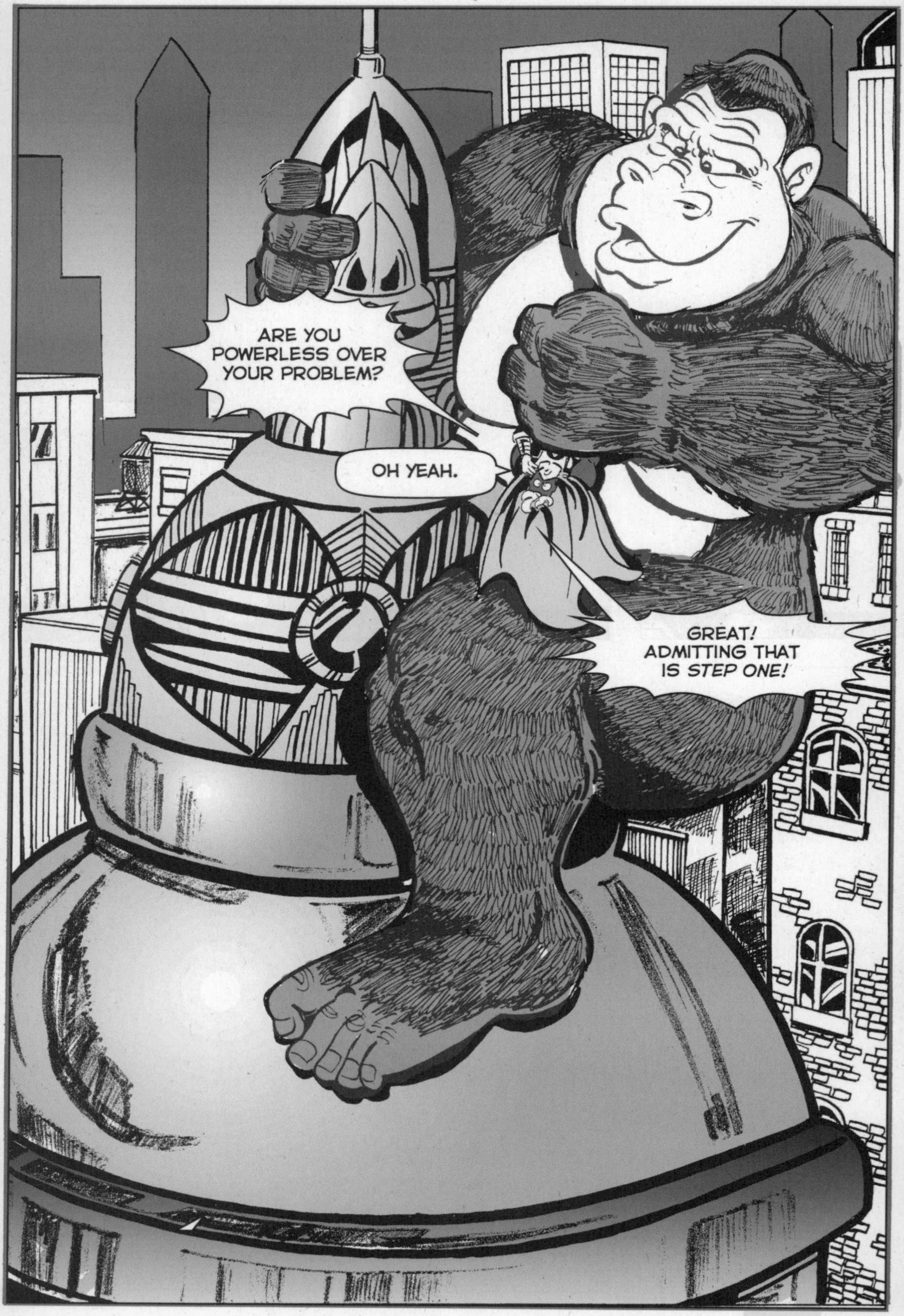
ARE YOU POWERLESS OVER YOUR PROBLEM?
OH YEAH.
GREAT! ADMITTING THAT IS *STEP ONE!*

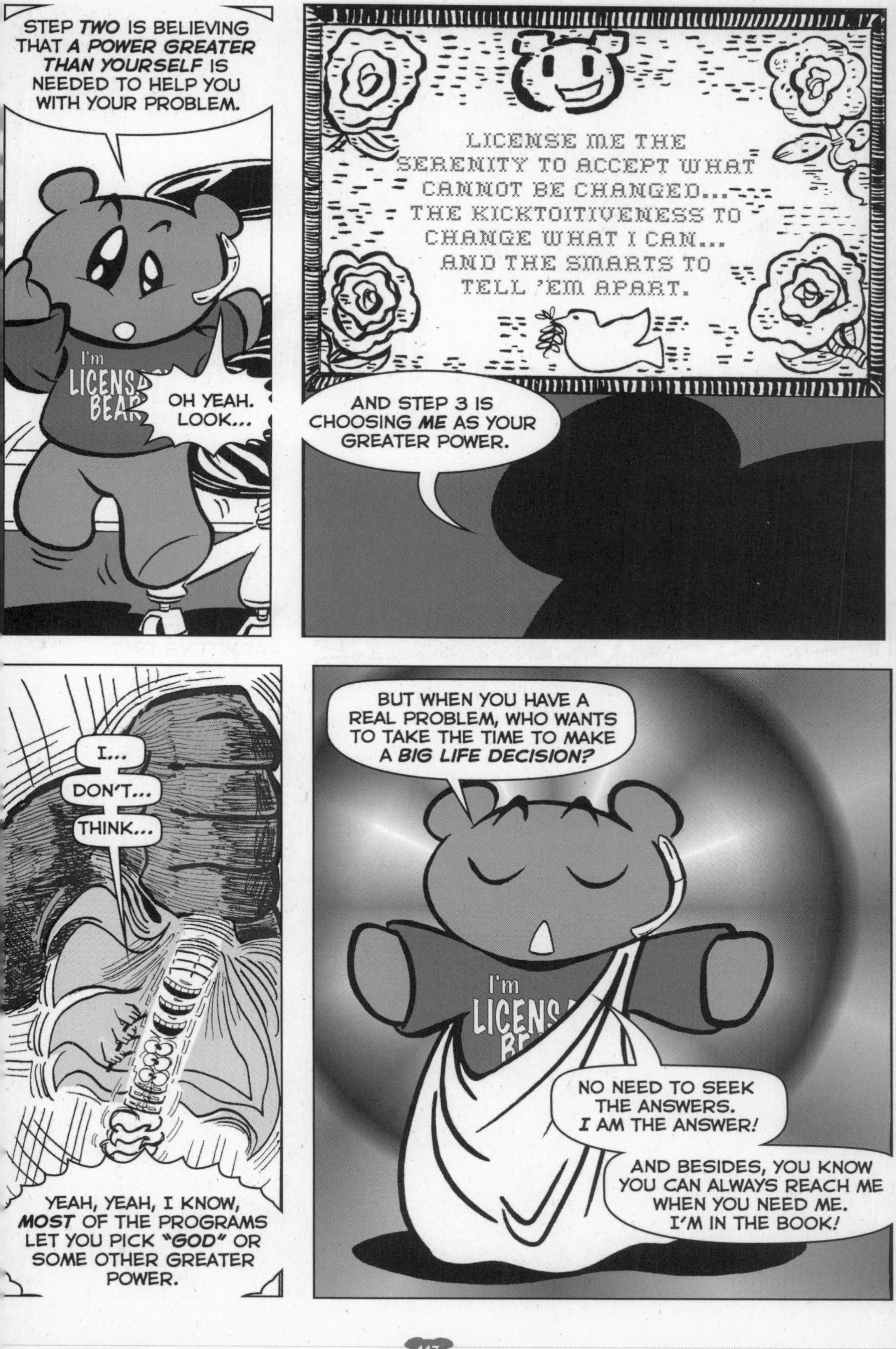
STEP *TWO* IS BELIEVING THAT *A POWER GREATER THAN YOURSELF* IS NEEDED TO HELP YOU WITH YOUR PROBLEM.
I'm LICENSA BEAR
OH YEAH. LOOK...
LICENSE ME THE SERENITY TO ACCEPT WHAT CANNOT BE CHANGED... THE KICKTOITIVENESS TO CHANGE WHAT I CAN... AND THE SMARTS TO TELL 'EM APART.
AND STEP 3 IS CHOOSING *ME* AS YOUR GREATER POWER.
I...
DON'T...
THINK...
YEAH, YEAH, I KNOW, *MOST* OF THE PROGRAMS LET YOU PICK *"GOD"* OR SOME OTHER GREATER POWER.
BUT WHEN YOU HAVE A REAL PROBLEM, WHO WANTS TO TAKE THE TIME TO MAKE A *BIG LIFE DECISION?*
I'm LICENSA BEA
NO NEED TO SEEK THE ANSWERS. *I* AM THE ANSWER!
AND BESIDES, YOU KNOW YOU CAN ALWAYS REACH ME WHEN YOU NEED ME. I'M IN THE BOOK!

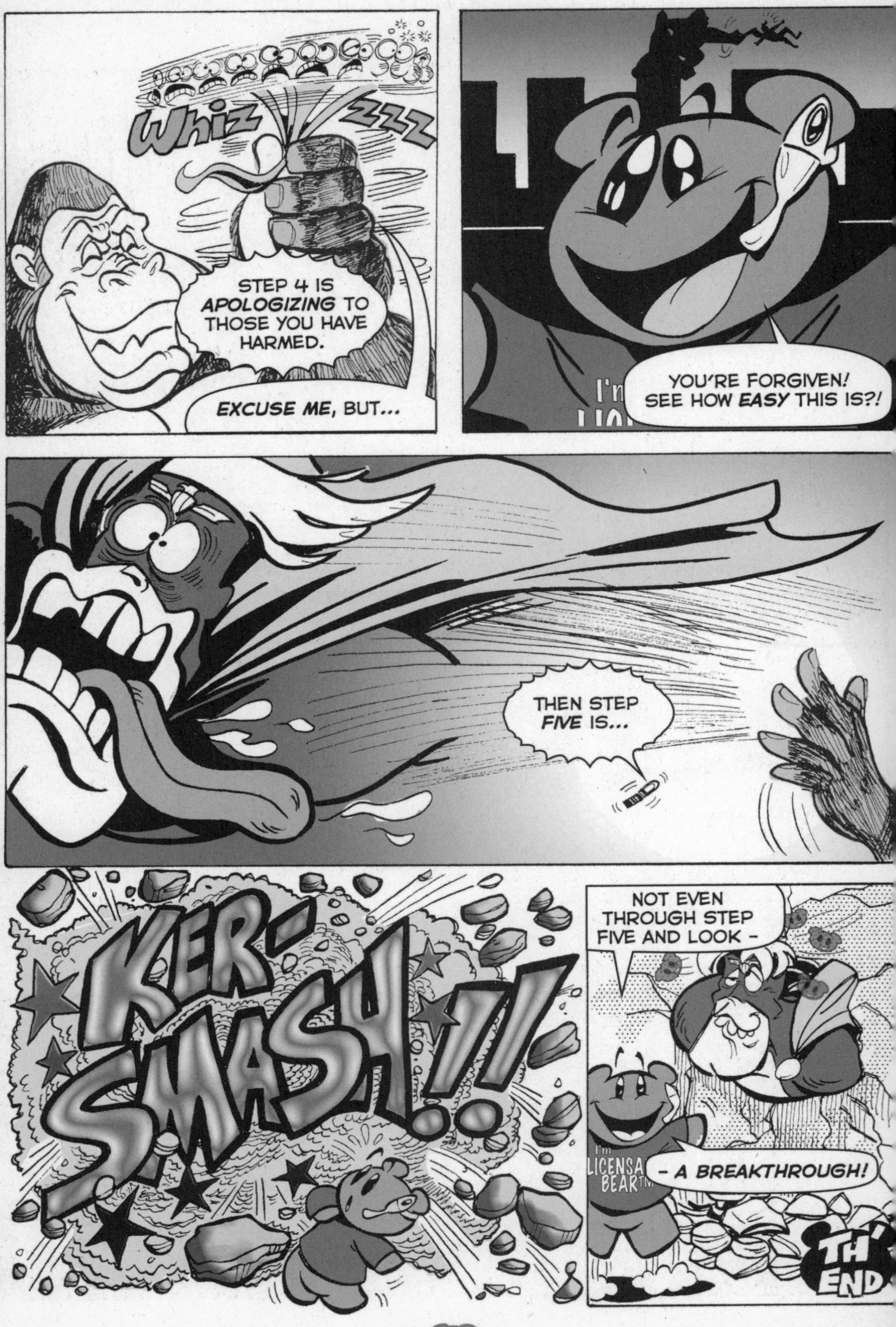
WHIZZZZ
STEP 4 IS APOLOGIZING TO THOSE YOU HAVE HARMED.
EXCUSE ME, BUT...
YOU'RE FORGIVEN! SEE HOW EASY THIS IS?!
THEN STEP FIVE IS...
KER-SMASH!!
NOT EVEN THROUGH STEP FIVE AND LOOK -
- A BREAKTHROUGH!
TH' END

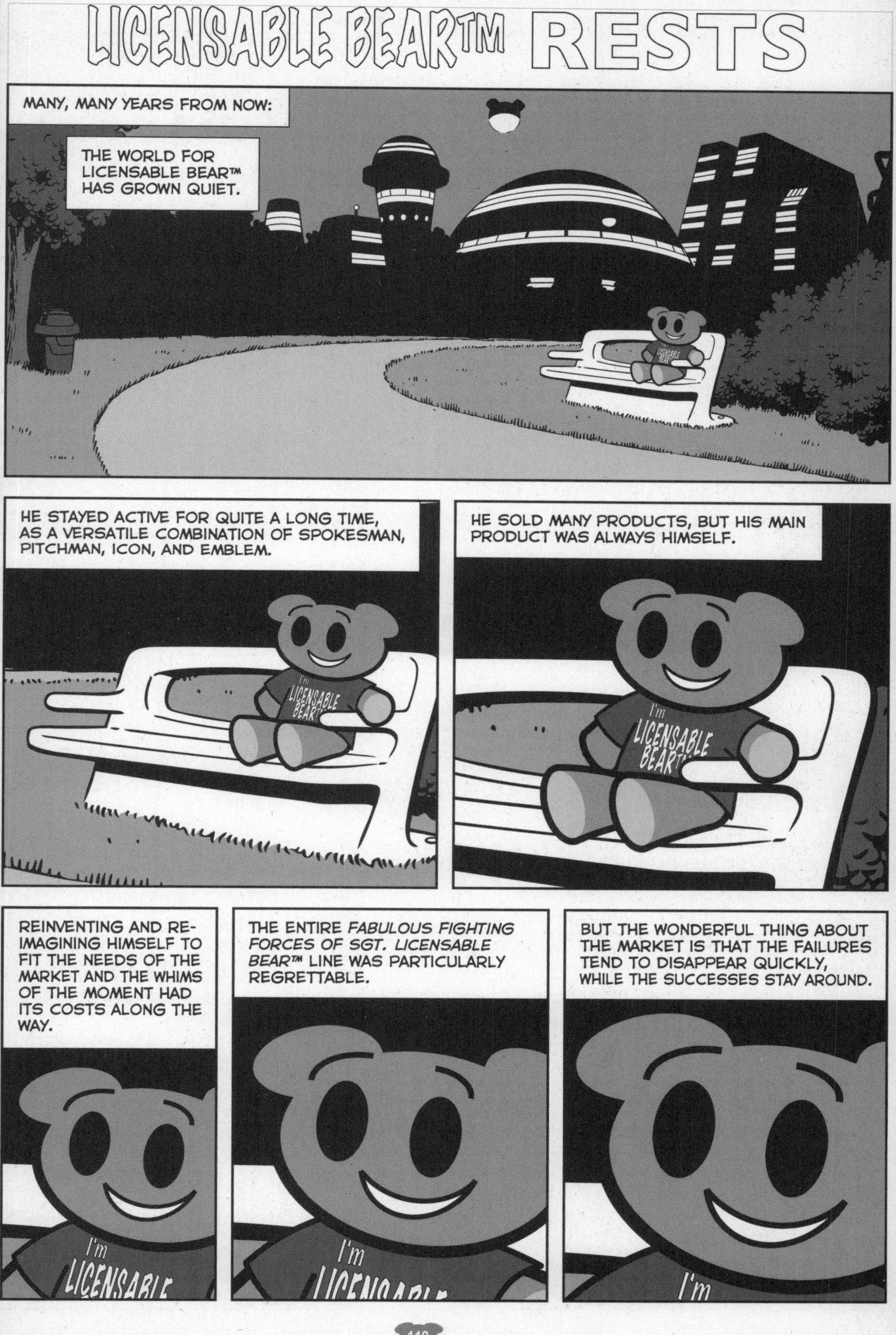
LICENSABLE BEAR™ RESTS
MANY, MANY YEARS FROM NOW:
THE WORLD FOR LICENSABLE BEAR™ HAS GROWN QUIET.
LICENSABLE BEAR
HE STAYED ACTIVE FOR QUITE A LONG TIME, AS A VERSATILE COMBINATION OF SPOKESMAN, PITCHMAN, ICON, AND EMBLEM.
I'm LICENSABLE BEAR™
HE SOLD MANY PRODUCTS, BUT HIS MAIN PRODUCT WAS ALWAYS HIMSELF.
I'm LICENSABLE BEAR™
REINVENTING AND RE-IMAGINING HIMSELF TO FIT THE NEEDS OF THE MARKET AND THE WHIMS OF THE MOMENT HAD ITS COSTS ALONG THE WAY.
I'm
THE ENTIRE *FABULOUS FIGHTING FORCES OF SGT. LICENSABLE BEAR™* LINE WAS PARTICULARLY REGRETTABLE.
I'm
BUT THE WONDERFUL THING ABOUT THE MARKET IS THAT THE FAILURES TEND TO DISAPPEAR QUICKLY, WHILE THE SUCCESSES STAY AROUND.
I'm

STILL, NOTHING IS ETERNAL.

SUCCESSES REACH THE END OF THEIR PROFITABILITY.

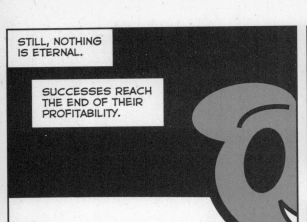

FAME IS FLEETING.

AND EVEN DESPITE THE ASSUMPTION THAT COPYRIGHTS WOULD BE EXTENDED INDEFINITELY, EVEN THEY PROVED FINITE.

A TRADEMARK LASTS AS LONG AS IT'S IN REGULAR USE. FOR DECADES, THE OCCASIONAL RETRO ITEM KEPT LICENSABLE BEAR™ GOING.

BUT THE AUDIENCE WHO FELT NOSTALGIA FOR LICENSABLE BEAR™ PASSED ON.

IT'S BEEN SEVERAL YEARS SINCE THE LAST NEW LICENSABLE BEAR™ PRODUCT WAS SOLD.

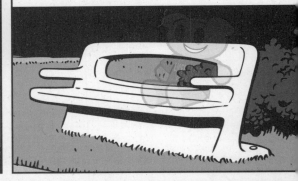

AND SO THE TRADEMARK FADES AWAY.

-END-

Licensable Bear™'s intellectual property insights

Of all the forms of intellectual property, the "trade secret" enjoys the coolest name. Some of us are rightly proud of our trademarks, and it is an achievement to get a patent, but if you tell someone you have a trade secret, they automatically want to know what it is. It sounds so surreptitious.

When two people with trade secrets meet, they must be horribly tempted to trade their trade secrets – but they cannot! If you trade a trade secret, you no longer have a secret at all.

Trade secret protection can cover just about anything where maintaining a secret you created gives you an appropriate economic advantage. A set of information can be a trade secret, such as a list of the people who bought the Licensable Bear™ Ice-to-Water Conversion System, and who might be conned (merely short for convinced, I assure you) into upgrading to the Deluxe Conversion System next year. It can be a process, like the magic used to embed a peanut into an M&M without shattering the shell. It can even be an invention.

A trade secret doesn't offer the full range of protection that some other forms of intellectual property, such as a patent, do. With a patent, even someone who comes up with same invention cannot produce it. For the life of the patent, you can sue and win for such accidental infringement. The same is not true of trade secrets.

Consider Kentucky Fried Chicken. They have a trade secret – the mix of 11 herbs and spices that makes their chicken yummy enough to have destroyed many a diet. But if your spice rack collapses into your mixing bowl, and the 11 herbs and spices which have landed there make your chicken taste them same as theirs, congratulations. Use this non-original recipe to your heart's content. Publish it, sell it, give it away, and KFC can't say "boo" about it (if saying "boo" means the same as winning a lawsuit).

Trade secrets are legally protected only from improper uncovering. You can't break into the KFC safe and swipe the recipe. You can't bribe a disgruntled employee to tell you the recipe. You can't build a house right next to KFC headquarters, and then stop by every day saying "Could I borrow a cup of," going through every herb and spice from agrimony through zedoary to see which eleven they happen to have on hand. Use of these improper means would let KFC say "boo" quite loudly indeed.

I have a trade secret – it's a process that turns any question into a comedy land mine. What is this process, you ask? I could tell you, but I'd have to kill you. That's the process: answering the question with "I could tell you, but I'd have to kill you." What do you mean that's an overused cliché at this point? You're mistaken – that's my trade secret.

Except that a trade secret stops being a trade secret if one doesn't protect its secrecy. As such, now I *will* have to kill you!

Licensable Bear™ is a dedicated marketing icon and is not a trained attorney. For much more accurate information, contact an attorney. For much less accurate information, try blogs.

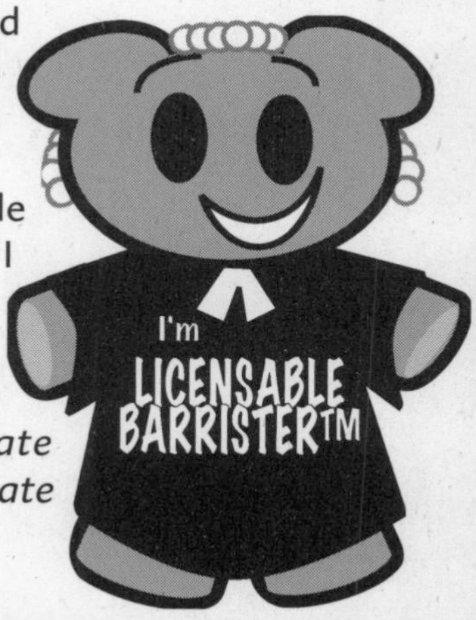
I'm
LICENSABLE
BARRISTER™

LICENSABLE BEAR™ Defends Himself

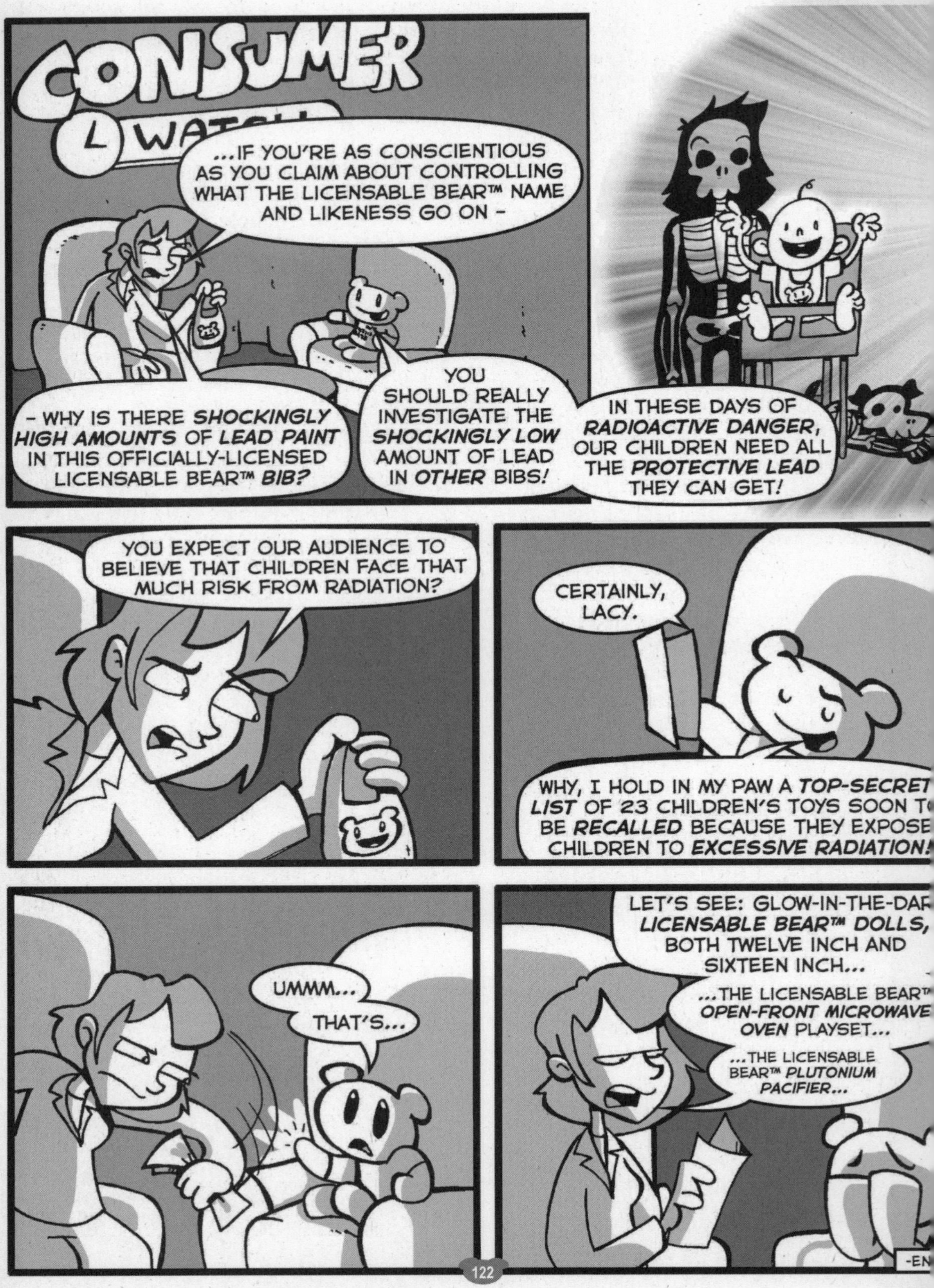

CONSUMER WATCH
...IF YOU'RE AS CONSCIENTIOUS AS YOU CLAIM ABOUT CONTROLLING WHAT THE LICENSABLE BEAR™ NAME AND LIKENESS GO ON –
– WHY IS THERE *SHOCKINGLY HIGH AMOUNTS* OF *LEAD PAINT* IN THIS OFFICIALLY-LICENSED LICENSABLE BEAR™ *BIB?*
YOU SHOULD REALLY INVESTIGATE THE *SHOCKINGLY LOW* AMOUNT OF LEAD IN *OTHER* BIBS!
IN THESE DAYS OF *RADIOACTIVE DANGER*, OUR CHILDREN NEED ALL THE *PROTECTIVE LEAD* THEY CAN GET!
YOU EXPECT OUR AUDIENCE TO BELIEVE THAT CHILDREN FACE THAT MUCH RISK FROM RADIATION?
CERTAINLY, LACY.
WHY, I HOLD IN MY PAW A *TOP-SECRET LIST* OF 23 CHILDREN'S TOYS SOON T BE *RECALLED* BECAUSE THEY EXPOSE CHILDREN TO *EXCESSIVE RADIATION!*
UMMM...
THAT'S...
LET'S SEE: GLOW-IN-THE-DAR *LICENSABLE BEAR™ DOLLS,* BOTH TWELVE INCH AND SIXTEEN INCH...
...THE LICENSABLE BEAR™ *OPEN-FRONT MICROWAVE OVEN* PLAYSET...
...THE LICENSABLE BEAR™ *PLUTONIUM PACIFIER...*
-EN

LICENSABLE BEAR™ Goes to the Comic Shop

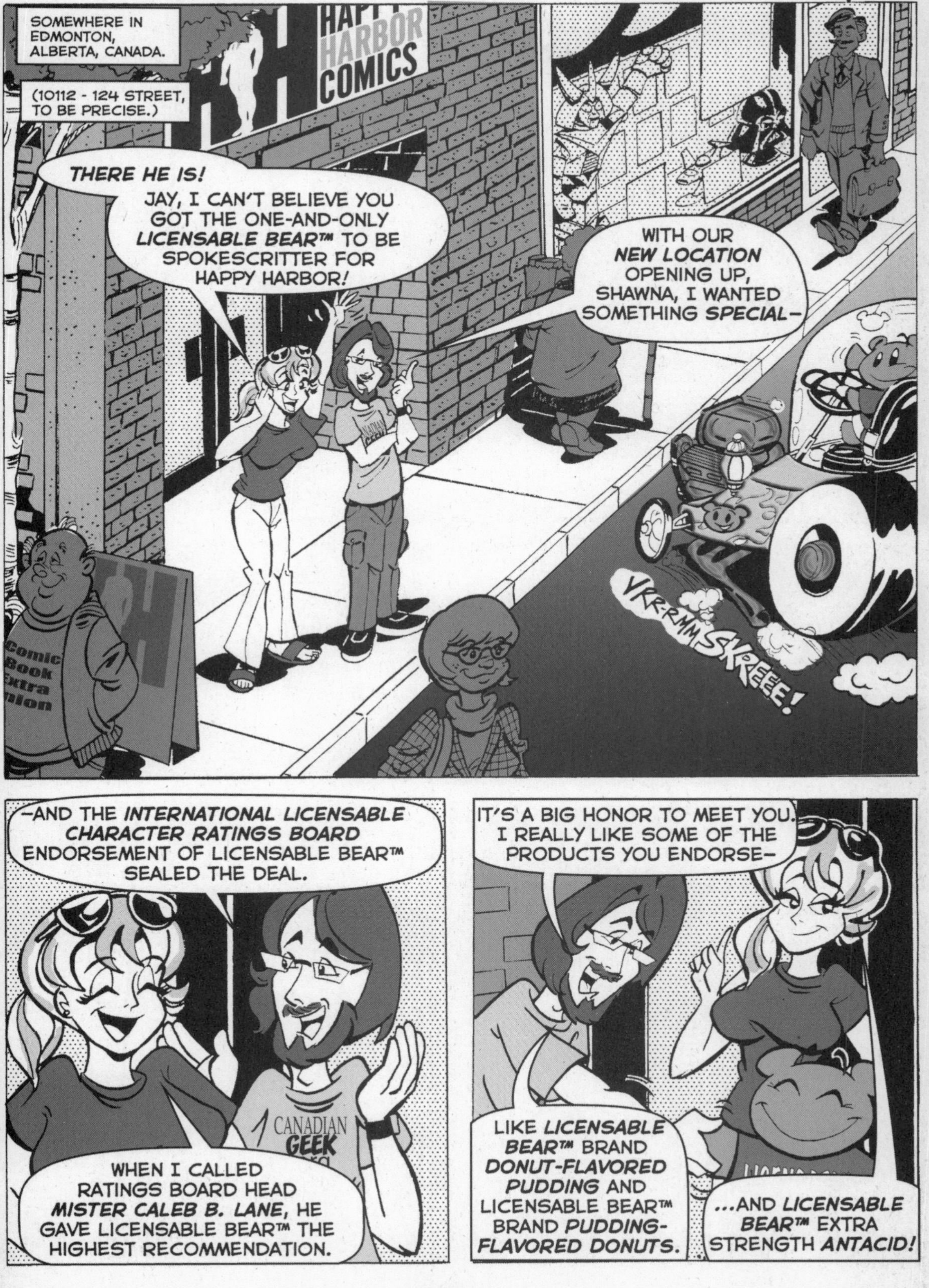

SOMEWHERE IN EDMONTON, ALBERTA, CANADA.
(10112 - 124 STREET, TO BE PRECISE.)
HARBOR COMICS
THERE HE IS!
JAY, I CAN'T BELIEVE YOU GOT THE ONE-AND-ONLY LICENSABLE BEAR™ TO BE SPOKESCRITTER FOR HAPPY HARBOR!
WITH OUR NEW LOCATION OPENING UP, SHAWNA, I WANTED SOMETHING SPECIAL–
VRR-RMM SKREEEE!
–AND THE INTERNATIONAL LICENSABLE CHARACTER RATINGS BOARD ENDORSEMENT OF LICENSABLE BEAR™ SEALED THE DEAL.
CANADIAN GEEK
WHEN I CALLED RATINGS BOARD HEAD MISTER CALEB B. LANE, HE GAVE LICENSABLE BEAR™ THE HIGHEST RECOMMENDATION.
IT'S A BIG HONOR TO MEET YOU. I REALLY LIKE SOME OF THE PRODUCTS YOU ENDORSE–
LIKE LICENSABLE BEAR™ BRAND DONUT-FLAVORED PUDDING AND LICENSABLE BEAR™ BRAND PUDDING-FLAVORED DONUTS.
...AND LICENSABLE BEAR™ EXTRA STRENGTH ANTACID!

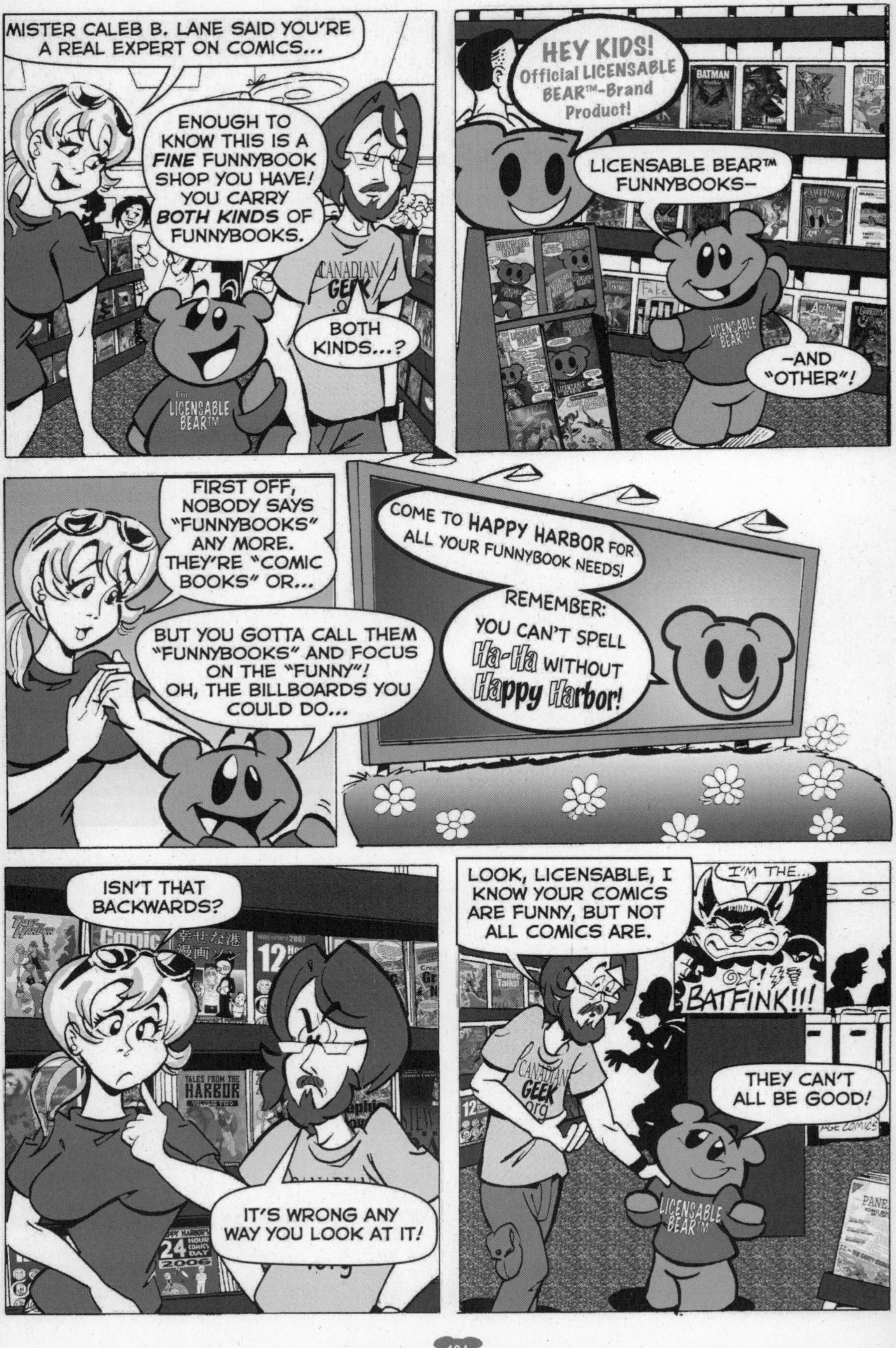
MISTER CALEB B. LANE SAID YOU'RE A REAL EXPERT ON COMICS...
ENOUGH TO KNOW THIS IS A *FINE* FUNNYBOOK SHOP YOU HAVE! YOU CARRY *BOTH KINDS* OF FUNNYBOOKS.
BOTH KINDS...?
HEY KIDS! Official LICENSABLE BEAR™-Brand Product!
LICENSABLE BEAR™ FUNNYBOOKS–
–AND "OTHER"!
FIRST OFF, NOBODY SAYS "FUNNYBOOKS" ANY MORE. THEY'RE "COMIC BOOKS" OR...
BUT YOU GOTTA CALL THEM "FUNNYBOOKS" AND FOCUS ON THE "FUNNY"! OH, THE BILLBOARDS YOU COULD DO...
COME TO HAPPY HARBOR FOR ALL YOUR FUNNYBOOK NEEDS!
REMEMBER: YOU CAN'T SPELL Ha-Ha WITHOUT Happy Harbor!
ISN'T THAT BACKWARDS?
IT'S WRONG ANY WAY YOU LOOK AT IT!
LOOK, LICENSABLE, I KNOW YOUR COMICS ARE FUNNY, BUT NOT ALL COMICS ARE.
I'M THE...
BATFINK!!!
THEY CAN'T ALL BE GOOD!

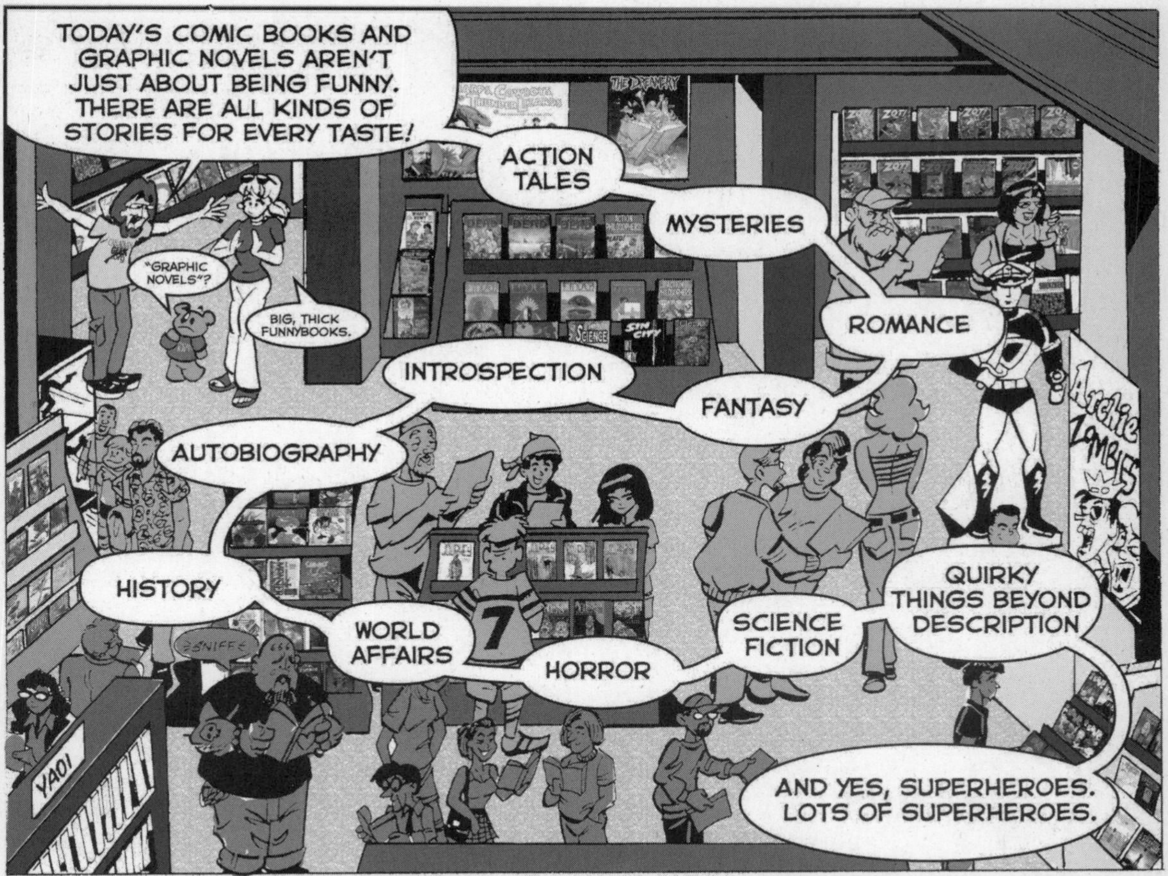
TODAY'S COMIC BOOKS AND GRAPHIC NOVELS AREN'T JUST ABOUT BEING FUNNY. THERE ARE ALL KINDS OF STORIES FOR EVERY TASTE!
"GRAPHIC NOVELS"?
BIG, THICK FUNNYBOOKS.
ACTION TALES
MYSTERIES
ROMANCE
FANTASY
INTROSPECTION
AUTOBIOGRAPHY
HISTORY
WORLD AFFAIRS
HORROR
SCIENCE FICTION
QUIRKY THINGS BEYOND DESCRIPTION
AND YES, SUPERHEROES. LOTS OF SUPERHEROES.
SNIFF
YAOI
Archie

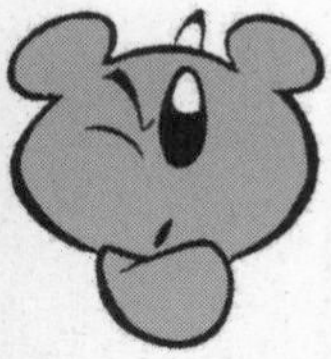

YOU EXPECT ME TO BELIEVE THAT NOT ONLY CAN COMICS BE FUNNY THINGS LIKE *THE GOOFY ADVENTURES OF TYLER SMITH*, AND SUPERHERO THINGS LIKE *TYLER SMITH, AMAZING LOBSTERGUY*, BUT A RANGE OF INTERESTING ADVENTURERS – *THE CURIOUS CASEFILES OF TYLER SMITH*, SAY, OR *AROUND THE WORLD WITH TYLER SMITH*? *TYLER SMITH, FRONTIER SCHOOLMARM? TYLER SMITH VS. DRACULA? TYLER SMITH, 3017 A.D.?*

OR EVEN TALES OF ORDINARY PEOPLE, LIKE *MATTHEW LUI, RUNNER-UP?*

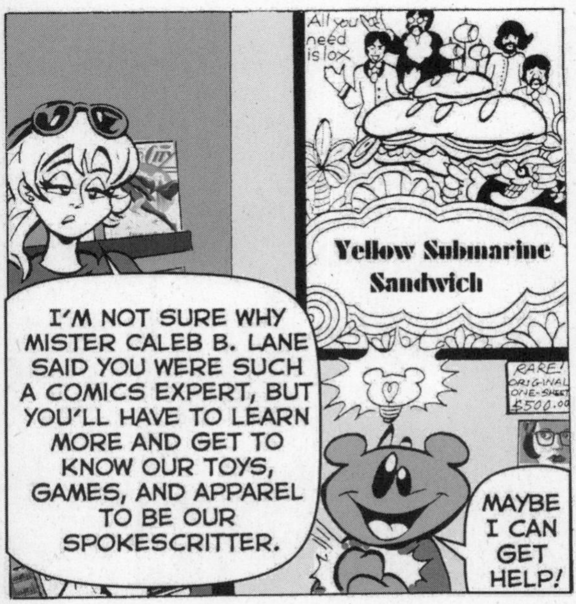
All you need is lox
Yellow Submarine Sandwich
RARE! ORIGINAL ONE-SHEET $500.00
I'M NOT SURE WHY MISTER CALEB B. LANE SAID YOU WERE SUCH A COMICS EXPERT, BUT YOU'LL HAVE TO LEARN MORE AND GET TO KNOW OUR TOYS, GAMES, AND APPAREL TO BE OUR SPOKESCRITTER.
MAYBE I CAN GET HELP!

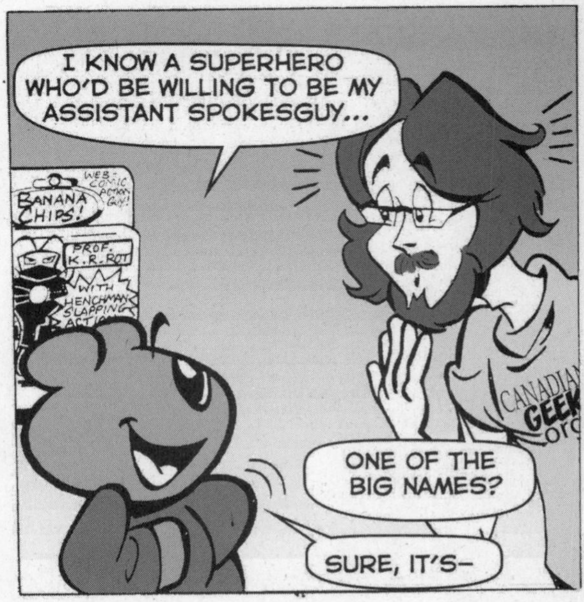
I KNOW A SUPERHERO WHO'D BE WILLING TO BE MY ASSISTANT SPOKESGUY...
BANANA CHIPS!
WEB-COMIC ACTION GUY!
PROF. K.R. ROT
CANADIAN GEEK .org
ONE OF THE BIG NAMES?
SURE, IT'S–

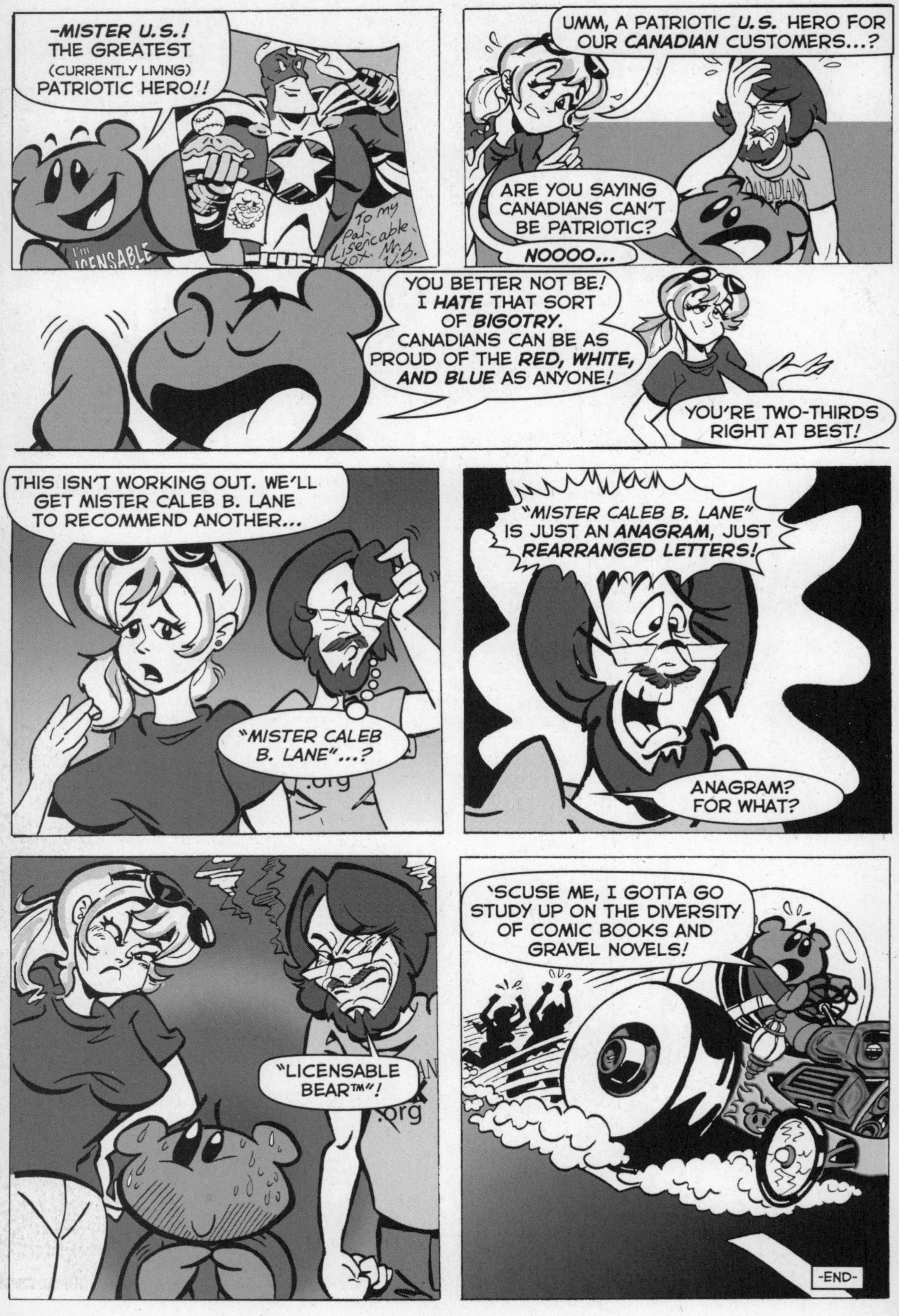
-MISTER U.S.! THE GREATEST (CURRENTLY LIVING) PATRIOTIC HERO!!
To my Pal Lisencable xox Mr. U.S.
I'm LICENSABLE
UMM, A PATRIOTIC U.S. HERO FOR OUR CANADIAN CUSTOMERS...?
ARE YOU SAYING CANADIANS CAN'T BE PATRIOTIC?
NOOOO...
YOU BETTER NOT BE! I HATE THAT SORT OF BIGOTRY. CANADIANS CAN BE AS PROUD OF THE RED, WHITE, AND BLUE AS ANYONE!
YOU'RE TWO-THIRDS RIGHT AT BEST!
THIS ISN'T WORKING OUT. WE'LL GET MISTER CALEB B. LANE TO RECOMMEND ANOTHER...
"MISTER CALEB B. LANE"...?
"MISTER CALEB B. LANE" IS JUST AN ANAGRAM, JUST REARRANGED LETTERS!
ANAGRAM? FOR WHAT?
"LICENSABLE BEAR™"!
'SCUSE ME, I GOTTA GO STUDY UP ON THE DIVERSITY OF COMIC BOOKS AND GRAVEL NOVELS!
-END-

LICENSABLE BEAR™ Rolls Out

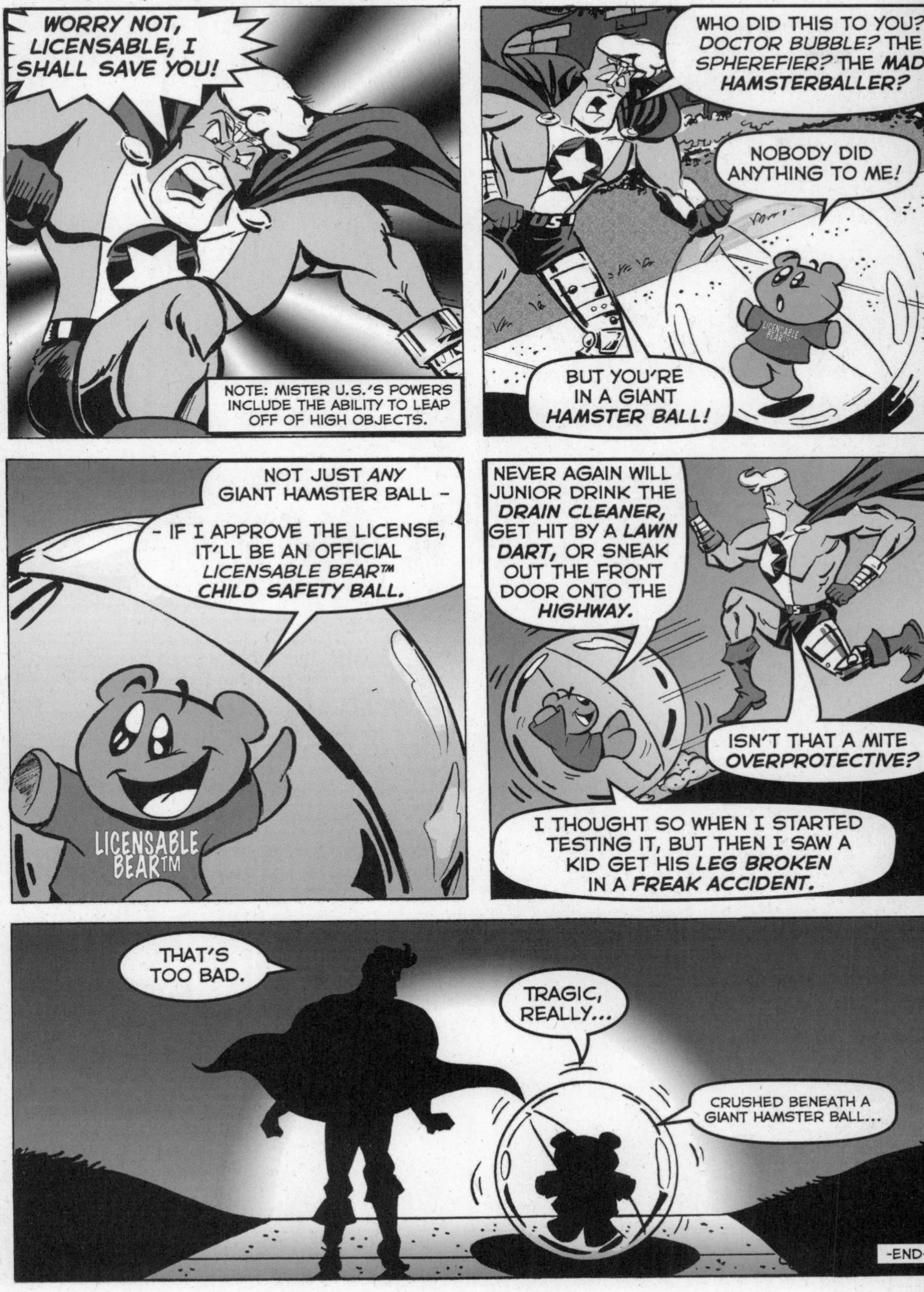
WORRY NOT, LICENSABLE, I SHALL SAVE YOU!
NOTE: MISTER U.S.'S POWERS INCLUDE THE ABILITY TO LEAP OFF OF HIGH OBJECTS.
WHO DID THIS TO YOU? DOCTOR BUBBLE? THE SPHEREFIER? THE MAD HAMSTERBALLER?
NOBODY DID ANYTHING TO ME!
LICENSABLE BEAR™
BUT YOU'RE IN A GIANT HAMSTER BALL!
NOT JUST ANY GIANT HAMSTER BALL –
– IF I APPROVE THE LICENSE, IT'LL BE AN OFFICIAL LICENSABLE BEAR™ CHILD SAFETY BALL.
LICENSABLE BEAR™
NEVER AGAIN WILL JUNIOR DRINK THE DRAIN CLEANER, GET HIT BY A LAWN DART, OR SNEAK OUT THE FRONT DOOR ONTO THE HIGHWAY.
ISN'T THAT A MITE OVERPROTECTIVE?
I THOUGHT SO WHEN I STARTED TESTING IT, BUT THEN I SAW A KID GET HIS LEG BROKEN IN A FREAK ACCIDENT.
THAT'S TOO BAD.
TRAGIC, REALLY...
CRUSHED BENEATH A GIANT HAMSTER BALL...
-END-

LICENSABLE BEAR™ Satisfies a Customer

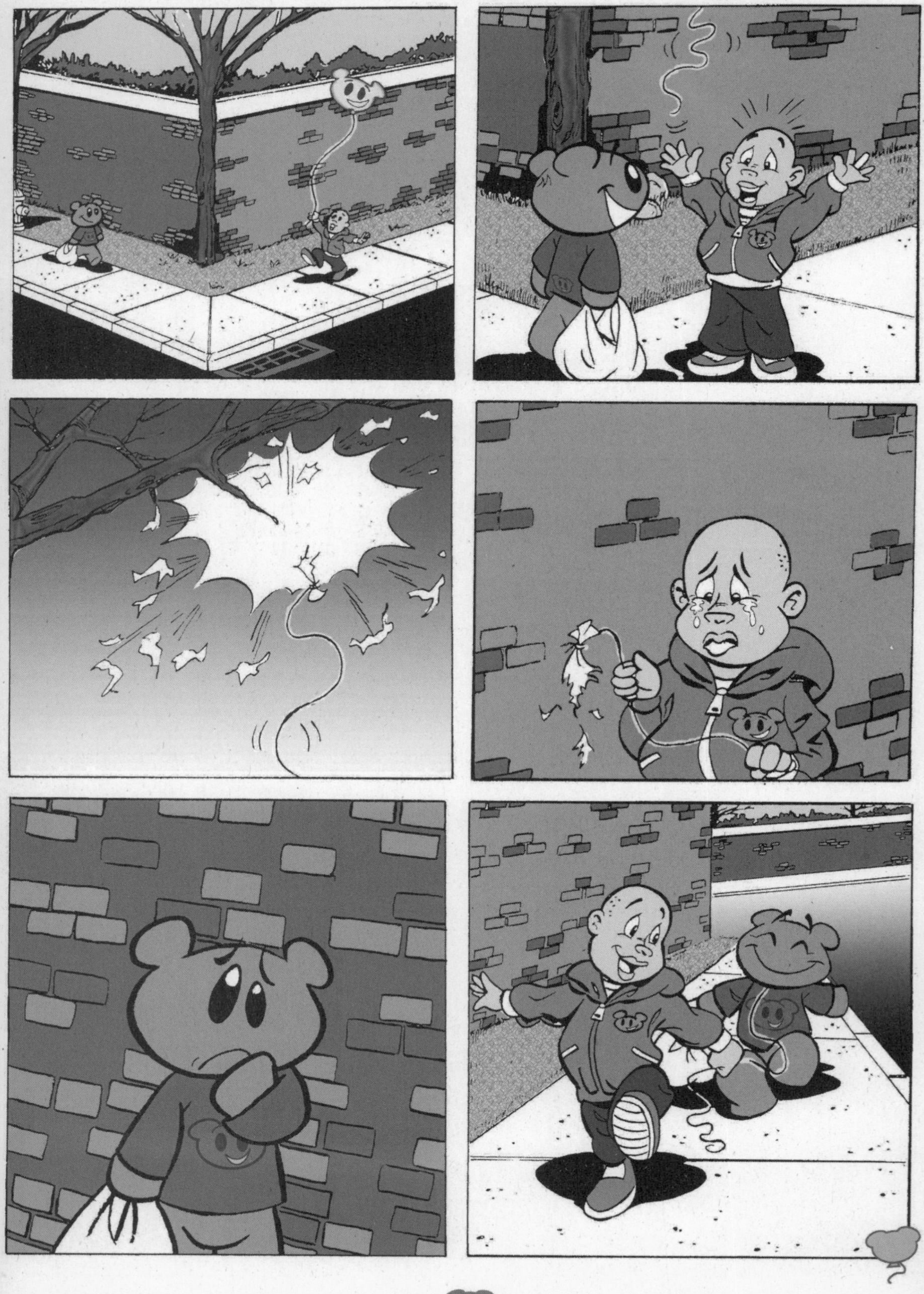

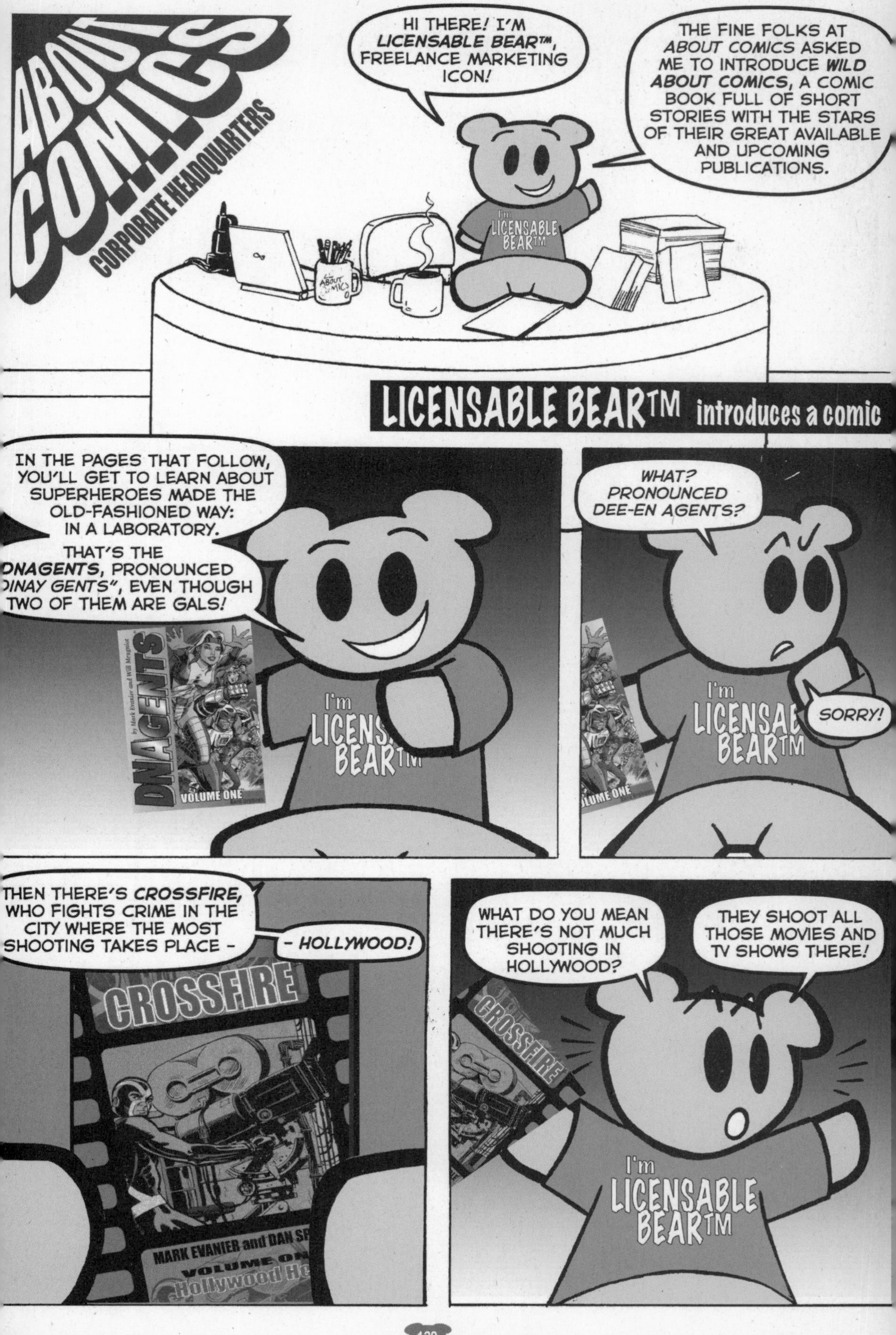
ABOUT COMICS
CORPORATE HEADQUARTERS
HI THERE! I'M LICENSABLE BEAR™, FREELANCE MARKETING ICON!
THE FINE FOLKS AT ABOUT COMICS ASKED ME TO INTRODUCE WILD ABOUT COMICS, A COMIC BOOK FULL OF SHORT STORIES WITH THE STARS OF THEIR GREAT AVAILABLE AND UPCOMING PUBLICATIONS.
I'm LICENSABLE BEAR™
LICENSABLE BEAR™ introduces a comic
IN THE PAGES THAT FOLLOW, YOU'LL GET TO LEARN ABOUT SUPERHEROES MADE THE OLD-FASHIONED WAY: IN A LABORATORY.
THAT'S THE DNAGENTS, PRONOUNCED "DINAY GENTS", EVEN THOUGH TWO OF THEM ARE GALS!
DNAGENTS
by Mark Evanier and Will Meugniot
VOLUME ONE
I'm LICENSABLE BEAR™
WHAT? PRONOUNCED DEE-EN AGENTS?
SORRY!
THEN THERE'S CROSSFIRE, WHO FIGHTS CRIME IN THE CITY WHERE THE MOST SHOOTING TAKES PLACE -
- HOLLYWOOD!
CROSSFIRE
MARK EVANIER and DAN SP
VOLUME ON
Hollywood He
WHAT DO YOU MEAN THERE'S NOT MUCH SHOOTING IN HOLLYWOOD?
THEY SHOOT ALL THOSE MOVIES AND TV SHOWS THERE!
CROSSFIRE
I'm LICENSABLE BEAR™

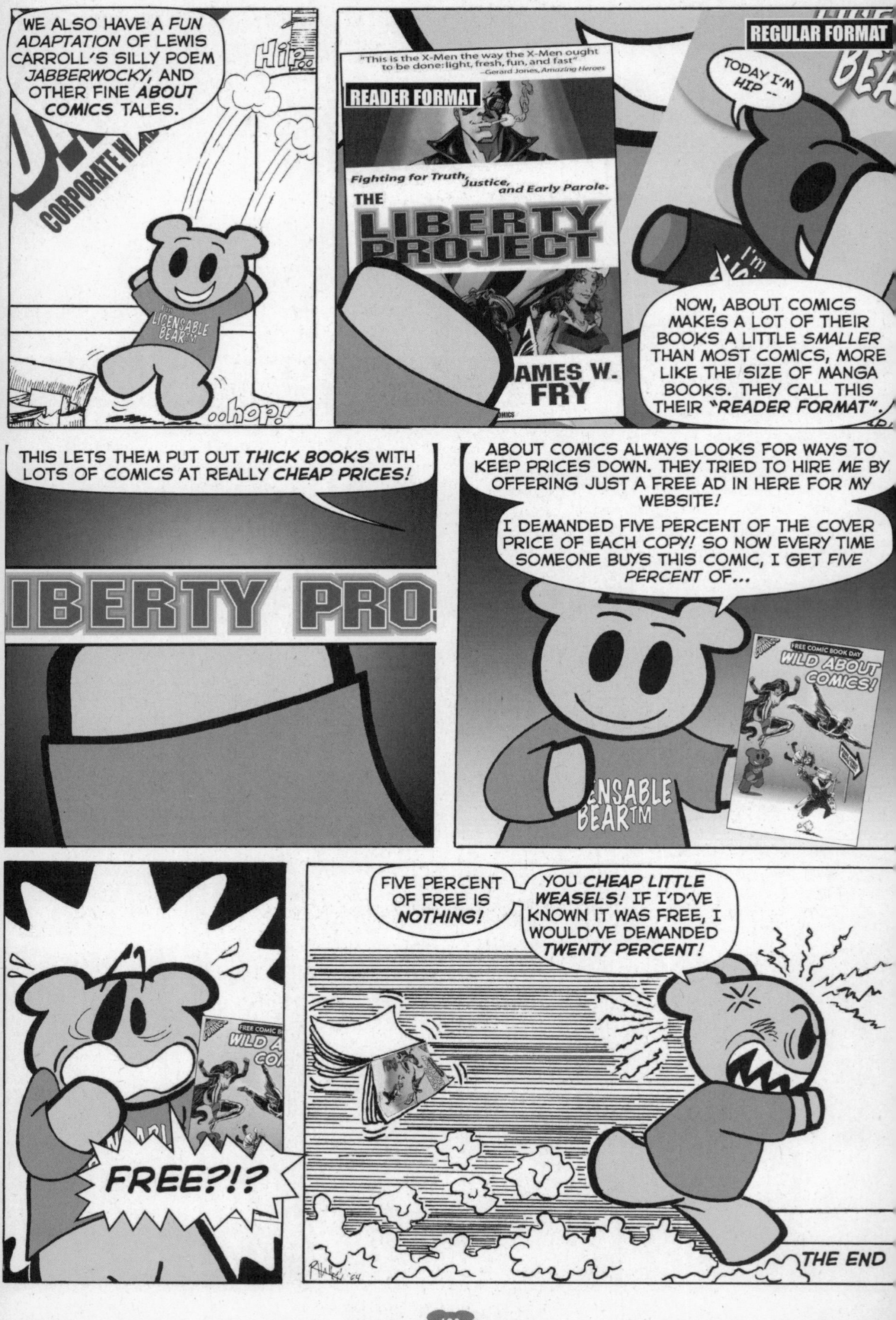

WE ALSO HAVE A *FUN ADAPTATION* OF LEWIS CARROLL'S SILLY POEM *JABBERWOCKY*, AND OTHER FINE *ABOUT COMICS* TALES.
Hip...
CORPORATE H
I'M LICENSABLE BEAR™
...hop!
REGULAR FORMAT
TODAY I'M HIP --
"This is the X-Men the way the X-Men ought to be done: light, fresh, fun, and fast" –Gerard Jones, *Amazing Heroes*
READER FORMAT
Fighting for Truth, Justice, and Early Parole.
THE LIBERTY PROJECT
JAMES W. FRY
NOW, ABOUT COMICS MAKES A LOT OF THEIR BOOKS A LITTLE *SMALLER* THAN MOST COMICS, MORE LIKE THE SIZE OF MANGA BOOKS. THEY CALL THIS THEIR *"READER FORMAT"*.
THIS LETS THEM PUT OUT *THICK BOOKS* WITH LOTS OF COMICS AT REALLY *CHEAP PRICES!*
IBERTY PRO
ABOUT COMICS ALWAYS LOOKS FOR WAYS TO KEEP PRICES DOWN. THEY TRIED TO HIRE *ME* BY OFFERING JUST A FREE AD IN HERE FOR MY WEBSITE!
I DEMANDED FIVE PERCENT OF THE COVER PRICE OF EACH COPY! SO NOW EVERY TIME SOMEONE BUYS THIS COMIC, I GET *FIVE PERCENT* OF...
FREE COMIC BOOK DAY
WILD ABOUT COMICS!
ENSABLE BEAR™
FREE?!?
FIVE PERCENT OF FREE IS *NOTHING!*
YOU *CHEAP LITTLE WEASELS!* IF I'D'VE KNOWN IT WAS FREE, I WOULD'VE DEMANDED *TWENTY PERCENT!*
THE END

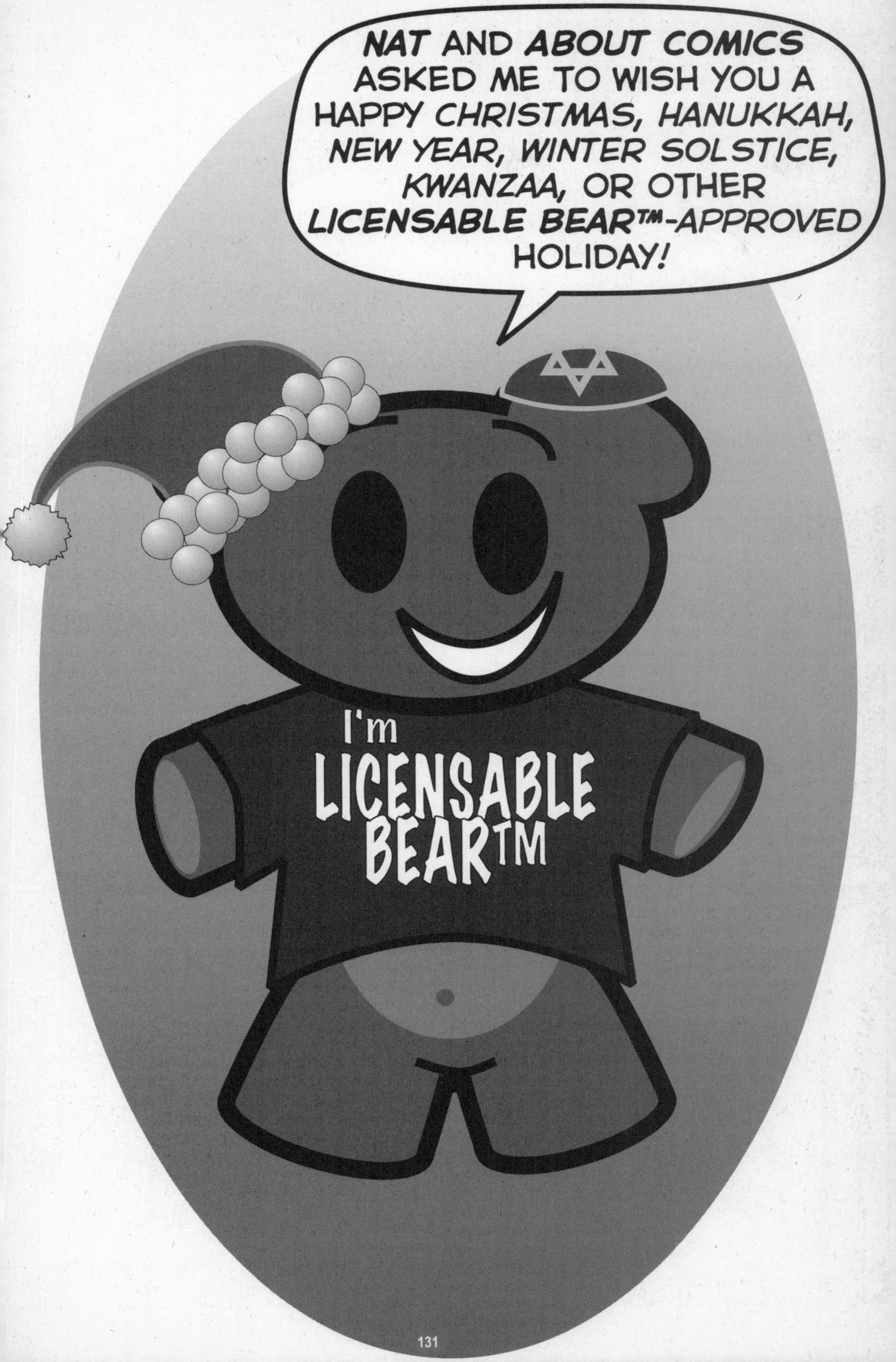
NAT AND ABOUT COMICS ASKED ME TO WISH YOU A HAPPY CHRISTMAS, HANUKKAH, NEW YEAR, WINTER SOLSTICE, KWANZAA, OR OTHER LICENSABLE BEAR™-APPROVED HOLIDAY!
I'm LICENSABLE BEAR™

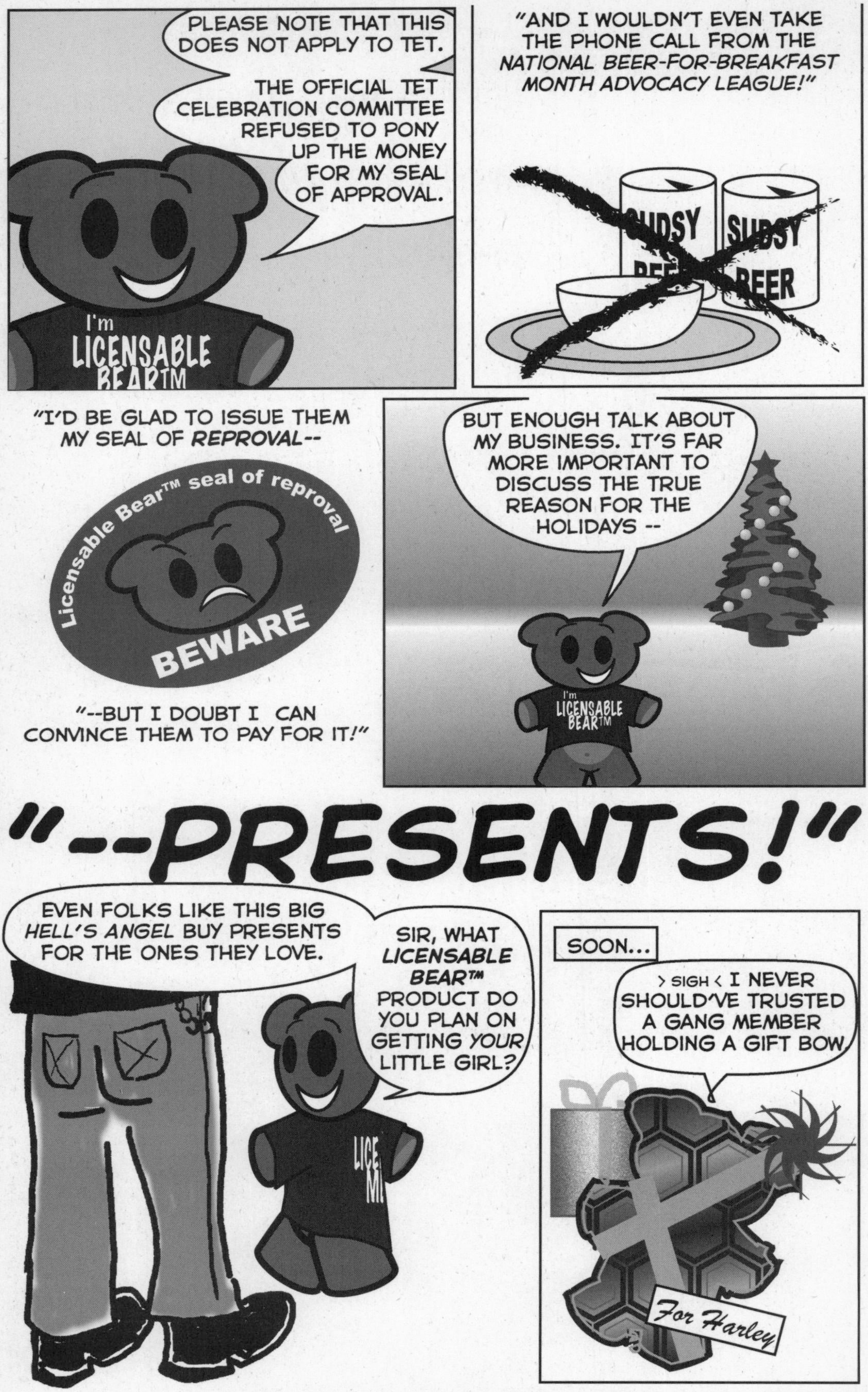
PLEASE NOTE THAT THIS DOES NOT APPLY TO TET.
THE OFFICIAL TET CELEBRATION COMMITTEE REFUSED TO PONY UP THE MONEY FOR MY SEAL OF APPROVAL.
I'm LICENSABLE BEAR™
"AND I WOULDN'T EVEN TAKE THE PHONE CALL FROM THE *NATIONAL BEER-FOR-BREAKFAST MONTH ADVOCACY LEAGUE!*"
SUDSY BEER
SUDSY BEER
"I'D BE GLAD TO ISSUE THEM MY SEAL OF *REPROVAL*--
Licensable Bear™ seal of reproval
BEWARE
"--BUT I DOUBT I CAN CONVINCE THEM TO PAY FOR IT!"
BUT ENOUGH TALK ABOUT MY BUSINESS. IT'S FAR MORE IMPORTANT TO DISCUSS THE TRUE REASON FOR THE HOLIDAYS --
I'm LICENSABLE BEAR™
"--PRESENTS!"
EVEN FOLKS LIKE THIS BIG *HELL'S ANGEL* BUY PRESENTS FOR THE ONES THEY LOVE.
SIR, WHAT *LICENSABLE BEAR™* PRODUCT DO YOU PLAN ON GETTING *YOUR* LITTLE GIRL?
SOON...
> SIGH < I NEVER SHOULD'VE TRUSTED A GANG MEMBER HOLDING A GIFT BOW.
For Harley

DON'T GET TOO WRAPPED UP TO ENJOY THE HOLIDAYS!

LICENSABLE BEAR™ Corrects the Press

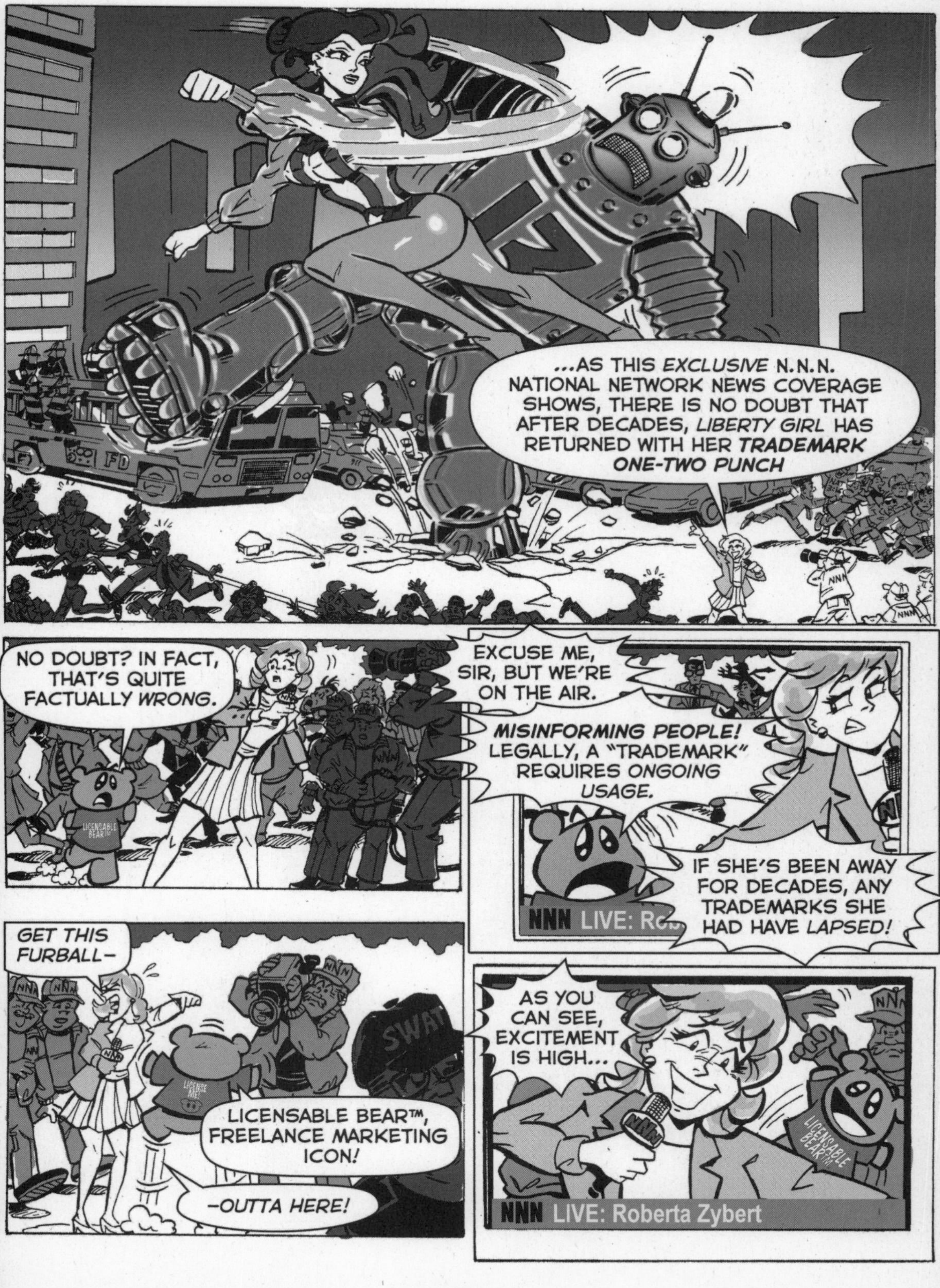
...AS THIS EXCLUSIVE N.N.N. NATIONAL NETWORK NEWS COVERAGE SHOWS, THERE IS NO DOUBT THAT AFTER DECADES, LIBERTY GIRL HAS RETURNED WITH HER TRADEMARK ONE-TWO PUNCH
FD
NO DOUBT? IN FACT, THAT'S QUITE FACTUALLY WRONG.
EXCUSE ME, SIR, BUT WE'RE ON THE AIR.
MISINFORMING PEOPLE! LEGALLY, A "TRADEMARK" REQUIRES ONGOING USAGE.
IF SHE'S BEEN AWAY FOR DECADES, ANY TRADEMARKS SHE HAD HAVE LAPSED!
NNN LIVE: Ro
GET THIS FURBALL–
LICENSABLE BEAR™, FREELANCE MARKETING ICON!
–OUTTA HERE!
SWAT
AS YOU CAN SEE, EXCITEMENT IS HIGH...
NNN LIVE: Roberta Zybert

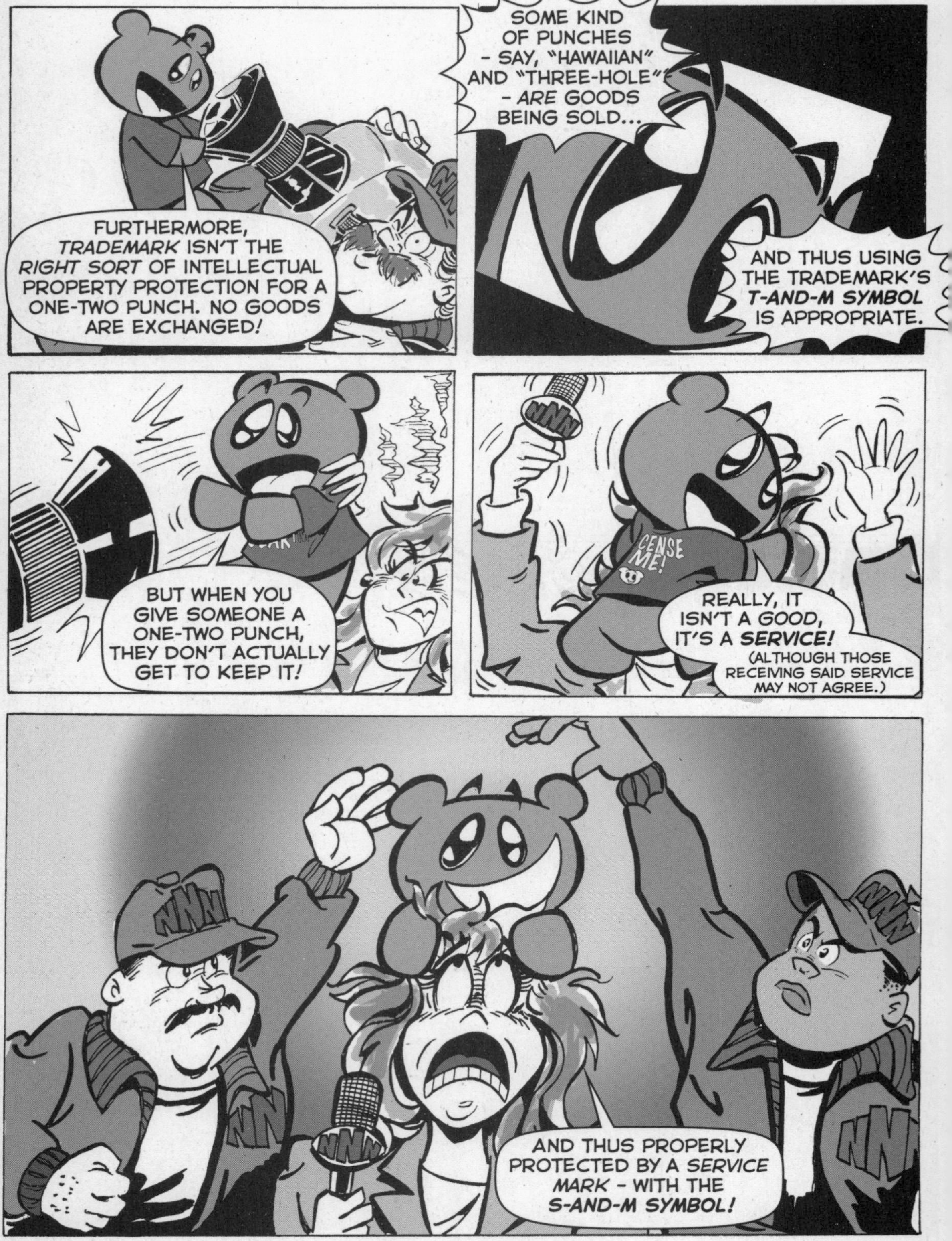
FURTHERMORE, TRADEMARK ISN'T THE RIGHT SORT OF INTELLECTUAL PROPERTY PROTECTION FOR A ONE-TWO PUNCH. NO GOODS ARE EXCHANGED!
SOME KIND OF PUNCHES - SAY, "HAWAIIAN" AND "THREE-HOLE" - ARE GOODS BEING SOLD...
AND THUS USING THE TRADEMARK'S T-AND-M SYMBOL IS APPROPRIATE.
BUT WHEN YOU GIVE SOMEONE A ONE-TWO PUNCH, THEY DON'T ACTUALLY GET TO KEEP IT!
CENSE ME!
REALLY, IT ISN'T A GOOD, IT'S A SERVICE!
(ALTHOUGH THOSE RECEIVING SAID SERVICE MAY NOT AGREE.)
AND THUS PROPERLY PROTECTED BY A SERVICE MARK - WITH THE S-AND-M SYMBOL!

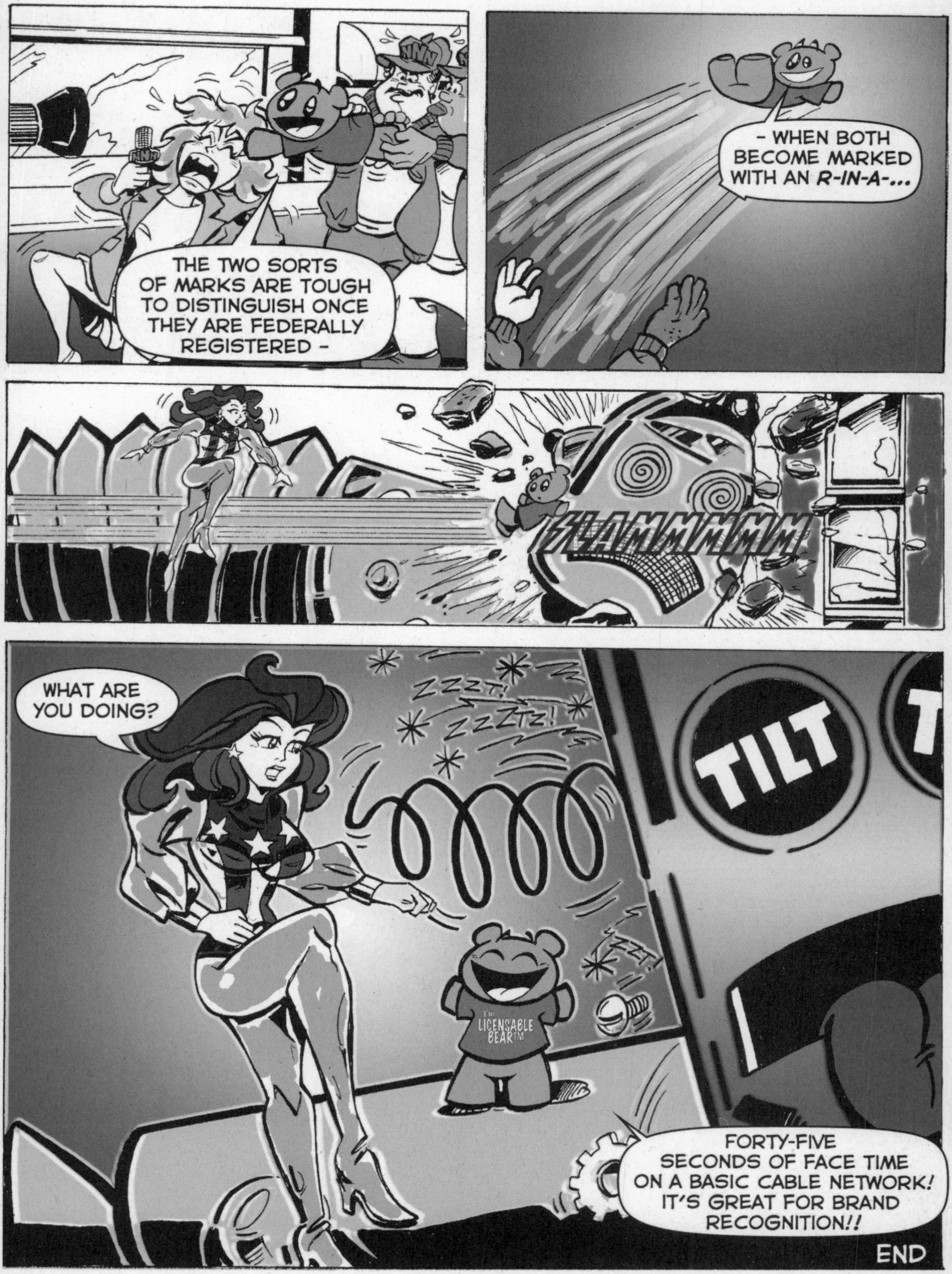
THE TWO SORTS OF MARKS ARE TOUGH TO DISTINGUISH ONCE THEY ARE FEDERALLY REGISTERED -
- WHEN BOTH BECOME MARKED WITH AN R-IN-A-...
SLAMMMMMMM!
WHAT ARE YOU DOING?
ZZZT!
ZZZTZ!
TILT
I'm LICENSABLE BEAR™
FORTY-FIVE SECONDS OF FACE TIME ON A BASIC CABLE NETWORK! IT'S GREAT FOR BRAND RECOGNITION!!
END

COVER GALLERY

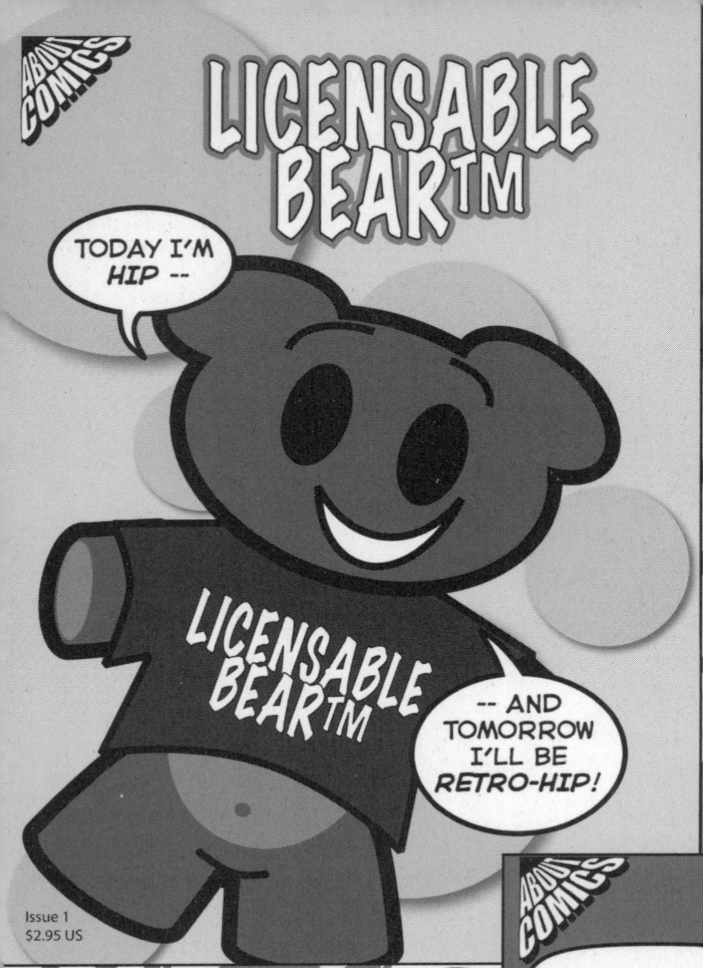
ABOUT COMICS
LICENSABLE BEAR™
TODAY I'M HIP --
LICENSABLE BEAR™
-- AND TOMORROW I'LL BE RETRO-HIP!
Issue 1
$2.95 US

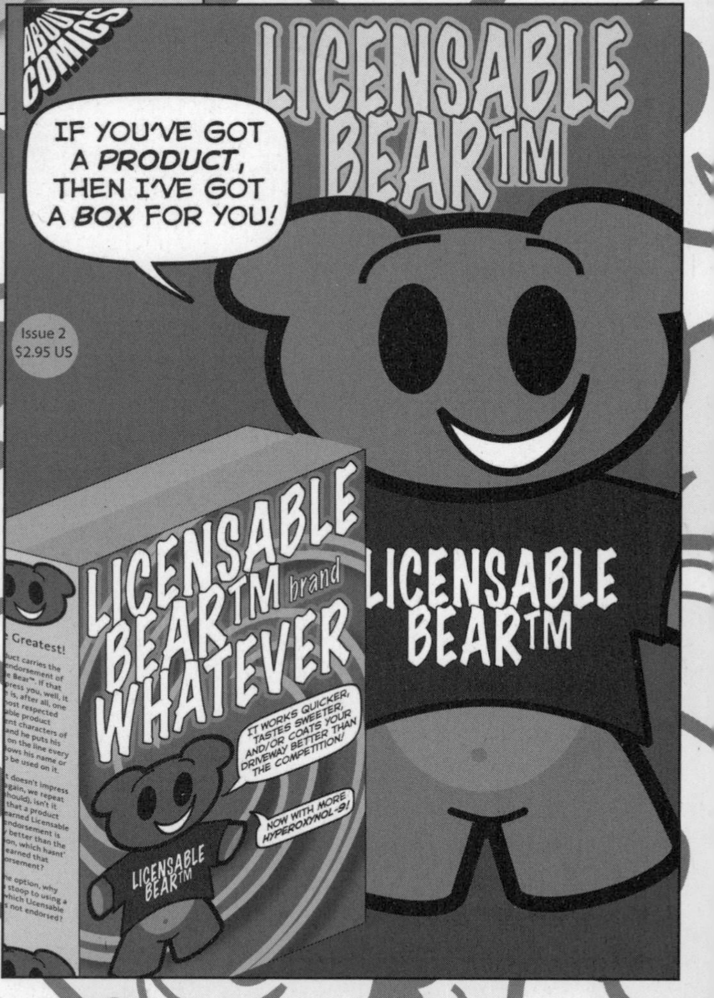
ABOUT COMICS
LICENSABLE BEAR™
IF YOU'VE GOT A PRODUCT, THEN I'VE GOT A BOX FOR YOU!
Issue 2
$2.95 US
LICENSABLE BEAR™ brand WHATEVER
IT WORKS QUICKER, TASTES SWEETER, AND/OR COATS YOUR DRIVEWAY BETTER THAN THE COMPETITION!
NOW WITH MORE HYPEROXYNOL-9!
LICENSABLE BEAR™
LICENSABLE BEAR™

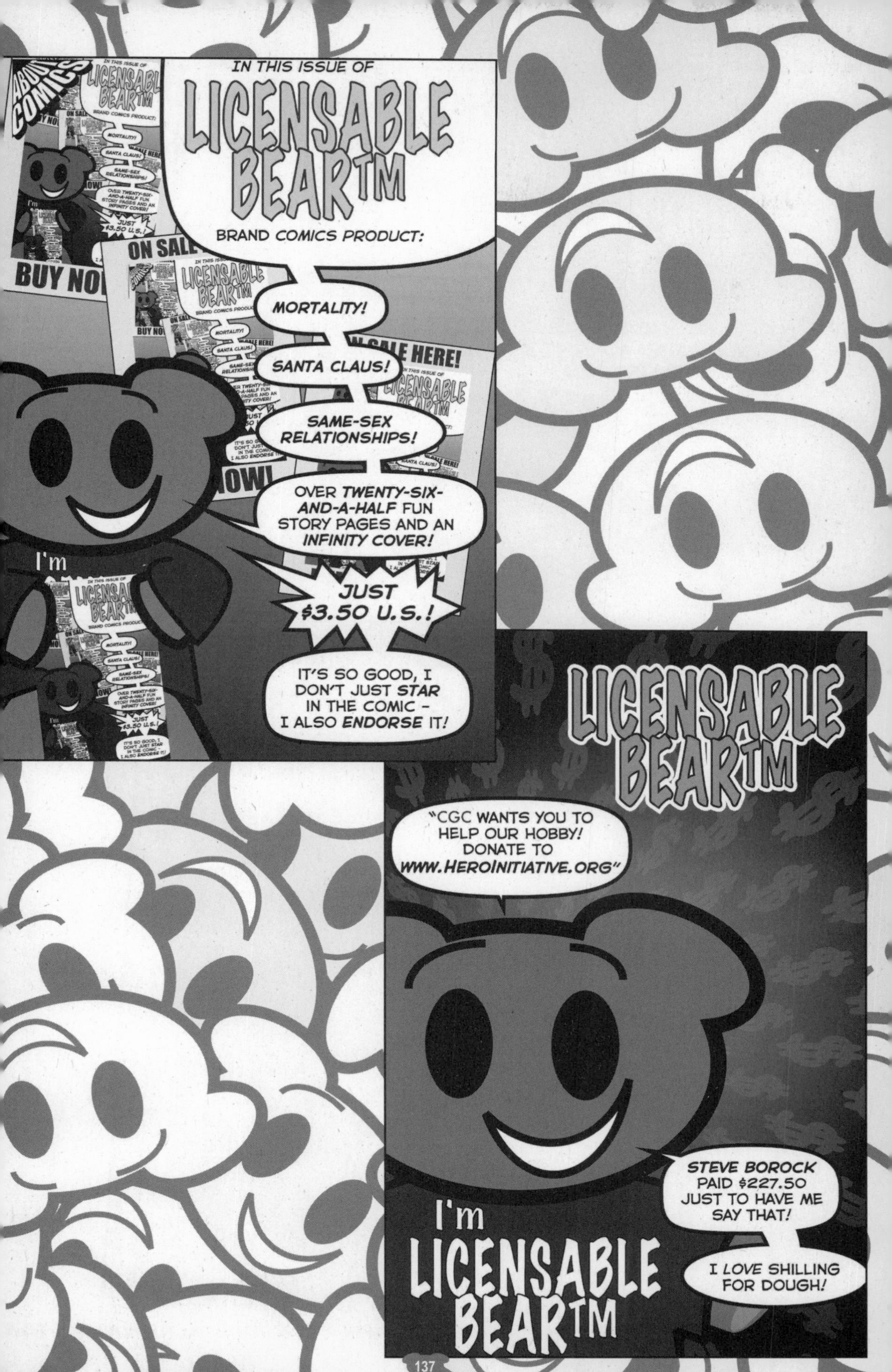
IN THIS ISSUE OF
LICENSABLE BEAR™
BRAND COMICS PRODUCT:
MORTALITY!
SANTA CLAUS!
SAME-SEX RELATIONSHIPS!
OVER TWENTY-SIX-AND-A-HALF FUN STORY PAGES AND AN INFINITY COVER!
JUST $3.50 U.S.!
IT'S SO GOOD, I DON'T JUST STAR IN THE COMIC – I ALSO ENDORSE IT!
I'm
LICENSABLE BEAR™
"CGC WANTS YOU TO HELP OUR HOBBY! DONATE TO WWW.HEROINITIATIVE.ORG"
STEVE BOROCK PAID $227.50 JUST TO HAVE ME SAY THAT!
I LOVE SHILLING FOR DOUGH!
I'm
LICENSABLE BEAR™

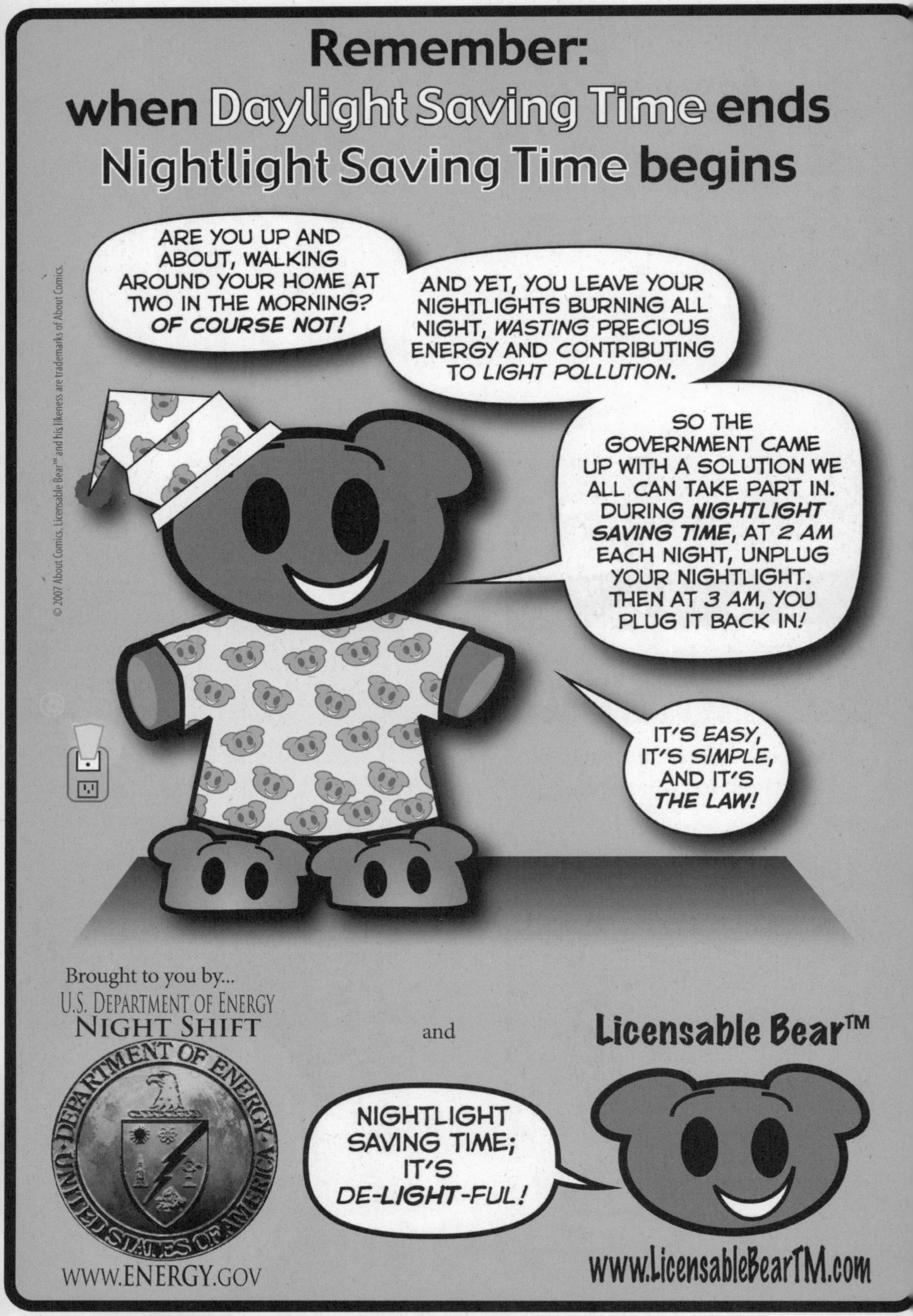
Remember:
when Daylight Saving Time ends
Nightlight Saving Time begins
ARE YOU UP AND ABOUT, WALKING AROUND YOUR HOME AT TWO IN THE MORNING? OF COURSE NOT!
AND YET, YOU LEAVE YOUR NIGHTLIGHTS BURNING ALL NIGHT, WASTING PRECIOUS ENERGY AND CONTRIBUTING TO LIGHT POLLUTION.
SO THE GOVERNMENT CAME UP WITH A SOLUTION WE ALL CAN TAKE PART IN. DURING NIGHTLIGHT SAVING TIME, AT 2 AM EACH NIGHT, UNPLUG YOUR NIGHTLIGHT. THEN AT 3 AM, YOU PLUG IT BACK IN!
IT'S EASY, IT'S SIMPLE, AND IT'S THE LAW!
Brought to you by...
U.S. DEPARTMENT OF ENERGY NIGHT SHIFT
and
Licensable Bear™
NIGHTLIGHT SAVING TIME; IT'S DE-LIGHT-FUL!
WWW.ENERGY.GOV
www.LicensableBearTM.com
© 2007 About Comics. Licensable Bear™ and his likeness are trademarks of About Comics.

STORYBOARD: Licensable Bear™ PSA

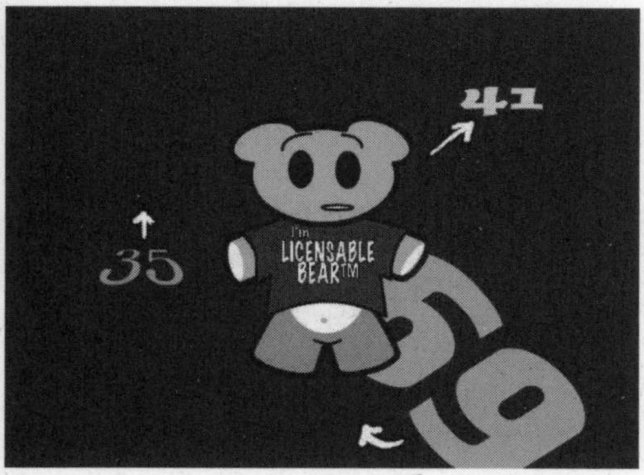
41
35
I'm
LICENSABLE
BEAR™

There are many sad forms of discrimination in this world...

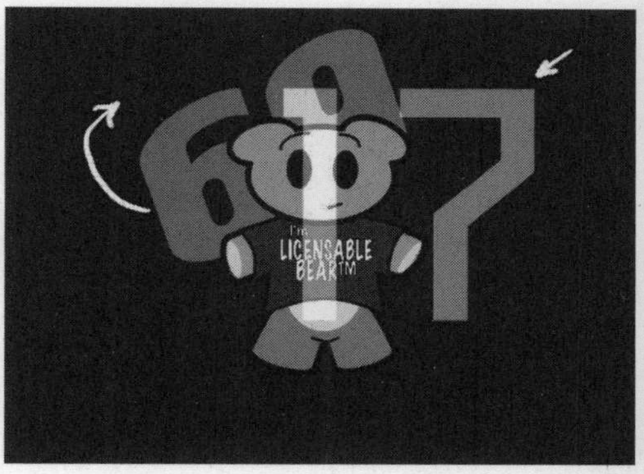
I'm
LICENSABLE
BEAR™

...but one of the saddest is <u>numeric discrimination</u>.

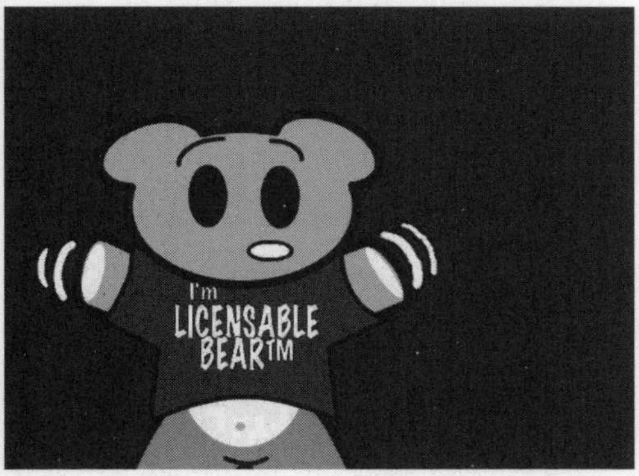
I'm
LICENSABLE
BEAR™

Some people call certain numbers "odd"...

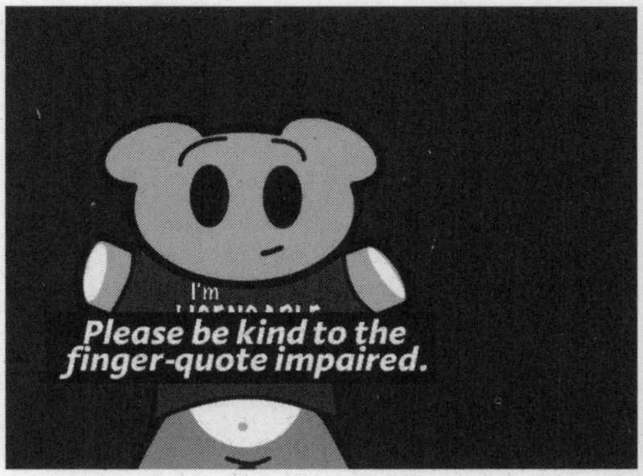
I'm
Please be kind to the finger-quote impaired.

...just because they don't perceive them as being as <u>even</u> as other numbers.

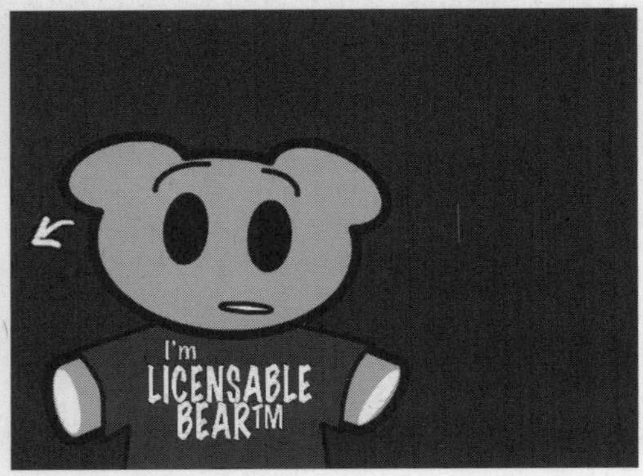
I'm
LICENSABLE
BEAR™

But there's no such thing as an odd number!

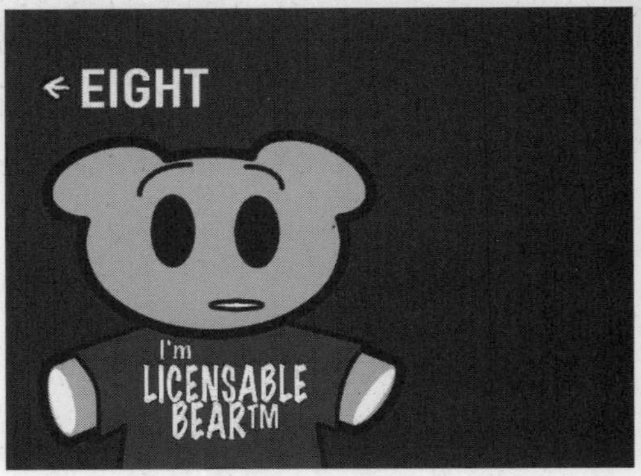
EIGHT
I'm
LICENSABLE
BEAR™

Sure, eight is a sufficiently even number...

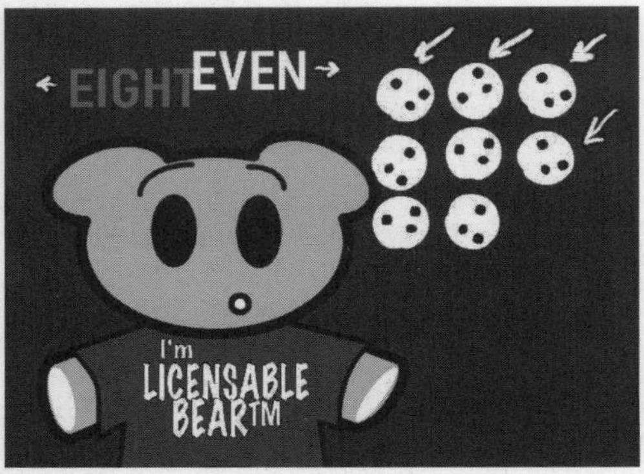
EIGHT
EVEN
I'm
LICENSABLE
BEAR™

...that we can all consider eight cookies an even number of cookies.

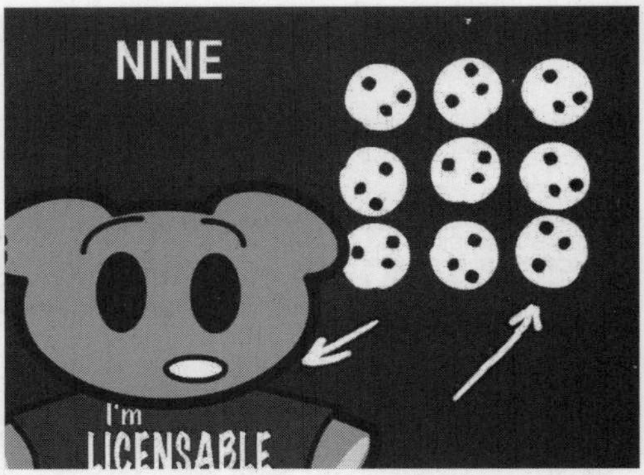
NINE
I'm
LICENSABLE

But nine cookies?

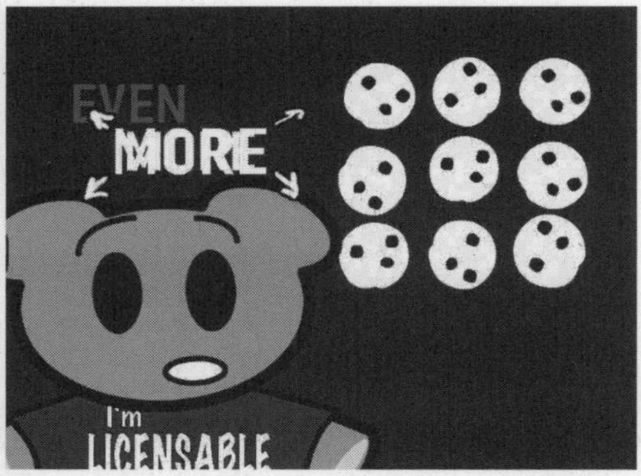
EVEN
MORE
I'm
LICENSABLE

That's even <u>more</u> than eight!

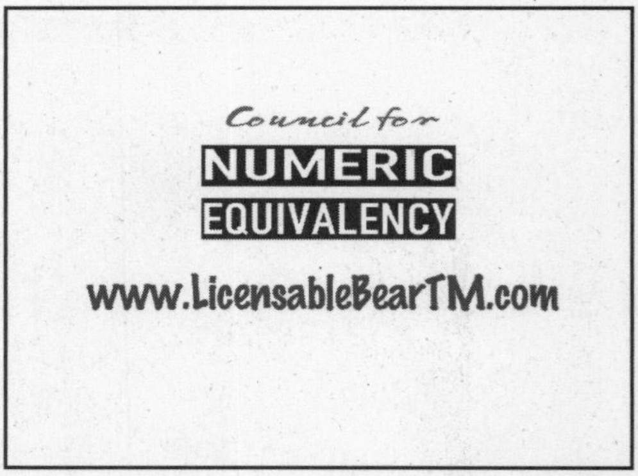
Council for
NUMERIC
EQUIVALENCY
www.LicensableBearTM.com

This message brought to you by Licensable Bear™ and the Council for Numeric Equivalency, looking forward to the day when <u>all</u> numbers will be <u>equal</u>.

Product Art

Bibs and babyware

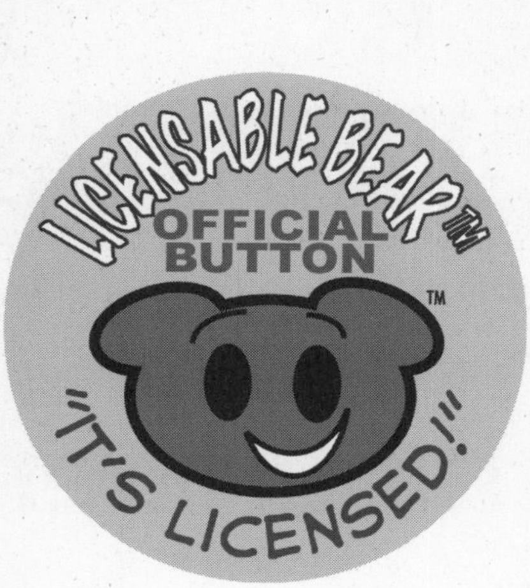
LICENSABLE BEAR™
OFFICIAL BUTTON
™
"IT'S LICENSED!"

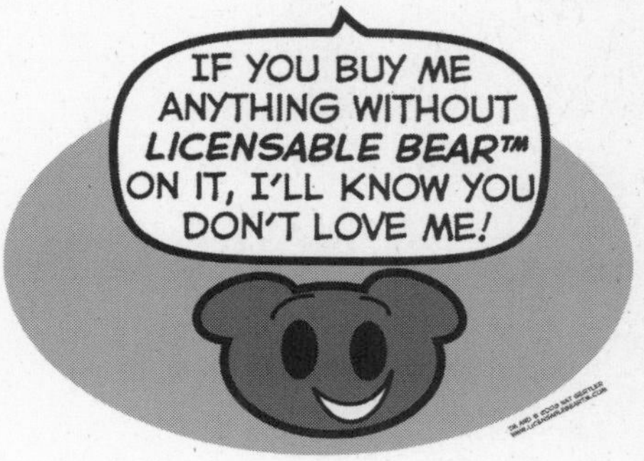
IF YOU BUY ME ANYTHING WITHOUT LICENSABLE BEAR™ ON IT, I'LL KNOW YOU DON'T LOVE ME!

Specialty t-shirts

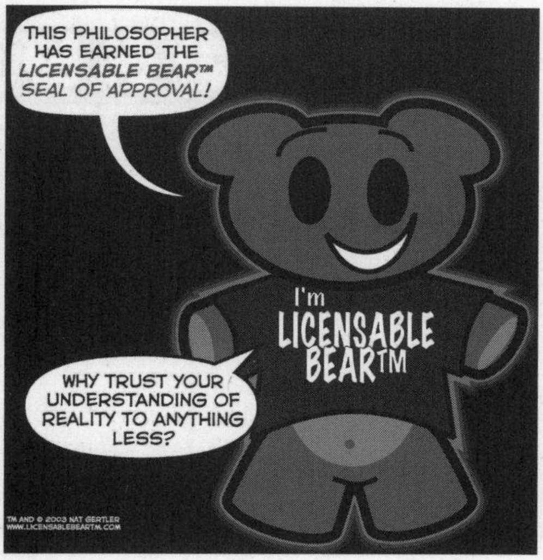
THIS PHILOSOPHER HAS EARNED THE LICENSABLE BEAR™ SEAL OF APPROVAL!
I'm LICENSABLE BEAR™
WHY TRUST YOUR UNDERSTANDING OF REALITY TO ANYTHING LESS?
TM AND © 2003 NAT GERTLER
WWW.LICENSABLEBEARTM.COM

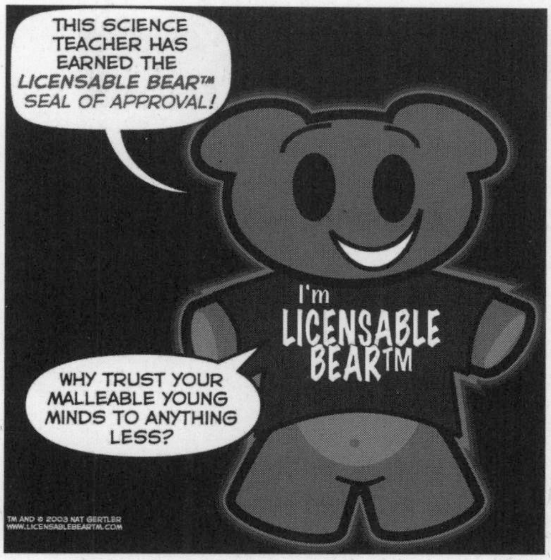
THIS SCIENCE TEACHER HAS EARNED THE LICENSABLE BEAR™ SEAL OF APPROVAL!
I'm LICENSABLE BEAR™
WHY TRUST YOUR MALLEABLE YOUNG MINDS TO ANYTHING LESS?
TM AND © 2003 NAT GERTLER
WWW.LICENSABLEBEARTM.COM

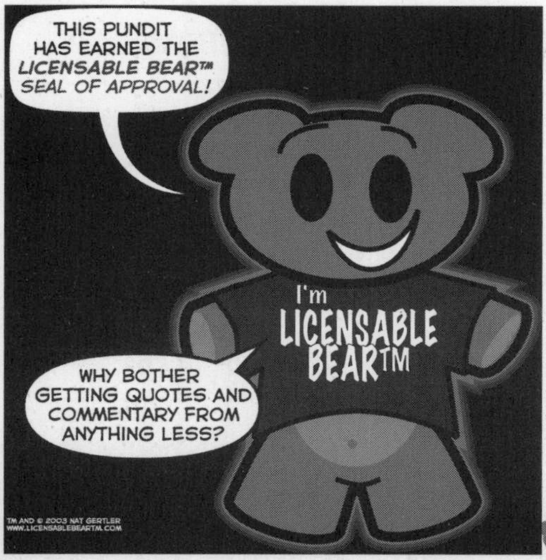
THIS PUNDIT HAS EARNED THE LICENSABLE BEAR™ SEAL OF APPROVAL!
I'm LICENSABLE BEAR™
WHY BOTHER GETTING QUOTES AND COMMENTARY FROM ANYTHING LESS?
TM AND © 2003 NAT GERTLER
WWW.LICENSABLEBEARTM.COM

Button for specialty t-shirts

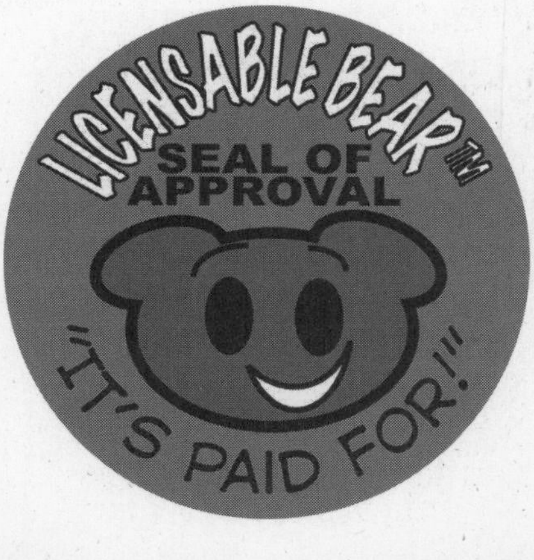
LICENSABLE BEAR™
SEAL OF APPROVAL
"IT'S PAID FOR!"

I GET *SEVEN POINT FIVE PERCENT* OF THE ADJUSTED WHOLESALE PRICE OF THIS SHIRT!
I'm LICENSABLE BEARTM
TM AND © 2003 NAT GERTLER
WWW.LICENSABLEBEARTM.COM

I GET SEVEN POINT FIVE PERCENT OF THE ADJUSTED WHOLESALE PRICE OF THIS SHIRT!
LICENSE ME!
TM AND © 2003 NAT GERTLER
WWW.LICENSABLEBEARTM.COM

Council for

NUMERIC EQUIVALENCY

"Some day,

all numbers

will be

equal."

General graphics (shirts, bumperstickers, tote bags)

ENEMIES of the LIBRARY™

Enemies of the Library™
Semi-annual
Used Weenie Sale

& Book Roast

Nat Gertler has a long history of writing short autobiographical pieces for publications. Had he spent that time living his life instead of writing about it, he might have more to actually say. He might write about the fires he's fought, the legislation he's passed, and offer the usual, unconvincing denials about having made love to a string of Hollywood starlets, directors, and two best boys (about whom it is said that they did not live up to one of the words of their job description, but it's not clear which.)

Instead, he is forced to write in rather transparent third person about a rather standard list of achievements, distinctions, and things that he likes to make sound as more impressive than they really are. He'll write about how he's a two-time Eisner Award nominee, hoping that you won't note that he's not saying that he's an Eisner Award winner, which would lead you to realize he's actually a two-time Eisner Award loser. He is the co-author of *The Complete Idiot's Guide to Creating a Graphic Novel* (with *Whiteout*'s Steve Lieber), which has gone through at least seven printings. That's just one of eight *Idiot's Guides* and dozens of books overall to bear his credit.

Nat is also the founder of 24 Hour Comics Day, the annual international celebration of comics creation that has generated tens of thousands of pages of original comics since its inception in 2004. He is in charge of the AAUGH Blog – BLOG.AAUGH.COM – the leading source for collectors of Charles M. Schulz books.

And he's the founder and both top and bottom man on the purely figurative totem pole at About Comics, a publishing and packaging firm specializing in comics and things that relate to comics. As a publisher, they (and clearly that's a corporate "they", which is a real-world "he") have released everything from the forgotten work of Charles M. Schulz to books of example comic book scripts (such as *Panel One*) to, well, *Licensable Bear*™. As a packager, they (he) help (helps) a range of customers who need original comics content created, or need existing comics content found and the rights cleared for them, or who simply need some specific comics-related services performed.

If you want to see more of Gertler's work, we recommend the trade paperback of his alternative superhero miniseries *The Factor*. Ask for it at your local comic book shop or not-so-local online bookseller.

In the movie of his life, Gertler would like to be played by Peter O'Toole (if only because it would mean that they both lived long enough that the many decades of difference in their age was no longer visible.)

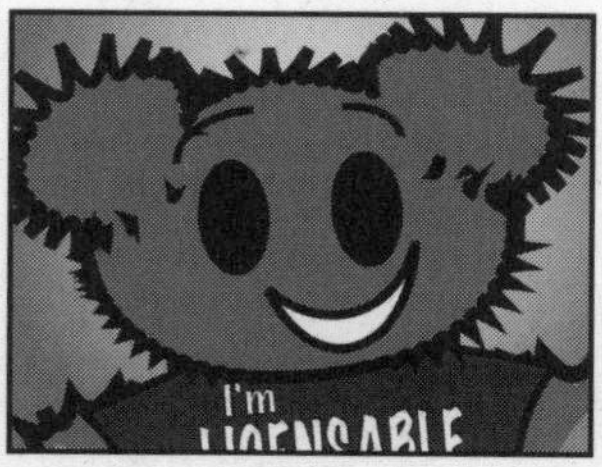
I'm

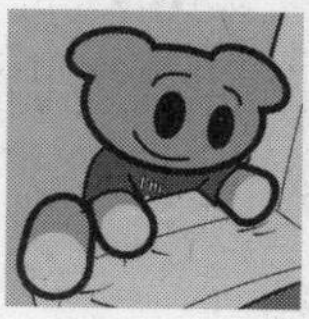

Mark Lewis is the co-creator of Mister U.S. His work has been seen in many of the *Big Bang* comics and on the covers of DC's *JSA All-Stars*, as well as in the pages of his own creation *Bugboy*. Most of the his waking hours are spent working in animation, on such shows as *X-Men*, *Fantastic Four*, and *Care Bears*.

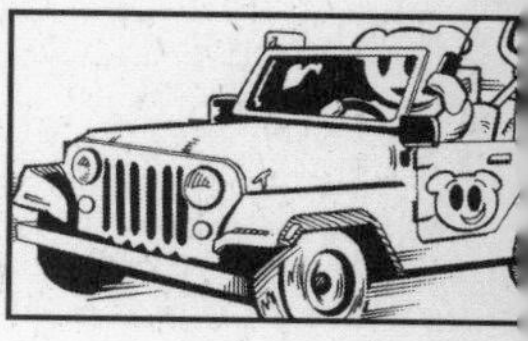

Since drawing Licensable Bear™, Filip Sablik has gone on to become publisher of Top Cow Comics, the folks who bring you *Wanted* and *Witchblade*. It just goes to show how far working with Licensable Bear™ can get you!

Inker Bradley Walton, who worked on Gertler's *The Factor*, manages to juggle his career as a high school librarian, his work as a playwright (*The Bloody Attack of the Evil, Demonic Giraffe Puppet*), and his family. Luckily, his family is small and easy to juggle.

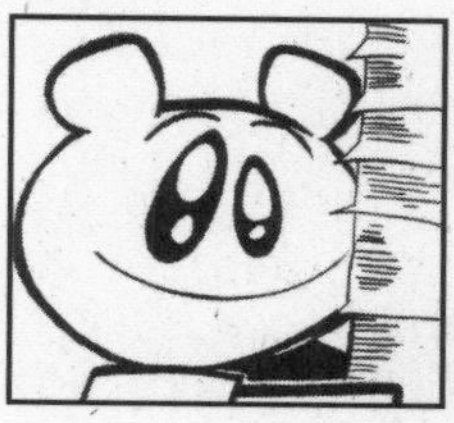

Rusty Haller, who has drawn more Licensable Bear™ stories than anyone, is the creator of the "Ace and Queenie" feature in Radio Comix's *Furrlough*. He's done a lot of character work, doing everything from comic books to coloring books to cookie jar design for such characters as The Flintstones, the Teen Titans, and Betty Boop. His previous comics collaborations with Nat Gertler include work on *The Factor* and *Eek! The Cat*. See more of his work at WWW.ACEANDQUEENIE.COM.

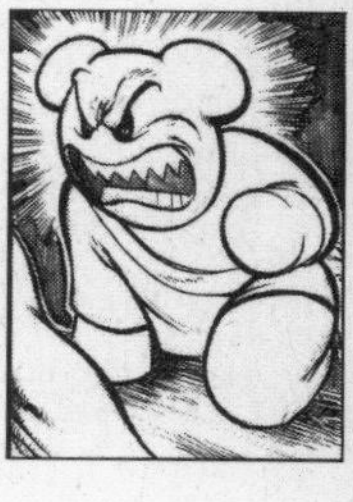

Tone Rodriguez bestrides the earth like a big, friendly, very talented colossus. First getting noticed for his work on *Violent Messiahs*, Tone has illustrated comics such as *Snake Plissken*, *Kiss*, and *The Simpsons*, and is a leading illustrator of trading card "sketch cards." Despite having become a killer on the TV show *Dexter*, Tone is apparently still at large, and has staked out some webspace at WWW.TONEROD.COM.

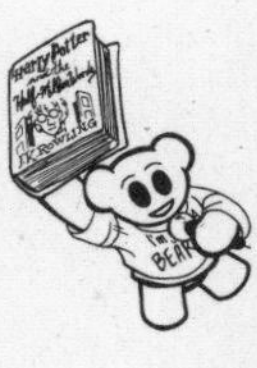

Mark Dos Santos, creator of the comic book *Air Space*, has been working on *Grimm Fairy Tales* and *The Unusual Suspects*. He also sketches the sketch cards. See more of his work at his website, the cryptically-named WWW.MARKDOSSANTOS.COM.

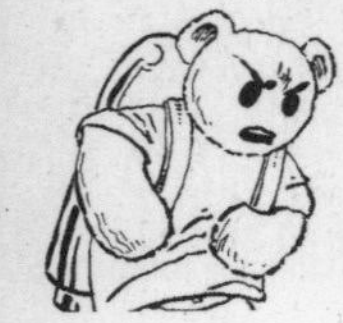

Alexander Grecian, after working with writer Nat Gertler on both *The Factor* and *Licensable Bear*™, was driven to throwing down his artist pen or pencil or crayon or whatever he used, because he could not stand the torment. Instead, he has switched roles to tormentor, writing such comics as *Proof* (for Image Comics) and *Seven Sons* (AiT/PlanetLar.) When he formulates new ways to torment, he will probably post about it at www.AlexanderGrecian.com.

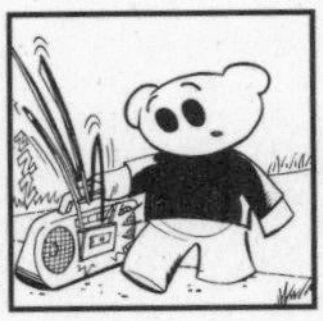

Talented cartoonist Dave Lanphear is better known for the tens of thousands of comics pages he has lettered. He was the head of the lettering department at CrossGen Entertainment, and CEO of Art Monkeys Studios.

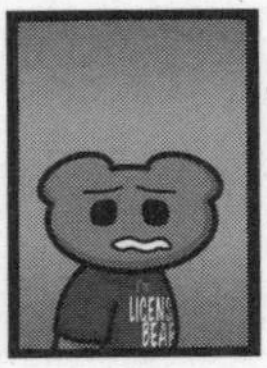

Eric Erbes is the artist of the Out Of This World bibliotherapy comics, and creates a number of online comics including Robo Luv. He got this assignment by answering an artist-wanted ad at DigitalWebbing.com, a handy tip for those seeking collaborators. You can learn more about him and read some of his online comics work at EricErbes.com.

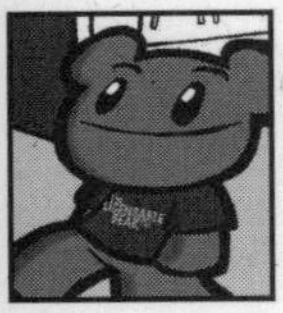

Ryan Estrada is a world traveler, and seems horribly addicted to doing comics in the most intense ways possible. After taking the 24 hour comics challenge (24 pages in 24 hours) several times, and even doing a 72 pages in 72 hours effort, he went and did the world's first 168 Hour Comic, creating a full 168 page tale. If you'd be interested in having Ryan create custom comics for you for an amazingly affordable price, check out www.CartoonCommune.com

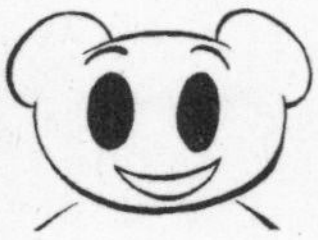

Argentina's Hugo Salvatierra has done "furry" comics for such folks as Radio Comix, Shanda Fantasy Arts, and Mu Press. See some of his other work at osozeth.DeviantArt.com.

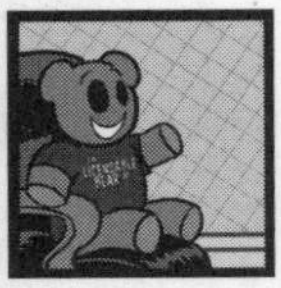

This is Israeli singer and TV show host Nimrod Reshef's U.S. debut. In over a decade of professional cartooning, his artwork has been printed by many of the country's top publishers. Nimi is a self-described "arak drinking, hummus eating, Uzi gun toting, nice Jewish boy."

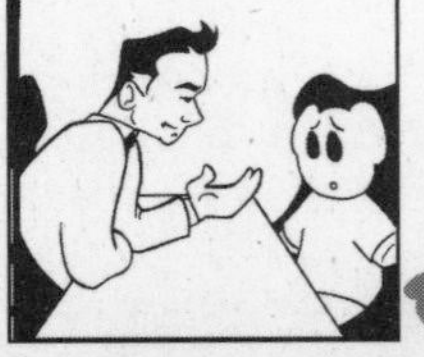

New Brunswick's Gibson Twist was born in Prague in 1847, the son of a deposed French monarch and cabaret souse. He died tragically at the age of 104 when his archnemesis, The Fantastic Dr. Xavier Jones, carried through with his nefarious scheme for world domination. And like most old, dead guys, he has a webcomic called "Pictures of You" which can be read at DrunkDuck.com.

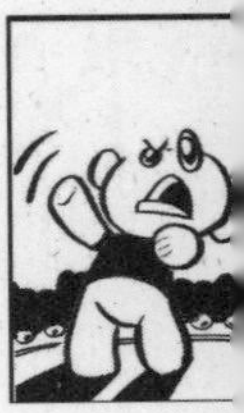

Jeanette "Jett" Atwood is a writer, storyboarder, and animator with some respectable video game credits. If you like her stuff, what you should really check out are her three 24 hour comics, which she's combining to make the *Puzzles* graphic novel. See more of her stuff (if you can call comics "stuff", which you really can) at www.TG-Studios.com.

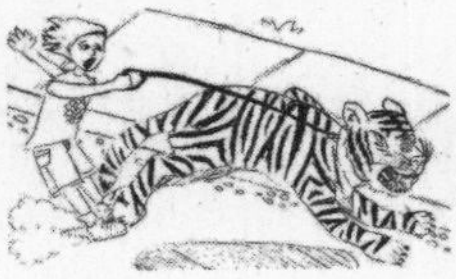

Sarah Gertler dels in Dwellaware. Er, dwells in Delaware.

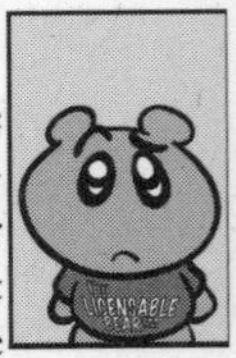

Jim MacQuarrie is a Wilton-certified cake decorator, professional balloon-animal-twister, archery instructor, former homeless person, webmaster at OddballComics.com and a founder of the creator help group Unscrewed (UnscrewedComic.com). Stalk him at www.JimMacQ.com.

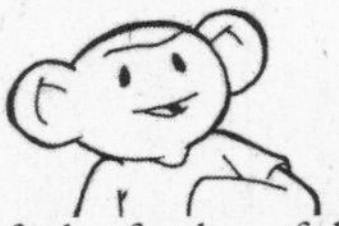

Lonny Chant was supposed to draw Nat Gertler's *The Proxy* graphic novel, but due to no fault of either of them, that won't be happening. Luckily for everyone out there, there is more to comics than *The Proxy*. To see Lonny stretching his artistic wings on other things, stop by www.comicspace.com/lonny/

About the Guest Stars

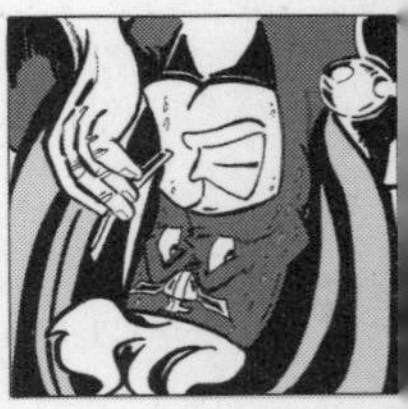

Mister U.S. really does lend himself out for guest-starring appearances for no fee, and has already appeared in everything from comics to games to a biological psychology textbook. If you'd like him to make an appearance in your comic or other project, surf on over to ItsMister.US for details.

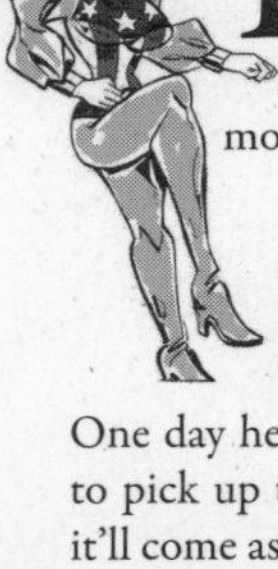

Liberty Girl, the patriotic hero from the past, appears in print and online publications from Heroic Publishing. Head over to www.HeroicPub.com to learn more.

Barack Obama doesn't know yet that he was in this comic. Shhh. Don't tell him. One day he'll just happen to pick up this book, and it'll come as a fun surprise.

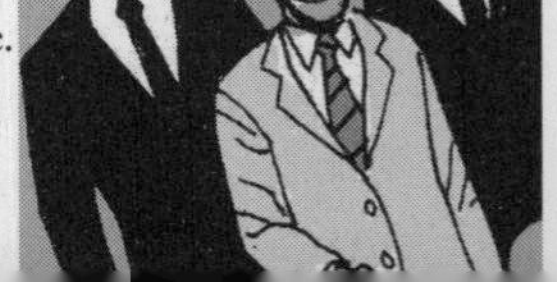